Vedas : An Extract of the Universal Values

VEDAS : AN EXTRACT OF THE UNIVERSAL VALUES

H. H. Swamiji Eraianban

GYAN PUBLISHING HOUSE
NEW DELHI-110002

Vedas : An Extract of the Universal Values

ISBN : 81-212-0767-3

Published in 2001 in India by
Gyan Publishing House
5, Ansari Road, Darya Ganj,
New Delhi - 110002

Phones : 3282060, 3261060, Fax : 3285914

E-mail : gyanbook@del2.vsnlnet.in

Laser Typeset at : Manastypesetter, Delhi-2

Printed at : Mehra Offset Printers

Contents

Preface

Thirumoolar, the author of the scriptural Tamil classic, *Thirumanthiram* (Sadhasivaahamam), was originally a Sivayogi called Sundaranandhar—He resided at mount Kailas, and once journeyed to the south to meet his friend and fellow disciple Agasthiar, who was living in Pothiya mountain. Standing on the outskirts of the Sathanur village one evening, he was disheartened to notice a herd of cows lowing miserably round the dead body of their cowherd, Moolan. His famous dictum, "Anbe Sivam"—"God (Shiva) is love"—motivated him to help the dumb creatures and so, by virtue of his yogic power he abandoned his body and entered the body of the dead cowhered, Moolan. The cows, on seeing their master come alive, were overjoyed and the ascetic in the cowherd's body led the cattle to their home in the village. Later, He returned to the spot where he gave up his own body, after finishing his task, he was surprised to find that his body had disappeared and understood it to be a play act of Lord Siva, who had a mission to fulfil through this devotee of His. So, he was forced to continue to remain in the cowherd's body. The Yogi who came to be known as Thirumoolar was immersed in penance under a peepul tree in Thiruvavaduthurai and drew crowds of disciples to him. Usually in Samadhi, he now and then uttered a verse which was recorded. And thus were the 3000 verses born, which gave shape to the text of *Holy Thirumanthiram* (10th Thirumurai in Saiva Sidhanttha).

Saiva Sidhanttha, a religious and spiritual path of devotion, set ablaze by Thirumoolar, was cherished and nurtured by the Nayanmars, and it helped greatly in the flourishing of Tamil culture.

Saiva Siddhanttha system pivots on the PATI-PASU-PASAM triangle Pathi or the master stands for God. Pasu is the individual soul in ignorance. And Pasam is the bondage of *maya* that binds the individual soul. These three are entities, hence Savia Siddhantha appears to be pluralistic realism. Suddhadvaitha is another name "Sudda" means unequalified and "Advaita" is "duaita" devoid of duality. These three entities though real in existence, are inseparably united with Him who is the Supreme reality.

Siva, the Pathi, also called Hara, Isa, Natha, Nandhi, etc. is the first cause. Sakthi is the instrumental cause in creation. And *maya* or *prakrithi* is the material cause for the world. This work of creation is likened to the potter who fashions the pot, the staff and the wheel used are the instrumental causes and clay the material cause for the pot: Siva and Sakthi are represented by the form of Sri Arthanareeswara swarupam. Sakthi is conscious, unchanging, eternal energy, the Svarupa sakthi of the Lord. The subtle distinction between pure matter (Suddha or Sattvika jagath) and defiled matter (Asutha or prakritha jagath) is *mahamaya* (Bindu or Vidya) in pure creation and *maya* or Asuddha Bindhu in defiled creation. Both are innert and different from Svarupa Sakthi, the essence of the Lord.

Siva, the Lord, is not just one of the Trimurthis of the purnas, but the source from whom the Trimurthis emanate. He is omnipresent, both immanent and transcendent and is called Viswaroopa and his vadhika—universal in form and beyond the universe. Again, He is with form and without form (Sarupa and Arupa), the Linga symbolizing the formless form of Siva. He, the Ashtamoorthi, embodies as the five elements and man; has eight qualities—Innocence, purity, self-knowledge, omnipotence and bliss, and Nirguna, having quality but not tainted by the *gunas* of *prakrithi*. He has five functions creation (Sristi), preservation (Sthithi), destruction (Samkara), obscuration (Thirodhana), liberation (Anugraha) and unlike Maha Vishnu, He does not take several avatars (Incarnations).

The soul is all pervading, eternal and a conscious agent capable of enjoyment, yet the fettered individual soul, who is called Pasu, by being bound to the world by the rope of avidhya, suffers because he mistakes himself to be finite, limited in thought, will and action. The bound soul thinks himself as a distinct entity from the gross, and subtle bodies he inhabits. But when liberated he gets restored to his original nature.

The three types of Pasas called Malas (stains) that bind the Pasu are *aanava mala, karma mala* and *maya mala*. The *aanava mala* that is beginningless and is the same in all, corresponds to *mula avidhya* or original sin. Aanava meaning nature of Anu or atom, not to size but finiteness, confines and limits the soul to the body and the sense organs and makes the Jiva forgetful of his natural glory and power. The soul, under the influence of Aanava is overshadowed by *karma mala* and that causes union of conscious and unconscious, indulges in all manner of actions, occuring merits and demerits and entangling himself in the cycle of the births and deaths. Maya mala, the material cause, gives the soul the means and objects of enjoyments. The effacement of *karma mala* and *maya mala* can be done only through strict spiritual disciplines and pure love of God. But *aanava mala* can be removed by God's grace alone. The souls are categorized into *sakalas, pralayakalas* and *vijnanakalas,* according to the *malas* that linger. The Sakalas have all the three *malas*. The *pralayakalas* rid of *maya mala*, are subject to *karma mala* and *aanava mala*: the *vijnanakalas* are the highest evolved souls, having only *aanava mala* from which they are liberated only through total surrender to the Lord and His grace.

Having shed all *malas*, the Jiva becoming one with Siva, is copervasive with Lord Shiva, shares all His glory and greatness, but has not lost his individuality and is unaware of it because of the overwhelming bliss. This state is compared to salt which is dissolved in water. When the Jiva identifies himself with matter, he becomes bound, and when he identifies himself with Siva he becomes Mukhta, but is not empowered for Panchakrithya which belongs only to Lord.

In Siddhantha, there are four paths of the ultimate. Chariya the first, called Dasa marga, the Lord path of the servitor leading to *salokya mukthi,* i.e., the devotee abides in the sphere of the Lord, involves services in the shrines like cleaning the premises, gathering flowers for worship, etc., the second, called Kriya, consisting of ritualistic worship, termed as *satputhra marga,* the path of the Lord's child, leads to *samipya mukthi* where the devotee is close of the Lord. The third, is Yoga, calling for contemplation, called Sakha marga, the path of the Lord's friend which leads to *sarupya mukthi* and the devotee attain the form and the various insignia of the Lord. These three approaches though preliminary, are rungs in the ladder that lead to Gnana or direct realization called Sanmarga and culminating in Sayujya mukthi, complete union with the Lord, Himself.

Place of Thicumanthiram in Saiva Siddhanta

'Thicumanthiram' provides the most sublime *mahavakyam* of Saivism—*Anbe Sivam—God is love.* The Nayanmars, the living commentaries on this statement, are singer saints inebriated with Siva Bhakthi. Their over-mastering devotion to the Lord expressed itself in adoration to the Lord and service to His servitors. The hymns spontaneously pouring out of their sacred lips, show their burning love of the Lord. For them love of the Lord implies love of all the devotees. Bliss shared is bliss multiplied, is stressed by Thirumoolar's declaration,—

"Yan Petra Inbam Peruga Ivvayagham"

May the worldshare the bliss that I have had) of (Let the bliss that I have got be multiplied abundantly and shared in this world).

His third dictum, the essence of the true religion which is catholic in vision *'Ondre Kulam: Oruvance Thevan'*—(The whole mankind is one family and the God, we worship is only one) or (The one race is mankind and the God we worship is only one). He goes on to declare that the body is the temple of God. So it is not to be despised but care should be taken as of a trust. His keen transcendent insight reveals His wisdom that the Lord has manifested as the world. That he is seen in everything, living and non-living and everything is pervaded by Lord Shiva. Thus saint Thirumoolar exemplifies Sanmarga as the path of gnosis.

I. Prologue: A bird's eye-view of Thirumanthiram

According to literary conventions an introductory section in praise of Lord Siva, the Lord of the Universe describing the powers the acts of grace, the immanence and transcendence and His various other aspects, embedded with philosophy and theology is exquisite poetry, has been given. The prologue brimming with Bhakthi, is a spontaneous out pouring of the soul in the presence of the majesty and the grandeur of the omnipotence, omniscience and omnipresence of the Lord.

In the prologue, the nature and import of the Vedas and the Agamas have been discussed. Many phrases and concepts which had later found their way as fundamental concepts in *Saiva Siddhantha* are encapsulated in the verses. In particular, the concept of monotheism slides imperceptibly into dualism and it is characteristic of *Saiva Siddhantha* to term the active arm of the monotheistic divine as grace (karuna).

Thirumoolar describes Shiva as 'Nandhi', 'Bull', which in iconography appears as the holy *vahana* of Lord Shiva. Again, Shiva is said to be the 'Lord of Maya-Land' that has its rise in the mind, which makes *maya* a principle of illusion. He introduces the concepts of the Pasupatha system (Pasu-pasa-pathi) and the important role of gurus, termed Natha here is elucidated.

Again the prologue gives us some insight into his life, wherein he mentions that he conducted his *tapas* under a Bodhi Tree in Thiruvavaduthurai. He eulogizes on Agasthiar, implying his leadership and his supreme Guru head of all Tamil Saivities, including Thirumoolar himself, and also makes him the pioner in bringing down Saivism from the north.

Thirumoolar introduces us to some important Saiva Siddhantha terms in Tamil. *Jneya, Jnana, Jnathra, maya, paryaya, mamaya, Siva* and *Agochara veeya,* whose important role and significance he expounds in Thirumanthiram. In some sections of the Payiram (introduction) details of the spiritual hierarchy and of the muths established by them are given. Nothing more about the location of the seven muths nor about the disciples except those mentioned by Thirumoolar is given.

He goes on to inform that the Saivite theology is both monistic (like Sankara's Advaita) and pluralistic too (like Madhvar's Dwaita). The one has become many. Again, the Lord Sadhasiva appears as the unmoved mover, one part of Him is in heaven and the other abides on earth.

II. Tanthra One (Karanakamam)

From Tanthra one, Thirumoolar launches out in full force on Saivite philosophy, mostly in the form of theology. However, the name of Siva is being superimposed parenthetically as the hidden power-entity on what appears to be purely secular concepts. The concept of grace, a theological concepts, pervades practically the whole of the text. A discussion on the three basic terms Pathi-Pasu-Pasam is initiated consciousness and *Chit-Achit* which are metaphysical concepts are dealt with consciousness is an essential aspect common to both Shiva and Jeeva, the former being 'the higher' and latter, 'the lower', *achit* (the ignorance of the *jeeva*) is to be broken as under before merging in the *chit* (the self-knowledge of Lord Shiva).

Details about the five senses (sight, sound, touch, smell and taste) which create the *achit* that stands barred from *chit* and the surrendering of this bondage in the Thuriya state which leads to the *jivan muktha* state of the Shiva Yogin or the Siddha are elaborately discussed. The nature of the Siva-*siddhas* and the thirty-six *Tathwas* (Tathwas being of the nature of categories that go to make up the manifested world) recognised by Saiva *siddhantha*, that have to be ascended to reach that state is described. Implications, that the ultimate is of the nature of cosmic space and that the essence of Jeeva lies in the self-same space in microcosmic condition, are made. The Agamic 'Carya' preparing the novice for the higher stages of the path to *moksha*, some special gems in the midst of common place advice and condemnation of *vama* Tanthra forms of worship are to be especially noticed.

III. Tanthra Two (Kamigamam)

In the second Tanthra, the importance of the Agasthiyar

cult to the founding of the Tamil *Saiva Siddhantha* system is indicated. The Puranic myths, especially the Linga Purana are in the nature of theology.

Siva's activities are classified by his devotees under five heads. They are creation, sustenance, destruction, obstruction and pervasion or salvation. Some terms that are encountered in Tamil Saiva Siddhantha philosophy and which describe creation are explained. The text goes on to describe the process and nature of creation, about Nandhi who supports everything in the world and about his destruction aspects that are the four forms of death: daily death, fated death, pure death and redeemed death. It states that the beginning and end of all things is void.

Some verses continue to explain the Lord as the Creator of mysteries, who pervades everything, who created all, Himself being the Param uncreated and how the body is created, and the principle of life placed within it. The rôle of the three *gunas* in the body, the 25 Tathwas that make up the Purusha within it and which are grouped in sets of five, the introduction of the 35 Tathwas into the body by the Lord, the six *chakras* and that (Aatharas) the divine Gnana is in the cranium, the confering of consciousness by may a, the evolving of desire and the rest are all delineated.

Jeeva is originally in pure Keva state in Thuriya, when Maya envelopes him and the Lord enters into Him. This Tanthra goes on to describe the categories of the Jeeva. There are three categories forming to classes: *vignanars* 4, *Prayakalas* 3. and *sakalas* 3. It describes that there are 9 gradations of *jivas* and 5 *malas* that are hard to get rid of. The nature of worthy and unworthy souls, and the way for *sakalas* and *jivas* to attain Shiva are described.

Kriya, worship is to be performed internally because the human-body has within itself Holy water and is also the Holy Temple, is depicted, Kriya is to be performed to the 'downward looking face of Lord Siva—'Adhomuka', the sixth face of Lord Shiva, an innovation of Thirumoolar. In conclusion the Tanthra, advice in the nature of *cariya* is suggested.

IV. Tanthra Three (*Veerahamam*)

This Tanthra begins with how Astanga yoga is to be

performed and what its fruits are. The description and the manner of operation of the eight great *siddhis* are to be found. The sadhaka's (aspirant) action of kundalini (yogic serpent) turning the body into a temple of Shiva, the attainment of immortality through Samadhi Yoga and the highest achievements through Samadhi yoga in yogic discipline and kaya (body) *siddhi* are all described.

Then comes discourses on special types of yoga and the varities of relationships between time and yoga. Kesari Yoga, the Supreme state of yogic bliss, Paryanay Yoga, the literal meaning being 'beside Yoga' (the Sanskrit terminology is Vamacara or the left handed yoga), and Chandra Yoga as another type of special yoga for achieving immortality are all spelt out in detail.

Thirumoolar discusses yoga more fully, thoroughly and with great frankness. He goes the full length of yoga and as known in his time.

V. Tanthra Four (*Sindhahamam*)

Tanthra four is concerned mainly with Manthras and Yanthras (Holy Mandalas). Ajapa, the silent Manthras, *Aum* and Sivayanama and the Bhairavi manthra, the manthra of Sakthi are elaborately mentioned and explained. The Dance of Lord Shiva (Sri Natarajan) is elucidated. An important *mandala* about the 'Thiuramalachara' which is a Yanthra, the '25 squares' mentioned that has its counterpart in the 25 Tathwas of the Saiva siddantha, and the mysticism of the letters of the alphabet, as well as the Siyanama and Aum manthra are to be noted. The Panchakchara and the six lettered Manthara *Om Namasivaya* come in. These manthras and yanthras give, it is said, the vision of Lord Shiva's Holy dance.

Kriya, the Puja form, that is connected with the Peeja Manthras and which does not refer to the external Vedic sacrificial system, but the inner Tapasic and Tanthric form is another subject matter that is dealt with.

The various roles of Sakthi in Tanthra as Tripurai, as Purna sakthi are enumerated. We are told of the lotuses of Sakthi. The two namely Shiva and Shakthi are conjoined as Shiva-shakthi and She is said to pervade the 16 kalas, to be the grace within Nada and Nadantha and is one with Siva in the Primal act of Creation. Her role as the support supported of the Yogic aatharas and her attributes are described.

This Tanthra continues the subject of Tanthric Chakras. They deal respectively with Eroli Chakram (Chakra of radiant light), Bhairavi Chakra, Sambhavi Chakra of 9 rounds. The central point in these sections is to relate the concerned Yanthra with the related Beeja manthras. The purpose of the whole is the obtaining of Siddhis, especially the highest of them, namely Samadhi. The relative Beeja manthra is also given. We find astrological concepts also linked with these Yanthras.

VI. Tanthra Five (*Vadhulahamam*)

This Tanthra deals with the nature of Saiva Siddhantha or Suddha Shivam and also provides a guidance to the attainment of it. It enumerates the characteristics of those who tread the path. Suddha Shivam is Saiva Siddhantha which is Vedanta. It goes to say that only after acquiring all knowledge (Jnana), practising all aspects of yoga, passing into the world of formless sound and getting rid of impurities can one evision the Supreme, the self-created, and be a true Saiva Siddhantha.

The Agma doctrine, is the four main states: Chariya, Kriya, Yoga and Jnana, in the path of Saiva Siddhantha. It is interesting the note the emphasis placed on *bhakti* as a Kriya. The path of knowledge is *sanmarga*, which leads to the Svarupa state. The path of yoga is Sakamarga and the path of Kriya is *sathputhra marga* as also *Dasamarga*, the path of devotion.

True lessons of Saiva Siddhantha are taught here. The end of siddhantha is union with Shiva. It is stated that there are four states of attainment namely, *Saloka*, *Samipa*, *Sarupya* and *Sayujya* and the starting point is Chariya (action). They stand respectively for God's world, God's proximity, God's form and Being one with God. Grace that illumines is an essential and for this.

Thirumanthiram criticizes six other systems, refutes their arguments before proceeding to establish the truth of its own inner faith.

VII. Tanthra Six (*Viyamalahamam*)

The verses in Tanthra six constitute the climax of the discussion of the previous Tanthras. The praise of the Saiva Guru is the ultimate aim of the Gnana stage, which is the summit of the Siva Siddhantha's upward journey.

The unity of the knower, the knowledge and the object of the knowledge which is achieved in Shiva, the Supreme, is established. A path to the ultimate by renunciation and Tapas, the latter considered to be an extraordinary path in Saiva Siddhantha, the correct way of practising Tapas and the misuse to which it is sometimes put are all touched upon. Even in Tapas, the Lord's grace is indispensable is the message given. Again, the meaning of the Holy Ashes (Vibhuthi) is brought out.

Finally, talks of the 'Siddantha-Vedantha' way and the characteristics of the 'Fit' disciple, one who is on the right path are indicated.

VIII. Tanthra Seven (*Kalottharahamam*)

This Tanthra is in the main concerned with aspects of yoga and kriya. The Adharas of yoga and Tanthra and dealt with under the symbolisms of the Lotus and the Linga, both, much favoured symbols in Hinduism. The Linga in its various characteristics of cosmic, microcosmic (Pinda), Sadhasiva, Athma, Ghana and Shiva is the subject of discourses. The nature of 'Sadhasiva' as distinct from Siva is importantly to be noted. Thirumoolar distinguishes between Sadhasivam and Shiva, treating the former as the Ultimate Formless (and beyond sound) power, and the latter as being not free of these attributes. At the microcosmic level, Sadhasiva is seated in the Sahashrara (1000 petaled Lotus).

There are many important verses in Sections 2-7 that throw light on Thirumoolar's metaphysics, epistemology and theology. Sakthi also plays as important role. As is to be expected, She merges in Sadhasiva, but remains as a separate entity, but all the same closely united with Shiva. She is found to be the first manifestation of Sadhasiva. The 36 Tathwas and 6 Athwas of the Agamas are mentioned. Sadhasiva is said to be the light of the life of all devas and the Lord of the sense gates of the body. His five forms and His five colours are described. Sakthi first evolves from Him. Then, the Vedangas, the Vedas, the Agamic paths, the Saiva truth, the Avasthas, the Rasis, the Tathwas and Supreme Truth that all evolve from Her and described. Sakthi is the kinetic and Shiva the potential aspect of God. The five sakthis seated in Sadhashiva and Sadhashiva who in turn is seated in shashrara is further mentioned. The only way of knowing Him is worship and as One Being, but the Tanthric path of rousing kundalini is also recommended.

Sections 8, 9 and 10, talk of Shiva as the first guru, of union with Him as the Supreme objective of kriya worship and of the Lord's grace, a most important tenet of Saiva Siddhantha. The following Sections, 11 to 16, stress the importance of kriya puja to Shiva, Guru and Maheswara, and about Holy men and the hospitality to be extended to them.

Concepts pertaining to kundalini Yoga make their appearance in Sections 17 to 19. They go on to explain what *mudhras* are and how they are to be practised. Again special procedures in performing Samadhi rituals for a fully accomplished *siddha* are prescribed.

Sections 20 and 21 belong to the branch of Tanthra, known as Vamacra. It is practised as a tanthric ritual by some sects. Thirumanthiram does no more than describe the ritual and the consequences to be expected of it with due warning as to the evils arising from making it a licentious act. Techniques to be adopted for such control are prescribed. The Gurus and the types of instructions imparted by them which on the one hand lead to good results, and on the other to evil are described in great detail.

The subject matter of Section 31 is mainly philosophical. The central point of the verses in these Sections clearly state that the "sun is the primal energy", which makes it Sakthi in short. Thirumoolar here refers to the Sun in this capacity of the source energy as Mahavishnu. Acquisition and control of Primal Energy is the objective of all Tanthras. As primal Energy the Sun's role in Tanthric categories and his path inside the human body is made clear. The relationship between the Sun and the Moon philosophically conceived is described. The Sun as the giver of Gnana and as manifested power of Sadhasivam follow naturally. This aspect is signified when the Sun is called 'Sivadhithya'.

Some aspects of the relationship between Shiva and the Jeeva as the two swans are considered in the following sections. The Lord is purusha and He is an Atom-within-Atom. He makes Tathwas, may a and Vaikari all illusionary and destroys all *pasas* by His Mighty dance. In the ultimate, He and Jeeva mingle and stand as one.

The Jeeva as soul and as *pasu* and the Lord as the giver of *gnana*, light to the Jeeva, in the form of grace, and as such stands beyond the 36 tathwas are next dealt with.

Section 37 is captioned 'In compassion for Men's Evil Lot' refers undoubtedly to the Lord's grace.

IX. Tanthra Eight (*Supraahamam*)

The subject matter of this tanthra is the nature of knowledge at various levels. The nature of the human body its essential ingredients and its experiences in various states are dealt with in the first two sections of this tanthra. It states that there are two bodies, the gross and the subtle. Eight constituents of the former are mentioned. There are also five *Indriyas*, three *karanas*, twenty-four *tathwas*, six *adharas*, nine *orifices*, eighteen *kalas* and the Jeeva's five experiences (Avasthas). Body substrates of Jeevas are in three stages of evolution. The position of the tathwas vary in the four states of jeeva awareness. There are 96 tathwas in all. In the Thuriya or the 4th state, he remains in *mouna*. Consciousness begins with Egoity and maya awakens soul from Primordial slumber.

Section 4 deals with 'Mid-Jagarat-Avastha'. In Thuriya, kalas and raga are roused by maya. God has placed 25 tathwas for jeeva and Vedanta reckons *tathwas* differently as 28. By breath control *tathwas* subside within body and *malas* are got rid of.

Adhvas (higher steps) are dealt with in Section 5. Thirty-six *tathwas*, 7 crore *manthras*, 51 *varnas* (syllables), 224 *bhuvanas*, 81 *padas* Primal and 5 *kalas* are all mentioned. The Dance of the Lord and Siva becoming by his grace are the fruits of Lord Siva. We come to know in the five states of Awareness, limitations of awareness are suffered by the Jeeva. And accordingly, mala contamination is the root of all evils.

Section 6 to 42 are full of metaphysical and theological speculations and are, therefore, of very great importance. We learn of Bindhu as the Power that permeates the Tathwas. Elaborations are made of the evolutions of Paraparam, the ascension of jeeva through the different states to reach Paraparam, the three *malas* that plague the *jeeva* and jeeva a prey to *thathwas* and *pasa*.

Descriptions of the *Kevala*, *sakala* and *suddha* states are made in Section 7. The cognition of the self and the respective cojoining in Sat, Asat and Sat-Asat are further elaborated.

Section 8 deals with *Para avastha*, that is experience at the highest level. The Lord as the Para, the sakthis are as the dynamic aspects of static *parapara*, the Eleventh state of consciousness of Para Nandhi beyond the ten avasthas and the nine manifestations of Para Siva are discussed. True knowledge and the way of self-knowledge through thought process are discussed. knowledge of Shiv, Sakthia and Jeeva that constitutes liberation and the gradation of the higher experiences in the different states are enumerated.

Section 13 describes the state of Pure Avasta which is totally deviod of *malas*. The rule of grace in achieving this state, the attainment of pure knowledge, the action of Siva who is seated within jeeva, the Maha Vakyam which conveys the message of the Gnana enjoyed in Samadhi state are other topics of discussions.

Thirumoolar repeatedly talks of the six ends providing an insight into the various aspects of these six centres. He also makes clear one of the fundamental differences between Vedanta and Siddhanta. Some details of the five other ways 'dear to Shiva' find a place in this section. The Vedantic formula *TatTwam Asi'* is played upon in different ways.

Section 14 is concerned wholly with the Pathi-Pasu-Pasam concepts using different imageries and the four Tapasvins. We are told of the talk of 'Head-and-Foot-Knowledge', of kundalini yoga and the equal validity of the two paths of *gnana* and bhakthi. The different concepts of the number three that dominate in various ways are explained.

Again the phenomena of cause and consequential experiences are briefly touched upon. The state and conditions of Upasantam are discussed in greater detail.

Section 30 emphasizes the importance of *tapas* for attaining Shiva, the Lord. This is a tanthra whose importance under the symbolism of eight petalled lotus is further dwelt upon. The declaration of the goal of Siddhantha to reach, the three Thuriya states of nine categories is a climax to the discourses on the subject.

Further, the denial of the value of mukthi which is the sign of evil and folly in men and the removal of *asuddham* leading on to the attainment of Suddha Saivism through Tanthra-yoga form the subject matter of Section 33. The Mahavakyam, *Tar-Twam-Asi* that provides guidance to attaining the Parahood, Vishu-Grasam or Total absorption and the Truth of the Universe are spelt out.

The ways of the Jnani's who are able to destroy karma, surrender desires, be possessed of Bhakti and then abide in Mukthi are described in Sections 39 to 42. The whole process of living, knowing, attaining moksha, etc., as a Divine experimentation sums up the whole of Section 43 in this tanthra.

X. Tanthra Nine (*Maghudahamam*)

To present a picture of the Divine Vision which is the ultimate aim of seeking moksha is the main purpose of Tanthra Nine. The dancing postures are the various aspects of the Darshan which are demonstrated in various ways. The dances of the Lord (Sri Nataraja) are of many kinds.

Thus, the revelation of the Darshan to the devotee leads to his attaing Gnanodayam (Dawn of Gnana) to the bliss of Sat-Chit-Ananda and to Swarupa Udhayam. It is said that it destroys fate. More details of Siva Darshan which also confers knowledge of Siva Swarupa are given. As such, a Siva Darshan confers the gift of liberation, termed Karma Nirvana, Nirvana a termed borrowed from Buddhism, is in Tamil Saiva

Siddhantha and Vedanta, a synonym for *moksha* which does not possess the non-substantial character of *sunyata*.

Thirumoolar diverts to the style of poetry peculiar to Tamil *siddhars* in Section 17 of this tanthra. The counterpart of such style of poetry can be traced only in the Sandha Bhasha of Bengali Baul bards. The Tamil *siddhars* are a peculiar brand of wandering ascetics, living on als. Most of them view Shiva as their Guru or Natha. Generally they are atheistic in their attitudes. They sing deeply esoteric songs which superficially condemn material values in language which often seem vulgar or even obscence, but are in reality deeply mystic. They practise a very higly systemastised science of medicine, called Siddha medicines, whose constituents are herbals though intermixed with mercury, gold, iron and other metals in some cases.

The text reverts to the glorification of samadhi and mystic realisation in Sections 18,19 and 20. The work ends on a note of religious passion over Lord Shiva in Sections 21 and 22.

Thirumanthiram is the sole essence and the nectar of our ancient four Vedas, i.e., Rig, Yajur, Sama and Atharva. Even though, it is 8000 years old, even today, it's immense value of literary and spiritually exhibits are outstanding and those who want to have abundance of linguistic vacabulary and those who wish to uplift their language style and those who wish to have spiritual awakening, this Holy Thirumanthiram is capable of fulfilling all the needs of the aspirants. It is not only a treasure or a classic to Tamil, but it is common to all, beyond sects, creeds, nations, language, etc. It insists all the essentials to make the human life, a meaningful one and thus we have to concentrate on this Tamil Classic *Sadhasivahamam Thirumanthiram-An Extract of the Universal Vedas* through proper reading with true understanding and adhering the principles in our daily life, it will ensure that our lives will have salvation merged with the Eternity.

On the whole, we once again salute the Holy name and Feet of Saint Thirumoolar and Lord Shiva, for the invaluable blessings showered on us to translate the classic into English and thus we hope that this work will show the miraculous depth of literacy of Tamil to English speaking people. May the Almighty's blessings be showered on all of us by all means:

Om Shivarppanam. **Swamiji Iraianban**
Tamil Nadu

Explanatory Notes

An Extract of the Universal Vedas—
(Thirumanthiram/Sadhasivahamam/Tamil Classic)

Invocation of Sri Maha Ganapathy

I offer my humble adorations to the Holy Feet enshrined in my consciousness; adorations to His Holy Feet who has five arms, whose face has the majesty of an elephant, whose single tusk rivals the beauty of the crescent moon.

Adulations to the God Head

1. He is the one—the uncreated Being who is the eternal-Shivam. He is two : Shiva and Shakthi. He confers grace on the Jivas. He stands as three, the triads being many; The primal shakthi evolving into three subsidiary shakthis; such as desire, knowledge and action. Again, the three Gods: Brahma, the Creator, Vishnu, the Protector, and Shiva, the Destroyer. Yet again, the three primal Gunas; Rajas, Tamas and Satthwas. As three, He is the entire creation represented by the three genders he, she and it. He is witnessed in all the four Vedas and in the four steps to God-Realization; Chariya, Kriya, Yoga and Gnana; He has conquered the five senses and is the five acts; creation, preservation, dissolution, obfuscation and liberation. He fills the six schools of philosophy and is the six steps to final realization; He is also the six Adharas (Moolathara, Swathistana, Manipooraka, Anaghatha, Vishuthi, Agna and Sahashrara) or pleasures. He pervades the seven worlds and is the seventh Chakra-Sahashrara which is located in the cranium. He manifests the eight pervasiveness through Earth, Water, Fire, Air, Sky, Sun, Moon and Jiva and remains so.

I. Special Introduction

2. You are the Holy one who sustains all life. You are the Lord of Her and Beloved of all the worlds. You are the One who spurned the Yama, the God of death and King of the Southern quarters. Of you, I sing praises and glory be to you.
3. You are the One who stands the same to all; You are the pure One, whom the immortal Gods adore. Even they, that daily stand beside You, do not know You. It is You, the same one that I seek, praise and meditate on.
4. You are the Truth of the vast spaces. You are the seed of the universal globe. You commanded me to seek and find You, and You are the haven of my refuge. I praise You by day and by night; and praising You thus, You dispel all my gloom, which has made me hold firm and in this strife-stricken world.
5. Wherever You search, You will find that there is no God like Shiva. There is none here below on this earth to equal Him is Glory; He is lotus like, of gleaming matted locks, fiery in splendour and is beyond the worlds, apart.
6. Without Him, there can be no celestials; without Him, there is no penance; without Him, the three Gods cannot accomplish anything. Without Him, I can never know how to enter the City's Gate—the Gate of Liberation.
7. He is the Primal first. He is older than the Trinity Three Brahma, the creator, Vishnu, the protector and Rudra, the destroyer. But, He is the peerless and unequalled Lord. Call Him Father as He is a Father to you. Inside you, He flames, in the form of a Golden Lotus.
8. He is hotter than fire and cooler than water; and yet no one knows of His abounding grace, he is very far away, and yet very close to those who are good. He, of flowing matted locks, is kinder than mother.
9. His matted locks that fall and gleam are wrought of golds; His name is Nandhi. He is my Lord and is

worshipped by one ever; But there is none whom He worships.

10. He spreads as high as the Heavens, holding the worlds apart. He is Himself the scorching fire, the Sun and the Moon. He, Himself is the mother that sends down the rains; He, Himself is the strong mountains and the cold oceans.
11. I look near and far; but around the first being, I see, no other God, mightier than He is; He is Himself the effort, and He is Himself the end of all efforts too. He is Himself the rains, and is Himself the rain-laden clouds. He is named the Nandhi.
12. Humans and celestials go after Gods who pass away. They do not realize that He of the forehead eye (Agni) is the Supreme, and is one pointed in His concern for His devotees.
13. Maha Vishnu who spanned the earth, Brahma, the one seated on lotus and other Gods could not fathom Him. There is none among those who measure the Heavens to measure Him. He stands transcending everything and everyone, bestowing all things with a glance.
14. He transcends Brahma on the lotus-seat, He transcends Mayan, Vishnu, the ocean-hued, He who transcends all, transcends Isan-Rudra. He transcends infinites space, yet witnessing all.
15. He is Brahma, He is Hara-Rudhra and is seated in every heart, and blossoms and is the Divine Effulgence which knows not any contraction, and He is the Eternal order.
16. He is of matted locks fragrant with konrai flowers. He is the One, who is with the Divine Mother. He is the One whom the devas and the celestials adore for anything they require.
17. The body and soul may intermingle, but the effulgence of the soul predominates. God fills the whole Universe, but His love for us stands Supreme.
18. The Supreme Lord seeing the devout penance of the king of Alagai, that is, Kubera, the God of wealth, made him the Lord, bestowed on him great riches, and

commands him to abide there in the land of Alagapuri and reign there.

19. All the fragrant seven worlds are His, but He chooses to remain in the cremation ground. He is sure to abide in our hearts, if we do sincere penance.
20. He is the One who in the olden days created birth and death, and if we take the path that leads to His abode, we shall find Him in the Holy hill of Kailash, which is resonant with thunders and fragrant flowers.
21. Sing His praise and become one with Him who is the Lord, and who is the source of all compassion, who rescues Vishnu, Brahma and the celestials from births, and who killed the trumpeting Gaja Mukhasura—the wild elephant-faced monster who challenged Shiva's Supremacy.
22. The Maya-world has its rise in the mind, the Lord of this Maya-world knows yet all our thoughts, but we do not think of Him. There are some who groan that God is not favourable to them. But, sure, God seeks those who seek to save their souls.
23. The God of fire, at one time threatened to engulf the world. He was contained in the northern seas by the Mighty Lord. In ignorant do not say that He is not the Mighty Lord, who is the Lord of all the Heavenly Beings, who, day and night, pours forth His Divine Grace.
24. Sing His praise, sing of His Holy feet; pour all your treasures at the sacred Feet of Siva ! and those who give up the clouded eye and disturbed mind, Siva will ever stand by them kindly and firmly.
25. He, of plaited locks is birthless and is full of vast compassion; He is deathless and never deserts those who come to Him. Kneel to Him, who is the granter of all joys; and kneeling, you shall find that all illusions vanish and the bond between you and Him becomes immemorial.
26. Adore the Lord who stands in unbroken continuity; the Lord who protecting the earth expanded all over it and stands transcending all; He sits in smiling glory on the

lotus of the heart, Holy be His Feet!

27. The infinite of lotus-face, rivals the rose of sunset. May His divine grace be ours ! and they who thus daily beseech Nandhi, He walks into their hearts and abides therein.
28. He, the All-pervading stands beckoning everyone. He is invisible to most people, but to them who freely give themselves to the Lord on High, He is the certain, immutable guide.
29. Oh ! who else is my kin but you? Come to me that I may see you. Let me not feel shy to embrace Your Feet ! For You who are pure and true, You ever stand as the axle-pin to the heart of Your servant.
30. Will my Lord draw me to Himself, just as the Heavens draw the rains? Doubting thus, many ask. But like a calf lowing for its mother, I cry for Nandhi for the sake of knowledge.
31. He is the Earth, He is the sky ! He is well ! He is the Heaven. He is the truest god, He is well; He is the inmost rapture of the sweetest song. From my heart from my hearts central core be sought only Him.
32. He is the Lord of the Gods and is our Lord too; He is the Lord who pervades all space, and he transcends the seven worlds which are ocean bound; No one knows his true nature. May we sing of His Divine grace!
33. The Gods whom this hoary world adores are many, the rituals are many and the songs they sing are many. But bereft of wisdom they know not the One Truth. These unillumined can but only droop at heart.
34. The Lord imparts to the celestials, the True path which is like the fragrance of the musk, which the musk-deer constantly emits. I chant the rich essence of His name when I sit or move about; His names that are thousand in number are like divine sparks.
35. If we tread the path of goodness as shown by Him, and sing His praise and adore Him, He the Lord of all ten directions, will protect and impel us in the right direction.
36. Nandhi, the Heavenly Father, is the unsurfeiting sweet

nectar. He is the unequalled, Bounteous One, First of time: Praise Him ever, and even as you praise Him, your reward will also be so.

37. I daily kneel and chant Nandhi's Holy name; He, the fire-hued one, stands envisioned flaming like the moon in the sky. He comes into me and throbs and breathes through by mortal flesh.
38. I will not cease to speak of Him as the Great One and the Rare One. I will not cease to prate of Him as the form unborn. I will not cease to talk of Nandhi as the mighty. I will never cease, for pure and great I am then.
39. He is the Divine Light, shining brightly in the devotees' hearts; He is the pure one, sporting therein, we shall praise Him and call Him our Lord; and adoring Him thus, we shall attain His grace.
40. You humbly and meekly seek the Feet of the Lord, who equals the serene rays of the purest gold. The All-fashioning Lord enters in such hearts that praise Him with songs of the humble heart and unpenurious tongue.
41. He comes to them who treasure His name in the deep confines of their hearts; He is the same Lord, who in His mercy, when deadly poison born of hate, spread over the entire atmosphere and threatened to kill all lives, swallowed the poison and saved creation from total destruction. He is the consort of Sri Parvathi of Gleaming brow. He comes like a deer to its fold.
42. The Lord's grace flows unimpeded to those who seek Him. One cannot achieve anything, even if one is able to orbit the world, without the grace of the Lord who is the consort of the Mother of reed shaped shoulders.
43. The Eternals' all-filling grace comes only to them that speak of Hara's Holy Feet and weep, again to them that daily muse at the Mighty Feet of the Great One, and yet again, to them that fixed in deep devotion, wait to serve Him.
44. The Devas (celestials) chant glory to the Holy Feet; The hymn of the Asuras (Demons) is glory to the Holy Feet; The humans too, echo glory to the Holy Feet and I too

glorified Him thus, and He shone in my love.

45. This sea-girt world will not survive, except according to the law. Happiness does not follow, except according to the law. Nothing can work against the law. If we adore Him who is the effulgent light, He will guide us on the path to liberation like the Sun.
46. His devotees praise and sing His Holy Feet, calling on His name oh, Hara! Oh, Shiva and describing Him as 'Twilight-Hued'. Yes. He of the primary hue, the first, the Infinite entered my being and held the centre place of my heart.
47. They who enshrine Him in themselves are equal to great sages and contemplating Him in their hearts, they will love and adore him. But those who do not think on Him do not get happiness, even as the kite sitting on a palm tree does not enjoy the palm fruit.
48. The pious adore Him who is the Lord of Gods. I bend my knees to Him and invoke His grace. He is Lord, our father, blessing us of earth. I seek Him, the lamp that flickers not.
49. Those who of soul and its limitations adore the Lord, are released from the eternal bondage that is inherent in the soul. They are thus able to cross the sea of *samsara* and reach the other shore of it (liberation).
50. I shall keep Him in my heart and adore Him, sing His name and dance with offering of flowers. I seek the Lord with singing and dancing for this alone I know and know only too well.

2. Glorification of Vedas

51. The central core of the Vedas proclaim that there is no dharma, barring what the Vedas say. And the wise ones ceased their contentious brands, intoned the lofty strains and won freedom's battle.
52. Brahma who spoke the Vedas is and Himself the author thereof. He spoke the Vedas only to reveal the great maker; He spoke them for the Holy Ones, for the sake of performing sacrifices; He spoke them, to mainfest

the True One.

53. In the beauteous Veda, aptly named the Rig, He stood as the moving mood behind. He, Himself stood as the eye of central vision, in the thrilling chant of the Vedic priests.
54. The Lord is neither *chit* nor *achit*. He is the Supreme path. He will bestow on us His grace, if we meditate on Him. This is the only path, the Supreme path, says the Vedanta.
55. The six Vedangas: firstly, Siksha that lays down rules for correct chanting of Vedic hymns; secondly, Vyakarana: that lays down the grammar of the Vedic chanting language; thirdly, Chandas: that deal with the cadence and number of Vedic hymns; fourthly, Nirutktha: that gives the interpretation of Vedic syllables; fifthly, Kalpa: that lays down the rules for their performances; and sixthly, Jyothisha : that prescribes the appropriate times for performing Vedic rites and sacrifices and the Vedas proclaim only Him. A few bother about it. Others consider it a privilege to follow many other Gods and thus waste their time.
56. Those who do not participate in the singing and dancing of the woman dedicated to the Lord and do not perform sacrifices or observe vows. Go to their destiny and become miserable.

3. The Grandeur of the Agamas

57. The Lord who consorts with His blue-hued Half has the twenty-eight Ahamas. Bowing low the sixty-six sages heard the Ahamas being expounded Siva's Fifth Face, known as Isanyam.
58. The Lord in His grace revealed the Sivagamas in a billion-million-twenty-eight number. In them, the celestials glorified the Lord's greatness. I too shall muse and praise Him.
59. The thoughts which pandits alone know, they spoke in eighteen various languages. The pandits' tongues numbering 18, are but what the Primal Lord Shiva

declared.

60. The sublime Agamas, seventy billion-millions though they be, were revealed by the Lord's grace. The Agamas like writing on the waters, were deep and baffling, eluding grasp, even to the Gods in Heaven.
61. The Infinite Shiva, revealing the vast Infinite, came down to earth, to proclaim His Dharma. Then, the immortals adored Him as Nandhi and He stood forth as the entire Agamas.
62. From Shiva, the Infinite manifests Himself as Sakthi and Sadhasiva again. He manifests Himself as Maheshwara, the joyous, as Rudra Deva, as Holy Vishnu and as Brahma. And as Nandhi, He begot the nine agamas. Thus, in succession, He manifests Himself from Himself into Himself.
63. The nine agamas so received are Karanam; Kamigam; Veeram the good, the high Sindulam and Vadulam. The other is Syamalam and Kalottharam, then the pure Subram and to crown it all the Makutam.
64. The Lord by His grace revealed the numberless agamas composed by the Sivagamas, yet if they know not the wisdom. He taught, the unnumbered fade away like writing on water.
65. When rain and summer and long drawn dews kept occuring and sustained the lakes, then did He in Sanskrit and Tamil at once, reveal the rich treasure of His compassion to our Great Mother.
66. At birth life comes into being, it stands preserved for a while and it takes departure; when caught in that momentary wave of flux, we get a glimpse of Him, the Lord who in sweet Tamil and northern tongue revealed life's mystery.

4. The Guru Hierarchy

67. You must seek the masters who received Nandhi's grace; first the four Nandhis, next the Holy Sri Vinayaga, then Panthanjali and Viyakrapadha, who worshipped in Sabha's Holy precincts, and include him (Thirumoolar)

to complete the number eight.

68. By the grace to Nandhi, I became Nathan. By Nandhi's grace I entered into Moolan. By Nandhi's grace, there is nothing that I cannot perform. I remained here below guided by Nandhi.
69. Malangan, Indhiram, Soman and Brahman, Rudhran, Kalanghi and Kancha Malayan come and as my disciples in succession, through imparting instructions to them.
70. The four Nandhis, each in his corner, ruled as masters; The four Nandhis held each his diverse spiritual treasure and each gave to the world what everything they had attained; And thus, they became the four immortal masters.
71. The Lord who is beyond birth and death, inspired me to instruct the twelve disciples. Yet, his surpassing greatness, of the three radiant lights, is never fully revealed; The Lord transcends what He revealed.
72. He, of the cool matted locks and coral hue, so spoke, that, you shall however, with purity perform the Holy rites, even if the Heavens may rain in eight directions. And speaking thus, He conferred His Grace on the Four Nandhis who remained steadfast.

5. Life-Sketch of Saint Thirumoolar

73. I bore Nandhi's sacred pair of feet high on my bowed head, thus I ventured to compose to Agamas, also by intoning His name loud in the deepest core of my heart and daily musing on Hara wearing high the crescent moon.
74. The mystic name of Sivagama flashed in my mind; I rose straight to the Holy Feet of Arul Nandhi; enthralled, these eyes witnessed in the Holy Sabha, the Surpassing Dance of Lord Siva, which smbolises the manifestations of the Universe as an activity, of Lord Siva, thus I lived and joyed for seven Yugas.
75. Oh Indra, hear what urged me to stay thus. In deep and true devotion I adored the Holy One, Parvathi Devi rich in penance the Divine Daughter of austerity of the

Universe and with unceasing ardour, I pursued her.

76. While I fasted here, I did not seek Sadhasiva, Tattwa, the Vedas and Muthanool (first book); I did not hold them in my heart, but soon my mind abandoning indifference, turned towards them and realised them all.

77. Oh Malanga, this it was that urged me to come here, to expound the Vedas and the Dance's Divine import; the Lord first unveiled these occult mysterious to Her of the asure hue and bright jewels.

78. She my saviour, named the Eternal Bliss, the Bright jewelled One, sunders all bonds of birth, I reached Her Feet, who is Shiva's treasure, Mistress of cool Avavaduthurai and remained steadfast in devotion.

79. Fixed in devotion I clung fast to Him who is Parvathi's half rooted form in devotion to Shiva who is in Avavaduthurai, I fast sought repose under Shiva Bodhi's tree—it is said that He, Thirumoolar, realised the truths of the Agamas and actually composed the work *Thirumanthiram* while contemplating Shiva/Sakthi while at Thillai witnessing the cosmic dance—in devotion I fast chanted the lyric spell of His countless names.

80. I remained prisoned thus in mortal coil for ages beyond count; I remained in space where day nor darkness is not. I remained immutably fixed at Nandhi's Holy Feet where Devas offer praises.

81. If in a former birth one does not do penance, who can say what the next birth will be; The Lord, however, gave me a good birth, so that I may sing His glory in sweet Tamil.

82. Entering the city of Nandhi, I sat under the Bodhi tree for ninety million Yugas worshipping the Lord of the Goddess of wisdom with the milk of wisdom.

83. To scale the heights, I sought the way countless Devas, Asuras and Humans take; conquering all wisdom, I grow into a Shiva-muni thus and came down here, a true Siddhar, through the cerulean blue.

84. By the grace of the Lord, I came to realize the inner

meaning of the Agamas, the greatest of the scriptures that thrill the heart, which are on par with the Vedas.

85. All the worlds may well attain the bliss. I have received, if the name of the lord chanted by the great ones is repeated; there will arise within the heart a thrilling unstruck sound which will lead to realization, when practised.
86. The Heavenly Beings forget not to chant the chain of holy hymns; the Holy Hymns revolve deep in their hearts and they with folded hands approach Nandhi, the Lord above and free themselves of the bonds of births.
87. He placed the digesting fire in the human body; He placed a cosmic fire to prevent the flooding of the seven worlds; He has given us the Tamil Sasthras to prevent the eruption of egoism. He who gave all these things is the Supreme.
88. Ayan and Mal (Brahma and Vishnu) toiled to seek His Head and Foot; baffled in their quest, they met again on earth. Achutha complained that he saw not the Foot and Ayan falsely claimed that he saw the Head.
89. Our Nandhi, the Infinite God, ever holds the bull, deer and axe, whose imagination is this earth containing moving and non-moving things has given me this opportunity, and on my head, he planted His Holy Feet.
90. So impelled, The 'Jneya'—'that which is to be known'; the 'Jnana' that is 'Knowledge' and the 'Jnathru' that is the 'known', the 'Maya' that is not an illusion, but a kind of 'purity' which hides the Lord from the vision of the imperfect and the Parayaya—the evolutes from 'Suddhamaya'—that arise in Mamaya, the Shiva and the Agochara Veeya that stands for Shiva's splendours here, all streamed out of me in full measures.
91. I have come by the Great path of Kailash, in the line of the Lord, Nandhi, the Blissful One who dances joyously, who expounded the above truths, who is the effulgent truth, eternal and limitless.
92. With Nandhi's grace, I sought Moolan, with Nandhi's Grace, I became Sadhasiva; with Nandhi's Grace. I

attained Divine Truth and with Nandhi's Grace, I remained so.

93. Who can know the greatness of our Lord. Who can measure His length and breath; he is the mighty nameless flame; I venture to speak of Him whose beginnings are unknown.
94. Unceasingly, I daily prattle the name of Nandhi, I praise Him in thought by day and by night as well, daily I yearn for my Master, the Light-hued, the Lord of the uncreated radiant flame.
95. Who can know the greatness of our Lord Shiva ! Who can truely measure His huge length and breadth ! He is the mighty nameless flame with fire and colour; I venture to speak of Him (Lord Shiva) whose beginnings and limitations are unknown.
96. I do not know the way singers sing; I do not know the way dancers dance. I do not know the way seekers seek; I do not know the way searchers search (The Almighty Shiva).
97. All, all, even Brahma who after Him created this huge worlds, seek the imperishable Light of Him, Shiva whose Luminous accents of Truth are spoken in words, whose heights of supremacy rise on the sweetest music.
98. Seeking liberation, the saints and celestials listen to his exposition at the sacred foothill, and singing His Glory, they gain realization, but others who are indifferent do not do so !

7. The Resplendence of the Three Thousand Holy Hymns

99. Moola composed three thousand Holy hymns in Tamil. Did He? Nandhi, reveals for all the world to know. Those who wake up early at dawn and sing understanding the meanings, will win splendid soft repose of the Bosom of the Lord Shiva.
100. The fine salvation of the diverse, works which are true and good is in the three thousand holy humns. All knowledge, special and general is in the Divine 3000 hymns which are original and wise.

8. The Spiritual Hierarchy

101. The Holy orders, spiritual and true are seven. of the first, Moola, sprung from the Himalays. Adorned in beauty, the nine tanthras and the three thousand hymns propound the word of Agama.
102. The immanent-living kalanga, Agora his very next, the good maligai Deva and the Holy Nadantha, Bhogadeva and Paramananda who conquested the senses and Moola who is breathing here they are all of the Eternal Hierarchy.

9. The Trinity

103. However much I may think, for ages and ages, of Him whose youth is eternal, Him who has no beginning or end, I cannot succeed. However, much Brahma and Vishnu may describe His glory. He (Shiva) too remains everywhere.
104. He, the First Being and He, the Eternal hued, and He of the glowing, original Lotus—real seat—though all the three forms and an integral whole, yet, the world considers them as separate, and quarrel among themselves.
105. The seed of this world Isa, becomes the Mighty God who is seated beyond the two karmas—good and evil deeds; the thoughtless so contend that Isa, Shiva, is 'this' and 'that' and the dross only know the basest low sediment.
106. Shiva, the First, then the three: Sakthi, Nadha and Bindu followed who flourished as the first three evolutes. They are all nine all together and yet they are all one and the same. All these are but names of Sankara, the First.
107. Thus if we but probe the soul of truth and lay it bare, then Aya or Mal (Brahma or Bhagavan Vishnu) and no alien Beings to us. The three eyed is but indissolubly kin to Nandhi. May all be blessed by the Heavenly Three.
108. While countless Devas stood around lost in matting prayers, I lay prostrate and adored the milk-hued one. Then, the Lord spoke to me that He is equal to Vishnu and Brahma, and that it is mine to give to the world the

grace of His Feet.

109. It is only by the grace of Lord Shiva, decked with Kondrai flowers, that the same essence exists in all the celestials and the humans. There is no God except He. So it is our only duty to enshrine Him in our hearts.

110. The ignorant do not know from where and how the first light that flamed into three and five did leap. So, blindly groping and lost in the maze of words, they assign graded ranks to Isa, Mal and Aya.

111. The Supreme is one; He is absolute and without lapse. In descent there of, He becomes Vishnu and Brahma; thus He the One ranked into many and by a conscious choice made a self-deduction.

112. In one part, He is Sadhasiva my Lord, one heavenly part of His residence in Heaven; the spirit that heaves in the body is one kingly part. His one part transformed all to motion.

1

Tanthra One (Karanahamam)

1. Divine Indoctrination

113. He, Divine Nandhi, Shiva's form/formless aspect of Sadhasiva came down from Heaven, from time immemorial, assuming human form, and karma to match, planted His feet of Grace on me. In doing so, he dispelled all my primordial impurities. He stood inside me, melting my yielding heart and filling my eyes with peerless bliss beyond all comparison and opening my inner eye to perceive the divine Truths.

114. Our Nandhi, Forehead-eyed, shattered to pieces all impurities by opening His Eye of grace. His eye, which sheds grace, is Sakthi through whom Shiva confers grace and is also the wielder of Shiva's power, at whose radiant light quaints all impurities. So transfixed He planted His coral feet on my heart and turned it to crystal.

115. They speak of the Three-Pati that is Lord, Pasu that is soul and pasam that is bondage. Pati, Pasu and Pasa are beginningless, that is eternal. But the Supreme God, Pati is untouched by *pasam*. But let Pati touch, that is when it draws near *pasu*, the *pasu-pasa* will not stand.

116. Like the rising spark of music that indwells within the bamboo, so too Lord Nandhi abides in this temple-body.

with sweet compassion gentler than a mother's, He shattered the three impurities, within, as like the Sun on the ocean of mercy rises and dispels darkness.

117. The Sun stone may well be surrounded by cotton wool. The stone by itself burns, not the wool, but when the Sun's rays fall on it, the cotton blazes into fire and shrivels into ash. So too, the imperative impurities wilt before the Lord's cathartic glance.

118. He removes all our impurities and transmutes our worldly existence into spiritual life. And dancing in the Chit-Sabha, the dance hall of the soul—He pours His grace, destroys the passions that bind the senses, and knowing the purity of the soul. He has come to reside therein.

119. Our intellect, meaning consciousness knowing not its true course is led with the senses, so finds itself in very deep waters. But inside our consciousness, there is a deeper consciousness drowned in the deeper waters of superconsciousness which the Gurupara, the Master Supreme stimulates by His Grace.

120. Like unto the swan that separates the water and parts from the cow's milk, so the Lord, Himself, alone, in this unique Sabha—the dance hall of awareness—departed and scorched like fire, the impurities that lay intermixed with senses, and thus roasted the seeds of the seven births forever.

121. Siva yogins are *jivan mukthas* who, by strict observation of the injunctions of faith in worship, yoga, etc. attain the final or Thuriya state complete liberation from bodily bonds, being dead to material circumstances, and even while alive being fully spiritual. They destroy the seed of birth and induce pure awareness in the waking state and in unbroken harmony they achieve tranced breath.

122. Sivayoga is to cognise 'Chit' (spiritual) and 'Achit' (material) to qualify for the yoga-penance, the self-attaining self-illumination and without deviation entering His Lordly domain—Samadhi in yoga; Nandhi of the nine yogas granted me this.

123. He made me see the truth that He pervades all; He granted me the vision of the world that even the celestials do

not know. He granted me the vision of his sacred feet that dance forever in the Holy Hall that is; the Universe in its' totality or Akasa (Ether) or space which is void, and the operating ground of the divine. He granted me this kind of His infinite grace and the Supreme Bliss.

124. Space intermingles with space, love drowns itself in loves; light dissolves in light. They alone are the elected, the Shiva-siddhars, who realize and attain this glorious state.

125. They are siddhars who perceive Shiva's world here below on earth. Deep in themselves they have realized and transcended Nada (Sound principle) and Nadhantha (the Ultimate sound). They are pure, eternal, and repose in unalloyed Bliss. Leading to liberation, they transcend too the 36 steps, postulated by the Saiva Siddhantha school of philosophy as Tatthwas, the five Shiva tatthwas arise in the 'pure maya' sphere, the seven Vidhya Tatthwas in the 'Impure Maya' sphere and the twenty-four Prakrithi Tatthwas in the Prakrithi Maya sphere.

126. Thus ascending high the thirty-six steps of Freedom's ladder, they walked into the peerless light of bliss. They saw Shiva, the inexplicable and remained pervasive as Sivam, witnessing all of Shiva's works. Having seen and realized they remained lost in divine tranquility.

127. They remained in Shiva, seeing themselves in all, thus they remained mutely gazing at Shiva's manifold works, in silence perceiving Time's three tenses: the past, present and the future. They remained lost in Divine tranquility—the end of all knowledge. They who realise it sleep in absolute knowledge.

128. Tranquility is seated in pure space, it does repose in pure space. Tranquility begins where Vedas end. There they abide quietly in self-realization.

129. Sleeping, they saw Shiva's world in themselves; sleeping they saw Shiva's yoga in themselves. Within them, they enjoyed Shiva Bhoga. How then can the mind of those who saw sleeping be described? Their state in beyond description too.

130. Hara (Lord Shiva), the First Being, bestows His grace

on you, even as you strive to reach wisdom's bounds. Shiva's grace matches human endeavour. The Lord like a flaming Ruby in the flaming sky dances in the unique sabha—the arena of space—for Uma, His Sakthi, to behold and enjoy.

131. Like the luminous emerald within the red ruby, like the emerald inset inside the ruby, He dances the Holy dance in the sabha-hall (Chidambaram) of the purest gold. What reward do those who adore Him get—Infinite rapture.

132. In this world, they received the great deathless way; in this world they attained the great birthless end. They received the unique gift of non-separateness from the pure sabha, the ineffable rapture, of non-communication with the world.

133. There is no one like our Lord Shiva-who knows distinctly the great and the small, the difficult and the facile. They who, like the tortoise withdraw their five senses under the shell, shall hear and see this world and the next, and all their impurities be dispelled.

134. Like the ghee subtely latent in the purest milk, the Lord speaks in silence into the waveless thoughts. They who in silence realize this shuffled mortal coil, become purity itself and mingle in the limitless light.

135. When the five senses, commencing with sound, retrace their evolution, the consciousness shall merge but in the cosmic mind. The understanding should be crystal clear that when one light merges in another there will be only light.

136. The dissolved salt emerges in crystal shapes; when the fierce rays of the Sun beat upon the water; that salt dissolved in the water becomes liquid again. So does the Jeeva get dissolved in Lord Shiva Himself.

137. The tiny atom, swimming in the vast Universe, knows no separate existence but merges into the vast. So the spirit abiding in each body, discovers its ancient home at the sight of His Holy Feet.

138. If you know that the Holy Feet of the Lord and are Sivam, if you only think that the Holy Feet of the Lord are Shiva's world, then you will realize that the Holy Feet of the Lord are freedom's bliss—life's goal; the Holy Feet are the sure and final refuge for the illumined souls.

139. It is only to see the Guru's Holy form, only to chant the Guru's Holy name, only to hear the Guru's Holy word, and only to muse on the Guru's Holy Being, will the soul thus receive its illumination.

140. The five senses will surely then come under your control, will surely then retread back to their native homes will surely then turn inward, when the soul meets the Lord.

141. All I see is Nandhi's two Holy Feet; all I think of is Nandhi's Holy divine Form; I think in all my thoughts of Nandhi's golden wise words.

142. Nandhi is the Lord of wisdom; those who kept our Nandhi's Holy name in their minds became holy. As the Lord danced, while the Vedas sang in praise, they beheld Him with enthralled eyes and reached the sacred shores of Heaven.

2. Transitoriness of Body

143. At first this body was mortal clay, then it was divided into two by the karmas, Good and Bad. Just as clear water falling from the sky mixed with the mud becomes muddy, the body was keeping well until evil entered. Thus men degenerated and became subject to birth and death.

144. When by use, this body, the roof of delights, falls to pieces with death, neither wife nor children, who all enjoyed follow the parting soul. Only the holy vigils kept, the austerities and wisdom gained, remain to go with him and save him. All others dwindle and desert us.

145. Kith and kin all gather together and wail loud and long; they now deny him a name and call him corpse, they bear him to the burning ghat and the body burnt. Then they take a ceremonial bath and the memory of the dead fades away with that and is soon forgotten.

146. The legs as two pillars and the central column as one single beam and the thirty-two siderial skeletal bones that extend sideways as reflaters support the body roof. But as the roof above decays and breaks, the breath of life fails to trace, its way to its mansion.

147. The body rots with gangrene and phlegm, the *Prarabdhas* leave the body. The bones turn fragile. After verifying

death by feeling the nostrils with the fingers, they cover the body and perform the cremation which included the offering to the raven.

148. The rich repast was laid and he dined and joyed, and in amorous dalliance toyed with sweet damsels; he moaned of a little pain on the left, and laid himself to rest only to be gathered to dust.

149. In the pride of pomp he built a stately mansion, in the rage of wealth he stepped into the palanquin and rode, in vain excess he gave away largesses in crores, and he roamed, but never called the name of God.

150. Cloyed in the surfeit of love, bodies were locked in close embrace and lips met lips; then, long cherished memories of this died. Soon the body was set on a bier while mourners mourned, the body, all passions spent, perished in the leaping flames.

151. The pulse failed and the mind lost its axle-hold. The five senses that enjoyed buttered sweets have left their homes, the fair-eyed beloved and the treasures that are dear have remained to stay, but the spark of life has quitted forever.

152. When the bonds of life broke loose, the roof went to pieces. The nine gates of the mansion closed fast forever. Time's painful march was fast gaining apace and as the hours passed by, one by one, they left him weeping.

153. He was the Lord of our land, he was the sole leader of our place. But now he is mounted on a palanquine for the ultimate journey's end. Mourners walk behind and before drum beats clash; thus extended the solemn show in ample length.

154. They say that behind the temple walls—the body—96 *tathwas* dwell safely. The 96 *tathwas* comprised the 36 internal *tathwas*, plus 60 external *tathwas* consisting of the 25 manifestations of the five elements: (1) Earth: skin, bone, tendon, flesh, hair; (2) Water: blood, fat, brain, semen; (3) Fire: food, sleep, fear, coition, sloth; (4) Wind: running, walking, standing, sitting, lying; (5) Space: anger, miserliness, avarice, obstinacy, malice; plus the ten *nadis* in the body: Ida, pingala, sushmna, Gandhari, Hasti, singhavai, Alambudai, purushan, guru and

sanghini; plus the ten *vayus* (air): prana, apana, udana, Myana, samana, naga, kurma, girihara, devadatha, dhanajjayan; the three desires: wealth, children, world; the five modes of speech: talking, memorising, singing, weeping, exulting; plus the three gunas: Sathwa, Rajas, Tamas; plus the four sound forms: Sukshma (subtle), Pasyanthi (incoherent speech), madhyama (emanating from the throat), vaikhari (articulation). They saw the temple walls crash and crumble, thence, without a trace, all alike ran away in haste.

155. Death strikes from life's enchanted cup. Cherished treasures of the heart, such as honeyed delights of dear wife, wealth and home remain behind kinsmen bear him on a bier, speed it towards the common burning ghat and discharge their burden to flames. Having done their part they hurry home

156. Witnessing the corpse from which the spirit has departed, men think it will not happen to them. They purse the tinsels of the world and degenerate without any karma getting extinguished.

157. Mourning friends, the spouse who weeps and all his dear children only follow him to the river's edge—they do not go even a step beyond; there and then sorrow drops its mark and the pyre is quickly lit. Then, the graceless band, whole-heartedly take a plunge in water.

158 The great potter wrought to shape this entire Universe of vast-compast treasure, from water clay. If a moulded pot breaks, men keep the pieces still. But if the body cracks no one will even care to keep it.

159. The body is fashioned out of numerous constituents—the five senses, the six chakras, the thirty joints, the eighteen sides, the nine ligaments, the fifteen rows, all are burnt to ashes, when finally consigned to flames. We know nothing more beside or beyond this.

160. In a pot, chopped to pieces, they placed the fruits of fig and the seeds of greens—seeds of greens are symbolic of unending karmas. The particular greens (Arai keerai etc.,) referred to here grow the more it is cut—it is mixed and ground to a paste and then consumed. The wailed loud and

bore the body away in haste.

161. This body has no roof about if, it has no standing ground (foundation) below it. It has two legs and a central beam to support it; but no cross beam exists; it is rudely thatched on top but unlined within. It is an empty vessel enwrapped in a karmic garb.

162. When the dancer's swaying shape and flashing feet are gone, the banquet hall remains deserted, unlit and unadorned. They now sing another song to a wailing tune, and, seeking fire, they fling the body to its consuming heat.

163. The foetus emerges, when three hundred days pass you know, dear friends that nothing remains of it now. For in 12 years time it has learned to smell the rich odour of life and at seventy, it has turned to dust—thus the show ends briefly.

164. When the flame is out, the lamp remains. Unaware, that the oil is spent, the fools lament aloud. They fail to grasp the truth, that night follows day. And thus immersed in sorrow they fall and moan, ever sobbing more and more.

165. The body and the soul, that the Lord of blooming Kondrai wrought (Lord Shiva), does not worship, the Divine. They lie neglected in the seventh Hell, writhing in pain and keen agony which cannot be worded. The kith and kin, who are of no avail, cry widely and shout and howl and sigh.

166. With the pride of life, man fills his fugitive years with horse and sword and outspread canopy. But even as the grawl cavalcade sweeps past, circling from left to right, the going breath of life expires.

167. When the energising soul leaves the body which is a leather bag, it does not matter whether the ravens feed on it, or the bystanders scorn at it, or drops of milk are poured on it and praised.

3. Evanescence of Wealth

168. Even before seize your elephant and car, your kingship and grace, and take away you riches, if you but seek the Lord's asylum, you need not do any other austerities, even while life pulses.

169. The radiant moon that animates life turns into massive

darkness. Likewise, why then speak of riches which cannot meet a better fate. If you unwaveringly seek the Heaven's king, choicest treasures fall at your feet like pouring clouds.

170. The shadows are useless to them, though they are with them and see their own shadows. Likewise, those who claim their wealth as their own are foolish. In the same manner, the life that comes with the body is sure to depart. But they do not see the light that lends lusture to the seeing eye.

171. The industrious bee hops from flower to flower, seeking, gathering and scenting its store of sweet honey, but soon the subtle thief digs and steals the hoarded wealth. Likewise, the same story is repeated to our earthly treasures.

172. Weigh well the pros and cons, and having weighed, one should not waver. One should not lose his bearings when caught in wealth's eddy; we should fling aside the transient trappings of earthly treasures and thus when the pale sergeant, that is death, comes, we should be ready for the great leap.

173. We cling very fast to our stock of cattle and gay riches which are all less stable than even the boat which upturns midstream, likewise, a bond ties the body to the soul and no one knows when it will give away.

174. However much of treasure we may leave behind us, our wife, children, brothers and sisters will only exclaim that we have left nothing much for them. If we devote our life merely to accumulate such treasure, at the end, when we are in agony no one will come to our help.

175. Our worldly desires grow, but there is none to find the truth, there is one state to hold, but nine exists for life to leave. Then old familiar faces come smiling to greet and bow; they are deceivers ever, for they abandon us without a reprieve.

176. Think, think of the Lord, when the vital spark leaves this mortal mould, there is no bribe to lure it back, the loyal servants of death are bent on a restless mission, do not consider anything that you pulse with Hot breath.

4. Fleeting Dazzle of Youth

177. They see the Sun rising in the East and setting in the West, day after day. Again, the tender calf grows, flattens for

a while and then dies, but they do not comprehend the world which is a wonder-pageant, and still, blind of eye, they never apprehend the truth.

178. Even as the years roll on, there is none who holds the Lord in his bosom. There is none to probe and perceive him who is profound, Even if Time's thread is stretched to its utmost, still they will not know the spark that kindles all the lamps around.

179. When youth had danced its way to palsied age, the chance to fill the years with more and more good deeds is scarce; so while life still throbs, fix your mind on Nandhi, into whose spreading locks the holy waters of Ganga pour eternally.

180. There was a time when fond damsels, who are the idol of wenches with budding and jewelled shaped breasts, bestowed their love on men who are to them slow sucked, cane's sugary juice. But now the sweetest cane has become bitter *nux vomica*.

181. The boy grows to become a youth and youth very surely decays to old age, but time's changes do not teach them that nothing abides. And so, in ceaseless pursuit, I seek His sacred Feet, who, transcending this world, presides beyond the Universe.

182. Day after day we wake to greet the morning; night after night we seek the night by couch; Eventhough God, who is good and great, may frown in wrath, His true devotees never miss the guarantee of His Great Love.

183. The five senses that dwell inside the body, may at anytime leave it. If the five senses become unsteady, the body which is the container of the senses also perishes.

184. We perceive only the external Sun and eye with which we see it. We do not realize the Lord within who stimulates both the eye and the Sun. Thus not knowing Him we pass from heaven to hell again and again, and pass away in the spring of our youth.

185 We, pitiable creatures do not think of the Lord who dwells within us with sixteen kalas—the kalas being a digit of the moon or a part. They are 1. Krupa (mercy); 2. Mrdutha

(gentleness); 3. Dhairyam (patience-composure); 4. Vairagya (dispassion); 5. Dhrti (constancy); 6. Sampat (spiritual prosperity); 7. Trasya (cheerfulness); 8. Romance (rapture); 9. Vinaya (propriety, humility); 10. Dhyana (meditation); 11. Susthirata (restfulness); 12. gambhurya (Gravity of demeanour); 13. Udhyama (enterprise, effort); 14. Akshoba (emotionlessness); 15. Audarya (magnanimity) and 16. Ekagratha (concentration). Then we wonder why we enter the mother's womb, and later pass away again and again.

186. In the days assigned to you and before youth passes away, pour out your heart, in songs of praise to the Lord. In the days that were assigned to me, I, wasted not the minutes away, but seeing all, remained apart from them.

5. Impermanence of Life

187. It is seen that the wanton buds, sprouting and blossoming on tender twigs, flash their beauty and all too soon die. Seeing this, yet they do not praise the Holy Feet of Lord Shiva. It is sad to note that they do not know when the sure call comes from the most high.

188. A field, that is the body, lay ready and ripe for the five senses to work on. The five senses watched, ruled and tilled that one body-field. But when the grim summons of death came from the Lord of death, all the five senses fled and quit the body-field forever.

189. The body likened to a musical drum has two rhythms, the right and the left breaths, keeping time; the five masters, the senses, inside the body make a display. But the Great king, the Jiva—dwelling within, when he departs the drum lie shattered like a heap of inert clay.

190. The Lord of this frail body, that turns to ashes, is Nandhi, the Lord of Vedanta dance. It is He who disports Himself in this crumbling frame. They who do not know that this body is an empty vessel, they also do not know what sustains and supports the life.

191. The Sun's rays visit all the ten quarters, but men who measure with their little sense do not know this; These men on earth—subject to birth and death—do not ponder nor

do they muse on the deep mystery.

192. Even a fine woven cloth gets torn after a time, the dark lock turn grey, the year begins and ends, this truth is not realized by anyone.

193. The body, a cooking pot contains the rice of nectar, the three fires are the Sun, Moon, and Agni and the five types of fire-wood are the pranas. As the days are passing away very fast, the rice of nectar should be got cooked without wasting time.

194. The bee that seeks nectar, flies high on top for its flower, and there, alone, it sucks the fragrant juice; Even so, they who seek the blessed divine grace, aspire for the Light that is beyond the visible reach of our eyes.

195. You should perform noble deeds in order to shape good karma; you must praise the Holy one, to reach the Holy land. This is the law, we need, the law for men who are blessed with this earthly life, to seek the eternal life.

196. Do not speak in envy, do not stray from the Dharmic way, do not covet others' riches with lustful greedy glances; attune your heart with pity, as you sit down to eat and share with others even before the feast commences.

6. Non-violence

197. There are many flowers available for the worship of the Lord; but the best is to refrain from killing even an atom of life; the best steady flame is the mind which is tranquil and the best place for worship is the heart where the soul resides.

198. The men who shout and yell to kill and stab another, will be bound with strong ropes by death's ruffians, and stationing them at the fire-gates of Hell, the agents will in turn torture and roast them in hell fire.

7. Abstain from Flesh-Eating

199. The agents of death, for all to see, bind fast the ignoble ones who do eat base flesh, and quickly push them into the fiery jaws of hell and fling them down to be there forever.

200. Detest and shun these horrid sins, such as killing,

thieving, drinking, lusting and lying. Those who attain the Holy Feet of Lord Shiva and the Eternal Bliss do not come to grief; such men forever repose in the bliss of wisdom.

8. Extramarital Relations Forbidden

201. Just as one, declining the luscious ripeness of the jack fruit, yearns for the tamer taste of the date which is thorny, the lusty youth covets the neighbour's guarded mate, when within his house, the dear wedded wife pines away.

202. Deeming the sweet ripe mango, which stands for one's dear wife, to be still unripe, though tended with loving care, they, whom the senses beguile, 'bury it' deep and climb up the gnarted tamarind tree, stands for other women, for the sour fruit, only to break their limbs.

203. Only those who are rolling in wealth, and such men whose intelligence is obscured by ignorance, yield to the sensuous charms of other men's wives; it is impossible to transform the minds of such men.

9. Evil Women—An Ignominy

204. Though the leaves of the nux vomica tree are fine, its wealth of fruit which is better on the tongue, is unfit to eat. Likewise, in passion's heat, do not ever pledge your wavering heart to them with rounded breasts and luring smiles.

205. Those worldly folk, who seek Comnutrial delights are like the eddying water sucked into whirling pools. The incontinent passion is such that it is fleeting as a dream; it is not real, so let not its siren spell be fool you.

206. A damsel so full of charm and tempting like a she-elephant, may embrace a lover with the ardour of grass that has received a fresh fall of rain. But if another more handsome man, looking like a celestial comes, She will ask the first lover to wait and desert him.

207. What are the joys that we seek or find in a woman's charms? is the question. The truly wise of heart pronounce their course thus: it is like the sugary juice from crushing mills in the hand, but in the body it is bitterer than, bitterest neem.

208. Those infirm of mind who, in vain folly, indulge in sex, are irretrievably lost in the lust of sex, sordid and rank, if they do not in good time and bind and restrain themselves.

10. Hoarding of Wealth—A Vain Pursuit

209. Life becomes a joyless desert when the riches, that have been accumulated to make a living by incessant toiling, have all gone away. Garments are torn to tatters and loved ones and dear friends, with no more love to spare, forsake you. And you, with nothing more to give or ask, void of glory and pomp, neglected by others, walk like an automaton, a sad man.

210. Even as the day dawns, men strive to fill the stomach pit; with needed tools, they seek hard to step the hungry void; But whatever the way of life we pursue, our only way is to praise Him; and surely then that pit, meaning the birth pit, is filled when what in us is impure, is swept off.

211. In order to fill the stomach's stony pit, they seek the precious gold; but little do they know how hard it is to fill birth's pit; it can never be filled with precious gold. Only when you attain true wisdom to rule that pit, then that pit is filled, and life is washed clean of primordial impurities for ever and rendered fit.

212. Our kith and kin, pursue us unrelaxing, and the bondage they forge with us is more stern and is relentless as karma. So, before life leaves the body, in good time, you should light the lamp of wisdom, and thus intent, keep close to that new-lit track.

213. The six tastes harry him, the five senses malign him giving him countless miseries, the pursuing karma through birth after birth tortures him; thus he learns to despise life and finds refuge in the Lord alone.

11. Pertaining to Sacrificial Fire

214. The riches of the spreading sky and earth are free from obloquy; all the directions and the hosts of Gods who hold sway there, all flourish in the wake of victory, when true Brahma, commencing with Vedas pursue the sacrificial

way.

215. The Vedic Brahmins who, intent on salvation, perform holy sacrifices, give before they eat; they stand supreme, even in true knowledge. So too in conduct they lead-heading straight to the one goal.

216. When the sacrificer in the company of his consort, maintaining the discipline of yama, etc, offers oblations to the outer fire and the inner fire, they proceed along the correct yogic path.

217. When in rapt devotion they chant manthras morning and evening, the two Goddesses—Gayathri and Savithri—in smiling grace stand with them. Then, the karmas, good and bad, like two birds springing from one seed, depart fluttering in great haste.

218. The egoism in us is burnt away, when the flame emerging, from the sacrificial fire fed with ghee, enters our heart. Salvation dawns on us the moment this truth is realised, for this is the Supreme path.

219. All our sins fly like a wick with that is fast consumed in a flame, all our diseases that karma brings in its wake fade away, and all evils that our karmas bring in its train are scorched—they all fade and fall in the rising sacrificial fire.

220. Formly holding that vast riches are a grevious curse, they hungered for the Lord who gives us the richest treasures; in order to achieve the undying wealth they performed all sacrifices, and waited, hoping and dreaming for the immortal prize.

221. He is the pure flame; He is the immortal Lord; He is the radiant flame who resides in the core of the heart; He is the Lord whose eyes are the Three flames: the Sun, Moon and fire. He is the transcendental Lord of the seven worlds, who is the master of the Homa's (sacrificial fire) cool flame, and besides all this, He is my heart's kin.

222. My Lord resides as flame inside the fire of Homa (sacrificial fire). He is seated inside the flame of the funeral pyre too. He is the two fires in the sky—the Sun and the Moon. He is the fire of the Homa that scorches karma and checks the sea of karma from expanding, just so He is also

the fire that was contained by the Lord in the northern seas, when the devas and asuras churned the ocean for Ambrosia.

223. They who striving in true penance everywhere, raise the sacrificial flame, conforming to Vedic rities, tireless and unsparing in kindling the Holy flame, their's is the true eternal flame and their names become immortal.

12. Righteous Path of Brahmins

224. They are Brahmins who perform the six duties, such as to learn, to instruct, to give alms, to receive gifts, to perform sacrifices and to persuade others to perform sacrifices. They tend the glowing fire and pray thrice—morning, noon and evening, daily. They stand firm on the holy path and perform the rituals chanting the Vedic manthras and hymns both morning and evening.

225. Intensely eager, to imbibe the noble doctrine of Vedanta, they merge in Pranava, which transcends the three syllables. And having the vision of the Lord who is Nadhantha—transcending sound, Vedantha—beyond the Upanishad and Bhodhantha-transcending the pasu-pathi-pasa complex, they merge in Him and be in eternal bliss. The vision of the Lord is the finite end and there they grow into unending bliss.

226. The meek, holy Brahmins, in order to seek the heart of truth, they chant the noble hymns, with their minds centered in the holy Gayathri and the mysterious Savithri. They do not drown in maya, for they are mounted on love's chariot and are lost in love's sweet ecstasy.

227. They the spotless Brahmins, pondered deeply on Pranava's (Aum) great holy way. Inspired and guided by the Guru's grace, they recited the mystic lay and the rituals prescribed by the four Vedas. And thus they attained pure, pristine manifestation realization of the pure form of self-manifest existence (swarupa).

228. The truth, penance, the realization that he and we are one, the intense control of the senses and the getting rid of the body-mind couples—all these help to attain the Brahmic state.

229. The Brahmins who yearned for the mystic truths of Vedanta, heard and listened, but still they yielded to the sway of desire on them. It is true Vedanta, only when earth-born desires are all crushed and those who have truly grasped Vedanta, have all their desires burnt away.

230. Do thread and tuft alone prove or make a Brahmin state? It is not so, for the thread is but cotton and the tuft but hair, the true thread is Vedanta and the true tuft is knowledge. These virtues belong to them, the Brahmins who truly see to these things.

231. I assert that those who are devoid of truth, bereft of pure wisdom, lacking sense-control, inert spirituality, empty of devotion or failing to grasp the divine truth, are not Brahmins, but are only mad fools.

232. The Holy Path is neither *chit* nor *achit* (real/unreal) state. The true Brahmins transcend the state of consciousness. Inspired and guarded by the Guru who leads the way, they reach the blessed Holy state; the pure Brahmins abandon all actions and rituals and glide into Thuriya Samadhi state.

233. Only those who chant the Vedas are true Brahmins; it is only the Vedanta preached by true Brahmins that is lofty. The true Brahmins realize that if other texts which are defective are read it is only for a show.

234. The Holy Brahmins who embrace the pure life, ponder well on truths mark the end of the Vedas. If they tend the sacrificial fire both morning and evening, then their land does not wane, their king's earthly empire grows ever.

235. When the light of Vedanta dawns, they are freed from karma, then, they scale up the path to the light of Nadantha; when thus they reach the Lord of Bodhantha light, they attain salvation and *siddhis* come to them.

236. They see the truth when the 'you' and the 'I' merge in one, then they seek the triumphant Lord seated firm and serene. Past all babbling words of sweet-sounding praise such alone, the worshipful grace they attain.

237. For those who partake of only the havis offered in the Homa, their internal and external attachment vanishes; their egoism and mind ceases to wander elsewhere; like Brahma who seated in the lotus they enjoy bliss.

13. The Rule of Kings

238. The ignorant king and death are cast in the same mould. Nay, to tell the truth, the tyrant king is worse, for more justly than the foolish king, Death claims his due. But the witless tyrant obeys no laws, but kills in murderous fury and death, does not approach the truly good men cast in a finer mould.

239. If he who rules the state fails to seek the Divine way or fails to strictly observe the Holy Law daily, then, day by day his land, enveloped in folly, decays and day by day the rulers' wealth declines and dwindles away.

240. If one refuses the holy life, then the holy garb is of no use. The truest garb is theirs, when the outer guise and the mind are in accordance with each other. If the king rules justly and he restrains those who go off the holy way, then he and they attain salvation.

241. If Brahmins flaunting the thread and tuft lead an unholy life, due to unredeemed folly, then that land droops and fades, and the glory of its ruler runs to waste. So, the king, scanning deep in the light of wisdom, shall cup the thread and tuft, kept and possessed for empty show.

242. When senseless fools donning the sacred thread and wearing matted locks, pretend to possess wisdom by chanting phrases, the ruler of the state shall, with the help of wise men test such men and for the good of the country, impart words to them dressed in wisdom.

243. It is the duty of the ruler to protect the cow, the woman, the true sacred Brahmins and men in holy garb whom the divine acclaim. If he ignores the duty, his name shall be ever cursed and his hell shall be irredeemable.

244. If one seeks the high salvation and true treasures, then, he should, awake or asleep, unceasingly pursue the holy way, it is to be known in truth, that of the labour done in this seagirt world, only one-sixth of the produce is due, to the king.

245. When a ruler protects his state exceedingly well, the subjects are duty bound, to incline themselves to the same end. But when the enemy, in the lust of pride, invades the

state, then, the king should leap like a leopard to defend his domain.

246. With the breath held in control, letting the inward fire to rise upward and with the mind turned to samadhi, one should reach the moon and qualify of the divine, nectar that flows from there. Instead, like inebriates, if one madly consumes heady liquors, then, such a man should be justly punished by the ruler.

247. Those who do not abide by their faiths that they profess, shall, besides the judgement they receive in the life beyond, by punished on the earth, in terms of Agamic law as revealed by Lord Shiva, by the just ruler of the land.

14. The Glory of Rain

248. The outpouring fertilising flood of rains, makes tree and plants bloom enriched with sap; The areca palm, coconut, cane, green plantain and even the nux vomica—all stand laden rich with crop.

249. The mountain torrent rushes down from the heights, boundless like the love from the pure heart, foamless, stainless, clear and crystalline, it is fit for bathing the Lord.

15. The Glory of Benefactions

250. Do not hoard, but give freely to all. See that food is served to others before sitting down the eat; the crow calls its brood to share its food. Do not discriminately over much, do not eat in greedy haste, however, sweet it may be.

16. Exaltation of the Charitable

251. The who seek and adore the Feet of Lord realise the self; they who most freely give in charity realise the self; they who cognise the Tathwas realise the self. They who realise the self become kin to the Lord in dear amnity.

252. It is easy for all to offer a green leaf in worship to the Lord, it is easy to give a mouthful to the cow, it is easy for all to give a handful of food to others, before sitting down to eat, it is too easy for all to bestow good and kind words on others.

253. The food that is given to feed the needy-that alone is

true charity; they who find out this simple truth are true men. But they who hoard in silence, like water in a pool past access, are blind to the ways of charity, for they eat and gorge alone without giving to others.

254. If you do not drive away ignorance and fill your mind with wisdom, then in days of plenty you will not give in charity. What awaits and avails it, though wide awake, if hell-fire spreads around you, or if you are impoverished of heart.

255. Even when knowing little of yourself, earing nothing for your good, and even unmindful of the poverty of tender youth taking no care, Death's stern relentless summons arrive. So, before death steals upon you, let noble charities that you perform, declare your redeeming goodness.

256. He had no kith and kin, who renounces everything, he who is dead, has no delights, likewise, the Lord denies His presence to him who is without charity, the Lord is known to him, only by the measure of charity done by him.

257. Some by doing such noble deeds; they overflow in charity; they become noble Gods in the high esteem of human beings. Death comes to many who hold this fleshy body their dear God, and it says to them, that He, death, is their Supreme God.

258. Our life's boat flies across the foaming sea of Karma: to dispel this laborious strain from life's vain battle, the twin path ways are the glory giving *tapas* and charity, which are the heavenly escorts to us and our dear kin.

259. Our earthly desires that know no end, are attached only to worldly objects. One's Godly way of life and the following of the noble way of charity, even the little things that one gives, are the sure prop provided for the life hereafter; take all the rest meakly as the Lord's gift for the day.

17. Ways of the Egocentric

260. The ripening nux vamica falls profitless on the ground, such is the barren wealth of those who deny charities. These hardened sinners do not know the truth. With usurious greed they deeply bury their treasures.

261. The aeons pass, the unreturning ages fly away; the alloted span of life dwindles away daily and this irksome body, as if squeezed by some unknown power, perishes, yet, seeing this, they do not learn the way of charity.

262. Those who deny doing charity do not know to praise the Lord's fact, nor can they enter the precincts of the city of Shiva's grace. Their ears are inclined only to those who preach falsehoods, and they stand enslaved to sin, being condemned to the hot embrace of hell.

263. Such is the lot of those who do not give in charity; that they fall a prey to consumption, anaemia, asthma and colic pain. Fleshy ills, sore throat and snake and thunder do not approach them that relieve the needs of others.

264. The Lord is adored by all the world, yet some do not praise Him; it is they who deny even the smallest bit to the needy poor that they do not care to tend the grove even with one potful of water. They will stand for ever in hell, their and is very near.

265. The persons without charity go unescorted, alone, on the last lap of their journey. Journeying thus, they miss their track and get caught up in birth-cycle in this world. They do not know how to dispel the karma that binds them, and so slip and fall to be irretrieveably lost.

266. They whose heart melts in charity, see the feet of the Lord and by their steadfast faith, attain the might of Swarga. But those sinful ones bereft of charity, helpless, forsaken are engulfed in low passion and pass into eternal night.

267. These two: Bliss and pain—are woven into the web of life. They are the results from the devising of our own deeds (past karmas). Even knowing and having seen that bliss from giving, yet the fools do not give in charity. They become shrivelled of heart and remain unwise to charity, not knowing its glory.

268. Think always of giving and gifting and you will become the Lord of blemishless glory, immune from death and birth; you will enjoy bliss, unearned by your worth deeds. Do not deny and cause pain for then you stand condemned as animals.

269. Do not seek wealth that many reckon as life indeed,

nor waste your days flattering silly minded fools of dark wisdom; but turn your feet to the Eternal Home and praise the Lord and then you will prove to be a true bowman by hitting the mark straight.

18. To be Love-Intoxicated

270. The ignorant prate that Love and Shiva are two entities. But none do know that Love alone is Shiva and when men come to realize that Love and Shiva are the same, they ever remain in Love of Lord Shiva, and Shiva they remain.

271. He is the great dancer smeared thick with burnt ashes. He wears leopard skin gleaming brighter than gold, and adorned with the tender crescent flashing rich with argent ray; at His Holy Feet, I remain entwined in Love.

272. You may turn your bone to fuel, your flesh to meat and left them roast and sizzle to gold-red blaze; you gain nothing by these strict austerities. But unless your heart melts in the sweet ecstasy of Love, you can never attain the Lord who is a treasuretrove.

273. They of intense love will surely have the vision of Hara; they of compassionate heart will attain the grace of His Holy feet of praise. But the world-burdened will only see life's revolving wheel (wheel of birth and death), be lost in the mazes of horror and enter the trackless ways of Hell.

274. Worship the Lord with heart melting in love, seek the Lord with pure love for He is the source of all Love. When we direct our Love to God, He too approaches us with love.

275. The Lord who sports honeyed kondrai flowers on His Head. Who was self-born before the beginning of times, and who abides even after the *pralaya* (final destruction of all). He, came to me out of His great compassion.

276. Many do not know Him who first wrought this world. He wrapped this world, born of his Lordly grace, in infinite love. In this evil-ridden world, He, the Lord of limitless space, filled out life with his unending Love.

277. The effulgent light emits beams of purest gold, so, plant that deep and firmly in your heart. If you, in yearning

song, thus worship Him and seek Isan's grace, then be sure that there is no end to His copious blessings.

278. He cause birth and death too in its wake, we see this mystery occuring daily, and yet mankind cling to life in deep desire. They do not call on Him, nor do they seek Him, calling Him-father, great and kind.

279. He is inside Love, He is in outer nature; He is also as the body. He is the past and the future: He is the Lord of the Rishies; He is the precious one who resides inside Love. Only those who reside in Love will find the free refuge in Him.

19. Siva Cognises Those who Love Him

280. He knows what we scorn and what we gain; The righteous Lord in love rewards us as befits our merits. Being well-placed, He wards His grace to such, who, with burning zeal and heart full of love seek Him alone.

281. The Lord gave us this earthly life to attain supreme bliss, but we spend it in doing deeds that bring misery; yet if only we have love for Him, we will put an end to our rebirths.

282. There will be spiritual glory if we have love and the grace of the mother will come to us; so one should give up attachment to the body-mind complex and ardently seek the Lord.

283. Like the sweet love experienced in sex-act, so too, succumb yourself to Him in the Great Love. Thus, all your senses are stilled in this sublimed Love. This becomes that, bounding in supreme bliss.

284. Even the enlightened *siddhas* standing close in banded group, did not know the Supreme Light in splenderous glow; but He gave the bliss of salvation and the splendid vision, to them whose hearts did overflow in intense devotion.

285. I saw the feet of the Lord, decked in adorous kondrai blossoms; I saw the feet of the Lord dressed in dark-elephant skin; I saw the feet of the Lord abiding on a lotus blossom; I saw the feet of the Lord within the intense love in the core of my heart.

286. The heavenly beings praise my Lord God as one who outspreads into myriad forms and things; they praise

Him as the Great Lover who is inside Love and savours the tributes of Love. It is very sad indeed that few seek Him or are led to Him.

287. Those who know nothing but only the cycle of birth and death, think that through worldly love they can attain the Lord; but the Lord is beyond birth and death and it is only through true devotion he can be attained.

288. The Lord God knows them who by night and day, seat Him in the care of their hearts, and adore Him in exalted love; He comes and in close proximity, stands before them as inner light, as they love Him in actionless trance.

289. It profits little if, intermittently, you pursue the Divine Light, but I will, unceasingly, seek the Greatness that has no end. To merge in Him, My Lord, my heart's precious Life and treasured delight, is the Holy bath.

20. Erudition

290. I discerned the meaning of life and its close knit union in the body. I sought the Lord untold by the devas, in the depth of my being. Denying nothing, He stepped straight into the inner care of my yearning heart; and thus I gained the great learning of being free from fleshy bondage.

291. When the learned-wise sat in deep meditation, they obtained the inner eye in their deep illumined souls. What they saw and spoke in contemplation, they imparted to others, and in turn opened others' eyes leading to high wisdom.

292. While yet life exists, adore the Lord of existence, prove in action what you learn to clear all sins. In unfaltering accents worship the Lord and you will behold a jewelled lamp which is beyond compare.

293. Men of learning abandon the worldly ways that fetter them. They praise the Lord day and night unremittingly. Practising and flourishing high on the coiling-snake like *kundalini*, they achieve firmness of mind and also of body. With the glory of youth, as if they have been alchemised on herbs.

294. The Pure Light comes as our guardian angel from high; the pure word dressed in beauty comes as our guardian

angel, the pure rich fragrance comes as our guardian angel. But it is the pure knowledge that comes as our guardian angel, which is the best and which leads us to all the above.

295. If the learned yield to the outer things of life, then all the lore is fruitless for them who fail to scale the heights with holy books to guide them. It is best to lean on the rod of *vairagya*, for the birds of desire fly away then. And yet men in ignorance cling to them and forever lie instupor.

296. Even as the sunstone radiates luminous sparks, those who meditate on the Lord become effulgent, the education we acquire will help us to meditate in the spiritual field of the moon.

297. In life's journey He is a support and rare Eclixiw. He is an unfalling guide in all the seven heavenly globes. But to those who are ignorant of mind He is no support at all. He, the mightly being who is great and kind is a sure prop.

298. If desire you must, then seize the Lord in desire, for all things are obtained if you get the Lord's grace. Like the deep-skilled devas of flaming light, the truly learned attained heavenly bliss.

299. He, whose body is shaped of the five elements, owns the seas and the high mountains. He is the best of the immortals who, through endless ages mounts the powerful bull, to arrive at the hearts of His devotees.

21. Audition and Retention

300. Listening to Dharma and to the words of Holy persons, listening to God's valorous acts and to the many manthras of the devas, listening to the lous reports and the peerless decade of the Lord whose body gleaning bright as gold, are all to attain the sate of Lord Shiva.

301. No one knows Him who is there, the Lord of all Devas and the supreme divine being. If there be any such, let him chant His praise, listen to the holy word and realize Him, for whosoever praise, listen to the holy word and realize Him; for whosoever chants His praise and realises Him, he stands aloft and envisions (envisage) Him in his heart.

302. Vishnu obeys and builds at Nandhi's bidding; at

Hara's bidding, Brahma obeys and creates, those who obey Shiva's bidding, they become devas, if you crave to achieve the fruits of your action, then you are chained to attachments.

303. The pious mortals who praise the Supreme Lord, rise to the state of immortals in time to come. Those mortals who do not fail in penance, receive His joyous grace. Thus the Lord of rare penance, rarely awards the Supreme prize.

304. Talk of Him ever, adore His name and prattle in praise of the Lord who gave us birth and death. Then the abiding light of His dear presence, like fragrance in flowers, comes in grace to you.

305. To seek excellence, listen then to excellent things, and follow the true mandate of wisdom—if your mind awakes to these, and if, you do not slip or stray away, then the Heavenly Lord, unhesitatingly will be yours forever and will never forsake you.

306. Those who think that they can attain the Shiva-Bliss through the senses, are like children who play with sand considering it to be rice. Those who cannot understand that He cannot be pointed out objectively will remain ever ignorant.

307. Life and body provide sure support for the soul, listening to worldly holy things is a sure prop and resting place. The one refuge to seek is Shiva's Holy feet with thoughts of Shiva, and with this supreme support to aid you, you can wholly afface rebirth.

308. He is the first being to them that exalt His name; sufferings persist for those who scorn His Grace. If you do not lose yourself in rapture and chant His great Glory. He stands a veritable stone-cow in complete silence.

309. The heart and the tongue met in unison to cognise the Lord: though he is in diverse shapes, we should find Him in unity. Then eventhough you are shaken in life like an axle from the pin, at that time seek the primal Lord in love and bind the Lord to yourself.

22. Illiteracy (Ignorance) Non-Learning

310. The Lord approves with His benign eye of grace even the unlearned, if they are blessed with the vision of the

Supreme Truth. But if the seeming learned fail to hold the truth, and are blind to the divine rays of True Love, they are indeed unlearned.

311. The truly learned live pursuing the one and only path. But others say that these are many paths of knowledge. The Supreme God is present in all places—and those who are unaware of God's pervasiveness are unlearned.

312. You fix in your heart as abiding joys things that are transitory; even so, you deem this mortal body which is frail, as enduring stuff. Though the Lord God pervades all life, He and His Light are absent from the hearts of the unlearned.

313. Bereft of all power I fell into karma's griefs, by not learning the ways of Hara, I fell into dark abysmal depths, also I did not learn to stamp the great benefactor in my heart. I learnt only to dance down the primrose path to hell.

314. The truly learned seek the path of Dharma and strict penance, because they knew full well that life is a fleeting vaporous mist. But the ignorant who are in truth this world's sordid knaves, sport in carnal joys mixed with karmic misery.

315. Just as there is the fruit of knowledge above, so too within us there is the same fruit; not knowing this men search for and analize earthly fruits and thus exhaust themselves in useless writing.

316. It is not possible to have a vision of the Supreme, without knowing the 36 tathwas and their scope. Wisdom can dawn on one, only by knowing the tathwas. Only those who go to the limits of the tathwas and have a vision of reality can be called educated.

317. The fools devoid of learning are unfit for us even to see them; the fools devoid of learning, their words are unfit for us to hear, the fools devoid of learning, find their friends only in fools, the fools devoid of learning, do not come near wisdom at all.

318. Though learned, they are fools if they are not acquainted with Sivagnana, they do not give up kith and kin and they do not strike at the root of ignorance, for their eyes do not turn to the different quarters. But they alone who truly reckon and are wise in love, win the truth.

319. Even to the immortals, the First Being is the Light Divine, the great Supreme God is the Light that devotees seek; some proudly claim that because of their good learning, they know Him truly well, yet, they do not catch the faintest gleam of His Light.

23. The Path of Justice

320. You do not have wisdom, unless you stand in the path of justice. To those who stand in the middle path, hell does not open its gates. They are heavenly beings who stand in the path of justice. In the noble fellowship of the just, I too walked their way.

321. Vishnu, the blue-dark cloud-hued being stood in the middle path; Brahman who chants the four Vedas stood in the path of justice. The wise saintly souls stood in the path of justice. He, our Supreme Lord, stood in the middle path.

322. Some became saintly, because they followed the path of justice. Some became heavenly beings, because they stood in justice. Some attained Siva-state because they stood in the path of justice. And so, I too stood, unfaltering in the good company of the just.

323. What He creates, none but He alone destroys; the just bore aloft His Holy feet on their devout heads. Those who chant the pure name of the Lord with ardour, and cling to Him thereof, they meet in the society of the just.

24. Abstaining from Liquors

324. The cow that is fed on broth of rice does not wander from tank to tank, the cow that is denied its drink of broth grows weak and lank. Those who swill the neat toddy, go astray from righteousness, for Sivanandha, the supreme bliss, which is far and away, is the truest drink.

325. The soul-hydroptic for the Siva-Samadhi state is lost in sweet rapture; it overflows in the bliss of the ever sweet nectar of Sivanandha. When you are fed on such nectar you do not lose the pure self-bliss, but forever you thus sit and lie below the Holy Feet.

326. Lust and drink are fit for only the wicked. In unholy

ritual they drink and lose their senses. But the wise drink the nectar streaming from the mighty Lord's Feet, which destroys egoism and bigotry.

327. Those who belong to the Vama sect, drink and perish; the *vama thanthra* is also referred to as 'Pancha Marga' since the rituals call for the application or use of five ways namely Mithuna (copulation); Matsya (fish); Manisa (meat); Madhu (liquors) and Mudra (parched rice, but really meaning the adoptation of various esoteric signs); the lustful ones are wholly lost in sensual delights. But the pure souls find the light of sacrifices in their inner flame; They who chant His true name, approach Him fast.

328. Those who do not see the inner truth, do not know about the Pasu-Pasa, also, they do not dwell in the Lord's bounteous divine grace, they do not seek Shiva yoga, in the clear light of wisdom, for they who soak themselves in liquors can never appraise the truth.

329. The fools who swear by their faith that number senses, who yield to the heady of drink—they neither seek nor see Mamaya's Home, for they are bound by the felters of maya (Maya in Shaivism is of two kinds; 1. Pure Mamaya which is creative and corresponds to *icchaśakthi* of sanskritic culture; and 2. Impure mamaya which includes within itself all the efforts, such as time and the impure souls. But recovering from the hold of maya, they merge in the Lord and are free.

330. The fumes of wine bring stupor and they destroy the truth, and make us seek the false, delusive joys of lust. Such men do not advance to attain the true wisdom, of sweet compact reason. Will such men ever attain the truest eternal bliss?

331. Though lost in meditation and rid of the cycle of day and night, and dead to outward things, yet, they do not drink of the nectar of bliss, and I, caught in maya which causes night and day, struggle to reach the bliss of the Lord's feet and that knows neither night nor day.

332. Some religious sects in order to seek *sakthi,* consume ritual drinks, but *sakthi* dies when the over-powered senses swoon; True *sakthi* indeed, finds its birth Sivagnanam in order to merge in Truth-wisdom-Bliss, and to it is immune to other

things.

333. If the aspirant (Shiva) imparts the grace, we also have the grace of Sakthi. In the same way, if Sakthi imparts Her grace, we also gain the grace of Sakthan—Shiva and Sakthi are shown as united in the Ardhanareeswara form (Androgyne). If we hold both, Shiva and Sakthi in our hearts, then truly, the eight siddhis will shine on us.

334. When all Tathwas and egoity are past and gone, and the truth of the self is realised, we come void of false penance, and are immersed in the truest joy; we are also rid of worldly lure and have drunk full of the heavenly bliss. This is indeed, true Siddhi and unalloyed Sivanandha.

335. The yogis, who hold their breath in control, yearn for the nectared delights of contemplations' Moon (Cranial Moon). They seek the eight *siddhis*; but the witless fools are they who yield to drinking and thereby let their senses swoon in its heady joys.

336. Unfold the petals of the Holy master's Lotus Feet, open and drink deep the nectar that gushes from that spring, Lead the Yoga-breadth up through the spiring channel and thus ascending in Samadhi, reach the Divinehood in Holy meeting.

Tanthra One Concluded.

2

Tanthra Two (Kamighamam)

1. The Sound of the Body (Agasthyam)

337. The celestial beings hailed the Supreme Lord and bewailed to him that the earthly-orb swayed from its epicentre and that it was dangerous on its side swerves (the south of India was depleted in weight by the exodus of the world's inhabitants gathered, to witness the Holy wedding of Shiva and Parvathi, at Mount Kailash in the North. The earth-orb swerved from its epicentre). And the Lord spoke to Agasthiyar, Holy Sage, who sat inhard Tapas, amidst the blazing sacrificial fire, to hasten to the swerving side of the globe and be seated there, to redress its balance (such is might of the Tapas of rishis, that the spiritual weight of one soul devoted to Shiva, equalled the physical weight of the sole population of ordinary millions).

338. Unfailing at dawn, with the Sun that is in the High heavens, Agasthya lights the divine fire. He is the Holy Muni of north from where the primal fire was born; and He is the all-pervasive radiant light.

2. Eight Heroic Deeds of Lord Shiva

339. The celestial beings moaned thus to the Lord that,

Anthaka, the Asura, equal to and even frightening unto the God of death, whose name he bore, and armed with invincible divine boons acquired by prolonged penance, was harassing all the worlds. And the Lord, lifting high His charm trident pierced Him straight to certain death.

340. Daksha, the giant king of the Himalayas, the son of Brahma erred fatally. To defy the Lord's primacy was his deadly sin—to establish this he performed a sacriligious sacrifice. And the Lord smote his head and consigned it to the sacrificial flames. And then thinking that such incidents are needed for this world, to serve as an object lesson, He so fixed a sheep's head to the trunk and let him live in this chimerical form.

341. The Lord's feet are all pervasive. They support all the worlds and they sustain all life. That the heavenly beings may know this, He, in mounting anger, nipped the head of Brahma—that is, Who was as five-headed as Shiva, and had one head pinched away with his finger-nail by Shiva who assumed the aspect of Bairava—and demanded Achutha, that is Vishnu, to drain him blood into the skull, when they both defied His supremacy.

342. The Lord pervades all, He fills my heart too with joy; He spoke the Vedas and all the scriptures. Him—the Haughty Jalandathara—the giant, and foster son of Varuna the Sea-God, who became a boon that no one else could kill him, and so, harassed the celestials, who in turn complained to Shiva—challenged in duel, and the Lord with His too marked a circle, and into it He saw the monster's final end—Jalandathara was destroyed by himself, for when he lifted the circle to his head, it changed into a powerful discus and destroyed him.

343. The Primal Lord who wears Ganga's sacred water on His matted crimson locks, destroyed the three cities, (the three cities with three flying fortresses were ruled by three giants. Flying their fortresses they landed on the cities of the celestials and destroyed them. Shiva, all the while with a smile on His lips, reduced the three cities to ashes). Thus, the ignorant recount the legend of the three cities. The three cities are the

triple impurities: egoity, karma and maya. It is these that He burnt, but who knows this truth thereof.

344. Seeking to rival the Lord's might, the Heaven's beings lit the three fires and performed an unholy Homa. The sacrificial blaze roared high; and from inside it arose an Elephant, Gajasura, of evil power, whose hide the Lord peeled off. They knew not why the Lord did it. And the Lord smole for the very fire to consume all those who aross from that fire.

345. He coursed the kundalini fire, coiled in Moolathara, upward to hollow on top. In that very fiery Yoga way, He scorched the God of death. The reason for Shiva to scorch Yama, the God of death was, because, he promptly threw his noose around Markandeya's life, at the age of 16, when fate had declared that he should die, not caring that the virtue of victim was immersed in Shiva worship. At the sight of Yama, the devotee clung fast to the Shivalingam Moorthy. The death-noose thus encircled Shiva as well and His wrath erupted, rousing the kundalini fire from the *Mooladhara.* He spurned Yama forcing him to a regretful retreat by the heat of His divine fire. The heroic feat happened at Kadavoor, the Holy shrine here below.

346. It is said that when the work of destruction ceased over the entire Universe, the Lord Shiva was seated in yoga. His thoughts stilled in deep meditation. And soon Kama, the God of sexual love, came there, to tempt the Lord by shooting His shafts of love. But He, in the Yoga way, foiled the Love-God's wiles. This He did at Korukkai, the divine shrine.

3. Linga Puranam

347. Sakthi said, that of a certain will She espoused Her Lord of Divine Feet; saying thus, She incarnated as the Mountain King's daughter and performed severe penances, in intense adoration to the Primal Divine Shiva, Lord, for all the celestial Beings to witness, and for all earthly beings to delight.

348. The Lord is mighty; He destroyed the Flying Fortress, So do not despair that He is beyond your reach, for sure He is the Lord who abides with abounding grace in them who

are true seekers.

349. The Lord is the primal one, He is the effulgent light. Brahma, that is Aya the creator and Mal-Vishnu, the preserver went seeking Him around the boundless oceans for an immeasurable period of time. Thereupon, Shiva granted the Divine Disc to Achutha (Mahavishnu) and the Eternal sword of Gnana to Brahma.

350. The ten-head giant Ravana, of peerless might, lifted the lofty mount Kailash, the seat of Shiva with his twenty shoulders. But the Lord, gently pressed His toe down, and so, the giant Ravana screamed that the Lord, Shiva is eternal. It is said that the Lord released him from under the huge weight of the mountain and blessed him, when Ravana played on his Veena and evoked repentant melodies from the Sama Veda in adoration of the Lord.

351. Dandhi, a brahmin cowherd boy, knew the way to the life hereafter. So, he would make *lingam* images out of sand, and in adoration, would pour on it the five products of his herd of cows. His father seeing the precious milk and other products of (milk-buttermilk, ghee, butter and curd) the cows being wasted, beat the boy and kicked off his fond images. Dandhi flew into a blind rage and smote the parents offending leg with a sword (axe). And so, the Lord, seeing this, blessed Dandhi bedecking him His own garland of kondrai flowers to sport it forever. It is said that at the appeal of the celestials, Shiva revived the dead father too.

352. With face drawn in care and hearts stricken with grief, the Devas together rushed to the Lord and cried that they bowed only to Him, the Lord. Praying thus, they prostrated low; and He of unsurpassed renoun told them to rise up, and not to fear.

4. Sacrifice of Daksha

353. The Heavenly Father in boundless fury, walked into the raging blaze of the unholy sacrifice of Daksha, in an attempt to denigrate Shiva. When the Lord rose in great wrath, the Devas who participated in the sacrifice ran helter-skelter in all directions, deranged—some losing their heads, others their

face, the nose, the shoulders, the teeth, the hand and other limbs, their depraved worship was unconsummated.

354. Hari, in vain attempt to quell the confusion that ensued, rising bragged that it was not Shiva, but himself who is the beginning of all things. Because of this, he fell into the fetters of consuming passing. Then, he repented performing tapas, and the Lord who has no beginning nor end bestowed His grace on him.

355. And so it befell, indeed it befell at Daksha's sacrifice, a wonder though it is, truly that is what befell there; thus the Lord does lend His grace in the knowledge of each according to his desert.

356. And thus it was with Brahma, Vishnu and the rest of the Gods; and thus it is that they came to be what they are; and thus it is that they are there; and thus the Lord does sit serene within, to reward the heart that truly seeks Him daily.

357. While the heavenly beings sang of Him as He sat in serene rapture, He came rushing to me along the highway of bliss that opened, in the manner that is yoga, like the Kundalini fire that shoots upward as from the Moolathara, to the crimson spheres of the Sahashrara.

358. Many of the high and handsome lacking in the grace of the Lord, met with disfigurement and destruction. Thus all these Gods—Hari, Brahma and Daksha, the Sun, Moon, Fire and Indhra all lost head, face, nose, hand, shoulder, some limb or other.

359. The celestials who audibly chant the sacred manthra, use the silent *pranava* (Aum) to rouse the *kundalini* from the *moolathara*. By chanting the Pranava, they control the mind and with the help of Ajapa Japa they rise to the heights.

360. Many of the immortals prayed to the Lord to protect the nine sacrificial pits for the holy ones to delight. And like Lord, bending His Mountain-bow, shot shafts of fire at the city of the Asuras, destroying the evil ones, that they may never rise again.

361. The ones learned in the lores may well waver, but you do not waver; melt in love for our primal lord and you will for sure have him; He destroyed the unholy sacrifice of

Daksha and yet turning back as they repented and prayed, He our Lord of Holy speech, blessed them all.

5. Deluge (Total Destruction)

362. Contending for primacy, Hari and Brahma fought each other, when the cataclysmal deluge at the end of time, in other words the end of the Yugas, swallowed the black mountain tops. And then from amidst the floods, there arose as an immeasurable mountain of light, the One Lord, manifesting the Truth and even blessing both Hari and Brahman.

363. The Lord stood high amidst the surging flood, as a flaming mountain, for the Gods to know His primacy. The mortal ones powerless to stand the radiant glow of the fire. Mountain rushed in trembling fear to the surging waters. The Lord then spoke to them telling them not to fear and that they would be saved.

364. As the smell of the ocean subsided, the sea of immortals and Devas sang praises to the Lord. They did not know that He who created the Ocean and the firmament rises beyond to the Ocean of His benignant grace.

365. The Lord, He creates all, is Himself the uncreated being—there is none in the world here below that thinking thus holds Him to his heart. Oh ! how compassionate He was, when He placed the primal fire to quell the tides, when the oceans ebbed and roared.

366. Brahman that is seated on the comely lotus sauntered in the Lord's path in the manner unreasonable of a sinful wretch. The Lord sought Him and in the ways approved by the gods, gathered alms in his severed head.

6. Boon of the Discus (The Magnificence of the Sudharshana)

367. Filled with arrogance as being the Supreme Guru, Vishnu vaunted about his egoism; then the Lord Shiva of the Silver mountain made the discus fly away, and it orbited around the seven worlds.

368. He, the Lord Shiva, bestowed the divine discus (Sudharsana) on Damodhara, but the potency of the weapon

was far too much for him to hold. And so he prayed to the Lord in fervour, and the Lord split its power into two.

369. The Lord split His power into two, one Half he gave to Vishnu as a Chakra, and the other half as the body to Sakthi non-separate on His side—and thus He remains.

370. Damodhara aimed his discus (Sudharsana) at the crescent-decked head of Veerabadhra that destroyed the depraved sacrifice of Daksha, then, the doughty Lord sentforth a sneese and behold, a gusty tempest blew and the discus fell down powerless against the Supreme God.

7. Skeleton and Skull

371. Shiva is the Lord of all celestial beings who wears bejewelled crowns of dazzling beauty; but, how is it, that the Lord bedecks Himself in skull and bones. For, if the Lord wears not skull and bones, they may turn into dust forever; that they may yet be redeemed.

8. Seeking Crown and Feet of Shiva

372. In ignorance, Brahma and Vishnu, each bragged as the Supreme Lord; then Shiva stood before them a pillar of fire; and they both searched and screamed in vain to behold His feet.

373. Yet, through His abounding grace I knew the Lord; He is the one who fills the seven heavens, who stands as a pillar of fire, the one pervading the seven worlds, He of the bejewelled throat.

374. The Lord is life, body and consciousness; He is Fire that enveloped the far firmament, transcending the Sun and the Moon. He pervades the cosmic space—thus His form of Your is Holy, and is the support of the vast universe.

375. He stood filling cosmic space and the two—Brahma and Vishnu trembled in fear. They went searching for His entire form. The one sought the crown and the other His feet but neither found them.

376. Vishnu, the adored of the Devas, asked of Mahabali for three feet land and Brahma whom the Rishis please in hymnal praise, the two contended in ego to gain the primacy.

377. Both, the four-headed God seated on a Lotus and the comely Lord who sleeps on the dark sea, are of the same essence as the Great One who cognises all, as the life within is unto the fleshy body.

378. Know now the truth of the divine flame that enveloped all and hold fast unto that; then you may receive the sceptre to hold domain over the earth and the grace to follow in heaven above.

379. To the celestial beings that prayed to Him, the Lord granted the sword of protection. But they do not know Him entirely as I who became His vassal. He granted Himself to me, He granted me bliss and the grace of His feet as the final prize; the celestials do not approach His feet thus.

380. The Lord is inscrutable, He defies the infinite vistas of time, the four-headed Brahmin prayed to Him to reveal His Self and to decree his fate on his bowed head. And the Lord far surpassing the dazzle of the Sun at the end of time, revealed Himself as pure Light.

9. Creation—Microcosmic

381. Paraparam that has neither beginning nor end consorted in pure consciousness with Paraparai; and in that pure light arose Param; and from the union of Param with Parai immaculate Nadha was born.

382. Nadha united with Bindhu; from this union, of Nadha-Bindhu did Shiva and Sakthi appears; Gnana arose from Lord Shiva and Kriya from Sakthi and Iccha (desire) arose from Bindhu itself.

383. Maya appeared from Sakthi, and the two mingled like a jewel and its lustre; He who make the Maya appear, remains far, far away beyond description.

384. Paraparam and Paraparai conjoined far, far away in the distance of time. After that, did Nadha conjoin with Bindhu and further on Sadhashiva united with Sakthi; Ana Sakthi acts on the *prakrithi* Maya (material) sphere. This sphere is known as (Maan) 'Mahat'. Thus was Mahat born. From Mahat evolves the five elements, earth-water-fire-ether and space and thus mahat is the finite support of these five elements.

385. Space evolved out of Maya, then, air from space, water from air and from water the earth's hard crust, thus they, the five elements formed in succession. The five subtle essences (Tanmanthras) appeared from maya and from them, the five gross elements (Bhoothas) appeared. The present world has arisen from the Vyahruthi Bhu.

386. Shiva, the He/She, creates all the universe. He has five sons—the five manifestations that are Sadhashiva, Maheswara, Rudhra, Brahma and Mahavishnu. He, the Holy one that creates all the Universe is Himself the Lotus-seated Brahma who became the creator.

387. Together in looks united in full, were the Holy Nandhi that is Sadhashiva and the Sakthi that evolved Mahat, and from this union arose the universe like a blossom opening gently.

388. Water emanated from fire, light emanated from wind, sound emanated from space, the earth emanated from water, this is the way the five elements evolved.

389. The primal one who is the Lord of the celestial beings, in co-ordination with Hari who swallowed and spot out the seven worlds and with Brahma, the four-headed creator, created of yore, this vast universe.

390. The supreme one who is aloft the Mount Kailash with Hari in the Ocean bed and with Brahma in the blooming lotus, created life by pure consciousness.

391. He is the first cause, He is the all-pervasive in Love. He is Vishnu; He is Brahma. He is the Veda, the sound and matter—the cosmos. All are the diverse manifestations of the ever-compassionate one.

392. He is a rare ruby; He is easy of reach; He is the one Lord. He is easy of love. He is the light within Brahma and now I know why it is easy for the creator to so do it.

393. The holy one in grace so ordained death and birth, He, the compassionate one, in that hour when by His throught, He commences the act of creation, He fills and pervades in all the eight directions.

394. The Immaculate One creates all; and as He created me too, He animates within me, is a support to the body, He

creates the bodies and *milieus* for Jeevas too according to their karmic desert. Truly, this is the Lord's act of divine justice.

395. In the act of creation, He stands adorning Himself with death's bones and kondrai's blooms gleaming as pure gold. His resplendent form out-shines red-hot gold. His form which is a vast refuge for all departed souls. He enters within Shiva and cognises all.

396. When He and She commence play, the play of the two produces all; there are changing seasons and the produce is diverse. When He and She join in Holy union, the act of creation is complete.

397. Shiva pervades Rudhra and functions as destructor; He enters Vishnu and functions as protector; He pervades Brahma and functions as creator. The other three, are just shells in which He works.

398. The Five Gods Brahma, Vishnu, Rudhra, Sadhasiva and Maheswara; in order to perform the five acts such as, creation-preservation-destruction-obscuration and redemption, as one from the other in causative succession, were born out of the union of Anava Sakthi with Bindhu, and being born of Anava Sakthi they were not free from the taint of the individualising Malam (Aanava malam-impurity).

399. Maya in union with the Bindhu yielded the rest of the three Mayas (Sudha-Asuddha and Prakrithi). The Bindhu was born of Nadha and Nadha was born of Parai, and all this takes place in the creative play of Parasiva, the ultimate.

400. They are the five elements beginning, withspace; they are the five manifestations beginning with Sadhasiva; They all originated from the Eternal Maya and they perform the functions allotted to them.

401. The honeyed Sakthi Thripurai evolved from Bindhu denoted by the orderly triangle; it is She that became the compassionate Sadhasiva; it is She that performs five merciful deeds.

402. She is the diverse names of Glory of Maya Sakthi. She is Mononmani, the ample bosomed; She is Mangali, the ever auspicious; She is Varani of elephant form; Arani of haunting forests, Mohini of tempting beauty and Poorani the

perfect being. She is the cause-effect conjoined in one, She is consciousness beyond consciousness.

403. Sadhashiva that stood as One animated Maheswara, and then Hara, Hari and Brahma. Thus did the One become the five.

404. The One alone created the seven worlds, the One alone spanned the seven worlds; the One alone survived the seven worlds and the one alone pervades body and life.

405. Our Lord is of the hue of red lotus, Our Lord is of the hue of crimson fire. He sundered the chain of births, that the dark cloud-hued Vishnu bound in *pasa* and consigned to the flower-bedecked crowned *maya*.

406. He is Nandhi, the great, who pervades life in all the eight directions. He brings body and soul together in birth. He is even in the heart of those who doubt Him and from there He seeks them; I have known Him perform this very often.

407. The One family (The trinity) creates the seven worlds; the one family preserves the seven worlds; the one family destroys all the seven worlds; the one family pervades all life and body.

408. Shiva together with Sadhasiva and Maheswara, stirred and commingled the impure family (of matter). The two then besought of the Lord, They asked what they should make, they pleaded to the Lord to command them. And the Lord Himself then spells it out.

409. And so, through creations He filled Himself as life within forty-eight lakhs of species. Then the men who are in doubt ask how this can happen, are truely condemned to the enveloping darkness.

410. The Sun, Moon, Agni (Fire) and the rest of the celestials the space-air-fire-water-earth-the sound-word-mind and the like were all born of Maya in union with Bindhu.

10. Preservation

411. He pervades as light and darkness, He pervades as fame and blemish, He pervades as body and life and He pervades as my constant thought.

412. He, Himself stands as space and celestials; He, Himself stands as body, life and matter, He, Himself stands as Sea, Hill and dale-through the entire creation in unbroken continuity, and He, Himself is the Supreme Lord of all worlds.

413. The Lord, indestructible, and continuous, pervades as body, life and world, as sea, cloud and cloud-laden sky. The Lord stands in majesty as the majesty, the true way that never closes.

414. He is Nandhi the great. He is the pervasive life in all the eight directions; He is the One who brings body and soul together in births; He resides even in the heat of those who doubt Him and from there He seeks them. This I have known Him to perform often.

415. The Lord takes diverse forms at the end of each aeon. Once He stood as pure light, once as the tempestuous typhoon, once as incessant rain and once as Vishnu, floating on the deluge, who is an aspect of Shiva/Sakthi.

416. He stands as love, wisdom and meekness, as pleasure and pleasurable union; He stands as the beginning and end of time. He stands filled as five elements and He stands in divine love.

417. He fashions all the worlds in minute detail. He, Himself fashions life, conferring birth; He fashions things both big and small—the cauldron, the pitcher and the pet. He, the Almighty architect fashions these and more.

418. He is the corporeal body and He is life within the body, He is pure spirit and He is infinite space. He is radiant light and He is consciousness inside. He is Nandhi—He supports me, animating life within the body.

419. It is indeed, a miracle that staggers imagination, to sustain the myriad lives in countless universe. Not less so, even after the end of each aeon, when after each total destruction of the cosmos, He draws the *jivas* in Himself and sustains them until the next cycle of creation commences. He sustains the yogic path that leads to the seventh state of existence.

420. You may well seek Him through rituals before fires; distant only He shall be, so seek Him in yearning love binding

low on the ground hanker after Him life after life and the Great One shall grant you the immortal body.

11. Destruction

421. With fire and Lord burnt all space, the Lord burnt the Oceans with fire; He burnt the Asuras with fire; for truly, fire is the Lord's shaft on hand.

422. I witnessed at the end of aeons that His Dayas, moments of repose, are three, of them one is Kalpantha. At the end of time, all things fell uprooted in destruction. At that time, this orb was then like a boiling rice pot; its mountains and valleys alike were all burnt to ashes.

423. The fire that resides in the *Muladhara* spread over all these—the earth on which we tread, the eight snow-clad mountains, the seven seas whose ebbing tides roar and on everything else. And, the spreading conflagration turned the earth and sky to look alike, and the shapes they took are not to be wondered at.

424. The grace of Bindhu descended from the cloud-clad mountains and pervaded the universe and all the quarters. It entered the Pranava and abides as the Kundalini in the Mooladhara.

425. There are four forms of mergence. The first is in deep sleep, the daily mergence. The next mergence is beyond sleep, the pure mergence is when the *jiva* remains completely actionless and the ultimate mergence is in Sivasakthi.

426. What transpires in the four forms of mergence is in daily mergence, the gross and subtle bodies are transcended, in the next mergence, the *mayaic* body is annihilated, in pure mergence, the mind and cognates merge in the Infinite and in the Ultimate mergence. Redemption Death Shiva's grace truly descends.

427. The senses are silent in the daily mergence, in the next mergence the soul leaves the body; the soul remains completely free in the pure mergence and in the final mergence there is union with Lord Shiva.

428. These are the four, mergences, the daily mergence is in deep sleep; the next mergence that gives the soul a longer

rest; the pure mergence that puts the soul in primal quiescence and the redemption mergence that steeps the soul in Lord's grace.

429. A plant, which is the soul, sprang out of the void that is Shiva, as *jiva;* it returns to the void in the final state. Yet, it shall not be void again. In that void, it will remain, become exhausted, and then it shall die, that is the fate of the Gods—Hari and Brahma too, who do not survive the holocaust of Samhara.

430. Scorch the gathering karma and exhaust them. There is One who annihilates them and the city is the body He fashioned where He does it. He pervades everywhere. He placed the mind and cognate *tathwa* group besides. He gave us ample wisdom to discriminate. By uprooting all karmas alone can the birth-death cycle be ended.

12. Concealment

431. He is the One who is within us all. He is the light within; He does not move even a wee bit from within. He your heart are thus together one, but the heart does not know His form.

432. The Lord who gave me life that is so sweet, also imprisoned me in miseries of *pasa.* He fashioned a skeletal frame and clothed it with flesh and skin. Then lighting in the spark of life, He hastened to annihilate me, Why is it so ?

433. The Primal Lord fashioned this body with built-in subtle organs of senses, together with Hara, Hari and Brahman who all assembled together. We do not know the treasure that He has enshrined here in.

434. The Lord is the light of our eyes. He loves us; He is the primal one. He is male-female and the neuter. They do not seek the path with melting hearts and tongues praising Him that leads to the celestial lake.

435. The primal Lord blesses all denizens in the earth below and in the heaven above. He dispels the darkness from the black chamber of the soul; and radiates the pure rays of His dazzling light within.

436. The world is full of contradictions of sounds, desires

and forms, but within this diversity there is the unity which the Lord of beautiful form very well veils away from our vision.

437. I held my Lord who is concealed in me; I adored Him in the depths of my heart, and behold He revealed Himself unto me and blessed me here below. Those here below may well adore Him, revealing the abounding rapture and enduring love that pleases Him too far.

438. The Sadhasiva that stood as one animated Maheshwara and then Hara, Hari and Brahma, thus did the one become the familial five in number.

439. He is the pure one, the Siddha in whom *pasa* lies prostrate. You should be firmly seated on land here below and seek Him in felicitous ways, so that you may vision the land, beyond not doing this, you are like one who is seated on the banks of holy Ganges, yet remaining unwashed and impure.

440. The clay is one, but the receptacles are many. God is one, He pervades all species. The eye sees several things; yet, it does not see itself. Similarly, the Lord is concealed in us. The Lord's concealment in us is so mysterious, is one of the five actions of God. It has a purpose, and that the Jeeva to seek. It is by seeking God, that God can be seen. Thus it is, but we see not the God in us.

13. Dispensation of Grace

441. Know this, that, He is the wind that blows in the eight directions. He is the wavy Ocean that girdles the earth, He is fire, earth and sky. He is the one that binds and unbinds the body that holds precious life—the *jeeva* and who seek the Lord, having experienced pleasure and pain in life, are bestowed grace. This bestowing of grace leads to the *jeeva's* redemption or liberation from the cycle of births and deaths, is the Supreme Act of Almighty God. The attainment of grace can come through total surrender in loving prayer, through the yoga way or through the realization that the all pervasive God is the object of all knowledge. And when it comes the *jeeva* is cleaned of all primordial triple impurities.

442. He, who seeks the luminous Nadha atop and savour of its sweetness, will no more know of death. The Lord is the seed of all, of the sun, moon and fire, of the vast universe, the Sole Architect that builds all as well.

443. The potter mounts the clay on the wheel and fashions as he conceives. Our Nandhi, the Lord is also the potter who moulds the world this way and that, the way His fancy takes.

444. He is the Lord Supreme who, the bull (Nandhi) for His Mount, mighty demons for this army. He is boundless in his munificence. He gifts the world for us. His goodness alone is goodness. He who is of matted love, dwells in the thoughts of all.

445. He created seven worlds in fondness for us. In love for us, He created the seven aeons, the five elements and He created this body and breath in love for us.

446. In olden days, He created the seven worlds. He created the countless celestials in the past. In olden days, He created numberless species; He who created all in olden days stands Himself uncreated as the Primal Param.

447. The Primal One created the five elements, the past endless aeons and the countless heavenly beings; the Primal One created and sustains them all as well.

448. He is one with the infinite space of the seven worlds and yet transcends it. He cannot be indicated as this or that for He, Himself becomes the various things and *jeevas* and helps them to go upwards, and remains the Supreme leader of the world.

449. He is the Light within and the body without. He is the beloved of the immortals above, their precious object. He is the Holy Form, the Adorned One of the saintly beings here below, He is the pupil of your eyes, the object of all knowledge.

450. He is the cosmic form that no one knows. He is the infinite space that fills the Universe; He is the space in the tiny pot too. He pervades all in close union as inseparable as the water in milk, His Goodness is indeed impartial—I knew of His bliss which is unweared.

14. Creation of Embryo—the Microcosm

451. He conjoins to my dear life that He awakens, the twenty tathwas that departed from me in the past life. Thus, He creates, even as He created the Macrosm, the Universe of the human body also, seated within the globular womb (the mother's womb). He, the Primal One created knowing what I am to be.

452. The Kundalini fire abides above the Mooladhara. The infant lays there in the water-filled (alaintaic fluid) womb, its tiny feet entangled. It lay in patience waiting that the sweet life may seek its onward course that He has ordained, releasing the ten *pranas.*

453. This body was then ordained, when two parents/ united in pleasure. He, the Heavenly Lord ordained at the hour of union, the sorrow-house of vexing *pasa* when that is to be.

454. Only they who have seen birth's finals alone know how Purusha of the twenty—five tathwas entered the corporeal body. No one else knows that which, in twin form, rushes within and seeks the woman's birth-pit.

455. The vagina opened when the penis pierced and together, they—the five pranas, the five elements, the five *tenmanthras,* the five gross and the five subtle sense organs all rushed in, and they all lay concealed in the centre of the forehead.

456. Just as the breeze spreads the fragrance through the surrounding air when the flower blossoms, so does the *prana* breath, when He blows in, extend over the *jeeva,* to be unfolded gently all the destined hour.

457. If these—the eight constituents of the subtle body that leave ultimately, the hundred and eight Tathwas that sneak in with the Purusha immersed in them, then the nine orifices and the Kundalini that coils like a serpent are not driven in by the divine charioteer into the infant body, then truly the infant will be born less than human (say a pig).

458. When in the union of sex, the male flow dominates in force, the infant is born with tamasic qualities of Rudhra; when the flow is in the reverse, the Sathwic qualities of Hari

dominate; when the two flows in balance, the Rajasic quality of Brahma prevail; He is born to Kingship fit for ruling, in whom the three *gunas* have a proportionate sway.

459. When two united in accord, there from their vital flows emerged the infant form. But when the *jeeva*, who is myraid bodies has dwelt of yore, now enters into it, then it is dominated by mind. Maya pervades it subtlety.

460. There is the pregnant: womb, the soul lay in primordial quiescence (Thuriya state). In Holiness and in truth the scriptures say that from state Maya and Her tribe—maya's eight evolutes—Desires and the rest, aroused it and conferred consiousness.

461. He erected the frame with skeletal bones; He fastened it with circuitoos tendons; He cemented it with blood and flesh; The Lord thus fashioned this body mansion, for dear life to dwell in it. From this day on, with increasing endearment I seek Him.

462. He is milky white in hue, He is effulgent like the Sun; He is benignant; He pervades the entire body and diffuses His tenderness. This, He ordained in diverse ways contained the rage of life in the Mooladhara.

463. Even on the day, when, ruinous karma trailed after the *jeeva*. He designed numerous ways of preserving it. He surrounded the foetus with water and kept it safe from the burning fire of the Mooladhara; He drew charmed edding circles around the budding life, and so preserved it safe and cool from harassing pasa. The absolute stands as sentinel, guarding the child in the womb.

464. The vaginal flow, surging alike, is met with by the silvery semen that well up, and then the infant is born inhaling eight and exhaling four finger— length of breadth. The child born measures eight spans of its own finger length and so out of the twelve finger— lengths that the *prana* breath constitutes, only eight are inhaled, the other four are exhaled.

465. The Holy One entered into the union of the two. He made a veritable bundle of delusions, by gathering twenty-five Tathwas, and fashioned the (five) sheathed body. Indeed, His gift was munificent.

466. The five-senses along with their foolish ways are born in this body. After death, the senses end with this body. So does the *Jeeva* that permeates macrocosm, also surely end in Nadha.

467. He mounted my life as on to a lead-like device; and there He planted with balance-like precision, the five subtle senses and the other thirty tathwas. He, thus fashioned a body, a steaming cauldron as it were with nine openings.

468. In union's rapture, the couple kneaded the clay for Him to fashion, the tenement of sorrow, with nine channels and eighteen tathwas; the kiln burnt and the pitcher emerged. In this act of fashioning the corporeal body; the divine architect provides for the subtle body that consists of eight Tathwas; the *purusha* body into which eighteen *avasthas* or states enter.

469. No one knows the six affictions (centres) that are placed within this body. Only seek the Great good that wells up therein and understand the *siddhis* within them; know this, that this flesh body is nothing but only of five elements.

470. He is the One who fashioned this body and He breathed life into that body. He set the nine gates, the nine orifices, the Kundalini fire coiled in the Mooladhara Chakra and the Prana breath that measure twelve *mathras* in length. To crown all, He lit the fire of divine Jnana, in the lotus-like Sahashrara Chakra in the cranium. The Lord made all these, and in intense endearment, I salute only Him.

471. The Lord is limitless and He kindles all life from the primal womb of His Sakthi. The liquid seed of causation is stirred by the Nadham, Mighty Himself. He endows it with the expansive form and it attains the manifest form in Bindhu. I seek Him in Heaven and on earth.

472. In the Union of the opposite sexes the light of life truly shielded is born. The individual life is but a bubble in the Primal life's infinity watery expanse. It is but a shadow of the Divine Light encased in the subtle body that is made of five protean senses (*thanmathras*) and the three internal instruments; mind, will and intelligence.

473. Of the eight organs of the subtle body, five are protean senses and the other three are cognitive instruments, that is,

mind, will and cognition. Know that the dear Lord who fastened this body-bag with the sticky glue of desire, will unfasten it too in time.

474. The Lord made the body and it assumed a name and form. Then, He created the earth and the many Tathwas, for the *jeeva* to seek his redemption—So say the Vedas.

475. It is no one else's grace, but only Hara's, it is nothing else but only the grace of Hara's that, He bestows life. He bestows too, the loving care of the twin foster mother.

476. Sakthi, the conjoint cause of creation and the luminous One that dispelled total darkness, together with Shiva, crated the myriad lives, their genus and their species. And having done that, they pervaded them too. Oh ! Your magnificence has no parallel.

477. The seed of life burns as a steady flame in the womb. It takes shape as any one of the three—male, female and hermaphrodite. How the father and mother were at union, even so He printed the sex. That Luminous One was righteous indeed.

478. If the masculine flow dominates, the infant is born as a male; if the feminine flow dominates, then the infant is born a female, when the two flow in equal force, a hermaphrodite is born, when the masculine flow gushes in plenty, then the infant that is born will sway the entire world. And when the masculine flow is scenty, nothing indeed is the conception.

479. If after ejaculation the inhale-breath of the male spontaneously extends five finger-length, the infant that is born lives a hundred years, when the breath stretches to four finger length in measure, the infant lives to the age of eighty. The yogi who knows the science of breath control; if he indulges in sex act will regulate the vital flow according to his will.

480. When after intercourse, the man is short of breath, the offspring will be born a dwarf, short in stature. When the breath blows freely, the infant may be born with defective limbs. The issue will be born a hunchback when the man's breath halts in mid-act. All these breath patterns do not apply to woman's breathing rhythm.

481. When at the time of union, if the mother's bowels are exceedingly heavy, a dullard will be born; if urine exceeds, a dumb will be born and if both exceed a blind will be born; thus it is according to the mother's conditions for the off-spring to be born.

482. If the male breath runs dominant on the right nostril, the infant will be born a male. On the other hand, if the male breath runs dominant on the left nostril, the infant will be born a female. If the descending current, Apana, comes up from the lower regions of the body system twine will be born. If the breath rhythm run in equal measure, through both the nostrils right and left, the baby born will be a Hermaphrodite.

483. If the breath run in equable measure, in both male and female, the infant born will be exceedingly handsome; when the breath rhythm falters in both, there will be no conception at all.

484. The damsel bore the infant seed in her womb, nourished by bright milk that is fed by Sakthi that grew inside in the centre between the eyebrows, and beaming like the golden rays of the rising Sun, it took the appropriate form.

485. In ten months it attains its full form and then it lands on earth at the appointed time, and grows; Maya fosters the body, but who knows the formless Maya.

486. The man did not know when He planted the seed and She who received the seed did not see it. Only the Creator knew, but He did not tell anyone. The Lord who reveals truth is also there, yet, I did not see Maya. Her stealthy conduct was very cunning indeed.

487. Seeking pleasure the two met. The infant seed was born and bred in *pasa's* misery. It then grew to manhood here below. And having grown to stature, it may well seek the ancient one that was before all the worlds were.

488. The cuckoo bird leaves its egg in the crow's nest; the crow suspecting nothing, hatches it and nurses it. It does not remove it nor does it reject it. It does not even ask why. So does *maya* perform this act of fostering the young one in the womb.

489. The Lord is the Primal One. He protects the *jeeva* at

all stages; the root, the shoot, the plant and fruits. Thus, He blesses all life and to each, He grants his own life's pleasure, and He accordingly stands will each one.

490. My Lord is of infinite greatness, yet He is within the littleness of this fleshy body. He is beyond the ken of celestials, yet He, Himself shall appear before you in prayer and penance.

491. Like the salt that emerges from the vast wavy sea, the individual body is formed out of Tathwas that arose in Parasakthi. To be born thus is the mighty grace of Him indeed, hence, birth and life itself is a valuable gift.

15. The Three Classifications of Jeevas

492. Life blossomed out of the play of Sakthi-Shiva; and the *jeeva* who was in the state of pure *kevala* of Thuriya quiescence was freed and consigned to the folds of the two *mayas*, and the Lord then entered the *jeeva's* thought and suffused his being with Divine Spirits.

493. The *jeevas* are classified into three groups basically, according to the degree of impurities they possess. The Vijnana (abbreviated form of Vijnana Kala) is a term more commonly used in Buddhism, meaning ordinary or individual consciousness as opposed to *prajna* world or universe consciousness. The true *vijnanars* are of four groups, the *pralayakas* are of three groups and below are *sakalars*, according to the state of their evolution, who are of another 3 groups. Thus *jeevas* are grouped ten in all.

494. Vijnanakalas, the most highly evolved souls, are of four classes. Those who are in Kevala state are no longer affected by *karma* or *maya*, they are amendable to Anava alone. Next are those who are self-realised, but are still conscious of the self. Then, there are those who have reached the ranks of the eight Vidyesvaras. And finally are those who rank as the seven crores of Manthras Nayakas. All these possess impurity of egoity (self-consciousness) to some extent or other, Only those who are rid of impure egoity are the truly realised beings (no more are they *jeevas*).

495. Below the Vijnanas are the Pralayakalas. Of the three Pralayakalas, a class are those who attained Mokthi. They are

the Jivan Mukthas, who have attained enlightenment during their immediate incarnation. The next group are those bound by the twil *malas* (egoity and karma). Yet another category are the hundred and eight Rudhras. The third major classification of *jeevas* is the Sakalas who have all the three *malas*.

496. The Sakalas are of three. They are encumbered by all the three malas (impurities): Anava, Karma and Maya. Among the three classes, there are those who have attained the miraculous powers of *siddhis*. The next are those who have attained neither and are still powerless to conquer the three impurities, but are simply immersed in the world by sound and other sensual experiences.

497. Those who have rid themselves of the five hard *malas* become Shiva; they become blemishless, eventually they become *siddhars* and finally attain the state of Mukthi; they uproot the bondage of *jeeva* and end their cycle of births. They alone are, who have realised the truth of peerless Tathwas.

498. Vijnanakalas are of three gradations: those who alone abide in quiescent Anava, (the *pralayakala* among *vijnanas*). So are the Pralayakalas of three gradations. And the Sakalas too are of three gradations. Thus there are nine major classifications of *jeevas*, evolving in separate gradations.

499. The Vijnanakalas may by their karma assume corporeal form and it is but by performing holy deeds they acquire the celestials frame and the higher *gnana* form. Thus by their constant striving they gain perennial wisdom and in the end become Shiva, Himself.

500. Having and rid themselves entirely of Anava Mala and lost in consciousness of the memory of *jeeva*, they become Bindhu and Nadha, they attain the highest heavenly abode which is the goal of oneness with Shiva Tathwa. Although all three groups; Sakala and the rest of yore possessed the Primal triple impurities: Anava, Maya and Karmas.

16. The Souls Par Excellence

501. Give just as weebit to a Sivajnani and you shall attain Siddhi, *mukthi* and heavenly bliss; you give a world of gold to the witless, and you shall become poor losing all joys.

502. Death waits for the due moment and seizes lives; But the Lord seizes the life of death itself, such indeed, is His prowess. He blesses all who know Him truly and they who sought Him become immortals.

503. I did not give Him up even while I was in the womb. I did not forget the truth of His Holy Feet. I gave up all falsehood, and sought the feet of the Lord of matted locks, that are like a self-effulgent lamp that needs no oil feeds.

504. Those that are destined to be, let them be; those that are destined not to be, let them not be; those that are destined to get let them go, and those that are destined to come let them come. The mighty Nandhi shows all and witnesses all; He does all appropriate things to those of tender love for Him.

17. The Unmerited Souls

505. You may feed her with fresh grass and you may even tender her well, but the barren cow can give no milk. Even so is the act of giving unto the unworthy souls who are neither good nor holy. They are like a crop that is raised in improper season. They do not flourish nor do they yield.

506. Give only those who follow the way of Yoga, Yama and Niyama, and to those who abiding in constancy adore the Lord. To give to those who have no love for God is indeed a heinous crime.

507. He, who gives to God, to the Guru and to the great Ones who are rid of passions will become a Gnani. The burning hell is not for him; it is destined only for perpetrators who are steeped in worldly pleasures, who do not know of the dire consequences and who will never get God-Vision.

508. You may give away wealth as massive as a mountain; and yet if you give it to those that do not adore the Lord, both you and the receiver will be condemned to perdition to reach the Seventh Hell of ineffable pain.

18. Hallowed Waters

509. Within this body of ours there are many water fronts that are holy. Yet we men do not take gentle dips in them and

drive away our karmas and get purified. Instead we vainly roam will and dale in search of purificatory baths. We are such witless men with confused minds.

510. The Lord will appear delicious cool to them who love Him dearly; He will never appear to them who are steeped in worldly pleasures. But surely He does abide in the thoughts of yogis who control breath and Gnanis who see doubt-free.

511. The Lord is within them, yet they do not know Him; they are all of false faith; the flow of their evil deeds in limitless; their evil deeds will go down, down the deep drain, never to know its destination.

512. They who adore Him, reach His heavenly abode. It is thus the immortals know of the Primal Lord. Even as God is within us, the Ganges, the holiest of waters is also within us. It descends from the Lord's Crest in Sahashrara within the cranium. So bathe in the yogic way, in the pellucid waters of the sacred Ganges and be purified of the triple, impurities and become holy.

513. They dropped gold into the sea and looked hard for it in the pond; there is nothing worse than this indeed to match their folly. Do not seek the Lord elsewhere. Nandhi is within you, as firm as rock of many ages. Yet they do not know Him and do not seek Him, for sure they are lacking in grace.

514. The black *guna* enters the body as frame of Tamas, the red *guna* enters the body as Rajas and the white *guna* enters the body as Suddha Sathwa. The purification of these three *gunas* by the grace of the Lord is bathing (real) in the holy waters.

19. The Sacrosanct Temple (Consequences of Damaging Temples)

515. Let them who transplant a Lingam at an established shrine beware of the dangers it wroughts; even before the transplant is completed, the kingdom will fall to destruction and diaster and foul leprosy will torture them. Thus did Nandhi, the Divine protector declares.

516. Even a single stone's place moved away from the

temple, wall shall spell ruin of the crowned king. He may be a sage, he may be one learned in the Vedas; if this crisis is sure, then the ruin is also certain. So has the Lord ordained.

517. The rains will fail, epidemics will spread and the mighty king will lose his prowess, if the poojas in the temples of the Lord falter. All this is sure to happen, if worship in temples of Shiva who spurned the very God of falters and the ruler will be held responsible for the dire consequences that follow.

518. Harm befalls the ruler, when worship ceases in the temples of Lord Shiva. The rains become steadily scanty. Theft and robbery abound in the land. Thus did my Holy Nandhi declare.

519. A priest who performs the Lord's poojas, if he is a priest only in name, then deathly wars will rage in great fury, fatal diseases will spread and famines will stalk the land. Let the poojas be performed by true priests—thus did the great Nandhi declares in truth.

520. The celestials hailed their Lord, their God, the Primal Lord and prayed to Him to help them and save them from the might of Padmasura which is deathly. Then out of the fifth face emanated His son—Subramanyar with six faces; and the Lord the six-faced God of coral hue to proceed to battle and smite the enemy Padmasura. Six-faced God is Muruga (of the Tamils), who becomes Subramanya (Vedic Natham) or Kumara in Sanskrit, the reference is to the wars waged by Asuras and Devas to be found in the Puranas. When things appear to swing in favour of the Asuras, the Devas approach Shiva for aid and He sends His Son Kumaran (Devasenapathi—General of the Army) to their aid.

20. Darshan of Downward-Looking Face

521. He sports the garland of white skulls, His spreading locks are matted; He supports the vast Universe and fills space in all eight directions; Shiva is blue-throated (Thiruneelakandam) darkness suffuses on the throat of His downward directed face. They say He swallowed the deadly poison that arose at the time of the churning the 'Mighty

Ocean' by the Devas and Asuras; and that it stayed in His throat. But those who do not know the truth and are ignorant. The inner meaning is that Shiva alone knows 'The Knowledge of the Truth' is verily the goal of Self-realization.

522. Oh You men, who live in falsehood and flattery in this seagirt globe, do you know why His throat gleams darks? Only He who made it so, knows it, when you speak the truth, He will make the celestial beings bow to you.

523. Inside the primal fire, Nandhi rises in the centre and stands as Shiva. Gleaming, He pervades all worlds; He who ambulates the world in all glowy, has hue of the twilight Sun. He is the Lord of the Downward-looking face of Mukhalinga, introduced by Thirumoolar. Shiva is described as the six-faced God (Athomugam-Face) which is not known elsewhere. The implication is that this is the compassionate face of the Lord, Shiva.

524. The ancient one of Adhomugha created this vast universe here below; In this aspect of five-faced manifestation, Shiva is Sadhasiva. In Adhomugha, He animates all life. He is Lord, conjoint with the Adhomugha Sakthi of lotus eyes and is best Lord of aeon's end.

525. Listen to how Adhomugha blossomed into a gigantic flower; then it transformed itself into a hundred worlds and then, with limitless energy impregnated and animated them. And then, the Lord, as Adhomugha, remained as their support as well.

21. Malignity of Lord Shiva

526. Those who rid themselves of all doubts in their thoughts and have attained Gnana and seek Him in intense love, shall reach the world of the celestials; if the low-born think any the less of Him, then their fate shall be dismal indeed-like the parrot in the claws of the cat.

527. The Devas and Asuras wasted their lives and finally died. They did not attain thus Gnana. Even the Devas cannot find liberation unless they adore the Lord Shiva. They who adore the primal lord in intense devotion alone can attain truth.

528. The Devas and Asuras not only defied themselves and one another, they defied the Lord and met destruction. Do not defy the Lord, however little, not even for fun, for they snow-ball one into ten.

529. A sad fate overtook the rishis who were learned in the Vedic lore. Knowing that God is within them, they presumed they, themselves were God, and forgetting all thought of Him, they plunged into distracting pleasures (The reference here is to the rishis of Ḍarukạ forest, who ignored Shiva and performed unholy sacrifices).

22. Abuse of Guru

530. The lowly ones do not care for their parents, using foul words they abuse their kith and kin, neither do they follow the Guru's behest. Indeed no one else other than those who revere the parents, kith and kin, and the Guru are in truth blessed.

531. He who speaks derisively of the Guru who taught the wisdom of the one-letter manthra (Om), will be born a lowly cur; and having led a dog's life for an entire yuga, he will be born a worm again, and then shall be consigned as a dust.

532. Those who have done exceeding harm to shock such people as a virtuous wife, a true devotee and a great *Gnani;* will in a year's time lose their wealth. I swear upon Holy Nandhi as this to be the truth.

533. Those who wounded the feelings of the Holy Guru who taught even one letter of the manthra will be born a dog. And after a hundred incarnations as dog, he will die as a human outcaste.

534. If Gurus who are devout of God are caused pain in the heart then the country, the people and their greatness will as all one be destroyed. Even the thrones of the heavenly king, Indhra and of the mighty kings here below, will alike crumble down. I swear by our true Nandhi, this sure.

535. Do not utter falsehood in the presence of a holy guru. For them, goodness and wisdom will depart, the time honoured path of righteousness and all else that leads to prosperity will

be forgotten, and the land will fall a prey to famine.

536. One who throws away the precious gem in hand and instead carries a heavy stone or one who prefers the bitter poison which is fatal, the likes of such a one is the one who follows the path of karma, when compared to Gnana, for the Gnana Guru is the real Guru.

23. Vilification of Shiva Gnani (Maheshwara)

537. The Lord's devotee lives by alms, those who show animus to him, however humble his condition may be, and those who abuse him as they will, shall fall into hell that is lowly.

538. Those who the Gnani, are rid of the benefits of good deeds that they have done; those who revere him as holy, are rid of the harm of evils done by them; those who reach the Gnani's presence will verily taste Shiva Bhoga.

24. Patience

539. In the hearts of those who are firm of mind, lie the varamus lizard of the yoga called Vairagya or steadfastness. Their Vairagya is compared to that of the varamus lizard, which tenaciously holds to the object it seizes does not severe, however hard you pull the reptiles. Their firmness lies in besilging nose and tongue in the Kechari Mudhra, where the tongue stops the nasal orifice in yogic breath exercise. Troubled thought is a torture. The only thing that stands still is exceeding devotional patience, Vairagya or firmness in divine thought alone is bliss. They who possess such firmness of mind are yogis.

540. The Lord seated on His throne was of milk-white hue; Celestial beings in countless numbers stood surrounding Him; Hari and Brahma too, whose king He is, bowed low at His Feet and prayed for His grace and the Lord blessed that they shall highly prosper on earth.

541. The Lord who is our King, is of ripe wisdom, they swell as unto a army in all directions and pray to Him. He creates the fleshy body. He is the Primal one of the celestial beings. If you adore in earnest Love, He will grant His grace.

542. The Lord is the Supreme Yogi. Inside and outside

home, by gentle and forceful means, the Lord prepared You-I constancy of yoga. He created all. He dances on the cremation ground as well. His plays are many and varied. Such is His play.

25. In Pursuance of Company of the Holy

543. The Lord blesses those who seek Him. So I walk with those who go after God, live with those who sing His praise; I consort with them and seek them and their Holy Feet.

544. In distress Your thoughts may quiver like a tender aspen leaf. What avails you if you are distressed. Without love for the Lord, man is in perpetual distress. Oh my heart! yet you do not love the Lord, Do you accompany me to where the Lord succour ?

545. The *gnani's* seek the Lord of the Celestials and they who seek the company of the *gnanis* will attain Shiva Truth, will indeed walk in the path of virtue and will be truly blessed. To resort to such Holy company leads to supreme bliss indeed.

546. The Holy are kin and of the Lord of flowing matted locks, whose fame envelopes all worlds. They reach the golden feet of the father, and He blesses those who seek Him in the silence of their hearts. So reach the almighty king for you shall attain the regal goal.

547. I walked with Holy men. I am a devotee of the Lord's devotee who reached the City of the Fire-hued Lord sporting divine weapons. The devotees who stood at heaven's gate saw me and announced me to the Lord. They prayed to Him that He was the refuge and the Lord welcomed them all to come in and took them all into His bosom.

548. Only eminent devotees will master the karmic eddies of birth; only they will realise the self and will achieve the state of immortality. Only the Supreme devout will enter and be in God. I joined to consort with them who are rich in grace.

Tanthra Two Concludes

3

Tanthra Three (Veerahamam)

1. Ashtanga Yoga (Eight:Folded Yogic Nature)

549. It is very difficult to expound the science of yoga because it is a vast subject. It is a science of breath—closing alternate nostril and counting time in appropriate measure. The secret of yoga was revealed by Nandhi at length; initially to the four sages, Sankaka, Sanathana, Sanathkumara and Sananthanar. The eight-fold science of great yoga (Iyama, Niyama, Aasana, prayama, prathiyahara, dharana, thiyana and samadhi) is eight-limbed, that is of eight organic parts and so is know as *ashtanga yoga*.

550. Herein I shall reveal the ways of Yama and Niyama, the upward coursing of how the kundalini energy from the Mooladhara reaches the thousand petalled Lotus from the Shahashrara in the Cranium peak through the six adharas within the body and the secret of Kevacha, Nyasa and Mudhra—the paths to reach the state of Samadhi. For this purpose, there are number of gestures by movements of the limbs of the body 'Mudhras' as they are termed. The Mudhras are the language in which the body speaks to the deity.

551. Do not waver this way or that. Follow the way of the eight-limbed yoga, for it is the sure path to reach the state of

Samadhi on *gnana* or enlightment. They who tread this blessed path shall reach the peak of gnana and they shall no more be born in this vile flesh. All karmas are ended forever.

Thirumoolar identifies Samadhi with gnana. This is similar to Buddhism where the Ultimate which is to be realised in Samadhi is prajna, at which duality disappears and Gnana, the essence of the individual merges in the essence of the universal.

552. The eight steely limbs of yoga are Yama, Niyama, Asanas etc., are numberless, wholesome Pranayama and Prathyahara alike, then Dharaana, Dhyana (Meditation) and to triump all is Samadhi. Each step is preparation for the next. Yoga holds the key to the attainment of Samadhi or the unitive trance.

2. Iyama

553. The Lord of matted locks, cool and coral hued, in His aspect as Sri Dakshinamoorthy (southward looking deity) taught the four Rishis—Sankaka, Sanathkumara, Sananthana and Sananthanar who were immersed in devotion. The Agamas descened to them from Nandhi. They received the title, Nandhi and were included among the Nadas (Masters). They were taught to perform the holy Iyamas, even if the heavens may pour in torrents in all eight directions.

554. The way of Iyama consists of a number of do's and dont's. The man who stands in Iyama's ways does not kill, he does not lie, he does not steal. He does not drink nor does he lust. He possesses marked virtues, being good, being just, sharing the good things of life with others, being meek and knowing no blemish. Iyama is the background, the ethical preparation for the onward march of the path of Yogic exercises.

3. Niyama

555. He who stands in Niyama should know the path. He should first have steadfast faith that the Supreme being is the first cause, that He, the first being is the central meaning of all Vedas, that He is the light divine, that He is the fire—the Kundalini fire, within that light and that He, who shares

Himself half and half with His Sakthi, are both inseparable and indivisible and that there is divine justice in the play of Shiva/Sakthi oneness.

556. Niyama is the next step. The One who observes Niyama's ways practises the initial ten virtues. He ardently cherishes purity, frugality of food, patience, forthrightness, truth and steadfastness. He abhors killing, stealing and lusting.

557. Furthermore, Niyama consists of the ten more practices. With these ten, one perfects the way in Niyama. They are tapas, meditation, serenity, holiness, charity, vows in Saiva ways, Siddhantha learning, sacrifices, Shiva pooja and pure thoughts.

4. Asanas

558. The next step is the practice of asanas of bodily postures. Asanas are postures practised for 'health and lightness of body'. They give 'Drdhata or Strength'. These *asanas* are numerous. Among them eight are rated high, especially Svastika; it commences with Padmasana. He who perfects these postures, verily becomes the master, for sure.

559. Padmasana is the 'Lotus' posture. The practitioner sits cross-legged with soles of the feet turned upward; the feet are drawn up close on the opposite things. The hands are stretched to the feet. This is Padmasana that is famous even in the far flung places on earth.

560. Bhadrasana is the 'happy' posture. The right leg is placed over the left, and the hands are stretched over the calf of the leg, and an erect and firm sitting posture is observed. This indeed, is Bhadrasana.

561. Kukudasana is the 'cock' posture. The feet are lifted onto the thighs and controlling the breath, the body is raised on the elbows, and a firm immobile sitting position is taken. This Aasana, however, is not included by Thirumoolar in his list of Aasanas which are in number seven (important). Kukudasana, literally means 'cock' posture.

562. Simhasana is the 'Lion' posture. Stretch the hands over the calf of the legs, lift the chin upwards and fix the gaze on the tip of nose. Thus should be Simhasana posture be

done.

563. These seven asanas—Bhadrasana, Gomukhasana, Padmasana, Simhasana, Sothirasana, Veerasana and Sukhasana, along with the eminent Swastikha, constitute the eight highly rated asanas. However, hundred and eighty asanas are reckoned in all.

5. Pranayama

564. Mind is the master of the five senses; he is the head of the home called body. He rides a steed to his destined goal. That steed is the 'Prana Breath'. The steed carries the masterly one and throws away the feeble one.

565. The Jeeva is great. He has two steeds—the Indakala and the Pingala breaths that run in the left and right nostrils, to master, but he does not know how to master them. If the Lordly Guru lends His grace, the steeds will become tame.

566. The steed of prana breath flies faster than a bird. If this steed is controlled, it gives pleasure that is far heddier than wine; it activates the body, it infuses vigour and dispels laziness. I have said the truth, let those who are wise listen to them.

567. The Prana should merge in mind and together the two should be stilled. Then there shall be no more birth and death. Therefore, one should learn to direct the prana breath in alternating streams from left to right and then he shall taste the nectar of life.

568. Inhalation of sixteen *mathras* of breath by the left nostril first is Purakam. Retention of sixty-four *thanmathras* of breath thus inhaled in Kumbakam. Exhalation of thirty-two *mathras* is Rechakam. Thus in *pranayama*, the breath is inhaled and exhaled from left to right and back from right to left with retention in between. A *mathra* is a specific time duration, a measure in time approximately a second. "Yoga suthras of Patanjali" says, "A *mathra* is the time which is taken up by thrice turning up one's hand over one's knees, and then snapping the fingers once."

569. If you control the breath within, it turns crystal-hard and young, however old your body may be. And with the

benign grace of the goodly Guru you may well become lighter than air.

570. Practise Pranayama in prescribed measure wherever you are, then the body will not perish. As you inhale, control and exhale in the prescribed measure, you may well become a triumphant Lord, with the conch of victory, heralding your achievement.

571. They know not that the science of breath consists thus of inhalation, exhalation and retention both ways. They who know the science of breath are destined to spurn the God of death.

572. In Poorakam, the breath is inhaled deeply so that it pervades the upper, lower and middle regions of the body within. In Kumbakam, it is retained around the navel centre. In Rechakam, it is absorbed within in due measure. Those who practise the science of breath, Pranayama, thus reach the grace of the Lord who swallowed the deadly poison.

573. They who control breath thus—inhaling sixty manthras by the left nostril, retaining forty-six in the Homa-pit of the navel and exhaling thirty-two by the right nostril—have truly seen the light of truth.

574. Inhale deeply and steadily; this prana fills the ten Nadis; then exhale slowly and see to it that the body does not stir. Retain the Prana breath and move the Apana breath downward. Thus sit exact and vanquish death.

575. The breath rises within and wanders as it lists, control that breath and it purifies the body within; then your limbs shall glow red and your hair turn dark. Purification by breath control is an important—element of the *pranayama* exercise. The body does not decay and God within shall never leave you.

576. The prana breath like the pair of damsels, runs in and out constantly within the body-house. If and when twelve mathras are inhaled, eight mathras exhaled and four mathras retained, you shall be made divine in Lord Shiva.

577. The twelve mathra breath is an elephant that is awake day and night. The *Mahout* that is Jeeva does not know the elephant; the *mahout* should learn how to control the elephant

and when he has learnt to control it the elephant knows not night and day—it exists in eternity. The elephant symbolises 'ego' and it is in this sense that Shiva is said to have killed and skinned the elephant.

6. Prathiyahaara

578. The next step in Astanga Yoga is Prathiyahaara or withdrawing the mind and looking inward. Practise the mind's withdrawal step by step and look inward. The good that is many, You will see within, one by one. And you may then meet the Lord, now and here below on this earth, whom the ancient Vedas still search everywhere.

579. Prathiyahaara is the restraint of, and subjection of the senses of the mind, which is thereby steadied. The mind is withdrawn from the objects of the senses. It helps in the act of breath retention below the navel. They know not the divine art of fixing twelve Mathras long breath below the navel region. Prathiyahaara is a rare art that helps the practitioner to achieve and advance on the yoga path. Once that art is learnt, the Lord enters within shouting in joy.

580. Two finger length above the Mooladhara, two finger length below the six organ and four finger length below the visible navel, there is *kundalini* within, a flaming lambent fire.

581. If you look twelve-finger length below the nose-tip and concentrate and meditate, the mighty siddha yoga shall be yours and your body shall be imperishable.

582. If meditating thus, you glimpse luminescence at the Vishudhi centre at the throat region, know you are destined for unalloyed bliss; if at the centre of the throat you behold lunar light, then your body will be intoxicated in divine joy.

583. Close the Mooladhara orifice below, centre your thought on Sahashrara orifice above and meditate on that; fix your lance-like vision on that vast space. Thus practising yoga, you shall vanquish time.

584. The Kundalini fire lies two finger length above the anus and two finger length below the sex organ, if you can meditate on the light that burns there, you shall be one with Lord, who ends all birth.

585. Separating the ego from the Maya, separate the Maya from the Lord, dissolve it away; then awareness, contemplation and loss of ego arise, which constitute the glory of *prathiyahaara*.

586. If breath that is exhaled is contained within, the thoughts too are contained there and the Lord shall not leave you. Pranayama aids the practise of Prathiyahaara.

587. In the act of Prathiyahaara all the world will be visioned. You should be rid of the despicable darkness and seek the Lord; if your thoughts are centred firm, You shall see Divine Light and be immortal thereafter.

7. Dharana

588. Control the mind from getting diverted towards the senses and concentrate on the *chidakasam* within the spiral column; the eyes must not see nor the ears hear, this is the way to eternal attainment of life.

589. The Heavenly waterfall ranges from the peaks of the cranium. Unceasing cascades course the prana through the spinal channel. There on the stony arena (of Mount Meru within) the Lord performed His timeless dance; I withnessed the unending light of bliss.

590. Sakthi is the damsel of the Vedas; She belongs to the astral land of cranium. He, Shiva is the bridal Lord; He sleeps in the land of the Mooladhara. He should be gently aroused and made to meet her. Then you shall forever be young. I know this truth upon Lordly Nandhi, forever and ever.

591. For the practice of Kundalini yoga bind the Mooladhara, raise the *prana* breath upward, course it through the spinal hollow and in aptness retain it within, and like a stork at the head of the stream sit calm in singleness of thought; You may well live forever and ever.

592. When Pranayama is practised in proper time-measure; the breath retention will stand appropriate with *prana*, he who retains breath that is *prana*, time and life shall remain inseparate with him.

593. There is a treasure in the thoughts of those who observe silence; they who open their mouth wide drive the treasure away windward; but they who are wrapped in silence

drive it to the lunar peak, it knocks there with its horns and if the gates of the cave do not open, it turns tail in fear.

594. If breath that is forked in and out is directed and centred on the mind, you may sleep well in the spacious bed chamber of the body cave that has two doors and seven windows; and long-long you live there too.

595. Oh you fool ! Eventhough you wake and pray, You can achieve nothing if out of the ten ways (ten kinds of *pranas*) that fill the body five leave by exhalation. Only those who control breath in ordained measure, will surely imprison mind-monkey with the body-fortress.

596. All those who came before have met their final end, Is there any guarantee of any other fate for those who come after ? What then is to speak of the millions and their life to be ? This is a great delusion. The sandy bank will never hold firm.

597. Truly, Dharana is practised in stages. That is, contain the body's harassing five senses in the five elements; then, to contain the five elements in the cognitive internal organs, next, to contain the cognitive internal organs in their *tanmathras* and finally to contain the *tanmathras* in the uncreated being.

8. Dhiyana (Meditation)

598. Dhiyana has been defined to be the state of the Antakharana (mind) of those whose *chaitanya* holds to and is occupied by the thought on the object. Having cast away the thought of all other objects. Dhiyana is born out of perfection of Dharana; When the ten, that is, the five elements and the five senses are contained, one by the other and Buddhi the internal organ in turn is contained by the senses then Dhiyana is born. Dhiyana is of two kinds. First, Para Dhiyana and that is centred on Sakthi, next, Shiva Dhiyana that is centred on Lord Shiva. These are the two ways of Dhiyana that should be initiated by the Guru.

599. Through Dhiyana, the quality of mental realization *(pratyaksha)* is acquired. It is of two kinds—Saguna or meditation on a form *(murtic)* and Nirguna in which the self is its own object. There is an ancient one that pervades as Nadha through

eye, tongue, nose and ear and the intellectual organ. Inside the palatal cavity, He shows the cosmic light. He gave the fleshy body and that we be redeemed.

600. In the undistracted gaze, that is in Dhiyana the light, the *gnana* form of Shiva, appears. Gaze and gaze to one's heart's content, mingle and become one with it and get into the heavenly stream that surges to the infinite spaces of void space, and envision the uncreated being.

601. They do not meditate even for once on the mystery of the jeeva within the body, they do not meditate even for once on Shiva within the Jeeva; Even for once, they do not meditate on the mind where Shiva dwells; Even for once, they do not meditate on the lotus within the lunar sphere. Alas ! they do not perform Dhiyana at all.

602. Dhiyana is a lamp. It is Dhiyana that lights all the lamps within. The lamp of mind should be lighted. It lights the lamp of mind and dispels the darkness of egoity. It extinguishes the fire of wrath and brightens all lamps within. From then on the main lamp—the mind's lamp—is indeed an undying lamp.

603. They may well practise yoga for eight thousand years, but still they do not see the Lord who is as sweet as ambrosia and dear like the apple of the ye; look within in Dhiyana, for Dhiyana is seeking God within, and if you seek Him within. He is enlightened within you even as your reflection in the mirror. It is seeing Shiva's reflection in the Jeeva mirror. All practice of yoga is vain without the seeking within.

604. Taste the fruits of Dhiyana, therefore, let the eyes be fixed on the tip of the nose. Then no more sorrows befall you, your body does not perish, You shall have no agitation at all, no feelings and no seekings. There is no more the feeling of 'I', and you and Shiva become one.

605. They who can fix the gaze on the nasal point and retain the roaming breath within can thus still the *nadis* and sure reach the goal. There is no fear of birth for them. Thus Dhiyana leads to the cessation of birth.

606. In Dhiyana the varied subtle sound experiences of these ten—bell, sea, elephant, flute, cloud, bee, dragon-fly,

conch, drum and lute—are heard for them alone who have stilled their mind in God.

607. In Dhiyana, other sound experiences, such as, the roar of sea, the thundering of cloud, the trumpeting of Elephant, the euphony of lute, the music of the orbs that glow in the vast firmament, the melody of the flute and the resonance of conch, all these are heard by the true yogis alone.

608. Those who realize God obtained the fruits of God-realization. They alone get the Godly qualities; they join the company of the immortals; pasa vanishes for them; they become immanent in all life and hear even the subtlest sounds, even as fragrance emanates from a flower.

609. Yoga leads to Nadhanatha, The end of Nadha is Divine Sakthi, the end of Nada is grand yoga; Natha's end is the final goal; Nadha's end is the Lord is seated.

610. The primordial darkness of Aanava flees as the kundalini fire glows in the six Adharas followed by the five Indhriyas (sense organs) in tameness. Those who involute their substrate in Tammathras and they in turn in Nadha, shall reach the feet of the Lord who is the refuge of all.

611. No darkness invades the mystic bed-chamber that is eternal day light; there is a way that this body be not consigned to the fire-chamber. The way to ascend to space lies through meditation and the light of this knowledge is prolonged by meditation. The even living light in this lunar region knows no end.

612. Having abated not in the rules of vows, the yogi who has learned to meditate, coursing the kundalini through the spinal column and passing the three *mandalas* with equal felicity, he, the yogi lives forever in the fleshy body. Hence perfect meditation leads to immortality.

613. There is a way of reaching to three Mandalas. It is meditation that leads one across the three spheres. There is in each Mandala its respective God and one should be blessed by the appropriate God and only then each Mandala will lead to the other.

614. The three Mandalas are in the dark chamber of the drooping heart. To transcend each Mandala is to be exalted.

He who pierces the Sushumna Nadi and becomes one with the Mandalas, shall know no wearness.

615. He who uproots the three *gunas* and is able to control breath in the Mooladhara, coursing it alternately through the left and right Nadis in the prescribed measure of time, will be made immortal by Him who is the King of Heavenly beings.

616. The petalled Heart-centre is four finger-length above the tremulous navel-centre. The throat centre is still two finger length above. Deep meditation on these centres leads to God. Those who can meditate on it in Sea-like depth will sure know Him, the Lord of corporal body. When the yogi shifts his centre of thought from the Mooladhara to the Anahatha (heart centre) and from the Anahatha to the Vishudhi (throat centre), then he transcends the thirty-six tathwas, becomes united with God.

617. Transcending the thirty-six unreal Tathwas, destroying Maya's thick layers, the yogis are transformed into pure Gnana by grace and themselves become that inseparable grace. They who achieved thus were the good souls that knew the way of dhiyana, Meditation.

9. Samadhi

618. Samadhi is the final goal in Astanga, the eight-limbed yoga commencing from yama through niyama, asana, pranayama, prathyahara, dharana and dhiyana. Samadhi is the consummation of the eight Siddhis. Those who persevere in the path from Yama to the end, will alone attain the end, Samadhi. When it is attained, the miraculous powers (Siddhis) come to the yogi of themselves. (eight Siddhis:—Anima, Mahima, Karima, Lahima, Prapthi, Prakamiyam, Isathwam and Vasithwam).

619. Samadhi is to reach the Meru Peak of Sahashrara. When the yogi is in the Meru peak of Sahashrara, Bindhu and Nadha flourish there, and Samadhi is born when he unites with them. Then the respendent light of endless Gnana will be visioned.

620. Where there is mind absorption, there is life's breath, Where there is no mind absorption, there is no life at all.

They who, in rapture sit in mind absorption are verily fixed in the absorption of yoga. That is, it is only through Samadhi, *manolaya* (Oneness of the mental tranquillity) is reached; all things are absorbed in unitive consciousness.

621. They who sit in the Samadhi of pure consciousness vision the mystic woods and the blooming pond; they roam in the royal expanse of space and there at the foot of the fertile Meru Mountain, they bridle their horse of breath to a stop.

622. On top of the spinal column in the centre, a unique habitat is built. It has three compartments (spheres of Sun-Moon-Fire). and four doors (the cavities where the Nadis—Ida, Pingala-Sushumna end and the fourth cavity of Brahmarandhra or the final entrance to Sahashrara). They sit within these in Samadhi. Then the yogi visions the vast space through the fourth door on the top and from them on, there is no more word such as death for him, not even in his dream.

623. There are five mystic regions, eight mountain ranges and six yogic centres that hold them. With thought centred on Him, the yogi well see Him standing there; partaking of the grace of His all-pervading Feet, they shall be immortal.

624. The life-breath is trapped within the locked body. Course it to the land that knows no desire. They who fix their gaze on the true coal will reach the mango fruit that hangs there in the garden—the yogi climbs the mystic mango tree within, and tastes of the fruit that is Shiva, for Samadhi leads to Shiva.

625. The celestials beings churned the ocean but with the dark mountain and partook of ambrosia's. But they did not climb the heights of the mystic mountain nor did they take part of the ambrosia that flows within; for they do not possess the unwavering mind that soars high in Samadhi. There is a way to vision the Lord. Ambrosia in Samadhi leads to God. Only the yogi in Samadhi finds it. In Samadhi with breath halted, the yogi becomes one with God, Himself.

626. He, the primal one is our own, He taught the four Vedas, He is the light that glows within the purest gold. Devoid of all desires they approached Him, adored Him in love and

climbed high the mystic tree. With their breath halted in Samadhi they became one with Him.

627. Beyond the Mooladhara which is triple angle shaped, is where time and space mingle; high above the centre, opposite the forehead hangs the crescent moon of myriad shape and peerless beauty. The yogi visions his mystic moon in the Sahashrara Centre.

628. The yogi bereft of distracting thoughts, then, ascending the way of kundalini and seeking the YIGH majesty, Him, the creator that is beauteous light that created all and reading the mystic moon in union, the yogi becomes one with the uncreated being—This, in truth is the tranquillity of Samadhi.

629. When Samadhi is attained, Shiva is attained, Sakthi too will be caught in its fold. In the tranquillity that is attained in Samadhi all distracting passions will be dispelled. Like a balance, the mind will attain perfect equanimity and the grace of Sakthi will flow unhindered. All this is for those who are in deep Samadhi.

630. He stood as the peerless pillar of light, when Jeeva merges in Lord Shiva in Samadhi, Brahma that creates and Vishnu of the Ocean-hue, both stand adoring the Yogi.

631. To those who are in Samadhi many yogas come to them of themselves and the eight Siddhis come to them, unsought too. But the yogi transcends them all. He walks with God. He becomes One in God, Himself.

10. The Harvest of Eight Limbed Yoga

632. They who seek the Lord of matted locks decked with flowers will sure reach the abode of Gods: The Lord that mounts the Bull and dances to His consort's delight blesses his devotee, saying that He would grant to His devotee what he seeks. The fruit of Yama is reaching the abode of the Gods—Devaloka.

633. Hold fast unto His Feet, adore them with love, sing His praise, study His sacred lore and constantly think of Him. You shall reach the world of Shiva, where you will be received in full regalia by the concourse of the sacred Rishi. In short, the fruit of Niyama is reaching the world of Shiva.

634. The Lord's grace is infinite, He elevates His devotees unto Indhra who is the Lord of the celestials. And the Yogi shall be received in pomp and honour, with the beating of drums and playing of pipes, all glory and bliss shall rain upon him. Here, the fruit of Asana is the attainment of the status of Indhra, the King of Devas.

635. The devotee shall be received by throngs of celestials when he reaches the world of Shiva, They shall hail him and shall welcome him as their Golden Lord who has come there; and the devotee shall reveal in rapturous pleasure. This is to say, that he who practises *pranayama* will be honoured by the celestials in the world of Lord Shiva.

636. When the devotee reaches the world of Shiva the celestials who stand in eight directions ask who he is. And Hara answers that the entrant is His devotee and that he is His own; and the noble Devas fore gather and hail him as well as if they have met Shiva Himself. It is said that the end of *prathiyahara* is to reach the world of Lord Shiva, and to be recognised by the Lord, Himself.

637. By seeking the good path the devotee turns away from the path of death. They walk the path of truth and seek the path of liberation. They are of limitless bounty. The celestials my well roam in eight directions, but perforce they have to come to the earth's way of the devotees and seek Him there.

638. He is the refuge of Vishnu who sleeps (Yoga-Nithirai) on the ocean, of Brahma who creates seven worlds, of Rudhra who brings dissolution of all life and of the Devas who revel in bubbling nectar-which is to say that in Dhiyana the yogi reaches all the worlds of Brahma, Vishnu, Rudhra and Devas.

639. Transcending Jeeva's caused limitations and accepting the causal Tathwas by extinguishing the causal sources themselves, do the *tapasvins* (who do penance) thus unite in the uncaused being. This in truth is supreme Samadhi. This is to say that in Samadhi, the Yogi transcending the limitations of the caused experiences, himself becomes the causal Tathwas, and ultimately unites in the uncausal being.

11. The Eight Great Siddhis

640. Pray and seek the Lord in eight directions, adore the Lord with constancy in eight directions and in meekness perform in eight directions, when you attain great Siddhis in eight directions. Siddhis are supernatural powers which the *tanthric sadhaka* (aspirant) gains through his yoga. They are usually eight in number and are classified into the lower and merely psychic, and the higher the fruit of long periods of fruitful training. The former are involved in self. The latter are available to those in whom the self is dead. They include clairvoyanace, clair-audience, telepathy, recalling one's former lives and those of others. As it is, it is forbidden to use these powers for one's personal benefit.

641. The Lord is the prized being of all celestials, as I sought His Feet in devotion all my blemish vanished and I visioned the mystic space. Nothing is impossible for me now. He blessed me with eight great Siddhis and ended my birth that is to be.

642. By the grace of the Guru, I realized that if the fire in the Mula is united in the Parakasa trouble will ensure you. So I took up the practice of Sambavi and Kesari yogas and attained the eight Siddhis and Shiva's abode 'Kesari Mudhra' is the name of yogic posture in Tanthra, which bestows spiritual attainment and enables one to overcome disease and death. And 'Sambavi Mudhra' is related to Sambhavi diksha which is a form of higher initiation which is concluded and conducted by the mere touch or glance or will of the Guru. It is connected with the secret cult of Kamashwari Devi.

643. It is but wisdom that the elements, Kalas, Time and Maya escape unentangled in them. You should embrace fast the Truth of the Lord that created and unending one and then you can transmigrate into the mortal coils of the beings of others. Transmigration is another one of Siddhi powers (Tanthric) through which one can leave one's own body and enter into that of another.

644. Karma yoga is several, several in number; they count up to twenty thousand eight hundred kinds, and all that they can give us is only physical work. That is to say that in the

course of the practice of the eight lined yoga, eight siddhis or miraculous powers appear. The siddhis are far superior to what results from the numerous karma yogic practices.

645. The breath of Prana measures up to twelve units on the Moon's *nadi* to the left (Idakala) of the twelve-exhale four, the other eight saved is retained within, and if this is practiced continuously for twelve years, then the eight great siddhis shall abide with you ever.

646. A devotee but paves the way for birth again when he abounds in the wealth of men around him. Nor does he realize that Siddhi cannot be attained by art, learning, genius and subtle wisdom. It takes the Siddhis to attain fullness, at the end of diverse melodies heard in yoga for twelve long years.

647. In the seventh year of his practice, the yogi becomes fleet of foot like the wind, his foot fall does not touch the ground, then, he divines the thoughts of other beings; then in the eighth year, he becomes eternally young, forever bereft of greying hair and wrinkled muscles; and in the ninth year of practises, he transmigrates into the bodies of other mortals.

648. In the tenth year of practice, the yogi can expand and contract into space, in the eleventh year, he can assume the form, he meditates cn; and in the twelfth year, he masters entirely all the eight Siddhis. He, then gains the powers to roam the worlds—seven above and seven below, and take one cosmic-form spanning all spaces.

649. The eight great Siddhis that are enumerated are: The yogi himself is the atom; himself the cosmos; He, Himself is light; himself heavy; he himself is invisible air; Himself migrating into the mortal bodies of others; He, Himself possesses the prowess of the truthful one and is Himself immanent in all.

650. The yogi assumes the size of an atom and enters into the lives of several beings, and then returns to his original form, but either way he is not affected in the least. This stage is reached in Anima Siddhi and from there, He rises further into Nadha chanting AUM and thus hastens towards Mukthi (liberation).

651. The Days are counted by sixty *astral nazhigai* (1

Nazhigai is 24 minutes) and the year by three hundred and sixty days. So the yogi should meditate incessantly through time thus reckoned and see the Light in the Manipooraka-yogic centre.

652. The yogins who turned their thoughts to Shiva, who became Shiva-suffused, who attained Mukthi by silence that leads to it are Siva Mukthas. They abandoned the five senses in search of divine purity with their thoughts centered on the cosmic dance.

653. The nine *vayus* (air) in the body are equal. The tenth, Dhananjaya, is superior. When the nine accord in their channels life and body too accord well.

The airs are ten in number: Prana, Apana, Samana, Udhana, Viyana, Naga, Koorma, Krikara, Devadhatta and Dhananjaya.

Prana, the vital force, takes the help of air and performs ten functions; the Prana moves always the Heart, the Apana in the sphere of the anus, the Samana in the naval region, the Udhana in the throat, and the Viyana pervades the whole body. These five principal *vayus* (air) known as Pranadi, belong to the inner body.

The five external Vayus, such as *naga* air performs the function of belching; it gives rise to consciousness; the Koorma opens the eyelids; it causes vision, the Krikara causes sneezing, it causes hunger and thirst; the Devadhatha does yawning; the Dhananjaya pervades the whole gross body, sound is produced and it does not leave the body even after death.

654. Dhananjaya pervades the other nine airs; within the body it permeates two hundred and twenty-four *nadis;* If Dhananjaya air does not function in this manner, this body will swell and burst. Here, the importance of two airs is mentioned. This is a part of Ayur or Siddha Veda which was used specially in the medicine of the Siddhas.

655. When Dhananjaya functions in disorderly manner boils itches, leprosy and anaemia and like diseases that show swelling appear; again paralysis, hunchback, arthritis and diseases of eyes that show bulging all appear.

656. When Dhananjaya malfunctions the eye gets disease like cataract and glaucoma; but Koorma air is necessary for

the eye and if Koorma does not permeate the eyes, It receives no light at all.

657. The One spark of Divine Light that is God, animates through the *nadis* that pulsate in the ear, eye and heart. The Gods, Rudhra-Vishnu and Brahma animate the three *nadis* and are respectively seated thereby.

658. Within the fleshy body that has nine gates, there is a centre, where the nine *nadis* meet. For those who can contain the nine *nadis*, their vision is not just nine, but they are several, several in number.

659. This lesson is told to those who are wise to learn, that is, to kindle the Kundalini fire that burns luminously in the Mooladhara and send it up through the Sushumna the central spinal column, then course into it the Prana breath that runs through the sun and the moon Nadis; This is the way to reach the seven mystic worlds in the cranium.

660. Oh Jeeva, in lust you see woman and sadly enough you are caught like a fawn in a net. You should know how to make the central *nadi* the breath way. You kept the seed (Bindhu) for sale, may your own be to consume. It should be conquest of the Bindhu through the *nadi*.

661. They who raise Nada within the *nadi* behold and vision the one being in a flash; there they imbibe the mystical nectar, vanquishing all beseiging foes.

662. The nine virgins, states to be: Vamai, Sreshtai, Raudri, Kali, Kalavikanni, Palavikanni, Palapramadani, Sarvabhuta—damani and Mononmani, all sweet as nectar, joined the Mother Kundalini up on the stalk of the mystic lotus bud. One by one, they climbed the floors and reached the Victorious top, *purna sakthi* and there they were transformed into perfection.

663. Sakthi that is Poorna (perfection) filled Herself into three chambers seven times; Poorna sakthi is Adhi or Primal Sakthi. The nine lovely virgins became a hundred and five, and as the cause of Vishnu, Brahma and the rest of the Five Gods. That is, she evolves as Icha, Kriya and Gnana and fills, by pervasively expanding, the seven Adharas, including Sahashrara.

664. The damsel thus blossomed the expanded, but if she chooses to hide Herself within, the five elements and all that expanded out of Her will evolves in the reverberant primal soul, Nadha.

665. When the breath as in the nadis is made to course in alternation from left to right and passes beyond the six yogic centres barrier, there, Sakthi of the lightening form is sealed amidst the cool flame, You are merged in her.

666. If you sit in realization thus with senses controlled and thought centred in oneness; then the prana breath that comes circling again and again will gently merge in the jeeva, within that Jeeva, the dancer dances and I stand seeking Him there.

667. I coursed the breath upward through the Sushumna *nadi* and I sought Her to the accompaniment of Nada's sound (Aum) and there the damsel was. I had her and then seized and bound the enemies shielding Her; thus I possessed the jewelled lamp of undying Flame.

668. The eight great Siddis are : Anima, Lagima, Mahima, Prapthi, Karima, Prakamiyam, Isat wam and Vasitwam. They are enumerated in this manner: 1. Anima is to become as tiny as the atom within an atom. 2. Lagima is to become Light as vapour in levitation. 3. Mahima is to become big in unshakable proportions. 4. Prapthi is to enter into other bodies in transmigration. 5. Prakamiya is to be in all thins, Omni-pervasive. 6. Isatwam is to be Lord of all creations in omnipotence and 7. Vasitwam is to be everywhere in omnipresence, 8. Karima is to become with sole Omnipotence.

669. The eight Siddhis are attained by the eight-limbed yoga when the breath is controlled accordingly, when the Kundalini Fire is coursed up through the Central *nadi* and passed beyond the Sun's *mandala* (Region) to the Moon's from there, the ambrosia flows that may be drunken greedily.

670. Not only will the eight siddhis be attained by the eight-limbed yoga way; but the goal-*siddhis* leading to *mukthi*—behind the *siddhis* too will all be attained with effortless ease, if only Tripura Sakthi grants Her grace.

671. They are Siddhas who together with the eight Siddhis

attain the Divine; they reach Paraloka and within them they vision the dear Lord then they reach Him truly, rising beyond the eight boundaries. The true God lies beyond the eight Siddhis.

672. They who can alternate the course of the breath from the left to the right and send it upward, unerringly through the spiral cavity to Mount Meru at the top, then, to them, Kaniya Loka, the world that is reached by Anima and the rest of the eight Siddhis will come of itself.

673. If the yogi succeeds in preventing the nectar that flows from the sphere of the Moon from entering the solar sphere and preserves thus for a year, then, he will attain Anima Siddhi—he becoming lighter than flimsiest cotton and he will be invincible too.

674. If the yogi meditates on Thani Mayaki (Aadhi sakthi) till the Tathwas associated with Her subside and continues his meditation for five years then he attains the Siddhi that is Laghima—the power to penetrate anywhere at will.

After attaining Anima siddhi, the yogi should persevere for five years to attain the Laghima siddhi. This is the power to render the body light at will; It is the power of levitation. It is the mastery over the element 'Air'.

675. When the yogi attains Laghima Siddhi, He will glow with divine light suffusing a radiance that is milk-white. In Laghima Siddhi, the yogi visions the heavenly glow that is true. The heavenly glow is otherwise known as Melliyal Sakthi (Sakthi of tender form).

676. A year after attaining Laghima, when the Tathwas and yogis, take their refuge in the tender Sakthi form he attains Mahima Siddhi—the power to expand one's consciousness to the largest atom or form. It is the power of greatness referring to the element, 'Fire', the mental plane. It is the mastery over thought, over the lower mind, over the creative urges of the mind. The attainment of this mastery truly implies greatness. Height is the dimension which symbolises truly this plane. It also requires greatness to overcome the adversaries on this plane, which is myths and fairy tales take the form of giants.

677. Having seen breath transformed into Light. Time does

not move anymore for him, it stops, The yogi conquers time. The past merges into space. Of the future, He becomes the Lord. From him emanates Gnana, and he visions Tattvanayaki (Sakthi of Tathwas).

678. All Gnana grows through the yogi; all the world flourishes through Him; all thins prosper through Him. He, himself stands in the grace of the Lord. The finite attainments through Mahima siddhi is got.

679. The yogi who thus stands in Mahima visions the Mother of Tathwas (Tattwanayaki) and the celestial Bhutas. If the yogi thus perseveres continuously, retains his vision, for a year, he attains the divine *siddhi*—Prapthi. It is the power to obtain any desired objective, to give indefinite extension to the subtle body or its members, the connection of a being with his organs as their presiding deity known as attainment, Arrival of the goal, deliverance, discovery, good fortune, juyful meaning. This particular achievement refers to mastery or rulership of the earthsphere.

680. Having visioned the dazzling light of Sakthi, the Siddha perceives the vast cosmos. So in Prapthi, the Siddha sees the vast cosmos unfolding like a flower, while the past merges into space, the future time stops forever.

681. The experiences in Prapthi Siddhi are inexplicable. There is no coming, no going, no ageing, no death, no delay in seeing the light of breath (Nadha). There is nothing described in particular. Thus it—Parasakthi visioned in Prapthi—with the Siddhas who have attained this Siddhi.

682. Parasakthi resides palpably within when Prapthi is attained and all Tathwas flee. A year after attaining Prapthi Siddhi, Prakamyam is reached. When the Siddha is thus for a year, he attains the power to transmigrate into alien bodies.

683. The yogi does not know how the being within becomes the radiant light. That light is already within the Mooladhara. With it they can see the Light of Shiva above. The Light above leads them to effortless liberation who thus seek. It is easy for salvation to be attained after Prakamiya.

Prakamiya is the capacity to derive enjoyment from everything heard or seen, the power to exercise an irresistible will upon the minds of others, the power to obtain more than one expects, to maintain a youthful appearance for an unusual length of time. It is the mastery over the element water, the emotional or astral plane.

684. A year rolls by after Siddha attain Prakamiya Siddhi and he perseveres in his adoration. Here the yogi is suffused with the light of *nadha,* and visions the Sadhashiva Sakthi, with her army of *bhuthas.* After attaining Prakamiya Siddhi, Isithwa Siddhi is attained. It consists in the power to control and create. It is the power of mind over maya.

685. At this stage the Siddha becomes the rays of the moon, its cooling softness. He becomes the moon's Kalas, then merging in them he, himself becomes the moon.

686. The power Isithwa confers on him are enumerated. He acquires the power to create, to preserve and he himself is the Lord of destruction, He and Isa become non-separate.

687. If the Siddha contains the five elements, within the cool Kalas of the moon, then in a year, he shall attain the rare power to perceive the true one.

688. A year after attaining Isithwa comes Vasithwas or the power to perceive the true one. He can become immanent like God in all that comes within his reach.

689. In the days the Siddha stands thus in Vasithwa Siddhi, He become radiant as the Sun. When he attains the rare vision of the True Being, his body becomes golden, his sense organs die and he visions the Narkodi Sakthi (Sakthi that appears like Glorious tender vine). Vasithva is the power of command and control, resulting from non-attachment to objects, self-control, self-restraint and power over the elements. Indeed, it is the power which controls *maya,* and the achievements of that power, controls, and restrains the All contained in the Self, and the self contained in the All.

690. After attaining Vasithwas Siddhi, the Siddha perseveres in the knowledge of Sakthi and of Shiva who shares Her body. And then after a year, he attains the powers to visit all worlds that hang from the golden stalk of the cosmic flower; then sitting inert like a flag of stone, the Siddha attains Kamaru Tathwa or Kamava-Syithwa Siddhi.

Kamaru Thathwa is the consummation of any and every desire, the power of suppressing desire; it is the achievement of the fulfilment of the heart's supreme desire, which is liberation from bondage, and the salvation from suffering by the annihilation of all desires. It is God-realization, It is the power which subdues the primordial kama or desire, the primal cause of existence. It is the Supreme Nirvana State.

691. Having attained Kamaru Siddhi, He will receive the power to pervade in all space just as the flower's fragrance. The devine fragrance shall be His. He shall be transformed into Mayasakthi. He shall be the Lord of light that everyone adores.

692. Having visioned the Divine Light he abides in it as in his mother's home. He visits the myriad worlds; he sees the Supreme light of Shiva who has His home amidst ghosts and ghouls.

693. He who has mastered the eight high Siddhis will be the Lord of the entire globe. His garland of victory shall be gleaming. He will be its beacon-light. His *prana* shall turn into peerless light.

694. Prana pervades in five hundred and odd *nadis,* then the ten and then the three. Sakthi pervades *prana* after the eight Siddhis are attained. The way *prana* mingles in *jeeva* is through Sakthi of the tender vine.

695. When the *prana* breath pervades the whole body, it draws the nectar within the Shahashrara and ambrosia flows like a river in the head. It pervades the *nadi* channels which are thousand three hundred and five in number. The Andaras (Yogic centres) are the way to the thousand petalled Sahashrara, the twin breaths Idakala and Pingala show the way.

696. Above the twin/petalled centre is the seat of Sadhasiva Sakthi. The Agjna Chakra between the eyebrows is the twin petalled centre. When the twin breaths Idakala and Pingala, ascend beyond the Agjna Chakra, the Sahashrara, the thousand-petalled lotus, is reached. On it are inscribed all the fifty-one letters. The fifty one letters in time became the Five letters (NA MA SI VA YA).

697. In the Agjna centre is seated Sadhasiva Nayaki. Her

awe inspiring faces are five and she holds ten deadly weapons. Without the aid of the five letter manthra, no ascension is possible from the two-petalled agjna centre to the thousand petalled Sahashrara. The five letters in time become the One letter (AUM).

698. She is the Tathwa Nayaki, is the One Being, when the breath ascends united through the spinal cavity. Then that one breath will reach the thousand petalled Sahashrara. Think of Her and you shall live a thousand years.

In the Sahashrara is the one being Tathwa nayaki. When the twin breaths pass beyond the twin-petalled agjna centre it begins to flow in a single stream though the Sushumna cavity; it is then that the Sahashrara is reached.

699. The *prana* that causes upwards through Sushumna reaches and meets the Kalai Nayaki in the Sahashrara and there it mereges with the fifty-one letters, then with the Five letters. Prana that merges in that Sakthi remains exalted. That is the final end of prana.

700. Before it coursed upward, the life breath that rose with the Thani Nayaki filled the five hundred and thirty nine *nadis*. And there it remained in Sakthi, totally absorbed.

701. When the pracious *prana* reached Shiva, it pervades the two hundred and thirty nine *nadis*. And then it reached the five letters where *prana* finally merges in the five letters.

702. In all, by the time, the *prana* travels and reaches *Sakthi* emanating from the four petalled Mooladhara where the kundalini fire is, it will have pervaded the seven hundred and twenty-nine *nadis* within. This introduces the concept of the general topic known as 'Varna Mala' by describing how 'prana' merges in the five letters.

703. When the *prana* courses through the six *adharas*, there will be nectar. Then the *prana* reaches the seventh centre of the Sun, and further it courses on to the eighth centre the moon, when the *prana* reaches the peaks of the Sun and the Moon, the *prana*, that is, the yogi attains Samadhi in the ninth centre.

704. The moon and the sun are in the uncreated being. The yogi who visions the moon at the mystic junction of the

three *nadis* is merged in light. He attains Samadhi that had its beginning at the navel centre. (Samadhi means the saturation with the almighty).

705. The manner in which an aspirant for yoga Samadhi should conduct himself is by following these ways: To give up thoughts of women, to think no more of kith and kin, to be meek in learning, to abound in Gnana, to be sparing of speech, to listen to deeds of Siddhi and to sit unruffled.

706. The prowess, of the one who has mastered the science of *Prana* and has attained Yoga Samadhi, is as follows—He vanquishes age and death, acquires the power to transmigrate at will into other bodies, to confer paradise to the dead, to assume the divine form of Gods and to become learned, acquiring mastery over the twenty-one branches of Sigagamic lore.

707. Seeking the Lord by going on pilgrimage to the four corners of the Seagirt world, thereby wearing away the soles of their feet is vain. Only those who seek Him in intense love shall know the city of the Lord.

708. Gods Brahma, Vishnu and Rudhra, Maheshwara, Sadhasiva, Bindhu, Nadha, Sakthi, Para Bindhu and Para Nadha in successive Atharas and Niradharas seek the feet of the Ultimate.

709. A yogi enjoys all unalloyed bliss beyond the Adhara Yoga. Adhara Yoga consists in worshipping the appropriate God at each of the centres, and ascending them one after another, reaches is where Sakthi and Shiva reside, shedding their sixteen Kala of mystic Moon. Ascend still beyond is Gnana, the Effulgent-Light Divine. Yet beyond this is unalloyed bliss, defying speech and thought, and which is reached through Niradhara Yoga.

Each of the successive *adharas* (Yogic centres) has its presiding deity—in Mooladhara; Brahma, in Swathistana, is Vishnu; in Manipoorka is Rudhra; in Anahatha Maheswara; Visuddhi-Sadhasiva, in Agjna, the Aparabindhu, in Sahashrara, is the Paranadha; Sakthi and Shiva. Still beyond are the Para Bindhu, Para Nadha, in effect, the centres are eleven in number. Only the first six kundalini yoga and reaching the seventh is known as Adhara centres above the seventh—they are known as 'Sthanas'. When Prana reaches the Paraparam in the space this is known as Dvadhasantha or the twelfth end. Prana's ascension beyond Sahashrara to the Dwadhasantha space, known as Niradhara Yoga—appearing apparently beyond the 'Yogic centres' of the body.

700. They who practise Yoga through the breath *nadis*, will in one flowing moon and sun become celestial beings. The Lord will reveal Himself to them who perform it truly and unceasingly.

701. They who control breath will pervade all unseen. They who pierce the Mystic Lotus sending their breath up through spinal column will taste of its fragrant nectar and will never know death.

12. Unfaltering Kala

712. In intense love seek Him, the Lord of the Forehead eye that showed the path of Divine Love. The Ganges in His cranium, plait will flow in grace, and in exceeding love, He will be your saviour.

713. Your thoughts will be firmly rotted in the Lord when your inner organs of cognition are controlled, when you control the sixteen *kalas* and control the *prana* within.

714. It is important that the *prana*, in yoga practise, is kept up without wavering straight through the Sushumna *nadi*, in a steady shyth, as a steady flame, like a still stone. They who know how the Lord stood comingled with *kalas* know the true way. This comes only by anchoring the thought on the Lord. By steadying of the prana, the vision of the Lord wears the moon that has sixteen *kalas* is obtained.

715. The Lord of Bhootha hordes, when the life breath is coursed upward through the single Sushumna channel. And Sankara of matted locks appears before you mounted on the sacred bull.

716. He is a true Sadhaka (aspirant) that knows not the time that passes in Samadhi. He looks forward to the big time ahead, thus directing His breath through the single Sushumna channel, to the space in the cranium. There he stands, resolved

of all conflicts. This is the Sadhaka's state in Samadhi.

717. The practise of yogic penance should be directed toward that excellent state; if you succeed in coursing the breath into the lotus in the cranium. You shall gain the Lord that remains hidden in the Vedas.

718. The breath has three states As prana it courses upward in a single stream through the spinal *nadi* and then it spreads into the cranial space for the lotus to blossom there and finally it merges into the divine form there.

719. The Kundalini sakthi that thus arises makes her way aloft through the fleshy coil and yet it remains within the yogi. And it is she who creates the worlds of the Devas and churns the mystic ambrosia within. The yogi drinking deep of it turns the body into a temple of Shiva. The Guru's guidance is essential for knowing how to course the Prana through the successive Adharas. The guru can guide this upward journey.

720. No one knows how the breath that glows within merges in Nadha. When you know the mystery of how it merges, then you can reach the region where Nandhi holds His sway.

The message that Kundalini yoga turns the body into the 'Temple of Shiva' is a very vital one and has had very fruitful outcome in temple art, whose basic design resembles the pathway to the 'Garbhagraha' (Sanctum Sanctorium) which corresponds to the position of the heart of the human body.

721. As you pierce and break through the yogic centres you will clearly vision the Prana leaving the Kundalini Sakthi on its upward journey through the Sushumna; the Guru's guidance alone can guide this upward journey. This guidance you should take as a precious treasure that is gained.

722. If you control and absorb within the breath that rises twelve *mathras* long, you may well live thousands upon thousands of years on deadly land and sea; the body does not perish at all. I declare this as true, upon my Lord Nandhi, Immoratility is attained through Samadhi yoga.

723. When Prana and Sakthi depart one from the other, the Yogi experiences at this way, when the Prana ascends he experiences the audition of seven sounds; he visions five

colours; he smells three odours and knows two tastes. It is thus the Lord of light indicates these sumptoms to him.

13. The Path to Kayasiddhi (Making the Body Immortal)

724. If the body perishes, the Prana departs from the body and the light of truth is never reached. So learn the way of preserving the body as it God's temple. By doing so, you can learn to preserve the Prana too and see God within. The body according to Kayasiddhi (Kaya means body) provides the best, and probably, the only medium for attaining (Mokhsha' and therefore it has to be kept always in perfect trim through yoga.

725. There was a time when I despised the body, but then I saw God within, and I realised, the body to be the temple of the Lord; and so I began preserving it with infinite care.

726. Purification of the internal organs of the body can take place if the breath is used to flush the idea and Pingala Nadis by Pranayamam. The body must be kept pure. This is achieved by churning the intestines through the practise known as 'Suddhi'. By this, the heart gets purified, the bowels become clean. The breath should be controlled in the heart's region and it should be made to pervade the entire system; the body becomes impervious even to fire.

727. The body attains a wax-like suppleness by the practise of yoga. The effect of practising yoga at dust is that phlegm leaves the body; when practised at noon the wind that is treacherous leaves and when practised at down, bile is expelled. Thus all poison is expelled from the body. The body that is purified from the poison of the three 'humours' knows no greying or wrinkling.

728. The coils of the serpent kundalini are three; the airs that agitate the body are ten. The yogi who tightly controls the two bags of apiration, inhalation and exhalation, in the prescribed measure of twelve-finger length prana breaths, and sits unwavering in meditation, his body shall not perish, but he shall live a hundred years.

729. The secret of how to live for 166 years is to breathe by the right *nadi* (nostril) a hundred and sixty-six mathras,

then breath by the left a hundred and sixty mathras and then reverse the rhythm. If this is done in alternation, you shall live long, a hundred and sixty-six years.

730. If you practise transference of breath from right to left and vice versa. You can hear, in the body-temple where the sakthi is seated, mystic sounds from the forehead centre (*agjna*) and also, Lord Shiva will reveal Himself dancing to rhythmic music. This we declare as true in the name of Sadhasiva.

731. The Bindhu is pure by far, from it emanates the sound 'Ha' from Nadha that abides lives the sound 'Sa' repeated together continuously they become the manthra 'Soham'. The Yogi who chants it silently while breathing, surely attains the Holy ways.

732. Rouse the prana that resides in the navel centre by chanting Shiva manthra in silent meditation. Course it and upward to the Sahashrara, retain the breath in the Agjna frontal, then rouse the Apana breath by meditation. That way you become Shiva, Himself.

733. Two finger length above the anus where foecial matter does not leave and below the male reproductive organ is the Linga. This is where the Mooladhara is. Centre your thought on Mooladhara and meditate. There resides the Lord of the six Adharas. The inhalation and exhalation is referred to as Hamsa (Swan) made up of the two syllables 'Ham' and 'Sa', also sometimes reversed to read as "Sa" "Ham" or "Soham". This also is a part of Nadha philosophy. This Upadesha is rarely revealed. So do take it and vision the Lord.

734. They who effect the mystic union with the asure-hued Sakthi within will shed greying and wrinkling. They will regain youth for all to see. This I say is true, by the grace of Nandhi.

735. The seminal seed shall never be destroyed if it thickens by sexual abstenance, the life shall be long if the body is lightened by austere discipline, and many are the good, things that flow if food is eaten sparingly. Continence leads to Godhood. You may truly become the Lord of dark-hued throat.

736. If the kundalini that is in Mooladhara is sent upward often to reach the space in the cranium, your body becomes comely and youthful, a desire, object for damsel bedecked with flowers around which humming bees swarm.

737. The Lord, of yore, spurned the mighty God of Death who ever harasses life; the Lord rides the chariot of fire within; if you vision His Holy Feet decked with triumphal anklet, you shall live forever in the canopied terrace above.

738. The fire that I saw in Kundalini radiates four kalas. I kindled in prana and coursed it through the seven centres; it pervades the entire body, with divine life that suffused the fleshy body as ambrosia, I grew into a tender fawn. The yogi vibrates with youthfulness. He will frisk about like a tender fawn.

739. If you pursue in ardour the search for power to acquire *kayasiddhi,* then you shall flourish far and wide; like a seed of paddy planted in a million, million fields;. Meditation on appropriate manthra will being *kayasiddhi.* So you do meditate, therefore, single-minded on the manthra that conquere fate.

14. Revolution of Time on Kala Chakra

740. I am here in the moon's sphere, seeking the Five (Siva tathwas) mountain ranges. Leaving this, I reach the region of the twelve great space that lies in the sphere of supreme patti, and from there I pass on—to the farthest beyond all these I seek to search here.

741. Knowiedge comes in diverse ways. Knowledge come through the five senses, through discrimination, through judgement, through experience, through learning, through attachment—coming through all these in succession knowledge erodes the life span, without the knowledge of the person.

742. The stages are many when death-assails man; The critical ages in man's life span, when death may visit him are from twenty-five to twenty-eight; from thirty to thirty-three; from sixty to sixty-two and from hundred and beyond.

743. There are appropriate days for commencing yoga. The birthday of the practitioner and the Ist, 2nd, and 3rd and 8th day following it are considered as best suitables. If he

selects the most suitable day, his entry into the mystic home within, will be easy.

744. To all those who enter the land of yoga practice, should know that the practice consists in this, the measure of breath inhaled is twelve inches, having measured accordingly, you should consciously exhale eight mathras. Breathing in this measure, continuously, the four mathras retained suffuse the six adharas—centres with prana that ascends beyond the twenty-five tathwas.

745. God is beyond the Mooladhara of the four pointed centre. Beyond the twenty-five tathwas is His Guru. He is beyond the six yogic centres that rise like the spreading banyan tree. No one ever knows Him.

746. It takes a few days for the yogi to traverse the adharas and *mandalas*. The days that take to pierce the nine centres are this—after the kundalini has been roused, it takes the yogi twenty days to pierce the six *adharas;* on the twenty fifth day, his Prana pierces the seventy centre of the Fire mandala, in the 26th day, the solar mandala, the eight centre and on the 27th day, he pierces the ninth centre of the Lunar Mandala. These days are the ones for yogi's Prana to reach the nine centres.

747. On the twenty-eighth day, the yogi gains the vision of the three Mandalas, each apart, and on the thirty-third day, he obtains their collective vision. He should centre his thoughts further and vision the twenty-four *tathwas* that are below in order to discover the Earth and the rest of the elements.

748. The yogi should practise yoga in the time and order stated. Thus, if he does not aspire the successive time and in stages, it is impossible for him to become God, much less near to Him. There is no other secret that the Vedas hold. Do not trumpet this, but in meekness accomplish it.

749. They who do not know this way to the goal and try other ways are but fools. They search God with a blazing torch, while they are ignorant that within them is the hand-lamp. They who can kindle the kundalini fire within them will abide ever in this fleeting world.

750. The six *adharas* may be reached in two successive

stages of three each. The spinal-cord is like the girth of the little finger, tant like the blow string; the *adharas* are there. Traversing the first three you reach the heart's centre and there you should be fixed in constancy. Then from the heart centre, you journey further onward you reach the three centres that end with the forehead. There, you shall be firm like a painted picture.

751. The yogi should know the importance of Sushumna in yoga, the consciousness that is perfection, the sinners do not know its goodness. There is no doubt that this body is the product of ones evil karma;. yet it possesses precious stalk that holds the mystic and sacred lotuses, that blossoms in the three mystic regions within. Though its central *nadi,* the sushumna, perfect consciousness is reached.

752. The yogi who through the spinal column ascends the above *adharas,* sees the three Mandalas together, in bound in rapture. They who see this vision see the end of karma; those who do not see this vision, however great he may be, die to the cycle to be born again.

753. Hear how this body perishes, the man has a pretty damsel for his wife; and like the sun his prosperity spreads, he commands the respect; of all who bow to him; this a body that waxed in a life like this, became a prey for the prowing dogs to consume.

754. They who knock about do not reach the refuge of the one of blossom feet; they who cannot contain the kundalini fire within, their body become a prey to fire. They who know the way, coursing the kundalini fire through the spinal column, seeking His victorious feet, will not perish by the cremation fire but will see the heavenly dancer through their spinal hollow.

755. They who sought the dancer as their goal gained many good things; they were able to stand in the path of the holy scriptures. In eagerness, they sit seeking Him and experiencing His presence within, they become one with Lord Shiva.

756. The acquisitions that flow from single-minded meditation are countless. Furthermore, if you meditate thus,

well and deeply, for thirty-three days after the Kundalini Sakthi has been aroused. You will vision the divine dancer on the peak of mountain (Meru) of blooming Gold in the Sahashrara and become one with Him.

757. The yogi knowing full well where the Divine Dancer dwells, should raise the Prana from the ten petalled lotus of Anahatha centre to the eight petalled Anahatha, there he can see the Lord seated. Then, he lives the hundred years as promised in the scriptures.

758. They who thus attained radiance a hundred fold will live a thousand years in a robust body; and they who saw a thousand years thus may well live a million, trillion years. They gain eternal life through yoga.

759. They may well thus live for aeons and aeons, and they do not tire in their devotion, and they thus see the mind's end and within themselves they see Him as a non-separate entity; and as one with Shiva they live filled in divinity and so see to live countless ages of exalted life.

760. Some seek only to exalt themselves by pursuing worldly ways; Some by knowing not what they are doing, seek only the fruits of enjoyment; some strive after action with no thoughts of the goal whatsover; but none of them will see the sakthi of lovely eyes.

761. They who do not see Her waste away their lives. They who do not seek Her spend away this life in artful talks. They who do not vision Sakthi, their riches and possessions vanish away unseen and intraceable. This shows that worldly wealth is perishable.

762. They who do not see treasure that surpasses everything else, but seek the treasure that perishes will not vision Shiva. If within their melting heart they seek within, they will see the treasure, that dies not and can attain the imperishable Holy Shiva state.

763. He is the one with the forehead eye, who is birthless; know that He is Nandhi within. As he pervades all space in solitariness, He stands as Shiva; If only you seek Him who is the unwavering goal, shall alone attain the state.

764. The fruit of seeking is great. They who seek do not

know death, they do not know of any evil, they who seek will become the Lords of the heavens and the earth. They who seek should know as true and it may well be told to only those who aspire.

765. These are the things that are worthy to be told; Akara or the sound 'A' is Shiva; Ukara or the sound 'U' is Sakthi and Makara or the sound 'M'; Let these abide in your thought when practising yoga. Chant, the manthra 'Aum' continuously in silence. When you thus chant let the Prana rise upward through the spinal cavity in the Sushumna, Then, it courses through the six Adharas and you shall reach the Lord.

766. No one knows where the Lord resides. But to them who seek Him should realise that the Lord is within them. He resides eternally within them. So, seek Him, and when you see Him, He and you will become one and the same.

767. No one knows how He and you become one. Listen; this is the way how He and you become one, He is in your hearing. He is in your sight. He stands within the mystic circle (*pranava-Aum*) within you. So, seek Him and become one with Himself.

768. Do you know how to reach His abode. His abode is not beyond reach. Transfix your thoughts within you in the yogic way. The seven circles inside will open. The seventh Adhara is the abode of the Lord. He resides inside, sweet as sugar-lump.

769. In the Yogic centres (six), He is seated as Brahma, as Vishnu, as Rudhra, as Maheshwara, as Sadhashiva and as Sakthi. He, that is immanent thus can be seen by you.

15. Measurement of Life Span

770. Put your hand on the forehead and look to see if the breath rhythm remains changed or unchanged. If it remains unchanged, it is well and good. If you see it enlarged, it means death awaits you in six months, if you see it doubled, in a month shall life depart.

Indian astrology has developed a branch of techniques in measuring the life span based on observation of the breathing rhythm. This is known as 'Saravottam' in Tamil as introduced by Great Bhoga Siddhar.

771. Nadha and God are one in consciousness; only they who transcend Nadha will centre on God. So transcend Nadha and realize God. God appears in the heart of those who transcend Nadha. Knowing the breath rhythm is knowing the Nadha. This truth, I realized and so merged in Nadha.

772. The breath that is spent in vain; if made to flow upward, will give the good of concentration to the mind. From this steadiness and concentration of mind, Gnana will be, that is in the Sahashrara will beam, and the yogi becomes the Lord of the earth.

773. Nadi Suddhi (purification of Nadis) is an important practice in yogic breathing. There is no Jeeva who practises Nadi Suddhi; it consists in breathing from the left nostril to the right; and from the right to the left in rhythmic alternation. He who practises carefully visions Sakthi and has mastery of his five senses. He is sure to live a hundred years.

774. If the exhalation of the Prana goes outwards in six mathras length, the yogi shall live upto the age of eighty. If the Prana goes outward in seven mathras length the subject will live upto sixty years.

775. If the Prana runs out through the left nostril in eight mathra length, the life spans up to fifty years, and know that it flows out in nine Mathras length, leaving three Mathras inside the practitioner will live upto the age of thirty-three.

776. If the Prana is exhaled in ten Mathra length, the life-span here below is twenty-eight; if the exhalation is in fifteen Mathra length, then, you shall see him only for twenty-five years.

777. If the yogi practises retention of breath in ten Mathras length, he will be able to direct his breath into oneness upward into the Mooladhara. Thus, if practises for an entire day of thirty *naligais* (one *naligai* is equal to 24 minutes) he is sure to achieve oneness (Two and half *naligais* make an hour).

778. If the practise of this ten Mathras of prana retained inside is practised for two days continuously, the downward streaming *apana vayu* (air) will not encounter any obstacle and will not trouble him. If practised for three days, the yogi

is certain to by glowing and the asension through the six centres (Yogic adharas) will begin then.

779. If thus the practise is continued for four days, the four petalled Mooladhara will be visioned. If further continued, on the fifty day, the second and third Adharas, Swadhishtana and Manipoorakam will be reached by *prana*.

780. Two more Adharas (fourth and fifth) may be visioned together when ten days have thus passed. On the fifteenth day, collective vision on the five Adharas together shall be got.

781. The sixth Adhara (Aghna) will be visioned on the 12th day; on the twenty-fifth day, the three Mandalas (Sun-Moon-Fire) will be visioned. On the twenty-sixth day the two, Shiva and Sakthi will be visioned.

782. The one supreme being that collectively rises in all centres may well be revealed on the twenty-seventh day. In the twenty-eighth day, the ten centre together (the space) may be revealed in rare collective visions.

783. On the twenty-ninth day, if the journey upward is resumed; the *apana* will stand as an impediment for ten days. On the thirteenth day of the journey, the *apana* will take seven days to leave.

784. There will still be three days delay on the thirty-first day of the journey upward for the union with God. On the thirty-second day, there will still be an impediment for two more days.

785. Thus it takes a month and three days when the Prana reaches the cranial heights. It can be said that on the 33rd day, the Jeeva reaches the mountain of Meru. And from within the fountain of nectar Nandhi bellows aloud. And if he reveals Himself in the space within, the yogi will truly be one with the Lord Shiva.

786. No one knows the greatness of kundalini yoga. No one knows that it is the science of breath control par excellence. It spans the spaces within and measures the duration of Prana. He who knows it will meet with no death at all. It is the Supreme Knowledge, It unites Jeeva in Lord Shiva, who is All-knowledge. He is the knowledge of all worlds and all

life. He is the pure knowledge non-separate from them. That knowledge is within. Seek and divine it. It will glow in pervasive richness.

787. The Lord is the knowledge. He stands as knowledge of the five elements—air and the rest. He stands knowledge pervading all life and worlds and is non-separate from them. If you seek Him within you, that knowledge will glow in pervasive richness.

788. God, who is all-knowing, grants this world that is unreal. He grants the vision of His dancing hall to the good ones of high praise. All this is the work of His sakthi. She is the fragrant flower-bedecked grace, that is the consort of the Lord.

789. This body is full of desires. It is an ancient mansion haunted by respective births. End the bonds of desires as under, make the Pasa flee in a howing manner and then, Nandhi, the great will grant His eternal wisdom.

16. Breath Rhythm Pattern for Days of the Week

790. The breath rhythm differ as between the left and the right *nadis,* on different days of the week; The Prana dominates in the *nadi* that is to the left (Ida) on Mondays, Wednesdays and Fridays. On Tuesdays, Saturdays and Sundays, it courses high in the right (*pingala*) *nadi.* On Thursdays, the Prana rises high in the left in the waxing moon's fortnight, and in the right in the waning moon's fortnight.

791. There is a breath rhythm for glowing health. If on Mondays, Wednesdays and Fridays the breathing dominates in the left nostril, the body will not know any harm, and it will glow in health. The Lord Nandhi, did thus tell us in a delectable.

792. The yogi who knows to make the breath flow on the right nostril, on Tuesdays, Thursdays, Saturdays and Sundays is indeed God Himself. If this rhythm is not obtained in the days stated, let the yogi correct it by appropriate breathing exercises, force it into the right nostrils by his subtle skill, then, he will know nothing else but only joy, eternal bliss.

793. If on a Sunday in one fortnight the breath runs high

on the right nostril, in the next fortnight it runs high on the left. If on a Monday in a fortnight the breath runs high on the left nostril, in the next fortnight it runs law on the right nostril. Thus the breath rhythm alternates from fortnight to fortnight on two days—Sunday and Monday. If this rhythm is obtained the Prana derives its strength. Try to know this well and accordingly regulate the breathing.

794. The breath that rises in the right *Nadi* while it courses into the left when changed may know a sudded jolt and a trembling fear. In that case, the yogi may leave the practice and rest a while. If the breath flows faster than the appropriate rhythm on the right *nadi* itself, then the yogi should correct it from time to time and bring the rhythm back to the norms indicated. However, this correction is quite a feat. This is the correct rhythm and if this rhythm is obtained *Prana* derives proper strength.

795. Prana runs helter-skelter to the right and to the left *nadis.* If the yogi regulates it appropriately so as to reach the Kundalini, he shall stand before the infinite light. Thus said Holy Nandhi.

796. The Lord that you search is seated on the flower above. The ways of breath control are sixteen. The art of rousing the kundalini and coursing the prana through the six yogic centres is a consummate one. It reguires knowledge and with the mind united in intense thought. Concentration, the breath coursing upward in strength can pierce the Adharas. There are days and hours appropriate for raising the kundalini. For these, you will know to be guided by the mighty Guru.

17. Belligerent Week Days

797. The Soola (unholyness) lies in different directions on different days of the week. Thus, the Soola lies in the direction of east on Mondays and Saturdays; on Tuesdays and Wednesdays it lies North and on Sundays and Fridays it lies West. On Thursdays, it lies on South.

This indicates the directional dangers in the days of the week. Indian astrology prescribes certain days of the week as not proper for undertaking journeys or tasks in certain directions. This is called 'Directional Astrology'. The danger in the direction is referred to figuratively as 'Soola', it, literally means the 'trident'; metaphysically it means danger.

798. The menacing trident is in the direction of the South on Thursdays. The dangers of Soola have little effect of the alternations in the breathing rhythm are appropriate. Thus Soola has no effect if the flow of breath from the left nostril is low. No harm befalls if the flow from the right nostril dominates, much good may actually swell.

18. Kesari Yoga

799. How to practise Kesari Yoga which is the most important technique in kundalini yoga, is to control the spiration within and see that the breath is not wasted. It is to be bound tight, the source of the kundalini in the Mooladhara is dammed up and stopped so that breath does not escape downward as Apana. Lock the chimney up in the mouth, Bolt the breath-escape of this Prana in the mouth's upper cavity with the tongue's tip. Having blocked the escaps below and above, the Yogi sits erect in Yoga Samadhi and no more will there be death for Him.

After kundalini has been roused and the Adharas have been pierced, the yogi arrives at a stage when he seeks to drink of the divine nectar that flows from the astral sphere within. Kesari yoga otherwise known as Kesari Mudhra is a technical part of the total yoga practice. Literally, Kesari means to traverse in the sky. The word Mudhra means 'to seal', 'close', or 'lockup'. The Mudhra is a technique of locking the breath within the body. After the practitioner has purified his system and gained control of his breath, the technique of Mudhra is imparted to him by the Guru.

800. Jeeva, the washerman, performs the cleansing act on the square plank of Mooladhara (four-petalled Lotus). There, the yogi erects a bund so that the Apana does not leak out through the sluices. He then lets in the Prana stream upward to fill the body-lake within. Thus he sits looking upward and is now rid of all impurities.

801. They who can force breath through the spinal

Sushumna, alternating the course of the breath from left to right and vice versa, shall know no weariness at all. They can abolish sleep forever and attain God-Awareness. They will be alert all the day and night in divine consciousness. They will not die, they shall be immortal.

802. Nectar is found in Kesari Mudhra. If the tongue's tip is turned backward to lock up the cavity in the gullet, and then skillfully rubbed, the mystic nectar begins to ooze from the regeon of the moon. When it comes, it is to be managed with care. And that which flowed and roared may be preserved.

803. Fan the tongue's tip upward in the centre of the palate and there abides Jeeva and Shiva at the peak of the cranium from where the nectar flows. The three Gods, Brahma-Vishnu-Maheshwara, and the thirty-three crores of Devas will be visioned there. There shall be no death; this fleshy body will be without destruction, for a million, billion years.

804. The nectar of the flesh is a heavenly stream. So transform this fleshy stream into a heavenly stream. It springs from the lofty peaks of the cranium. They do not know how to make it flow. They who know the art will swill the divine nectar and will be free of doubt forever.

805. If you can send the breath of the right nostril and the left nostril into the upper cavity of the mouth, you shall know no death at all, you will not die. And then the gates of nectar will open. This *mudhra* confers lasting youthfulness and longevity. Greying and wrinkling will disappear for all to see. The yogi will be young, and this I say truly, in the name of Holy Nandhi.

806. With the guidance of the Guru if we ascend upward, we shall meet the Lord, we shall then hold sway over all the worlds. But they who let the restrained breath to escape out through the Suriya nadi (Right) and yet sit meditating, are surely decreed to evil-fate it leads to evil consequence.

807. They who sit bewildered overwhelmed by evil karma, let them perform the karma of tongue, that Kesari yoga prescribes, then there is no more room for death. Those who realize that karmas are useless, they do the divine work and enjoy the sweetness that is like that of the juice of the sugarcane.

808. The yogi's who have thus experienced divine sweetness, if they send the tongue upward in a bud like formation and make the coiled kundalini erect, then nectar begins to trickle from within and the body becomes sweet as sugarcane.

809. Twirl the tongue's interior upward into the cavity of the gullet through which saliva flows and drink of the nectar welling up, and remain chanting 'Sivayanama', repeatedly, in silence. The water that the breath brings flows pellucid as from the Ganges. Learn this way to make the heavenly nectar flow.

810. The yogis knowing the appropriate way worshipped thus within, received showers of grace that is ripe Gnana. If they only know how to bolt the door within and check the flowing stream, well then they become abiding cave temples within, 'cave temple' is esoteric language for the cranium.

811. He who takes his abode within that temple is kinder than mother for the entire world. He is good even when others are harsh to him. He is within them too, whom He deals with harshly. He is deadlier than fire itself to those of evil deed.

812. He is seated at the centre of the forehead of the yogi who performs with kundalini fire, He is in the golden city of the yogi who reaches the flower of the spaces of the cranium; He is in the imagination of those who sing of Him; He is in the intelligence of those who perform rare deeds.

813. The yogi is then in rapport with the mystic moon, beaming and shedding the sixteen *kalas*. He sees the two hundred and twenty four *kala* worlds within the divine mansion, that is his body, shedding argent rays. He sits supreme within in great accord.

814. The yogi visions Sakthi, within him, the kalas enveloping Her too, there she, the virgin, the divine fawn sits in the midst, Her visage shedding soft rays. She sits, Herself too streaming ambrosia down.

815. Within the golden regions of the cranium, the sparkling nectar flows in silvery cascades. It was there inside the astral sphere above all the time. They who can guard it from flowing out becomes eternally young. This is a blessing for sure.

816. If Sakthi who is like a tender vine of goodness resides within in haunting fragrance, then the Lord who is a treasure-house of Tathwas Gnana also stands united in amity within.

817. If the *prana* within is made to rise, through the Sushumna cavity to the blossoming lotus at the heights of the cranium, then the moon's mystic region opens and there the yogi remains for an indefinite, length of time, He lives long too.

818. A practice that aids in the successful performance of Kesari *mudhra* is 'Uddiyana Bandha'. As the *prana* stands in the moon's mystic region, the yogi should practise Uddiyana Bandha. He should arrest and dam up the course of the downward Apana; then the Lord in dazzling brightness of the Sun, with Kundala in his earlobe stands transfixed in their awareness, His dance having come to a stop.

Uddiyana is a Mudhra. It literally means 'flying up or soaring', being so called because the great bird, Prana, tied to it, flies without being fatigued. The belly above the navel is passed backwards towards the spine. The portions above and below the navel should be drawn backwards toward the spine.

819. The exhaling breath will be retained inside, the retained breath must be prevented from escape. In due time, the ambrosia starts flowing from the moon's region; if it is not checked it will merge with the Kundalini.

820. It is after this that the yogi can see light. If he but opens a wicket gate within the body-bag, the light will shine inside. If the breath that is controlled spurts there upward to the Sahashrara then this dark body will be bejewelled as a lustrous temple lamp.

821. Inexplicable are the experiences of Kesari yoga when the prana courses upward and the breath is still retained in *kumbaka*, in the mystic regions of fire and sun around the navel and throat, and thought should be transfixed there. It is not possible to say that what stood there, it is indeed indescribable.

822. Air, earth and water and all the five elements in the body may well be described. But when all these five elements combine together then, well may be the power of vision

resulting in distant vision.

823. I shall here describe the nature of that distant vision. The distant vision consists in attaining the grace of Sakthi of collyruim eyes in the first instance, and then thought should be centred on the fine divine light, that is the Lord appears and then may vision all worlds too appearing as in bright daylight.

824. The light (kundalini) shines, as bright and as day, twelve finger length below the navel. So say the Vedas, with that light they yogi light the nadha lamp above, and so becomes the great master of the mystic mension that rises within him.

19. Pariyanga Yoga (The Boon of Union of Male/Female)

825. The yogi anointing the woman's body with diverse unguents and decking her tresses with fragrant flowers proceeds in union to enjoy the damsel in heightened passion. But if he knows how to shoot the prana breath inward through the spinal cavity. Sushumna, their enjoyment never ceases.

Classical Sanskrit texts explain Pariyanga yoga with the use of a term 'Vajroli' and refer to it as a Mudhra Tamil Scholars call it a yoga, even as they call Kesari Mudhra, a yoga. The word 'Pari' means 'hard' and 'Anga' refers to the male sexual organ. In fact, this seems to be the main import of the Vajroli mudra as well as Pariyanga yoga.

In this Mudhra, the main object seems to be to restrain the flow of semen without loss of enjoyment through control of breath.

826. If breath is controlled delicious enjoyment results in sex union when they seek enjoyment. The breath stands still; as the full-breasted damsel and the fervant male seek enjoyment, the liquid silver (Sukhla-Semen) draws in the liquid gold (Shronitha-Female's secretion) and the yogi, masters the retention of his semen. The couple comingle in ecstatic passion the whole time.

827. In that conjugal yogi that is practised by the hero and the heroine, they drive the coach of breath, that has its wheels in the regions of the left and right nostrils, upwards there they collect the waters of the heaven and the organs do not

know weariness.

828. This then is the meaning of that mudhra; when in union of the conjugal act, the yogi does not let the semen flow, but checks it and retains it within himself. He becomes a master.

829. He becomes a master of all Gnana; he becomes a master of all enjoyment; he becomes a master of himself; he becomes a master of his five senses.

830. This is Pariyanga yoga that lasts for five Ghatikas—five Naligal time (two and half hours). At the sixth Naligal time, the damsel sleeps in the arms of the lover, in blissful union that fills her heart in an experience that defies description.

831. Successful practitioners alone can resort to Pariyanga yoga. No great yogi shall embrace a woman unless he has successfully practised the Pariyanga yoga, technique of the five Naligai time of duration.

832. If it is questioned as to who is the yogi who has accomplished this audacious yoga practice, the answer is, the Lord Shiva who wears the heavenly Ganga on His matted locks. Shiva, the Supreme Yogi, embraced Sakthi of embrosial sweetness of speech, for five *naligai* time, thinking and yet thinking not of the act performed.

834. For practise of this yoga, the apt age for the woman is twenty and thirty for the yogi. Then does high rapture ensue. The five senses of the woman desert her. He mind becomes exhausted when she reaches the climax. But the man knows no weariness, nor does his silvery fluid get ejected.

835. Pariyanga yogi is exalted. The yogi is who experiencing ecstatic joy, performs this mudhra unexcited. As so, he becomes radiant like the Sun; he is an acknowledged master in ten directions and an acknowledged head of the 18 Gana groups.

836. The youthful yogi, espousing wisdom that is denoted by Boodha (Mercury)—Planet who stands in the middle of the sun and the moon, when he embraces the damsel knows infinite joy. He has his red mouth burried in the mystic moon (practise of Kesari yoga) lest the silvery liquid flows ahead of the gold liquid of the female.

837. He, who, in perfect wisdom's beauty, embraces a

woman knows no grief. Although he is by the woman's side the silvery semen remains unspent and does not flow into the vaginal track of the woman.

838. This body, that malts wax like on fire, by sexual union, will not any more indulge in the act of when wisdom dawns on him. Those who have attained the wisdom of space will know no exit of the liquid silver.

839. The vision of space in Pariyanga yoga is possible when the yogi knows the space and the light in the space. Then his mind shall be as strong as a child of bronze. He visions the void after having tasted the nectar, through Kesari yoga with the guidance of Great Nandhi.

840. Who are those that rank high above ? They are Vishnu, Brahma and Nandhi (Rudhra). In the fourth rank is that Sadhasiva, who expounded this Pariyanga yoga to the slender-waisted Sakthi.

841. If you can reach Shiva and Sakthi inside the golden circle. Within the cranium and then join and unite in them, then you will be conferred with immortality, you will live on the earth a million, trillion years.

842. No one knows the techniques of breath control—inhaling, exhaling and retaining the inhaled breath. And those who know the skills offer themselves to the Lord entirely.

843. Knowing the way of self-oblation, the yogi if he reaches the mystic circle of Shiva and Sakthi, he reaches the true way; his hair turn dark and he attains eternal youthfulness; the one Sakthi will abide inward and in due course all worldly longings will be dispelled.

844. There is a lotus that neither knows land nor water. It is having no stalk or root, yet the lotus, this lotus blossoms. There is no city, yet there is a light above. The lotus that has neither the above nor the below is a flower none has heard of.

The Lotus is in Hinduism a symbol of many things, here of the skull (cranium) of the man/woman.

20. Amuri Dharanai (The Flow and Glory of the Urine)

Amuri Dharanai is practised in yoga. It is a technique of

urine therapy to achieve longevity. It is advocated for practice after Pariyanga yoga (or Vajroli Mudhra) for this requires advanced preliminary yoga preparation. In fact it is practised along with Vajroli and so it is called 'Amaroli'. He who drinks Amari, snuff it daily, practises 'Vajroli' is called practising Amaroli 'Auri' Tamil (is synonymous with Amari (Sanskrit term) meaning 'Deathlessness'.

845. The urinary liquid within the body is like a picot of small well dipped into a vast sea. If this urine is fed once a day in the appropriate way, life will know no distress at all. So well may you seek it.

846. The body glows in a year, if this clear divine water is taken inside. No harm befalls it, control of Prana will be realised. The mind will centre in Letter 'A' (Prana) and will be uplifted, and the body will be turned into gold.

847. Drink a hundred pepper measures (presumably a pepper measure is a drop) of this divine water, and men will know that there is no other medicine beyond this. Rub it clear on the crest of the head and your greying vanishes away and fresh black hair shoots forth.

848. The men who do not know the truth thus say that, the water on the banks of the body is like a mirage to be kept away from. But they who can drink the midstream, rid of foam and vows, omitting the first and the last portions that flow, will be immortal, and all greying and wrinkling will disappear.

849. Oh ! damsel of flowing tresses and slender forehead, this is a miracle you should hear. Mix pepper, amala, turmeric and neem in this water hidden in the body, and your body will be soft and the hair on the head will be dark ever.

850. He, the Nandhi called it the hero's recipe, heaven's elixir and Sakthi's potion. Some know it as the *medicament primus*. It is specific that is of radiant light that is hard to describe to the world at large.

21. Chandra Yoga

851. The Prana that runs in the body in gross. The two breaths run gross through the Ida and Pingala, they rise and

fall like the *kalas* what wax and wane. When the Prana ascend the Moon's kala, it turns subtle (Sushumna) and this Sushumna Prana is pure.

852. The kalas of the moon are sixteen, of the Sun are twelve and of the fire they are ten. The yogi experiences them all in the upward journey of the prana through Sushumna and the Kalas become his mystic knowledge.

853. The ten Kalas of fire are absorbed by the further twelve Kalas of the Sun; and together they are absorbed in the sixteen Kalas of the moon. Those who have learned to merge in the moon's Kalas, truly become masters of the earth, filled entirely with all Kalas.

854. You should know truly and well that there are the number of the Kalas enumerated. There are twelve kalas of the sun, sixteen Kalas of the Moon and ten Kalas of the fire.

855. All these Kalas the ten Kalas of fire, the twelve Kalas of the scorching sun and the sixteen Kalas that emanate from the moon, which are not alike merge into oneness.

856. The ten, twelve and sixteen are the Kalas that appear in the Agni, the Sun and the Moon. There are four kalas of the Star Jeeva and to enumerate all the Kalas in total, there are the fettering Tathwas too that are ninety-six in number.

857. All the Kalas from the left and the right *Nadis* are roused and passed through the central *nadi;* the Kundalini fire in the Mooladhara is kindled; all the *kalas* reach the cranium at the top and there in the Sahashrara, the yogi pays homage at the feet of the great one.

858. Two Kalas each of the fire, star, moon and sun and one Kala of Parai who is unto a star, together form the nine beams of Parai in the navel Chakra of the Jeeva here in this world.

859. These nine ! earth, water, fire, air, space, sun, moon, agni and star constitute Pranava (*Aum*), the way that is great.

860. When the moon wanes, the stars shine bright and when the moon waxes, they do not. Like the stars that are innumerable are the jeevas of the universe. The divine manifestation is like the Star of the stars.

861. The Kalas shoot and expand in the waxing fortnight

of the moon. In the waxing fortnight they shrink and become small. They who can know the mystery of the fifteen Kalas will reach the Feet of the Lord of indescribable glory.

Out of the 16 Kalas, 15 are the eternal Kalas of the moon. There remains one Kala always. That Kala is nothing but *chit* itself. We call Her, Tripurasundari. It is understood by this, that in order to rouse the kundalini, one should practise in the lunar fortnight alone, and not in the solar one.

862. Through the Kundalini yoga, the Kalas of fire should be roused. Merge them in the Kalas of the sun. Then merge them all in the Kalas of the moon. Finally, merge them all in the Jeeva Star, and all senses and sense organs will be rid. This truly is Chandra yoga.

863. The despicable men who do not know of the sixteen Kalas within the body do not seek to reach them. When death lays his trap, they fall then and there bewildered forever.

864. When the fire-kalas pass through the moon's nadi, the sun receives them; the Kalas of the fire and the sun together merge in the moon's Kala. When the Kundalini fire unites in Shiva, the Kalas of the star merge, and the Jeeva who resides the star, becomes all life.

865. Sitting unmoved, seize both the twelve female Kalas of the sun and the sixteen male Kalas of the moon and consign them to the Kundalini Fire, in this yoga an ecstasy beyond recount wells up.

866. Practise Nadi Suddhi by coursing the breath running in the sun's *nadi* on the right to the moon's *nadi* on the left, and vica-a-versa. If this can be done without erring then the yogi lives a thousand years and his body be well preserved.

867. The merger takes place in the ninth centre of the Moon's sphere. The yogi's heart resounds to the triumphant beatings of the Divine sound of the Nadha; there, the Lord, that is Supreme of all celestials stands in high exaltation. There, the yogi too shall stand as a starry (stellar) Light, and the Sun-shall blow the conch to announce his arrival.

868. The sun and the moon only measure time; The nectar of grace rains into him who has become great. When he travels beyond the spheres and knocks, he meets the Lord there in

His very own abode.

869. The Light of *Aum* rises from the navel-lotus. The Light of Aum is the finite Manthra, No one knows this; When they come to know that secret manthra, then the Sun, that is Jeeva stands before the eternal father, that is almighty, God.

870. It profits not to tell those who do not listen to advice, and they are deaf-mutes. If you only learn how to merge the primal Kundalini with the finite being then, the Holy One will appear before you.

871. The Kundalini serpent consumes the Kalas of the moon. The fire consumes the kalas of the Sun too. If you can resolve the conflict of the serpent and the moon merging the Kalas of the moon in the kundalini, then the Lord will never, never leave you.

872. The kundalini that moves up devours the moon. The yogi sleeps not until the serpent throws it out. He may sleep when the Moon comes out. Then his mind shall be as luminous as the full Moon. Then the mystic inside will shed its dazzling Kalas fully.

873. The yogi should not sleep until the moon comes out. He should not eat until the moon rises, he should not sleep until the moon moves; the yogi may sleep when only the moon moves.

This reminds us of a parallel of the Sasthraic infuction not to sleep and eat when there is a lunar (or solar) eclipse, when Raghu, the serpent, is mythologically said to devour the moon (or Sun) for a time.

874. The yogis who thus practise Chandra yoga incessantly conquer death; they will live in this world beyond aeons; They who practise in success this moon's yoga, are worthy of our obeisance.

875. The yogis traverse the spheres of the Sun and the Moon, and see visions of the past, present and future earth; And on that full moon day the nectar ripens. Time stands to a stop, until the moon drops back from the Kundalini.

876. Who knows that six of the waxing Kalas of the sun and six of the waxning kalas of the moon wake to life running to twelve *angulas* (30 centimetres) and the moon then drops

out. It is an indication that the moon has dropped out of kundalini's mouth.

877. If the yogi thus achieves this goal his semen does not flow where it lists on the day of the full moon; it firmly collects in the Mooladhara, and devoid of all passions, chanting *Aum* in the silence of his heart, he remains pure and is filled with total consciousness.

878. The moon reappears, now with the six waxing Kalas of the fiery sun. Six Kalas of the moon and four Kalas of the Kundalini. Thus, they are sixteen Kalas emitted in the full moon.

879. The sun's Kalas is emitted in the mingling of the male semen and woman's fluid; if the sun's Kala is low, the semen ejects quickly, but when the mind and body stand balanced they will never let the semen flow.

880. If the yogic course their breath with the mind centred in the direction of the Nadha sound that emanates from Shiva's conch, then the five senses that run blind will meet their restraint; and the interminable bliss of delectable nectar will never leave them.

881. Course the five pranas through the central Sushumna; on the bank of the river where the waters of the nectar flow; They who remain thus do not have death. Their Kalas are good and they are not time-bound.

882. Opening the springs where nectar wells up, the yogis walk toward the Lotus Feet that are as cool water; They, thus sit in undisturbed Samadhi; coursing through the spinal channel and alternating the breathing through the right and left *nadis*.

883. If the breaths of the moon (Ida) and the sun (Pingala) course their way unhindered through the spinal channel, the yogi's body shall be imperishable and abiding joys well up here below for him. This is the way of true yoga.

Tanthra Three Concludes

4

Tanthra Four (Sindhahamam)

1. Ajapa (Non Speaking Letters)

Thirumoolar, here expounds the secrets of manthras and yanthras. Manthra is the sound-body of a Devatha, deity, and Yanthra is its diagramatic representation.

The primal manthra is *ajapa*—that which is not chanted. As, we breathe in, we make the subtle sould 'Sah' and as we breathe out, the subtle sound of 'Ham'. These two constitute the Ajapa manthras. "Soham" or 'Hamsa' as it becomes by continuous repetition inversion.

The mute chanting of this unchanted manthra requires no special effort. Soham is, however, equated with the Pranava manthra *Aum*.

The exposition of the secrets of manthra and yanthra belong to the realm of Shiva yoga, are distinguished from Kundalini yoga expounded previously.

884. You are the Supreme Gnana: I praise and land Gnana that is our refuge. I adore the Holy Feet of the Lord that are constantly in my thought, thus I expound Sivayoga; Listen, I chant the one letter *Aum* that is dear to the Lord Shiva.

885. All the worlds developed from the one letter manthra *Aum* (pranava), that is Nadha. The two letters A and U became

Shiva and Sakthi. He became the Light (Gnanam) by the three letters A-U-M and the letter M, became maya, the term 'Ajapa' refers to a special form of effortless meditation. Every living being (jeeva) performs this *japa* (repetition) unconsciously, but constantly. This is called Ajapa Gayathri. This Ajapa Japa is performed in three places—in the Mooladhara-Anahatha- and Agna.

886. Chitrambalam is where the Devas reside, Chidambaram is where the Devas reside. Thiru Ambalam is where the Devas reside, the Sabha of the South is where the Devas reside.

The one letter manthra *Aum*, denotes the divine dance. It is Tandava, the grace act of the Mighty Lord performed in the Golden Hall of Chidambaram, the Sabha of the South.

The word Chidambaram, is of Sanskrit origin, and is made of up of two words 'Chit' (meaning mind and thought) and Ambaram (meaning sky or space). Hence, the world would mean Infinite Mind or the Divine Itself. The Tamilized form of Chidambaram is Chitrambalam. Moolar, Himself has pointed out in various passages, Shivas Mighty dance appeared first as a mental vision in the mind of yogic Sadhana hold Siddhars.

887. The Athbhutha (wonder) Dance is performed in the Golden Temple (meaning the Golden Sabha), the Ananda (bliss) Dance is performed in the Golden Temple, the Anavaratha (eternal) Dance is performed in the Golden Temple, the Pralaya (Deluge) Dance is performed in the Golden Temple and the Samhara (dissolution) Dance is performed in the Golden Temple.

888. The one letter *Aum* is the one which became Tandava Dance; the grace of the Lord became Thandawa. He who performed the Anandha Tandhava dance in the Golden Hall is the one and uncreated being.

889. He is the Cosmic Light. He is the Tathwas all; He stands as the Letters A and U (Shiva/Sakthi). He is the Divine Light for Tathwa Dance. He is for Himself and the support of all.

890. He is the uncreated Lord, the *Para* Great for all the worlds. He stands as *Na-Ma-Si-Va-Ya* in the sphere of the

Mooladhara. He stands as *Na-Ma-Si-Va-Ya* in the sphere of fire. In the sphere of the sun, He stands *Va-Si-Ya* and in the sphere of the Moon as Va-Si.

891. The Letter A and U are Si (Shiva) and Va (Shakthi, They are Supreme; They are space and beyond the reach of thought. They are vast space, of supreme intelligence. The Letters A and U are the final refuge and eternal joy. They are the letters where He performs His holy dance.

892. The three letters *Si-Va-Ya* are perpectual bliss; the letters Si and Ya are unitive Gnana itself; Si-Va-Ya is unalloyed joy. Many do not know these things. They who realize this in nov will behold Him in joyous (Ananda) dance.

893. A and U are the two letters; they form the manthra Si and Va. That all men of vast knowledge chant. These two letters Si and Va, are the source of the five letters. *Si-Va-Ya-Na-Ma*. The Thandawa Dance of dissolution merges in them. They are in the Mooladhara Triangle. From there they ascend to the rest of the yogic centres.

894. The letters A and U that are Si and Va, are Sadhashiva. They are the imperishable Agamas. They are the Godly goal. They are the shady mastwood tree on the banks of the Ganges; where bees in dwell. They are the Holy dance. They are the Divine teachings of the Agamas. They are the immaculate purity of the divine dance hall.

895. The pure letters are the Agamas; they are *pathi, pasu* and *pasam*; the pure letters are grace that is bliss, they are egoity, maya and desire. The pure letters are the sit of Divine Dance.

896. He, Himself stands as His Lord; Himself stands as His mountain He, Himself stands as pervasive. He, Himself stands as the Lord that is Himself. The is Lord is all.

897. He is the Lord who stands dancing eternally; He is the Lord who is the Holy One, He is the Lord who unfolds Gnana's honey-laden flower, He is the Lord whose Feet are holy beyond peer.

898. The Peerless Feet of the Lord are eight letters: the Peerless Feet of the Lord are seven letters; the Peerless Feet of Lord are fifty one letters; the Peerless Feet are manthras that

are seven times thousand. The eight letters make up five letters of Panchakshara (Namasivaya) and Bijaksharas (Om).

899. The seven thousand manthras became fifty and then into the seven with diverse endings; Thus of the seven thousand manthras that are chanted beyond thought. But ultimately have the seven and the two as vital.

900. There exist seven thousand manthras; but none of them are potentially divine. The two-letter manthra is this manthra that is Shiva's Holy form and all manthras are contained in this.

901. He is unto Himself in His Dance. He stands the letters A and U; He is the one for the Magic Dance of the Tathwas. Here below, He dances the dance peerlessly.

902. The Dance that is in the two letters is the joyous dance: it is the Dance of dissolution; it is the dance that leads to bliss; it is the dance that is Shiva Linga. It is the alchemy that transforms the coppery *jeeva* into the golden Lord Shiva.

903. Chant *Sivayanama* and copper turns into gold; The *chit* para (Supreme Intelligence) exists there in the *Sivayanama* manthra. Chant 'Srim' and 'Krim' and copper turns of gold. The holy temple alchemises copper into gold.

Srim and Krim and Beejas manthras for Shiva and Sakthi same as A and U, and Si and Va.

904. Thirumoolar (Thiru ambalam) chakra is fashioned in the manner by drawing six vertical and six horizontal lines, forming twenty-five squares, and in inscribing in each the five letters and meditate on it continuously.

905. This is the way to chant the manthra; *Sivayanama, Sivaya Nama*; if chanted in this way; there will be no more birth; with the Lord's grace you shall behold the eternal dancer and copper (that is jiva) turns into gold (Lord Shiva).

906. This Sivayanama manthra is golden, so do not chant it loud, just say it in silence and your body will glow red. If you take it in slowly, as you breath in, your body becomes gold; and in time, you shall behold the golden Feet of the Lord Shiva.

907. Not only shall you behold the golden feet of the Lord, you shall have noble children, I say that in the name of

the Golden Feet, the copper that is the Jeeva, will became gold that is Lord Shiva. And as you behold the Golden Feet, you too shall assume His form. So centre the manthra in your thoughts and witness the great Dance of the Golden Feet.

908. By chanting Sivayanama, you may easily transmigrate into any body; If you chant the manthras, the goodly sakthi will be your companion, the fiery Snake of *pasa* will leave you. This Holy manthra is the secret of the Holy Dance, so chant it inceasingly and intensively.

909. It is the Sushumna (subtle) manthra; chant it eight thousand times and you shall see the subtle path of Sushumna. You can destroy karma that is very subtle. You can enjoy the bliss of Lord Shiva that is the subtlest of all.

910. Chant the Holy manthra, thus: "One the Supreme Bliss, One the Supreme Bliss' and you shall have bliss. Bliss has its source in the five letters A:I:U:E and *Aum* and the vowels of life. The five life-vowels became the five-lettered manthra and joy that is within joy. Bliss lies in the five seed-letter; they are *Ham, Hrim, Hum, Ksham* and *Aum*.

911. The two letter manthra, A and U, is the body of the Lord. Chant it inaritculately. As the two suffuse your body, you stand transformed, the two letters that the Lord's corpus became the five letters U-A-I-E-O; that is Jeeva. The two letters that are the Lord's corpus became the five letters I-O-A-U-E that is Lord Shiva's Dance.

912. The Dance vowels are Si-Va-Ya-Na-Ma. The Dance letters I,U,A,E and O (m) became Sivayanama. The Dance letters I,U,A,E and O (m) became Namasivaya, the Supreme God.

Letters AU, AE, and AUM denote the five letters Si-Va-Ya-Na-Ma. The origin of the five letter manthra is traced to the letter-sounds in Shiva's rhythmic dance steps.

913. He danced as one, alone. He danced as two, with Sakthi, He danced as several that is, in all life and creation. He danced in three, the sun, moon and fire. He danced in seven, that is, the worlds that are seven. He danced on one foot and with the nine Sakthis. The arena that He danced on is Space—the adharas. He danced the dance of ruby.

2. Thiruambala Chakra

Thirumoolar now proceeds to reveal the *yanthra* or the diagramatic representation of the Panchakshra (Five-lettered) manthra (Namasivaya). He calls this the Thiruambala Chakra or the yanthra for the Divine Dance Arena. (The *yanthras* are referred to as chakras here).

The Thiruambala Chakras seem to be a cluster of several chakras. Its several variations are represented in different diagrams. Thirumoolar also lays down the rules for chanting the *beeja* manthras; and expounds on their esoteric significane. There is a diagram with 121 chambers filled by the manthra, Sivayanamá. This is called the Sivayanama Chakra.

914. To form the *chakra*, draw twelve vertical lines and cross them with twelve horizontal lines; thus hundred and twenty-one squares are formed. The Lord dances in this chakra. The numbers 121 of the square is 11, and there are according to the Vedas and 11 Rudhras (various forms of Lord Shiva).

915. He abides in His own letter "Si" the four letters conjoined are the great letters of His name. On the four sides of His chakra are His own five letters. He abides in the one letters, and so is Hara's manthra too.

916. Say 'Hara Hara' and nothing formidable happens to you. Those who do not know this, do not say 'Hara Hara'. Chant 'Hara Hara' and you will be a celestial. Say 'Hara Hara' and you know no more births.

917. In the Chakra, the letter 'Si' is in the eight directions. From that one letter in all the eight directions arose the vie Gods. The nine Sakthis and the Bindhu and Nadha. Thus, the manthra, the pure word flourishes.

918. No one knows how the Lord became conjoined with her, who, sits on the blooming Lotus. They who chant the aspirated letter, 'O' conjoined with the unaspired letter 'M', may well preserve their life for ever.

919. The Panchakshara (Namasivaya) is the abode of the Lord. The Panchakshara is the manifest of Namashivaya. Sivayanama is the subtle form. Thus, He is in that manthra both, in the manifest and subtle forms.

920. The Chakra is formed with lines six by six, the lines

inside are five by five: thus in all, they are divided into twenty chambers and in the centre of these in the letters 'Ma'.

921. The yanthra of six letters Om-Na-Ma-Si-Va-Ya is formed by inscribing the letter 'Ma' in the centre and above it describe the letter 'Va'. Surround the two letters by the letter 'O'. Split them in the centre vertically by the letter 'U' and place the letter 'Ya' on the top. Fix the letter 'Si' on both the sides, so that they look like two eyes. The letters 'Na' and 'Va' form the diagram's two feet.

922. Describe the Pranava letter (Om): in the centre on the top place 'Si', on the two sides place the letter 'Va' and 'Ya'. then inside inscribe Na-Ma-Si-Va-Ya and on the outer round figure the letters Si-Va-Ya-Na-Ma.

923. This is how the five letters are filled in the twenty five chambers of the Chakra. Write Si-Va-Ya-Na-Ma in the row on top of the Chakra; on the next row fill in the squares with Ma-Si-Va-Ya-Na: In the third row, write Na-Ma-Si-Va-Ya, still below in order comes the letters Ya-Na-Ma-Si-Va. In the last squares, are written the letters Va-Ya-Na-Ma-Si. Thus are the squares filled in the Chakra, with 'Si' to begin with and 'Si' to end.

924. Enclose fifty letters, two each, in the twenty-five chambers. Begin with the letter 'A' and end with the final letter 'Ksha'. With these fill the one letter 'Om' in the twenty-five chambers of the *chakra*. They are fifty one in all.

The letter 'Ksha' makes it clear that Moolar has the Sanskrit letters in mind. 'A' to 'Ksha' make fifty-one letters, in all; says Moolar, which would correspond to the Sanskrit system in one manner of counting.

925. Describe Hara, Hara on the outer circle and in the inner circle describe Hari, Hari; in the innermost centre place Om, the Ajapa, mark the ends of the circle by the trident sign.

926. Above each trident sign, inscribe the Beeja manthra 'Hrim', this surrounds the diagram Om. Write the five letters in the space between the trident signs; the Chakra thus formed, is indeed the Lord's abode.

927. Inscribe our name Moola, that is Om, in the centre, surround it in two concentric circles, in the space between

the two circles, inscribe the five letters, A.I.U.E and O. This denotes the five Holy letters—Si-Va-Ya-Na-Ma.

928. This is the yanthra for Moola Chakra, this is the famed Moola Chakra. The Chakra takes its loveliness only when the space between the two circles are filled entirely with the five letters that are stated.

929. As you describe the Chakra of this manthra (*Om*) the Lord as Guru will clearly instruct you the way to meditate on it. Anterior to the chanting of this manthra are the seed-manthras that pertain to the wind, water, fire, earth and sky. YAM, VAM, RAM, LAM and HAM.

Moolar connects the Panchakshara with the five elements and their corresponding Beeja manthras in Tantrism.

930. Conjoin the sixth letter U to the forty-eight letter S (a) 'I' add the Bindhu letter 'M' (.) to form the syllable Sum. In a similar way conjoin the fourteenth letter AU to S (a); add the Nadha letter Ah (:) to form the syllable Sauh; to follow chant these—SI VA YA NA MA, thus when you chant the Holy manthra; in its full form as Sum Sauh SI VA YA NA MA, the triple Pasas showing in distress take to their heels and go away.

931. Shiva and Sakthi interchange their Beeja manthra states. The Lord is seated in His consort's letter (SAUH) the mother is seated in Her Lord's letter (HUM). When thus the two are seated in amity, the holy beings comprehend the inner meaning.

932. Describe the letter 'A' and above it inscribe 'HARA', further, above place the letter 'E', then, the Linga form is shaped, centre your mind on it and course your breath above, you will indeed vision the Dance of Divine Light.

933. There is the letter Hau.and the letter Sau, everything is comprehended in them; No one knows how they are entwined. They who know the mystery of this union are indeed blessed of both, Sakthi and Sadhashiva.

934. The five lettered manthra (Namasivaya) is the seat of Holy Nandhi, it is the Holy manthra, is the Divine Chakra and it is the Lord's abode.

935. Many are the ways to see the mighty dancer, Shiva,

chant the first letter of the dance (Si), you will be one in thought with the dancer. This is truly the way to see the dancer.

936. Kindle the kundalini fire where is lies dormant, and chant the letter 'Na' that is in the chakra: then the symbolized 'Na' brings the Lord there.

937. She (Sakthi) Herself grants grace if you lift the kundalini upward; granting grace Herself places you high above in the Sahashrara; you should chant here syllable 'Ma' and you will in deed, be placed like a gem of serene ray.

938. The North beamed in radiant light and there the Lord of the Devas (Indhra) crowned in bright diadem stood, and the Lord revealed His letter 'Si' sparkling as the rays within pure gem: it beamed aloft for all to see like a light set on a mountain top.

939. He, Himself stands as the increased soft light, He, Himself stands as the self-existent Vedas; You chant His uplifting attributes and He, the unborn sage of the Vedas reveals Himself.

940. He, the Lord of the Vedas, gave us this birth, so that we might become the Lord of the Vedas; the Lord of the Vedas stands within the five letters and is Himself the five letters.

941. The five-letter form of Lord Shiva is this:— His feet are the letter 'NA'; His navel is the letter 'MA'; His shoulders are the letter 'SI'; His mouth is the letter 'VA' and His cranial centre aloft is the letter 'YA'.

942. Thus the five letters are of such greatness and Nandhi shone in it as His radiant form. You can see Him as the letter 'Om ' and He speards vide like a vast ocean.

943. The manthra spreads everywhere, the manthra grants its boon to all lives. If you but chant it in the appropriate manner, all hostility that harasses shall flee from you; it is the manthra that makes you mighty and strong; Invoke this manthra chanting 'Om'.

944. Invoke Holy Nandhi by chanting *Om*: kindle the kundalini fire and make it blaze, by chanting 'Na', so as to reach the goal. They who knew Him thus, truly saw His

Divine Dance, steeped in Supreme ecstasy for ever.

945. In the chakra, that is designed there are five letters in their appropriate places. There, He stands, the Parapara (the transcendent reality) who fills the fifty one letters.

946. Inscribe the five letters SI VA YA NA MA: in the next row place the letters YA NA VA SI MA: further on place the letters in this order thus: MA VA YA NA SI, SI YA NA MA VA and VA SI MA YA NA. Thus the Five letters stand permuted in the Chakra.

947. The letters that are placed thus are the five elements, they are the five colours too. If the letters stand in their appropriate order, He, for sure, stands within the letters.

Letters are said to have colours, perhaps because when used in *yanthras*, they are coloured differently. Usually, the colours are five, namely white, orange, yellow, green or blue and black. Colour symbolism is important in Hinduism. Hence, the five letters (Panchaksharam) are said to represent the five elements and are assigned individual colours each.

948. Thus stands the Chakra, and thus did it extend to the four corners of the earth. Nandhi who stands high aloft Mount Kailash, is the master of the comely Maya land: He, the Lord stands in the celestial arena and from Him flows the milk of grace, just as milk flows from the mother-cow to the calf.

The word 'Chakra' stands for 'a circle used in a variety of senses. These are different *chakras*. In rituals, Sadhanas in which male and female aspirants assemble and perform the rites of Panchamakara. The term Chakra is also used to denote Yanthras or mystic diagrams and again, the term is used to denote different nerve-pleasures in the body.

949. Significance of the Chakra is that, much good comes from within this Chakra. Within this Chakra, there are five names. This Chakra is the five letters of the Divine Dancer. This Chakra is where the Divine Dance goes on incessantly.

950. In the centre space there mark the letter 'A': at the top of the cranium place the letter 'U' and surround it with the letter 'MA'. On its 'leg' place the Bindhu letter 'SI' and on its horn place the Nadha letter 'VA'. You shall clearly know that this is the Shiva Manthra.

951. There are three ways of chanting Panchakshara. You commence with 'A' and 'U' and with 'Si' in the centre, that is: OM-Na-Ma-Si-Va-Ya. Commence with 'A' and 'U' and 'Va' and rest the regulated breath in, that is as OM VA SI YA NA MA. Then commence with 'A' and 'U' and 'Si' and rest in the following order, that is: as OM SI VA YA NA MA. As you chant thus, the Primal Lord '*Om*' appears rejoining.

952. The Lord is in *Aum* where the *adharas* and, and beyond. There, you shall see the Lord who reveals Himself of Himself. He is blemishless, the light divine. He is the whole truth. He is the alchemic pill of flawless gold.

953. When you chant 'A' and 'U' simultaneously, then, melting Mukthi does appear there: when he chanted 'Ma' Nandhi was with him. How shall He speak of his Father's greatness:

954. The knowledge of the Jeevas here below is like letters written on water. They do not seek the letter that is in heaven. No one knows that letter. They who know it, have ended their breath.

955. Course the breath through the central Sushumna and be within the centre of the garland of letters, when in the centre of that garland the Primal Manthra *Aum* that the Vedas speak of appears, then, Mukthi is sure indeed.

956. The unholy do not know the greatness of a great letter that is below the navel. Sakthi and Shiva are on the mystic letter below the navel. Even the creator (Brahma) knows it not: There it is Shiva with Sakthi, in total splendour.

957. 'HA' and 'SA' together form Hara's manthra (HAMSA). But no one knows the truth of Hamsa: when anyone comes to know the truth, he will know Hamsa as beginningless.

958. There is a great manthra that rises inside the heart's lotus: its roots lie deep in the navel; They who do not know it, do not come by it: they only prayed at sunset and departed with just a loud noise.

959. The 'HAMSA' manthra that is chanted within spreads in all directions. It is the manthra of life, the sustaining breath; it is the manthra in the heart's lotus. When chanted constantly that manthra in life's centre is truly likened to a mahout's

goad, that controls elephantine passions.

960. Nadha rises in formless space and Bindhu rises in Sakthi of slender waist. Together they form OM with the letter 'YA' in the centre. When this manthra SI VA YA NA MA is chanted incessantly, the manthra (*Om Sivayanama*) spouts Siva Bliss.

961. If Bindhu and Nadha conjointly reach the mystic moon inside the Lord-head, the heavenly ambrosia wells up, the manthra that rises there is truly the oblation to Shiva.

962. They who truly know are they who chant the six-lettered manthra (OM SI VA YA NA MA). They who do not know are they who do not chant the six lettered manthra. Even they who chant with no other letter, may be redeemed with this one-letter AUM.

963. Fifteen vowels are formed with the letter 'AUM', add the Nadha letter 'U' to Bindhu's luminous letter 'A' with the rest of the thirteen letters. They are now fifteen vowels. Together with the consonants, the primal letters are reckoned as fifty-one. This verse is inspired by the concept of 'Varnamala' (garland of letters) of the Sakthi cult.

964. When the letter 'A' that is Bindhu ascends upward together with the curled letter 'U' that is Nadha, then, Sakthi with the sixteen Kalas beams within and expands endlessly as neck, hands, legs and the entire body. Her form expands as the fifty-one letters too.

965. The letters fifty are all that the Vedas are: the letters fifty are all that the Agamas are. When the source of these fifty letters are known, then the fifty letters come to five letters.

966. With the five letters, He created the five elements, With the five letters, He created the diverse life. He supported the vast: spaces with the five letters and He abides in the Jeevas with the five letters.

967. They who continuously chant the Lord's Holy name, in high desire, for them the miseries of karma fly away: He, the Lord of matted locks, beckons them to come into Him.

968. He is the elixir of life: He is the eternal time, He is the melody in music and He is the song too. The celestials fervently adore Him. He stand in their thoughts. He abides

in the five letters too.

969. The vast spaces arise from the great letters, the five letters and sustains it, as the Supreme Letter. He stands as fire and life, as the renowned letter. He stand, as the rare resplendant, as the one letter.

970. He pervades the spaces and beyond, as the seed letter. He fills and sustains it, as the supreme better. He stands as fire and life, as the renowned letter. He stands as the rare resplendent, as the one letter.

971. The world takes form in the sound of the fourth letter (Va), the world is contained in the sound of the fourth letter. The fourth letter is the Holy way for them who chant it, incessantly.

972. The lovely Sakthi entered into my heart and there She sat rejoicing. Chant NA MA SI VA and think of what it brings: I clung to Her Feet and was transformed, and then, all my prattle ceased.

973. This corporeal body is made of the food of rice: offer it into the fire of OM and incessantly chant NA MA SI VA: this is the name of finite Sakthi: She, the mistress of Dharma stands revealed.

974. The five letters are the Lord's gift. He that assumed the eight forms, dances in it the centre, night and day, in eternal endearment.

The five elements plus the moon, the sun and jeeva are the eight forms of Shiva, or Shiva pervades in the eight directions.

975. The letter 'A' is Jeeva, 'U' is Para and'Ma' is Mala: thus it is in the three-lettered word *Aum*. Si is Shiva: Va is Sakthi and Ya is Jeeva. Thus is the three lettered word SI-VA-YA.

976 To chant commence with letters "NA" and "MA", with the letter "Si" in the centre and with the 'Intoned Letter'—VA in regulated breath, together with Om at the beginning of all. If you chant this even once, the Lord of 'MA' (Maya) will abide in your heart.

977. The five elephants (senses) roam about in the body-forest. The five letters become the goads for these five elephants.

The five senses can control the five senses. Only they who can contain the five together, can, reach the Primal Lord, Unafraid.

978. The five Kalas arose from the letter 'A' and the rest (AUM) arose from the five letters, leave out the letters 'Na' and 'Ma' and contemplate thus on "SI VA YA". You seek Nandhi in the Mooladhara; those who meet Him there with Parai (Sakthi) will not have any more actions to perform.

Santhiyatheetha, Santhi, Vidya, Prathishta, Nivirthi, are the five kalas.

979. Chant SI VA YA in love and you will be immortal; it is a rare yoga and Gnana as sell; together with it, the illumined Jeeva receives grace and He becomes Shiva; this indeed is true liberation.

980. Realize the truth of the five blissful letters and the transcendent reality will fill your heart, the truth is that you will be immortal. I cannot emphatically say that there is anything else other than these five letters that are your refuge.

981. Chanting 'A' and 'U' in understanding along with 'Si', 'VA' and 'YA' (that is as Om Sivaya) is truly the form of Shiva. They who understood 'Si', 'Va' and 'Ya' with 'A' and 'V' , have realised *'Om Shivaya'* as a great Manthra.

982. In your hearts' centre, hold the letters SI,VA and YA, and Na, Ma together with 'AUM', when the five letters are thus chanted, the Lord of 'Ma' (Maya) appears appreciatingly.

983. Seek to do all your actions chanting the five letters beginning with 'Na' (NA MA SI VA YA), by doing so, all the stubborn karmas are vanquished with these five letters. Those who chant in their hearts, the five letters beginning with 'Si' (as Si Va Ya Na Ma) then they will be one with the primal Sadhashiva.

984. The letters 'Nad' is Jeeva to the being (Na-Ma), the letters 'Si' is Para to the being (Si-Va). Even, they have no Tapas at all, may yet became Shiva, the Lord of Tathwas, by chanting Shiva as SI-Ya. This is the true-beyond doubt.

985. Know 'A' and 'U' together (AUM) in its depth and seek Nandhi in Gnana within. The five senses that are Wavering become your friends. Chant AUM and you become doubt-

free.

986. They know not well the letter eight (A) and the letter two (U). The ignorant ones,'do not know what eight (A) and 'two' (U) are. Eight and two (Aum) are only tend and this is verily the truth and in Gnana Siddhantha.

In Tamil, the numeral eight, is written as the letter 'A' and numeral two is written as the 'U'. Hence the play on the words 'eight' and 'two'. The illiterates are generally referred to as those who cannot count eight and two.

987. Draw eight vertical lines and eight horizontal lines. Thus in the central chamber that is formed, inscribe the Lord's six letter—OM NA MA SI VA YA. In the forty-eight squares, that remain, distributes the sacred letters and pray there.

988. To form the Shiva Chakra, place them—the Dhanavar, the Chatter, the two Sathirars, the two Guard-Gods and the rest of the fifteen Bindhu and Nadha and Shiva Gnana Natha—in all the appropriate squares. Thus is Shiva Chakra formed.

989. Some reached the Paraparam by way of their great penance: they surrendered their self to Him and they adored Him chanting SI VA YA NA MA; but I do not speak any more than a tiny bit of the Mighty Lord; Greatness. I am near Him only a little; beyond this, I know nothing.

990. Shiva is the first name, then the other three, and the other five follow. They are all nine, and yet they are one and the same; Bindhu and Nadha flourished with them. All these are only names of the First Sankara.

991. Draw lines to denote the universe that is a seed: there mark the sixteen Kalas, then the twelve kalas and then the ten Kalas that appear in the sacrificial rituals of Brahmian you should thus mark and chant in Chakra.

992. Ah, I beheld Him within the lotus of my heart, and I saw Him, I rose and met Him: then I lost my sense of the self. so you too chant 'Name', in undiminished endearment, betaking, to gracious ways of the eternal Lord.

993. Raining flowers on Him the Holy celestials meditate on the manthra that confers grace, they approach Him chanting His "Nama". Thinking of Him clearly as the apple of their

eye they abide and united with Him.

994. The six letters are the six faiths. The six letters multiplied by four and proliferated into twenty-four—they are the letters of the Savithri Manthra. Savithri has the first letter that is AUM. They who separately meditate on it, have no more travail of birth.

Savithri (Divine Creator) is also Sri Gayathri, the most sacred of all Vaidika Manthras.

995. Draw eight lines vertically and eight lines horizontally; Distribute the letters so that each occurs eight times in the chambers thus formed. Repeat it in the four corners and encircle the whole in Om. Meditate thus on the Chakra and the Lord of Uma will be yours.

996. Those who meditate, chanting the manthra 'NA' to begin with and 'YA' to end with, such as NA MA SI VA YA and chanting the prefixing manthra that has 'A' and 'U', that is, 'OM', will see the primal Lord inside their heads.

997. Figure out the five letter manthra with 'MA' to begin with, like this, MA, SI, VA, YA, NA—on a fresh plank of a Peepul tree wood, and in similar fashion inscribe it on a palm leaf and smear it with wax and warm it gently over fire, then centre your meditation on it, the concentration that you attain is strong that your enemies, for sure, will be rendered actionless.

This is called Sthambana (Inaction state) Chakra, Sthambana—stopping, checking, restraining the powers of fire, the flowing of water, the ferocity of wild beasts, etc. making a spirit or person stand immovable in one place and depriving him of the power of speech.

998. At the lower end of a plank of Kondrai tree wood inscribe 'NA' and 'SI' and on a palm leaf write the letter 'MA' and smear it with five ingredients—Ginger, pepper, mustard, garlic and asofoetida. Then bury it head downward in the hearth's fire, you shall attain the powers of Mohana (fascination).

999. On a plank of wood of the Pertia tree, at the north-west corner where Aiyanar has his temple, and on a dark leaden plate smear poison and inside inscribe the mark of Bindhu (dot) and surround it by 'OM', then concentrate on

the manthra Utchatana (the science of exorcism) will be yours.

This is called Utchatana Chakra—powers of expulsion; setting demons against a person to ruin him by magical incantations, or dislodging them by magical incantations, or dislodging them from persons or places.

1000. Smear a green palm leaf with the state five ingradients in a triangle chakra in the cremation ground and bury it at noon in the south-east corner, where the God of Agni resides. This manthra device for Marana (Death) is a spell to destroy enemies.

Marana—deprivation of life, killing either spirits or men.

1001. Smear a palm leaf with yellow arsenic and place it on a live plank, to serve as a receptacle, inscribe on it the letters 'A' and 'U' and chant the manthra eighty thousand times.

This is the yoga of Vasiya Chakras (making others, our own) Vasiyam—bringing a person under one's own power. control and influence, etc.

1002. Smear a palm leaf with silver power on a Thursday and inscribe the letter 'U', place it on a plank of the wood of white Jamun tree and face westward. Then chant the Pranava manthra (*Aum*) eight thousand times. This is the way to attain Akarshana power of bringing things and people to you.

Akarshanam—summoning or invoking a spirit or absent person visibly into one's presence.

These magical acts are exposited as eight in number. Besides, the six mentioned above, the other two are: Vidvedanam, or excitement to hatred: and Bhedhanam, causing dissension, discord, etc.

3. Archana

1003. Archana is worship with flowers, perfumes and lighter, along with chanting of the names of the Lord, and singing His praise. The appropriate flowers for Shiva worship and the perfumes worthy of the occasion are described by Thirumoolar. He also gives directions regarding the lamps to be lighted and the oblations to be offered. This kind of worship belongs to the Kriya path, will confer great blessings.

But Thirumoolar warns the Shiva yogis not to resort to the Kriya path, for Kriya only adds to Karma. The Kriya path cannot take the devotee any further. One can, at best, become a devas. That is but a step, as Devas themselves have to follow the Gnana path, if they seek to unite with Lord Shiva.

More important, says Thirumoolar, is worship in the mansion of the mind. Those who stand in the bhakthi path, also need not care for Kriya (action). To seek the Lord by way of the senses in vain. The Gnana way also leads to Nandhana (Nadhantha) the divine light. It alone leads to union in God.

1004. Worship with flowers; the flowers for *archana* are lotus, blue lily, pink lily, white lily, flower of areca palm, Mandarai creeper, Shoe flower (Mandaram) Thumbai, Vakulam, Surapunnai, Jasmine, Shenpagam, Padiri and chrysanthum. Dowership with these flowers with full of love towards God.

1005. To form the ten unguents, take musk, sandal paste, perfumed *Kumkum*, camphor, fragrant eagle wood and the rest and mix in water or rose water and make a paste. Then apply it on (the Chakra) and worship.

1006. Offer oblations in love, light golden lamps, spread the incense of fragrant wood and lighted camphor in all directions, then forget your worldly worries and meditate, and you will truly attain rapturous Mukthi (liberation).

1007. By worshipping thus, there is nothing that you cannot attain: by worshipping thus, you shall come by Indhra's wealth. You will attain miraculous siddhi powers and you will attain Mukthi.

1008. Such devotees have mastered all passions, even when other men's wives approach them, they do not touch them. Their mind is perpetually pre-occupied with offer of diverse oblations: prostrating low they worship, constantly chanting manthras; thus they abide in the mansion of mind.

1009. They who have been received by the Lord in His Grace do not seek the path of Kriya; they who do not desire to accumulate karma, do not seek to perform kriyas; they who are great Siva yogins and they who stand surpassing in loving devotion, do not seek kriyas (actions).

1010. Most do not know to reach Him by Divine Gnana,

they seek Him, in vain, by ways of the senses. But if you constantly seek Him, within you in the right way, you shall indeed be in Nadantha.

Thirumoolar identifies Nadhantha with the Gnana Margem here.

1011. Light and Darkness are together in the heart, so does it seek grace and ignorance at once: but the knowledge that is with in Jeeva is bereft of light: with the exception of those who have attained Divine Gnana, the rest despair of dispelling Darkness.

1012. With yourself becoming His self and Himself becoming Yourself; there is no more two selves, but as becoming the one Shiva: when it is thus, those who took themselves to the path of kriya if they take to the path of Gnana, they become one with Shiva. They who seek kriya may only become Devas.

1013. 'OM' rises from under the Navel, 'Va' rises from the throat when stretched, 'Na' has its seat in the forehead, Bindhu and Nadha are placed still above.

1014. The Jeeva has 'Na' and 'Ma' for its seats, Shiva has 'Si' and 'Va' that lead you to Him. Be rid of 'Na' and 'Ma' and seek the Primal one and He will be yours at once: the state of Mouna (utter silence) leads to becoming Shiva that is to reach true liberation.

1015. Yoga reaches its consummation in the flow of nectar in the seventh centre; the Gnana light is revealed in the eighth centre. Then beyond in the eleventh centre is the supreme Paraparam.Then beyond, for beyond is void, the Dvadashantha Infinite space.

4. Nine Sacrificial Pits (Nagagundam—Sacred Fire)

1016. To recount the greatness of the nine sacrificial pits is thus: The blessed fire will blaze in the nine sacrificial pits; all great things will arise in the nine sacrificial pits. Thus, I shall speak of the nine sacrificial pits.

The word 'Navagundam' (nine pits) is used in a double sense here. On the one hand it refers to the nine fire-pits used in sacrificial (Yagna) worship, and on the other, it refers to the human body, with its nine orifices.

1017. The sacrificial pits take different shapes. It is sometimes triangle-shaped. It is square shaped, pentagon shaped and hexagon shaped: it is made triangle upon triangle, we shall later relate, other pits that blaze in fire.

1018. By coursing the breath through the Sushumna, the kundalini fire blazed aloft: light emanated on top. It pervades the worlds and engulfs the entire cosmic space. The fire in the nine sacrificial pits is the same as the fire in kundalini within.

1019. The light that arises from within the sacrificial pit becomes the light. You attain the power of the sacrificial fire which is limitless, to create and dissolve worlds that are two times seven. I here state in one single book, the truth that is spread extensively over the ancient Vedas.

1020. The sixteen luminous Kalas will occupy sixteen points. in the sacrificial pit thus formed. Those who can see that fire within will not touch the breiling pasas.

1021. The five elements stand dancing in the fire, within and without, in the triangular pit. The humming orbs of the twelve Zodiac, will appear, for those who seek it, as a resplendent Light.

1022. The holy effects of the sacrificial fire—the head and face will glow in a halo of light. Fire will appear on the hand if so they will it and the glowing body trembling and shaking will give forth the shining Linga. The Divine Sakthi said thus, there is good indeed in the worship of the sacrificial fire-pit.

1023. Our Mother of high esteem, who radiant from head to foot stands in tenderness, said the 'word' (five letters) is great. The learned, though learned into the roots of learning, do not seek nor ask of Her, so they are in distracted confusion all the time.

1024. The sacrificial pit takes the shapes of a shining-bow and the crescent moon, the tongues of fire shoot forth like mystical serpents from the eight directions. And the kundalini too with its four petals flamed in me, filling my inside with radiant light.

1025. The fire reaches the feet of dancing Shiva: it flows as water of worship at His Feet. The fire reaches the eight mighty arms of the dancer, that fills the entire universe. It also reached the fire in the forehead of the Lord.

The kundalini fire reaches the Feet of Shiva within even as the fire from the sacrificial pit reaches Shiva above.

1026. The three-eyed Lord is the entire fire. The Lord of the Self-same eye, engulfs the entire universe. With eyes in all directions. He sees all the eight directions. He is the Lord, my father and He lives for all everywhere.

In fact, the sacrificial fire in Shiva Himself. His third eye is all fire, and the vision of the eyes spreads in all directions and touches all lives.

1027. The six orbs of fire arose out of my father. The six faces appeared before him. In Him is intermingled God Kanda and so He is His son. Thus should you connect in understanding.

1028. The Vedic fire, that is the kundalini arises within the sacrificial pit, that is the Mooladhara, when the controlled breath flows in unison through the Sushumna, then in the Agjna centre two petals open and unite in the divine Light. They who thus worship and vision, making the kundalini rise through the Sushumna are truly celestials of Divine Light.

1029. He pervades all the worlds as the light-splendrous, latent as the sparkle in a gem. He is immanent in all, for those who seek Him as the Light of the Divine Word. He stands as a beacon light on the hill top, and as the light with, in the eye too.

1030. The sacrificial pit formed within is a hexagon of six yogic centres. In its circle, the Thirty six thatthwas arise trembling, with these tatthwas under your command you can ascend into the very high Heaven.

This simply means that also within us is the hexagonal sacarificial pit, it is the hexagon of the six adharas and in it the thirty six thathwas arise trembling. The yogi, can reach the Lord, in the Sahashrara by transcending the tatthwas.

1031. Thus does He, and God, rise from the sacrificial fire pit; His feet are three, His hands are seven. His faces are two, His eyes are six, His tongues are seven, and His horns are four; He, the one that does not know any end.

This simply means, the Form of God that arises in the sacrificial pit—is described by Thirumoolar somewhat according to the lines recounted in the relevant Rig Veda Hymn—"There three His Feet, Seven His hands, two His Faces, six His eyes, Seven His tongues, Four His Horns and thus does arise the God of the sacarificial Pit."

1032. There is no space for the Endless one; there is none to take measure for the Endless One; There are no adequate words to describe the Endless One; Oh! Ya, (Jiva) knows the Endless one.

The numberal ten is written as the letter 'Ya' in Tamil, Hence, 'ten' here means 'Ya' which stands for jiva in the five letter manthra.

1033. The sacrificial pits are shaped thus, Decagnonal, Octogonal, Hexagonal and square. The fire blazes in them like a crimson lotus centre your thoughts, the kundalini fire within pervades the entire body as into its tongues lapped Siva-Sakthi.

1034. There in the sacrificial fire, appears Shiva with Parvathi, His consort with four spreading hands, five the legs, ten the faces, two the flowery feet, the shining crowns forty in number and twenty five the ears.

1035. His faces are five; five times five He measures the Tatthwas; There is the sacrificial fire pit that is upon on five sides. And so it is incumbent for, the subtle kundalini fire to reach the Lord is in the five-fold (Panchagni) Divine Fire, that is to truly attain Mukthi.

1036 . He is Mukthi, He the Light, He is the exticing Light in the thoughts of the fully learned; they who, with desires served, seek Him through the Light within will reach the goal and remain blemishless, ever after.

1037. The five Kalas of Lord Shiva are there in this kundalini fire pit within; the ten cardinal directions are there; the five elements too also there. Those who warm themselves at the fire of Kundalini have truly united in God.

1038. The Lord redeemed the several sea-girt worlds: you must seek the one great being for the celestials excelled in Gnana sacrifices and truly merged in Him, this is the unalloyed truth.

1039. The Lord who arises from the sacrificial fire pit is described thus, with two feet, two hands, the nose shaped as letter 'Ma' and with the third eye in the forehead, seek the Holy One within your head.

1040. The Holy One arose cherubic within the kundalini fire and He blossomed youthful in the middle: as the sacrificial fire blazed in this manner, the sphere of the forehead (Agjna centre) broadened and deepened and there He was with His Sakthi tender as vine.

1041. The sacrificial fire in the pit, spreads and pervades the macrocosm; so also the yogi's kundalini fire within spreads across the six Chakras and reaches the two-petalled centre (Agjna) where he visions Sakthi. The sacred fire, ascending further, reaches the seventh centre engulfing it from top to bottom unintermittently and there he visions the seven worlds, he has thus vastly gained all riches.

1042. Hold the fire that blazes as vast riches as your great Guru to reach your goals. When this Gnana dawns, the jeeva in earnest seeks the regal powers over the world.

1043. Many do not know and do not also seek in truth, the fire that rises and spreads everywhere. Those who have tended it within their body live long, very long, for ten million aeons, as it were.

1044. As in the nine sacrificial pits that transcend time, the yogi in his nadis raises the fire in the nine Chakras. Even as the seed of birth trembled in fear of it, so did the vast universe at the mighty yogic achievement.

1045. The shapes of the nine sacrificial pits are described. The sacrificial fire pit of four sides is likened to the four Sadhanas—Chariya, Kriya, Yoga and Gnana. The sacrificial fire pit of three sides is like the shape of fire; of semi-circular shape like the bore, the sacrificial fire pit of six sides is like the Adharas within, of eight sides like the earth's cardinal directions, of heart shape like the leaf of peepul tree; The sacrificial fire pit of five sides is like the letters of Shiva Manthra, of oval shaped like that of the golden bowl. Thus of yore the nine sacrificial fire pits are shaped, where you seek the Supreme Lord.

5. Shakthi Beedas—Tripurai Chakra

1046. The inner meaning of the six-pointed Chakra is as follows: Mamaya, Maya, Baindhava, Vaikari, Pranava *'Aum'* and the Inner Light (Ajapa) are the manthras in six clusters where Sakthi resides. And beyond them Tripurai is there.

1047. The manifestations of Tripurai are many:-Tripurai, Sundari, Andari, Kum-Kumi, Paripurai, Narani, the dark hued Easi and Mononmani. Thus the One Sakthi of diverse forms and many hues, manifests as several.

Sundari—the beateous; Andari—of the form of sky; Kum-Kumi—of red hue; Paripurai—Sustainer of worlds; Narani—Divine prowess behind Narayana: Easi—Sakthi of Maheshwara; Manonmani—Sakthi of Sadhasiva.

1048. In the three cities (Triangle) which arose of themselves She is the One of the three forms; She is the colour of Gold, red and white and She grants knowledge; enjoyment and mukthi.

1049. Tripurai confers Nadha, states Nadhantha. She expands as Para bindhu and gives rise to the cosmic Universe. She is Parai (Sakthi of Para); Abhirami (of surpassing beauty); and Agochari (beyond comprehension). She grants Gnana and Her grace of love as well.

1050. Describing Tripurai's Form, She wears anklets on Her Feet She is robed in red silk. Her breasts are contained in corsets. She sports arrows of flowers; a bow of sugarcane; an elephant gold and noose strings; She wears the diadem on Her lovely head and on Her ear She wears kundalas of bluish radiant gems.

1051. Her ears sport kundalas; Her brows are arch-shaped like a bow that kills; Her form is magnificent; It is of ruddy hue. She adorns Herself with neckless of Rudraksha beeds, garland of flowers, a glowing crown on which the crescent moon beams forth. Thus adorned She, the Chandika stands supporting the four directions.

1052. Tripurai who stands thus is Puratami (ancient One). She is Mohini (the enticing one) who beauty does not wane. On the crown of Her tresses is the damsel Ganga; Her eyes gleam with divine Gnana. She is Karidani (the one who attracts) who attracts in four directions. She is the immaculate one, seated on a circle of pure Lotus.

1053. She wears fragrant flowers on Her ample breasts, She is the source of bliss; She is the primal substance; She is Maya, Uma, Sakthi; She is Maha Parai; She is all these. She is the atom within the atom. She is self-manifest divine form. She is the embodiment of Gnana.

1054. There are no celestials that do not know Her; there are no rare *tapas* that are performed without Her. The five Gods can perform nothing without Her. I do not know how to reach liberation without Her.

1055. They who know Her say that Parasakthi's bliss is, They who know Her say, She is formless. They who know Her say that all actions flow from Her desires. They who know Her say Param is in Her. Thus say the wise of Her.

1056. Where the Lord is, there is His consort Mahadevi. She is there as protective life, where there is fleshy body, where there is space. She is there and beyond it too. She is everywhere, lordly over all things.

1057. She is Paraskathi, Mahasakthi. She is the power that supports all in countless ways. She is Sakthi that is pervasive. She is the Sakthi that protects through timeless aeons. She is the supreme pleasure that confers all blessings.

1058. All enjoyments emanate from Her; She is of curly tresses that grants Grace. She is Parasakthi that shares Shiva's form. She stands as support for the tender vine of Gnana, that Her devotees daily grow in their hearts.

1059. She of bouncing breasts is the support of all life. She adorns Her tresses with fragrant flowers. She is the One that the celestials seek. She is the girl of the hue of red coral. In intense faith, I hold Her dear in my heart.

1060. She, the Parai, primal Parapara, with ten faces, created all things and all diverse life. She is Sakthi and mistress of Divine Gnana who moves my mind, intellect, will and thought.

1061. She is the mistress of all worlds, who rules over my heart. She is virgin, is lovely as a peacock, and performs continuous tapas. She is all knowledge-conquered and stands filled in my heart.

1062. She who thus stands is bedecked in jewels; She entered my heart with the beaming *kalas*. She entered the arena of Holy Dance for the seven worlds to adore Her. She is Manonmani: the jewel of the inmost thought; She is ever-auspicious and She merges in me, never to be separated from me.

1063. She, the bejewelled One, merged within the Lotus of the heart. Manonmani, the jewel of the inmost thought merged in rapture of the Lord. They know not Mangali, the ever-auspicious one, who is the path to gather Gnana.

1064. She stands inseparable, as the light within, the mother of tresses bedecked with fragrant flowers, stand in union, in the Lord; they who then rise in adoration shall receive Her bounteous grace.

1065. She is the lady who is the embodiment of compassion. She is bliss-beauty (Ananda Sundari). My wavering heart is like tamarind fruit encased in a hard cover. Into it, She poured Her benignant glance and made it pure, She showed me the way to Shiva-state, made me radiant in Gnana and redeemed me.

1066. They say She is and She is not, yet She revealed Her form to me. They saw not when she stood filling the Dance arena at Thillai (Chidambaram). She stood as cause of cause pervading the three spheres (*Sun, Moon and Fire are the three spheres*).

1067. She—the Parasakthi—who stands as body and life, took me to Shiva-state; She, of the ethereal light, that holds the book of knowledge in Her divine hand, entered in me and stood one in my awareness.

"Holding the book of knowledge is in Hand" is in Hinduism, a description of Sri Saravathi, and in Buddhism of Tara; Moolar's Sakthi does not belong to any particular well-designed sect, but is lelectic, combining in herself the attributes drawn from many sources.

1068. She, our mother, of three eyes, that holds the book of knowledge in Her Divine hand, is of crystal form. She of comely white lotus, chants the Vedas: She is Parvathi, bear Her Feet on Your Head and adore Her with devout songs.

1069. She, the primal virgin, is with elephant goad and noose and cane of sugar, sing her praise, adore Her feet, beseech Her in this manner, meditate on Her and worship Her.

1070. She created all the diverse things; She is the sister of Sri Mahavishnu that protects all. She is the bejewelled mother, seated on the Lotus of Dharma, so chant Her name as Shiva-Sakthi, infinite number of times and you will see her light and all things past, present and future.

1071. She is the mother of tender form that pervades Medha and the rest of the sixteen Kalas; She is the Paraparai that shines in the Vedas and the holy scriptures; She is the widespread support of all that exists, she is the grace within nadha and nadhantha.

1072. Tell these men, all of you who were blessed by Her grace, how this mother filled of divine Gnana; rules all worlds, transforms your inconstant thoughts and makes you realize God-Truth. I adore Her Holy Feet forever.

1073. She of the visage of Varahi of Divine Boar grants all power and state. She that holds the pestile knocks the heart of evil ones, and the plough that prepares the soul of the good ones for the Gnana harvest. She, of the pearly teeth holds the rest of the insignia. She rises in their hearts, who meditate on Her truly.

1074. She is *Omkari*, the Pranava form. Her form is of indelible green hue. She became Ankhari of creative force and gave birth to the five Gods. She became Hrimkari and then sweetly lapsed into the music of Her Manthra 'Krim'. She abides in Her own Manthra.

1075. She, Tatparai, the Supreme Mistress of all creation stands as the uncreated being. She is the fourteen worlds that were created from Sindhu. She is the world of the celestials. She is the mind and the intellect and is Shiva-state too.

6. Bhairavi Manthra

1076. There are twelve Kalas of primal Bhairavi Devi. To the twelfth letter 'A', is denoted. Add 'A' and 'M' letter denoting Maya. Thus with letters twelve and two from OM to AIM they are fourteen. Her manthras lead to the end of sixteen Kalas.

The twelve Beeja Manthras are:

1. HAUM— 'Ha' means Shiva; 'AU' means Sadhasiva; 'M' means Sivaya who dispels sorrow.
2. DUM— 'DA' means Durga; 'U' means save; 'M' means mother of the universe.
3. KRIM— 'KA' is Kali; 'RA' is Brahma; 'I' is Mahamaya; 'M' means mother of the universe.
4. HRIM— 'H' is Shiva; 'RA' is Prakrithi; 'I' is Mahamaya; 'M' means mother of the universe.
5. SRIM— 'S' is Mahalakshmi; "RA" is wealth; 'I' is satisfaction; 'M' is Nadha.
6. AIM— 'AI' is Saraswathi; 'M' is Nadha.
7. KLIM— 'KA' is Kamadeva; 'L' is Indhra; 'I' is contentment; 'M' is Nadha.
8. HUM— 'H' is Shiva; 'U' is Bhairava; 'M' is Nadha.
9. GAM— 'G' is Ganesha; 'M' is Nadha.
10. GLAUM— 'G' is Ganesa: 'L' is what pervades; 'AU' is Thejas; 'M' is Nadha.
11. KSTRAUM—'KSA' is Narashimha,;'RA' is Brahma; 'AU' is teeth pointing upwards.
12. STRIM— 'S' is deliverance. 'T' is saviour; 'RA' is liberation; 'I' is Mahamaya; M is Bindhu.

1077. The end of that fourteenth letter is Bjairavi, In the Lotus of thought, She rises as Mahasakthi as beginning-middle and end; She is the beginning and end of all.

1078. The three Gods are contained there; They who meditate on Her wil not take to the path of fleshy lives who are thatthwa bound; The blessed ones who meditate on Tripurai become radiant Light.

1079. She is the treasure of Blessed Nandhi who is the Pure One, Meditate on Her for a month of twenty seven days and reach within the centres of fire, Sun and Moon. He who thus stands in Firm meditation become Shiva, Himself.

1080. Tripurai, who with gait rivalling that of the cow-elephant, is entwined with Shiva and is one with Him, He who meditates constantly on Her, will be with Shiva Himself, The Mighty Hero is the Lord is Nandhi. The devotees will be with Him in the Golden Mount of Kailash and all the worlds will adore him there.

1080. She is the Grace that Nandhi has realized. She expounds the Vedic Dharma with Justice and accord, He who meditates on Her for a lunar month of twenty seven days will envision Bhairavi Devi, blessing him with Her Trident.

1081. To describe Her form, She has four hands, She holds the trident and skull, the serpent, stoop and elephant goated with in Her Mighty Hands. Shestands one with Shiva. Neither Brahma nor Mahavishnu know Her form, For she is of Ethereal Form.

1082. She, of Ethereal Form is Vine-like, she is vangeful to these who err. She is true wisdom and true knowledge. She is green as a parrot, She is a bedecked in Jewels and Gem-like lustrous is Her Form and Her robe is plaited with several precious stones.

1083. Her crown is studded with stones brillitant like a million moons. In Her ears, She wears kundalas of radiant Gems. Her glance is like the gentle doe's and Her eyes are the Sun and the Moon, in rapture she glows as a red Gold.

1084. The supreme Sakthi, Arya, the Noble one is seated in the centre of the eight petalled Lotus. Eight Virgin Sakthis and sixty four beautiful damsels surrounded Her, entirely, encircling Her thus, they envisioned Her Glory.

1086. She who wears anklets, bangles, conch and discuss is the Supreme Pervasive in the eight quarters of the globe. She is Goddess Parvathi who sustains the universe and its eight cardinal points. She who is possessed of the wealth of Grace, is seated on a Lotus and compells our worship.

1087. Smeared in fragrant unguents, bedecked with beauteous flowers and dressed in new and comely clothes She, Sakthi, is in the Mani Manthra yoga that spells no word. There, where she is, you shall hear the sound of her conch for Yognas around, thus She is Tripurai; whom you seek.

1088. Like many jewels that are made of gold, so too the

Gods they conceive of are many, but She is the Supreme cause whom the three Gods, Shiva, Brahma and Mahavishnu adore.

1089. She is the Supreme cause; She is in Japa and in manthra chanting; She is in yoga; She is seated in the lotus flower of those who control their breath in Pooraka, Kumbaka and Resakha. She is Narayani. She is the End of the Vedas and that Nandhi revealed to the world in compassion.

1090. Do not commence with the little finger in counting manthra by way of doing Japa. You now reverse that by going to the third in the traditional way and seek Her, the mother of Tamil. Nandhi revealed this as the truth of Japa of the Nine Sakthis.

1091. Of the nine Sakthis said above the one is at the Crown; counting them in the appropriate order Nandhi, who of Yore, expounded the ways of the eight limbed yoga, laid down laws and rules of Japa way.

1092. She of tresses festooned with flowers and eyes pouring compassion stands protective within. She, the tender vine, dispels the darkness of the soul, She rises with thread-like column of smoke from the sacrificial fire of kundalini, reaching the heights of astral sphere and returning with ambrosia.

1093. Chant the manthra that is of Her heart (Hridhaya Nama) and say 'Na Ma'. The offering of prana that courses through the central Sushumna reaches the heights of the cranium top and there, chant Sikha Manthra (Sikhayai Nama).

1094. Chant the exalted Kavacha manthra, invoke that, for your body to receive protection, and then perform Soola Mudhra (sign of Trident) and chant Nethra Manthra (Netiaya Nama). Worshipping thus, rebirth will never harass you.

1095. These Mudhras are difficult to practise. Press the little finger in reverse direction, hold the ring finger and the fore-finger pressed together and insert the thumb in between.

1096. Take away 'I' from the Manthra 'SI', conjoin the Bindhu letter, 'M', to promote Pranayama practice do chant the Holy manthra 'Sam'.

1097. In this manner, chant 'Sam' to pervade the Prana of Jeeva and adopt the conch Mudhra. This dispels ('Ya's) the

Jeeva's *maya*. The Supreme Devi shall appear luminous there in the centre.

1098. She is Bairavi, the eternal, Neeli, the Blue-hued, Nishachari that sojourns in the dark. She enters into the heart that is purified of the three evils—lust, anger and ignorance, and of Herself She confers grace. Seek Her, the consort of the primal Lord in this world and She will bless you.

1099. The Vedas, the diverse, moveable, and immoveable creation, the five elements, the four quarters of the globe are all but the manifestation of the mother of three eyes (Sun-Moon-fire), the spreading darkness, the vast spaces, the several life species, the Light that is Parapari—all these are but the Primal Sakthi; She pervades all as one energy.

1100. She is the primal Bhairavi: the virgin in the kundalini, those who rouse Her, will in body and soul be one in God, their circle of births hare below will be snapped and they will beget a form, comely beyond words.

1101. She, the Mother of lovely tresses, of arched eyebrows, and Her eyes like blue water-lily, is the ambrosial bliss—Beauty (Anandha Sundari) who does reveal Shiva, the supreme to us.

1102. Having revealed Shiva to me, She spoke to me of that blessings that follow; She made my thoughts doubt free and infused joy in me. She made the divine light shine in me and redeemed me too.

1103. She who sports the garland of sixteen kalas, assumes as million, million forms. She, the good mother beams forth the three lights—fire, sun and moon and stands on the cool heights within the head.

1104. She is the good mother, the supreme mistress of all penance, the Manonmani, who dispels the darkness of *maya* by Her glance of grace. Gently stand and adore Her; by adoring Her. You shall have no more births.

1105. She, of shoulders slender as bamboo, of tresses laden with fragrant blossoms adorns the crescent moon for a jewel, She of pure matted locks holds the trident; She, the beautiful enters my heart is endearment and stands constantly in my heart.

1106. She is seated as virgin in the Mooladhara, She is the peerless mistress, the supreme mother who beckoned me apart and separated my impurities from me, cleansing my heart. She loved my heart and She entered it.

1107. From among the three Nadis (Ida, Pingala and Sushumna) She stands as virgin kundalini is thread like slenderness in the central Sushumna; She is the summum bonum of all virtues. She wears golden anklets on Her Feet, that sing in rythmic music. Thus, She entered my heart and slumbers there.

1108. As I was steeped in divine slumber, She, Manonmani, came and with Her arms bedecked with bangles drew me close to Her and transferred Her luminous spittle of grace into my mouth, and said that I, Her son, shall not slumber any more. She performed this miracle.

1109. She, who is of sweet speech, can be reached by rare penance. She is of maiden innocent speech, bejewelled in precious stones and attired in fine dresses. Those who seek Her Holy Feet, saying that She is their refuge. She, the goddess consoles them in soft speech.

1110. She taught me the miracle, quelled the terrors of my heart and fostered in me the divine love, She contained my desires in the Sushumna that bathes the Moon in full light and told me not to fear.

1111. She is the Supreme One of mighty penance, whom the *jeevas* seek. She of dark tresses is the causal being. She is Narayani who dissolves body, life and Pasas all at the same time. She is the awesome, one, She dwells in my heart.

1112. She, the virgin in endearment dwells eternally in my heart. She sports in my heart and reaches my head, shining there with Her radiant kalas.

1113. She, the full breasted mother abides in union, in Him, who wears the crescent Moon on His head, in Him, who has the third eye on His forehead. The flowery vine too, looking toward Him who is within the crest of Mount Meru, stands there.

1114. The sweet mother dwells in my heart, She then entered the four-finger Prana of retained breath and She joined Shiva in divine union. She, the ancient one performed rare penance.

1115. She is the beginning, She is the beginningless; She is the cause and the causeless; She is the light and the non-light. She is the bliss that is divine beauty, She is the supreme mother; She is samadhi, the transcendental end; she is Manonmani, the jewel of the inmost mind. She entered my sentience and abides in my heart.

1116. She, the bejwelled Mother abides there in my heart. She stands there in endearment saying 'NAMASIVA'; She dispels from me all thoughts of rank and status that Brahma and the rest enjoy; She destroys in me all speech that arises from ignorance.

1117. Alas ! These poor men spend their lives away, prattling in ignorance. But to all those who seek Her in constant devotion, She, the primal one, grands Mukthi. She has three fish-shaped eyes, red lips that warble sweet words; In grace, she reveals before me, Her face that is full of compassion.

1118. She stands in all three, in my mind, in my heart and in my intellect. She stands in my head, beyond the Sahashrara, She stands with in the bounteous lord; She, the Virgin that created all, stands as thought. behind Mamaya's concealed Light.

1119. She, the eternal virgin ceased not to be a virgin, when She made love and bore five children, and among them is Shiva too who composed books of truth. Oh ! this Maya is dark, dark indeed.

There is a play on words, when Maya is said to be "dark". She is so because, it is She who is the cause of delusion. Also in Tamil, 'Mayam' means blackness-of-Mayon—a Tamil name of Vishnu, 'Five Children' refers to the five gods of Panchayatana, namely Shiva, Sakthi Herself, Vishnu, Surya and Ganapathi in Puranic mythology.

1120. The Lord is space. Sakthi is dark. Truth is union in God. It is sheer-bliss for the holy ones who with double free mind adore the Lord. The primal one will sure bless Him.

1121. She is the beginning and the beginningless. She is the Para Sakthi and the Para Parai that shares half the Lord's form; She is the bejewelled supreme mother; She is the end of

Samadhi; She is Manonmani; the jewel of inmost thought; She blossomed exuberantly in my prayerful heart.

1122. Most do not know that She is the learning above all learning and that She is the beginningless Vedas. She is the creation and its diversities. She is the Tathwas, is the Primal one. She assured me that She is the kindred of the Jeeva.

1123. She is the kindred of the Jeeva and resides in the jeeva's spinal Sushumna. She is the mistress of sweet speech. She is the spouse of the Lord whom all praise highly. She is the comely one, dear to Shiva. She is the One whom I adore and She severed my hard karmas.

1124. She is the light that shines in those who have severed their hard Karmas. She is the truth of all those who reach Her. She is the Mother who took me into Her vassalage. The Lord is Her spouse and yet, She is beginningless.

7. Poorna Sakthi

Sakthi is another form of the Sun (the pure energy) possessed the twelve kalas, that is the twelve positions in the zodiac.

Poora Sakthi is the primal Sakthi. She possesses the full sixteen Kalas. She is the perfection. She is united with Shiva in the sphere of pure consciousness. Yet, She remains eternally virgin. This is the subtlest of the subtle mysteries of God. But, from it follows the great truth that Shiva is the father and Sakthi is the mother, and that mother and father are one.

1125. She is the beginning and she is the beginningless. She is the cause and She is the uncaused, She taught the Vedas to the Vedic sages. She is the self-manifest Light and She is the abiding Divine Light. She, of twelve kalas is Prana Paraparai who became half of Shiva's form.

1126. I measured the limits of space. I measured its beginning and its end; I measured the men and women everywhere in the spaces; I measured the Primal Lord of the vast spaces. In devotion, I measured His grace and knew all.

1127. No one knows that the primordial Sakthi espoused Shiva and that together they are perfection. She bestows Her grace on Her devotees. Meditate on Her, the eternal virgin, in the Mooladhara. For wherever She is, your yogic feat in breath control shall indeed be a great success.

1128. It is important to note that Sakthi is frequently referred to as a virgin, though she is said to be the consort of Shiva and mother of children. This is because the magical power of a woman is thought to reside in her virginity.

1129. The five massive elephants Jeeva, the Mahout with the good the Lord of many splendoured crown, (Shiva) who appears in the fragrant Shahashrara and the mother who is in rapturous union with Him, are all forever merged in one love-union.

1130. In the rapture of this union enters my father is subtle love: my mother Para Sakthi, in misery's broth of harassing Pasa, enters to the very marrow.

1131. Cease talking of the worldly creatures as 'my mother', "My father" in the possessive way of this world. Our mother and timeless father are here in union, as our unerring guide for us hereafter. Nandhi truly stood as mother and father in one.

1132. On the lovely Lotus-that blossoms in the cool waters is the four-headed God (Brahma); the years vouchsafted by Him here below are no more than a hundred. The mother of Gnana appeared seated on a lotus. She is the mistress of words, abiding in the tongue. Now it is Her command as to how long you live.

1133. Untroubled by Aanava ways, the devotees looking inward steadying their wavering mind and centering it on high; doing thus, when their egoity disappears, and when they realize the practise of praiseworthy Para they and He becomes One for ever.

1134. This mistress of the Tathwas arose of Herself, and illumined the moon in the astral sphere within; the light of kundalini rises brightly like a column of treadle, where that Shiva, the fawn dances.

The term 'moon in the astral sphere within' refers to the Chakras, or nerve pleasures in the body, through which when roused kundalini passes in tanthric Sadhanas.

1135. She, of fragrant tresses abides in the vast spaces

where neither night nor day it is. Seek Her and slumber in silence with grace and you will forever youthful transcending time and age.

1136. You will forever be youthful, transcending Bindhu and Nadha that do not approach Her. You shall be one with Para Sakthi and reach the finale Mukthi state; She, the grace divine confers all liberations.

1137. Parasakthi who stands with pervasive Para, becomes Gnana Sakthi and Iccha Sakthi, and when Kriya Sakthi arrives from Bindhu, the dancer becomes immanent in all of them.

1138. In form Shiva and Sakthi stood resembling the flower and its fragrance. This, they know not. Shiva was one with Sakthi when together they stirred the primordial Bindhu to commence the act of creation, then He in thought was one with Her. Thus, it was, my father stood.

1139. Shiva-Sakthi who in thought, thus commenced evolution expanded as Bindhu and Nadha; She wears the orb of moon as on Her matted lovely locks, She is possessed of Satthwa Guṇa; She is the beginning and the end. Thus Her form is divine.

1140. She, who is full-breasted of the milk of ambrosia, is contained in Shiva, She is in Jeevas, yet they do not know the way to reach Her, She wells up from within like a bright lamp and sheds Her light into them that hold Her dear in their hearts.

1141. He is Rudhra, fire and light, and He is my master; He mounts the bull in surpassing splendour. Those who have not seen Him, should get away from here. He supports the hearts of the aspirants who have seen Him.

1142. She is seated on the petals of the six *adharas*. She is seated on the petals of the flower of cosmos and on the two hundred and eighteen worlds above. She is the blessed one that is seated on the flower of the heart. She is the bejewelled one that is on the earth below.

1143. The bejewelled one is where Parama is; She is the light that shines high as resplendent pennon; She is dazzling like the lightening in the sky and all worlds whirl in Sakthi's way.

1144. That flower walked in the nine centres within, as nine Sakthis they were there: the Kundalini light arose through the central passage and spread in the Sahashrara into the lotus.

1145. That lotus in several folds is the abode of primal Sakthi; the lotus that lifts the soul is in the heart; when the lotus in the Mooladhara is roused, the lotus in the Sahashrara blossoms.

1146. The spark that arises in the triangular Chakra (Mooladhara) flies and spreads in the rest of the Adhara Chakras; and piercing the Sahashrara shines brightly; thus She pervades in all Chakras.

1147. There, She abides with ten faces in all directions: it is because of Her the wind blows in all quarters: even the five flames upwards and water courses downwards and everything functions properly because of Her.

1148. Her glances are like sharp arrows; She is the supreme mother, She is Manonmani; Her waist is as slender as a tender vine and Her tresses are bedecked with flower garlands. By far, She is very fragrant and Her form is red gold. Daily She looks at the Lord and prays.

1149. She, Sakthi, the Great Goddess utters the four Vedas; She dons Herself in fine robes. Her feet encompass the entire world; She stands elated pervading all worlds and Universe; She stands adorned with three lights: Sun, Moon and Fire.

1150. In Her form She holds the one Lord of all the worlds. She creates millions and millions of vast universe in Her thoughts; She is draped in cosmic light. She who beautifies all, I stood adoring.

1151. I pray thus:- 'Hail to you'. She is the mistress of all worlds; She is the mother of rare penance, is my prowess and is my mother too. She is bejewelled and Her countenance is dispelled of all passions. She is of soft finery who drives away fearsome death.

1152. She is of many pairs of hands bedecked in jewellery; She is the fountain of divine bliss. She, the beautiful, is Tripurai Devi of perfect loveliness. She is Mount Kailash that destroys all karmas. She, the primal One, is the One that uproots the karmas of all Her devotees.

1153. She is the damsel of sweet music, She is the tender vine of the limitless void. She is of infinite fame. She is the fruit laden green vine who drives away Maya that gives transitory fame. She, of abiding fame entered into my heart.

1154. Our Lord is eternally existant. She, Our Parasakthi followed Him, through 'heaven and earth', when at the beginning the worlds were created, and breathed life into all creation. This truly is Sakthi's work.

1155. They say that God is 'this' and 'that'. They do not know Him as the true one. They also do not know that He is the One who grants ultimate liberation. Those of muddled thinking do not know that She, the great mother bedecked of honeyed-flower on Her tresses, confers grace.

8. Sustentation Supported

1156. Kundalini blossomed into ninety-six tathwas in the four petalled Mooladhara. The four Adharas above have forty-four petals in all: Beyond is the Adhara, with sidereal petals. And yet beyond the Lotus Sakthi is seated. She, Herself is like a tender petal that supports all of them.

Shiva and Sakthi and mutually the support and the supported at once. They share their form, half and half entwined in divine delight.

1157. She, the benevolent mother, remains the 'support-all' looking aloft to Her own divine light. She spreads Herself over the six adharas (Yogic centres); She holds the Vedic truth in Her thought and centres on Her five letters.

1158. The benevolent mother remains with Her spouse sharing Her half with the Supreme God. Follow this, mother of divine light and gain Her support, and all sorrows will see their end and will become blemishless pure.

1159. The Lord of the vast spaces abides in the loving heart of the Mother, that bedecks honeyed-flowers in Her tresses; He shares Her is His form; and He arises from Her, Himself being thus a woman too.

1160. It is indeed strange to hear of woman espousing woman; for, from woman did man arise. When anyone comes to know the why of this, then no more will there be talk of Sakthi arising from Shivam.

1161. She is the great truth of silence and is the high manifestation of graciousness; She, Manonmani Sakthi, is a pure light. The blemishless light espousing God entered in me and delighted me.

1162. She is the virgin of delight: She, Manonmani is Sakthi, She pervades the world as woman and supports it. She is the mistress of the five actions is the fountain-head of the Vedas. The Lord expoused Her is delight.

1163. The Lord stood In delight, with forehead eye; The Lord stood in delight seeking to enter our hearts, the Lord stood in delight for all the worlds to delight. The Lord stood in delight with Sakthi, Her shoulders entwined in embrace.

1164. She is full-breasted and supple waisted; Her skin is yellow-spotted spreading all over; She is of pure speech. She is softed-footed like a feathery peacock. How shall I describe, how she entered my sentience.

1165. It is beyond description even for bedazzled Gnanies, to describe the fiery sphere that envelops Her. She is the supreme mistress of unconquerable act. She is Manonmani that is beyond grasp.

1166. He spreads as the high heavens, holding the worlds apart; He, Himself is the scorching fire, sun and moon; is Himself the mother that sends down the rain and is Himself the strong mountains and the cold oceans.

1167. They who reach Her, may well of divine compassion, be here on earth-below. Yet they should be regarded not as human beings, but they are higher than the celestials, for their qualities are divine and their composure is serene.

1168. She is the one omnipresent virgin that oversees the eight directions and pervades everywhere. She is the beginningless Parasakthi that are everywhere; the devotees pray to Her and praise Her in all the eight directions with fragrant flowers in their hands and songs in their tongue.

1169. The Moon within shines with virgin rays, the mansion where She is, is red in hue. So follow her, Manonmani, and you will reach Parasakthi in the cranium within the head, beaming with sixteen kalas.

1170. Parasakthi is the power that supports all and everywhere, She resides the region within the head in the cranium, She is praised in the Vyamala Agama as the 'Sakthi of the Night; She is the Sakthi that comes as Guru. I perceived Her form to be diverse indeed.

'Sakthi of the Night' refers to midnight worship with flowers as designated by the Viyamalagama school.

1171. She is the Yogini Sakthi who conceives the seven worlds, cognises all light and stands as its support. She joined the Lord, of Yore, in creative union and become Bhoga Sakthi. The union of Sakthi with Shiva is both yoga and bhoga. And then She became Param Herself that is, Parasakthi, undifferentiated form Lord Shiva.

1172. When this Sakthi and the great Lord of ours united together, the union of both was yoga and divine bhoga. It is in truth that, in this union, Manonmani Sakthi of fragrant tresses was truly in yoga.

1173. Yoga Sakthi is the pedestal of light within. She faces southward. Her navel is the centre of the cosmos. Her Feet are accordingly sublime. May you realize all this:

1174. She unites with Lord Shiva in the kundalini fire that is high in the cranium and from Shiva/Sakthi union arose Nadha-Bhindhu-Maya. Sakthi that is bedecked in bejewelled bangles rises.

1175. From Parasakthi, evolved the eight Sakthis, all of equal kalas—fourtheen. From Bindhu, She manifested the entire creation. All these are Her mutations. But, as ever, she remains the undiminished Param.

1176. Worship Her in the Vidhya Chakra for 27 days, continuously chanting the Rudhra Beeja Manthra. She, the white hued three-eyed Parasakthi, will appear bearing a mace and Her Mudhra of yore, accompanied by the eight Sakthis.

1177. Her Mudhras triple--Jnana Mudhra, Tathwa Mudhra and Anandha Mudhra. She is all pervasive. She is the Paraparai that Paraparam hold. She is the Sakthi and Anandha Sakthi too.

1178. She is like the fragrant tender vine; She is eternally virgin with budding breasts. She is radiantly red hued as kumkum. She bears the elephant goad and noose; the entire universe is the abode of this virgin.

1179. She is Manonmani, who is beyond the description of word and thought. She is the mother that has ghosts and Ganas for Her heavenly hosts. For Hara who surpasses all knowledge, She is the Mother, daughter and spouse at once.

1180. She is the cause and the caused at once, She is the Tathwas; She is the supreme spouse; She has ten faces that look in ten directions. She is the ancient one and that is enveloped by perfect Bindhu.

1181. Our Parasakthi has ten faces. She revealed the four Vedas with the six Angas. She as one pervaded the six Adharas and stands eternal. You must know that She is our lovely bejewelled mother.

1182. She is the virgin of arched eye; brows. She is the awesome one; She is the gentle, holy Devi who shines in seven worlds. She of ambrosial breasts is the mistress of Over-Soul (Shiva) and She knows no separateness from Her Lord.

1183. She is the Great Mother that is non-separate. She is the lovely vine that unites in the Mooladhara. She in Gnana, with senses centred and absorbed in union. Stood merging in the Jeeva within.

1184. She stood in the deep core of my heart and there dispelled the falsity of the five senses. She, the Mother of boundless bounty joined in union in me, and drew me, entranced, into the rapturous path of tapasvin.

1185. She, the bounteous mother, Bhoga Mahasakthi, confers Her grace and the sweetness of this grace, She grants from within. You must know this just as the colour cannot be separated from a flower. She remains inseparable from the Jeeva and as such abides eternally in the Jeeva.

1186. The Mother invaded my heart and resides therein perfect in tense union. And in that cranium centre, She was abiding in wonder. That, indeed is true union.

1187. Get rid of your desires that run thus—this and that, adore Her and well may you conquer even fate-look upward through the Sushumna and see Her the flower in the

Shahashrara, in the three spheres, of the sun, moon and fire.

1188. The Mohini ascends to the three spheres. At the top in the sphere of the sun of twelve kalas, She appears; She in Mamaya with fourteen Kalas; and in the moon's sphere the bright one, appears finite.

1189. Like the rays of the sun, the nadha arises from the moon sphere; from there it travels to the root of the tongue, and thence the light goes to the throat and then to the region of the heart, from where the articulate sound rises. The source for all of this, is the moon sphere where Sakthi is.

1190. With the sixteen Kalas in the moon sphere, is the beginning and the end, of where Sakthi is; it has no indefinite changes; it is of infinite beauty, reached by the mind and that is concentrated; it is a centre that is densely fragrant and there She was born, and there She abides in divinity.

1191. She, the bejewelled one abides there, in the finite centre. There, She abides as the Holy way, She abides there as infinite bliss, there, She abides, the great Mother, with all the worlds praising her and yearning for Her.

1192. Embracing together, the Mother and Her handsome spouse look inward and outward. In this Shiva / Sakthi union arose Maya and Her five sons, who arising with their respective Sakthis commenced their tasks—certain creation, prevervation, dissolution, defuscation and revealing grace.

1193. With many rituals, they perform many *tapas*. They should meditate on Her within their body vessel. Then the kundalini light within will ascend through the Sushumna cavity and subside in Her love.

True tapas (penance) is to meditate on kundalini Sakthi—to seek inward rather than to observe, in vain, the myriad elaborate and complicated rituals.

1194. She dwells in the flowers of the six yogic centres. The devotee should make them unfold and then the primal Manthra which is more precious than pearl, will arise in radiance.

1195. Her visage is of pearly white-radiance. She is Sakthi, Sakiri, Sahali, Jatadhari, She has three eyes in each face, She is with ten hands, She is the bejewelled mother who belongs to Paraparan. She stands as Goddess of learning in my heart; She is Sakthi (of powers great); She is Sakiri (of grace granting), She is Sahali (of manifest form); She is Jatadhari (of matted locks); She is Vithaki (of Gnana possessed).

1196. She pervades the three spheres of the Sun, Moon and fire: She is the head of all three together. She is light within and She does not abandon you even if you forget Her.

1197. The six Adharas (yogic centres) concealed within; there, with the white light of the Kundalini Fire, Shiva-Sakthi, of tresses bedecked of honeyed flower, stands mingled very intimately. She is the vine from Vishuddha and ascends to ambrosia in the Supreme Sahashrara.

1198. When that vine from the Vishuddha adheres/ reaches to the mark (agna) the Guru has shown, then, ambrosia flows, that is the form of Shiva of Anklet-girt feet, that is Divine Bliss. She, the bejewelled One, spreads it over the six adharas in order accordingly.

1199. She, the yoga Sakthi was seated as kundalini, the bejewelled One, the Gods that are three, as the shining garland of six yogic centres, as sixteen Kalas and as Jnana Sakthi, in the forehead. The congregation of Manthreswaras, all arrived to praise Her.

1200. That Sakthi is the Mother of Sadhaka (aspirant-yogi), the mistress of Mukthi, they do not know, and in vain they turned their devotion in other ways: they are wretches and like a beaten dog they howl and wail.

1201. To those who shall behold the Feet of the Holy One, seek Her presence and constantly meditate on Her, to them, the Mother of cloud-dark tresses will reveal Her lotus-like, Holy Feet and place them on their thoughts, blessing them with Her grace.

1202. Hold Her is your thoughts. hold Her on your head and in your presence: hold Her in the Mooladhara; hold Her in meditation that is undistracted by worldly thoughts and holding Her in the mystic junction of the cranium, enter into Samadhi.

1203. She of arched brows who resides in Shiva and the rest of the five letters, stands as the goal of those who enter in

Samadhi. Chant the manthra in endearing love so that, She will ever abide as the first of the nine Sakthis in your full moon sphere.

1204. Ascend all the six yogic centres, where She resides, in order, and daily approach Her of fragrant tresses. If Her manthra is repeated with the four—Pranava, Beeja, Sakthi, Kilakam, you can attain many good results.

1205. If you but with folded hands and pure devotion think of Her, whose form is tender like a flower petal, who is kundalini, the eternal virgin, whose eyes are painted in dark collyrium and who is surpassing sweetness, then, you will conquer the fruits of your twin Karmas.

1206. Think of Her, think of Her time and again. Think of Her deep in the heart and train mind towards Her, and reach Her; realize Her, the Holy only one in the world and She will make you bide here below forever, and you shall attain the eight attributes of Lord Shiva.

1207. Like a turtle, withdraw your senses; like a devoted vassel, be in loving constancy; chant 'AUM' and meet Her of shining fragrant tresses as She stands as Light, in your heart's centre. There, She stands, bedecked with flower, that is crescent Moon.

1208. In Her beautiful bangled hands, She holds the elephant goad and noose; She carries the ascetic pitcher and conch and dances in rapture in the heart. Course your breath through Sushumna, seeking the twin letters 'Si' and 'Va', that is the heart of the Rudhra Manthra.

1209. Brahma, Vishnu, Rudhra, Mahesa, and Sadhasiva all, prayed at Her Feet and attained their respective states: Kama, the God of Love, His brother Sama, the Sun, Fire and Moon all, all, be sought Her Feet and bore them on their heads.

1210. She wears the crescent Moon; the trident, and the skull; She is a long slender vine; She is immaculate and bejewelled. She dances as luminous Gnana through the central Sushumna nadi; She is the beginning of all Universe.

1211. From end to end of the cosmic Universe, there is nothing but the bejewelled Mother. It is all but Sakthi and

Shiva cojoined like Sushumna and Kundalini.

1212. The Lord consumed poison, while He let the celestials to consume ambrosia, their immortal state shall you reach and the joys of penance shall be yours. Piercing the Chakras, high in the Sahashrara, She entered the unopened flower above and sat there with the Lord.

1213. So that their high penance may wax, they walk from place to place, but soon perish. She is there in the four petalled Mooladhara, so stand there on top of the cranium and worship Her, for She is exalted of the letter AUM, and possesses surpassing beauty.

1214. She is the beauteous One, is the Divine Swan (so-Ham): She is there in the Manthra AUM too, She, the mother of Niyama constantly stands to succour those who chant the syllable NA-MA-SI-VA.

1215. She is a crystal statue of purest moon's rays; She is of rich pearl's radiance; She is of wavy tresses; She stands immanent to Jeevas as the pervasive Kala.

1216. The virgin stands comingling with her lover, She stands cominglying in all life and thought, in all learning and wisdom and is time eternal.

1217. She is the embodiment of eternal time. She pervades all thought and love; She is Malini (Uma), Makuli (Kundalini) and Mandhra Chandika (that blows away the troubles of Her devotees like a tornado). She is protectress and is inseparably united in Jeevas. She stands indivisible with Her protector.

1218. Parasakthi is half of Him, who sports golden matted locks; who peels the elephant and dances in trumph. Their heart is one, the hands are ten, the bewitching faces are five and the eyes on each face are three.

1219. There are thirty-six tathwas in the body with jeeva, among them the active group of the five senses constitute the body. Brahma and the hordes of eighteen gana-genres praise Sakthi who stands as the beginning and end.

The 18 Ganas are:— 1. Devas (Amaras), 2. Siddhars, 3. Asuras, 4. Daityas, 5. Garudas, 6. Kinnarars, 7. Nirutas, 8. Kimpurushas, 9. Gandharvas, 10. Yakshas, 11. Vinjayas, 12. Bhoothas. 13. Pisachas, 14. Antharas, 15. Munivas, 16. Uragas, 17. Akasavasis and 18. Bhoga Bhumidars.

1220. In the beginning She created the fifty-one Kala beings and stood as their life and soul: and He, the Lord stood there by the side of the jewelled one's side, in the Chakra of fifty-one letters (Sahashrara Chakra).

1221. Two are the centres where the Primal Lord is: One is the jewelled one and the other is the six adharas. As the mind reaches the six yogic centres. She is there in each with Her presence; Thus, She, of the flowing tresses stood in sweetness.

When Gnana is acquired, Jeeva's perfection is attained, she dwells in the six yogic centres. As Prana breath reaches, these yogic centres one after another, She can be visioned.

1222. She stood there for me to withness the seven centres within me being uplifted and enlivened. At the time, the ten breaths within me became one Prana breath; and She stood there, chanting AUM and imparting awareness.

1223. The Holy manthra 'AUM' that Gnana imparts within, is the sure way of union of God: thus Lord Shiva, the director and Sakthi, the consort of the director arise together in amity. Then She, the beloved of Lord Shiva (Sivakami Devi) blesses you.

1224. She is fire; She is the primal being and Isa too; She is the three spheres, She is the wind and the rest of the other elements. She fortifies jeevas and she renders them youthful through the practice of yoga. She, as Manonmani, stands bedecked in flowers, in the eyebrow centre of the Jeeva, radiant as the crescent Moon.

1225. She that stands the Manonmani in the eyebrow centre becomes one with the fifty Holy letters. She is Paraparai and parai too, She is of the five actions of creation, preservation, dissolution, obfuscation and revealing grace (redemption).

1226. She is Mohini who is vibrant and yogini who is amicable. They who reach Her stand at Her Feet adoring Her, and they unite is Shiva and they ascend to become that Para Shiva.

1227. She, the Golden Lady, abides as Anandha Mohini at the far end of the cranimum top. Hence, meditate on Her in silence chanting AUM, for in this way lies the redemption of life.

1228. She is the mother who gave birth to many faiths, She is Manonmani (the heart's precious gem) and Mangali, the auspicious. She is rare for any one to know Her. But to them, that seek Her, united in thought and word, She appears as subtle wisdom.

1229. She is the subtle wisdom to those who possess subtle intellect, and behind it there is the Lord's wisdom that is Gnana: the way of Sanmarga (Gnana) is the true way for those who seek Shiva state: this is the holiest way.

1230. The Gnana way becomes the Sanmarga (good) way, it drives away all evil ways and from that good way, all good deeds arise, Sakthi, indeed is the mistress of this Sanmarga way.

1231. None except Sakthi, Shiva and (I) Jeeva know the source of Mukthi—liberation. When you constantly meditate on Sakthi that ripend as AUM, and that paves the sure way to enter the centre high in the Sahashrara.

1232. Do not waste your lives thinking of this and that. Those who reach to the Good mother of tresses bedecked with flowers, in the Moon's sphere from where ambrosia flows, and pray there, may well conquer their decreed fate.

1233. They may well conquer their decreed fate, and conquer too their Kamaic Pasa; well may they conquer their desire-ridden senses, they may know all these, and that the mother conquers all of them.

1234. Through time interminable it was that Sakthi and Shiva stood as one, in the fifty-one letters. This is the state how the Mother of flower laden tresses and Her Lord of yore have been. In truth, this the truth.

1235. When Sakthi and Shiva united all creation, arose without seed; and thus it was the fifty-one letters and their respective deities acquiring Gnana, Jeevas attained perfection.

1236. The perfect Shiva and his consort of arched brow were seated there, in the Sahashrara, and the celestials stood praying to swill the ambrosia that flowed. And She stood there as ambrosia, radiant as the crescent moon.

1237. They who reach the eternal star become one with Her, of tresses festooned with garlands, fragrant Ganga, and

Moon. She stood in stellar brilliance, and men of Holy *tapas* prayed for self-realization.

1238. All Gnana appears in the thoughts of Jeevas who thus reach Her, standing face to face with Her that is bejewelled with their inner light realizing Her and uniting in Her.

1239. She of doe-like eyes and He of handsome visage appear together: so seek Her and She appears in the form the devotees conceive Her, and She grants the pure way and several branches of knowledge.

1140. Transcending all human knowledge; She stands as Vedic subtlety; She is Maya; She is divinely proud; She, the red-hued damsel is Sivanandha Sundari (Shiva-Bliss-Beauty). In endearing love, She stands as the pure way.

1241. Do not leave Her, the mother of precious jewels, who is the pure way. But with the Lord centre Her is your thoughts and there you will be absorbed in Gnana.

1242. The states of Brahma, Vishnu, Hara and Maheswara all only lead to AUM, if AUM pervades the six yogic centres and the three Mandalas, then you reach the nine centres within and you shall become honey-sweet divine, you shall sing in a rapture and shall reach the state of surpassing greatness.

The states of Brahma, Vishnu, Hara and Maheswara are illusionary. She is beyond all these. She pervades in AUM, in the Sahashrara beyond the six Adharas and the three Mandalas. There She confers the state of greatness, surpassing that of all the Gods.

1243. The celestials Vanavas and Dhanavas will come to you and worship your feet, and Indra and other Gods in the eight directions will therefore seek the way of worship to reach the Mother of tresses festooned in clusters of flowers, and Her Lord too.

Vanavas and Dhanavas are the children of Danu, their mother—asuras.

1244. Chant the Holy manthra of the Holy Mother, worship Her with fragrant flowers, burn incense, light the multi-flamed lamp and thus perform worship of Parvathi, the oblations that you offer in Archana are for the Lord of Divine Light as well.

1245. He, the Parapara, who is eternal, indestructable and immanent sustain all here below. She, Sakthi that holds the lovely parrot in Her hand, shares Her form with him. Adore Her, Parasakthi, sporting the wavy tresses.

1246. She, Uma of dark slender form is the good vine that has three eyes, is the mother of arched brows and is the Supreme mistress of Lord Shiva's ardour. Adore Her and be illumined and She the very Golden Goddess (of wealth) shall be at Your Feet.

1247. Parasakthi decked in garland of radiant gems, appears resplendent to dispel your darkness of Aanava. In love's intimate union, She sports with the Lord that is blue-throated; let Her be the goal of your heart, and follow Her close.

1248. The lord who is the consort of Sakthi is the Light of the world. He stands in me, this is the greatness of my love; He stands in Her too as the one inseparate form; He, with serpent and Ganga on matted locks is contained in Her.

1249. Lord Nandhi has several forms and so pervades several lives. Why does He, in this form (with Sakthi) appear so openly? This is indeed baffling, and a mystery why Shiva sports in joy with Her of bangled hands and bejewelled form.

1250. The Lord, the pure one of peaked matted locks and holy feet, that holds Ganga on His head, conjoins in maya and shares Sakthi in love; the great Sakthi; Supreme source of everything, embraced him in bodily union that all creation arose in union.

1251. I lost myself, as I realized Him as our Isa; as I united in Him, I became one with Him; as I embraced the Lord of all worlds; I remained in divine fulfilment and as I entwined my self at the feet of the primal one, I received the grace of His Sakthi.

Once He is realized as Isa, you unite in Him, You become one with the Almighty, Him. By embracing the Lord of all worlds, the Self is effaced.

1252. The great Manonmani is all greatness. The truly learned know that the true goal is the Holy Feet of the Lord. Those who know this truth exalt His Golden Feet as the unfailing refuge of life.

1253. My heart seeks the Lord in love, but, He, the sweet one is beyond the seven worlds, they say. This is the reason why I adore the Mother with fragrant flowers and melting love in my heart.

The yogi adores the Holy Mother Sakthi for She is more easily accessible than the Lord, who it is said, is beyond the seven worlds.

1254. Manonmani, the Supreme Mistress is the Mother of the headvenly home. She fashions the Holy home and stands there as Divine Mother. She, Maya, fashioned this body and She abides in this body home too.

1255. My Mother and Father united in love; had they not, then, my Mother and Father would not have even known me. But now, I sit with Mother and Father and I constantly adore my Mother and Father.

The yogi constantly adores the mother (Sakthi) and father (Shiva), who in love stand ever united.

8. Eroli Chakra (Chakra of Supreme Light)

1256. The four Nadhas arise from the radiant Bindhu in the four-petalled lotus in the Mooladhara. When radiant kala of Nadha suffuses everywhere, then does the Chakra of Supreme Light arise in the central kundalini fire.

Va(m), Sa (m), Sha (m), Sa (m) are the four Nadas. From radiant Bindhu in the Mooladhara the four-petalled Lotus arises Nadha. From Nadha in the central Kundalini there arises the Eroli Chakra.

1257. The letters in the Kundalini fire are mighty great, they rise to heaven, and they form a great Chakra. I shall now relate the way the letters are placed.

The mighty four letters in Kundalini Va, Sa, Sha, Sa form the basis of this great Chakra.

1258. The aforesaid Bindhu with twelve Nadhas stand as respective letters in the four petals of that Adhara. Chant the letters a hundred and forty-four times, they arise loftily and form as Chakra.

1259. The letter Bindhu and the letter Nadha conjoin and together fill the Mooladhara. When the conjoined letters are thus chanted repeatedly, they form the Earth Chakra. They form the Gnala (cosmos) Chakra.

1260. When the letter Bindhu and the letter Nadha conjoined, the Earth Chakra expounded and become Adhara (Mooladhara) that lengthened to immense distance; the letters thus expanded as Earth. The cosmos chakra expanded into five elements 'Ha' (Sky), 'Ya' (Air), 'Ra' (Fire), 'Va' (Water), and 'La' (Earth).

1261. The letters arose as Bindhu and Nadha, expanded as Chakra, lengthened into earth elements and water elements beyond.

1262. The Chakra lengthened as water element, then further as fire element, then, still further as wind element and further beyond as sky element.

1263. To speak of the astral letter, all other letters are contained in it; Know this that the astral letter is 'Ha', that is SIVANANDHA Bliss.

1264. Know that the Chakra is made with the commencement of four Nadas letters and twenty-five Bindhu dots, placed in the chambers, which thus makes the Sun Chakra.

Repeat the four Nada letters with Bindhu twenty-five times to form Soorya (Sun) Chakra.

1265. The letter 'A' and the other five letters that follow are the letters of the primal one; the six letters thus formed, are the letters of Sakthi; The middle letter of the first four 'Va' aforesaid letter of Sakthi (Va) is the letter of the fire element. Thus, it is with these holy letters.

The six letters commencing with 'A' are the letter of SIVA/ SAKTHI.

1. A, Aa, I, I, G,U.
2. E, E, AI, O, O, AU.
3. Va, Sa, Sha, Sa.
4. (AUM) Si, Va, Ya, Na, Ma.

1266. The letters of the radiant Chakra are a hundred and forty-four. The letters are but the six letter Manthra whose central letter 'Va' belongs to fire. This central letter is as radiant as fire flames. Thus are the six letters, first and last.

1267. The ultimate centre filled by 18 letters has neither

beginning nor end. So when the kundalini that was at the base ascends and crosses beyond the third centre from it (Anahatha) then the mystic sphere of the moon is visioned.

1. Eighteen letters—they are 16 letters of the moon's 16 Kalas and two letters (A and U) of AUM.

2. 13th letter—after the twelve letters in the 12 Kalas of the Sun are ascended, cover the moon sphere which absorbs the Sun's Kalas.

1268. There are three hundred and sixty days. They belong to the goat's group. The days are reckoned in fortnights of fifteen days. They come as the Centras 16 are two kundalini ascends; and they come as the 'sphere of the Mystic Sun' within is reached. The time is measurable by the Sun.

1269. The Sun travels through the twelve zodiac houses (Mesha-Rishaba-Midhuna-Kataka-Sinha-Kanni-Dhula-Vrischika-Dhanush-Makara-Kumba-Meenam) across the vast firmament. In time span a day is reckoned as thirty *naligai's* (24 minutes—1 naligai) time and in days, it is reckoned as three hundred and sixty in the full year round.

1270. The zodiac houses (Rasis) are determined in three clusters. With the goat 'Mesha' comes its group of three and with the twins 'Mithuna' comes its group of three. Thus, the Rasis in the zodiac are reckoned in three clusters.

Rasis in the zodiac are reckoned in three groupings: Goat (Mesha), (Bull (Rishaba) and Twins (Mifhuna)

1. The Mesha (Aries) group or path in this cluster are: Rishabha_(Taurus); Mithuna (Gemini); Kadagha (Cancer); and Simha (Leo);
2. The Rishabha (Taurus) path contains: Kanni (Virgo); Dhula (Libra); Meenam (Pisces) and Mesha (Aries);
3. The Mithuna (Gemini) path contains: Vrischika (Scorpio); Dhanus (Sagittarious); Maghara (Capricorn) and Kumba (Aquarius).

1271. When the Chakra is formed in the zodiac, it is filled by Bindhu, and Nadha too fills therein, then the Rasi Chakra is fixed in zodiac.

1272. The Bindhu letters arise with Nadha letters; When

the letters of Bindhu and Nadha are placed appropriately in each Adhara, then, the Taraka (steller) Chakra appears.

1273. When the Taraka Chakra thus assumes, its form as a star, then on this star a divine light beams from it; When Moon and Sun comes on to this state it becames the support of Sakthi, the supporter of all.

1274. Bindhu ascends on this Chakra, so does Nadha ascend too, and on Nadha ascends the flame of fire (kundalini fire). Beyond this, appears a light that is blue.

1275. This blue light enveloped all Universe, it became the light of the earth, water, fire, wind and sky; thus as it flamed and together, it pervaded everywhere as one divine light.

1276. The universe arose out of primal stain, expanded as diverse worlds, stands firm and it rests on Bindhu's strength.

1277. If Bindhu and Nadha arise in equal proportions: they together produce the balanced Beeja (seed); if Bindhu rises more and Nadha less, the Beeja becomes far more potent, that is, eight times more than Bindhu.

Nadha and Bindhu are stages of Sakthi in the movement towards the manifestation of the Self and objects, that is as the universe. Bindhu and Nadha produce Beejas, if Bindhu rises more and Nadha less, Beeja becomes eight times more powerful than Bindhu.

1278. The two Beejas arise from Nadha, one ascends upwards and with Nadha alike, the seed behind expands as caused Bindhu.

1279. As the Bindhu rises higher and higher, the Beeja seed goes in vain; but when Bindhu rises equal with the Nadha, it is drawn within to pervade the sixteen petals of the Vishuddhi adhara-yogic centre and here the Bindhu that expands becomes the seed of liberation.

1280. From the seed of Bindhu arises all Beejas; all life and this world too; from the Lord's feet (Nadha) arose the Bindhu seed.

1281. The fifty letters evolved from Bindhu and Nadha; the Chakra was formed from the letters; the Chakra and the letters stand within the body and truly, the letters are the

Manthras.

1282. To speak of Manthras and Chakras, they resemble the circle of fire that the tanthra glorify. Meditate on Pranava 'OM' that is the Supreme Manthra with its seat in the eyebrow centre (agjna centre). Reach this through Tanthra and there is no more bondage for you.

1283. The manthra that arises in the Mooladhara Chakra does not leave the eyebrow centre; when your egoity is discarded then you may vision the Pranava Manthra.

1284. You may vision Pranava in the Chakra that snaps your Pasa; it will protect all your thought and you shall perceive all directions. If you but know how to look for it then, it will lead you to the Supreme Truth that is subtler than subtle.

1285. The letter 'A' of Shiva and the next letter 'U' of Sakthi form the first two letters in the Pranava 'OM' Chakra. This Chakra is the earth, fire and the rest of the four elements.

1286. The Pranava manthra (OM) in the Chakra arises and expands into the six-lettered manthra. It is the Vedic Manthra that conjoins with five letters—AUM NAMASIVAYA—arises for those who are inclined this way.

1287. The Holy Sakthi is the presiding deity of this six-lettered manthra. If the aspirant's goal is the attainment of the Holy Sakthi that is likes fire (Kundalini) in there, then ensnaring Pasa will not harass him.

1288. Sthanbanan, Maranam and Vasiyam are the powers that arises of themselves there in the Chakra. No enemies come in the place where the Sadhaka-aspirant is. It is so for them who seek it within them.

1289. Vision the Chakra in the Mooladhara and centre the sound 'A' wherein, then, meditate on the benevolent Shiva within and course the Prana breath upward—thus contemplate on the six-lettered Chakra.

1290. As the Prana 'OM' manthra ascends in composed measure thus—a quarter, a half, a three-quarter and one full—the internal obstacles perish as it ascends. Thus it is for those who chant the enchanting manthra for worldly attainments.

As the manthra ascends in appropriate measures, the

impediments vanish. Thus is the manthra chanted for worldly purposes.

Pranava manthra is composed of Bindhu (1/2 Mathra); 'M'(1/2 Mathra), Natha (3/4 Mathra) and 'A' and 'U' (Full Mathra).

1291. The letters of this manthra belong to the divine dancer. Chant this manthra inside Uluva free of obstacles—then you will become the jewelled lamp in the Hall of Dance (Chidambaram-Sri Nataraja). Even at this very moment, do arise and chant Nama with love in the core of your heart.

9. Bhairava Chakra

1292. The Bhairava Chakra worship should be performed in ten days in the fortnight. The first six days, the eight, the tenth, the twelfth and the fourteenth days of a fortnight are the appropriate ten days. (Leave out the seventh, ninth, eleventh and thirteenth days). Then course the breakthrough the right nostril and do worship.

1293. As you thus worship Bhairava, the God appears with trident and skull, and blinds your enemy's eyes and drinks His life, and you may play with your enemy's body as with a ball.

1294. The Primal Bhairava that comes to bless the Jeeva holds the skull and trident, the drum and the noose too, and the severed head and sword as well in His hands.

1295. The Great Bhairava's form is ruddy bright; His hands are six and His look is blessed; He appears as shining truth in the hearts of the pure. So, adore Him in sincere devotion.

1296. Perform the Bhairava worship thousand times with drink and ecstatic dance, with sandlewood paste, fragrant incense, musk, civet and diverse unguents, Pray and worship Him thus, and He will destroy your enemies.

1297. As you pray and as you ascend the six yogic centres within, there shall be fight and obstacles. Pray for the ways things should be and all your wishes shall be fulfilled.

1298. To speak of Sambavi Mandala Chakra is like this: Form eight chambers, within the eight chambers is the Central Chamber, within the eight chambers of this central chamber.

This verily is the eye of the four Tathwas—Shiva-Sakthi-Nadha and Bindhu. When we see this holy state revealed then we will verily know all the worlds.

1299. The Mandalas that are formed by twenty horizontal and twenty vertical lines have two inner Bhupuras and two outer Bhupuras. The innermost Bhupura is formed of sixteen chambers.

1300. The Mandala is formed of twenty by twenty lines, in Bhupuras. Place four Lingas in each corner and place four flowers there. Thus the Sambavi Chakra is formed.

1301. The five letters are the embodiment of the fifty-one letters, Chant the pure five letters SI,VA,YA, NA, MA and you will lack nothing then.

1302. When the holy feet are yours, you shall want nothing, realize the Vedic Manthra AUM and chant it in steadfasteness. This brings the conquest over death, thus it has been said.

1303. Sambhavi confers such blessings as attainments of wealth, great state, pilgrimage to holy waters, delicious food, pleasant emotions, sound sleep and gold and you will see your favourite God. As the Mother of the Chakra blesses, all those will be yours of themselves.

1304. If you persevere in the way of the five holy letters, they will be yours. If you so proceed in this way, you shall achieve all you wish and you shall have no enemies in the world here below.

1305. For those who bow low to Her, enemies shall there be none and they will stoop before no enemies or be exalted in glee over them. No more are they harassed by karma and its untoward manifestations too. All good things will flow daily, as cool as water, and without any impediments.

1306. All may chant the five letters and worship the Chakra of Sambhavi. She is the bliss-form that no one has so far visioned. She is the earth, the sky, the Moon and the sentience that pervades body and life.

1307. The manthra AUM, that imparts Gnana within is the way to unite in God. Thus, Shiva (director) and Sakthi (consort of the director) together arise in amity and She, the beloved of Shiva (Sivakami Devi) blesses you.

10. Bhuvanapathi Chakra

Bhuvanapathi chakra is formed of fifteen letters. The fifteen letters are collectively known as Pancha-dasakhshari (This is also the Srividhya Manthra Chakar).

1308. The five letters beginning with 'Ka' are golden hued; the six letters beginning with 'A' are red hued and the four letters beginning with 'Sa' are pure white. The Manthras grouped thus to bliss below on this earth and to liberation above.

1. Ka, Aa, E, La, Ham (Vakbhava group);
2. Ha, Sa, Ka, La, Ha, Ham (Kamagaja group);
3. Sa, Ka, La, Hrm (Sakthi Group)

The colours mentioned indicate the colours in which the letters should be marked in the Chakra.

1309. If you but see the truth, this is it, this is the true God, there is none other than He; listen to what I say, this triangle (Chakra) is great like the ocean, centre your thoughts on it; bliss and Mukthi shall be yours and you will be Siva-form.

1310. The one Parasakthi belongs to the Lord as His part, Her form is Paravidhya; She grants Mukthi and Siddhis; Though the Parasakthi is one, She assumes eight forms indeed, when Shiva assumes the form of Yoga Guru.

The eight Sakthis are counted differently. Several delineations are as follows:—

1. Isani, Purani, Arthi, Vami, Murthi, Arini, Rodayithri and Janani.
2. Jayari, Vijayai, Jayanthi, Aparasithai, Siddkhai, Rathai, Alambusai, and Utpalai.
3. Vamai, Sresthai, Raudhri, Kali, Kalvikarni, Balavikarni, Balaparadhamani, Sarva Bhoodhathathmani.
4. Arini, Janani, Rodayithri, Kali, Tatpurushi, Vamai, Aghori and Sado-Jathi.

1311. The eight Sakthis belong to the eight limbed yoga; these eight Sakthis mingling become one (Parasakthi), when Nandantha is reached. The Bindhu that stood apart disappeard. These experiences do not reach the witless lowly ones.

1312. You must firmly establish the Yanthra and worship at the feet of the Yanthra Raja, chant the manthra, the Guru has taught you, perform Anga-nyasas (bodily gestures) and meditate. Inscribe the six-pointed (double) triangle on a copper plate. This will end your births.

1313. Place the letters Srim, Hrim and above these Rim on the six-angled diagram. Inscribe a circle to encompass the entire diagram and place the sixteen letters, inclusive of AUM.

1314. Describe more manthra letters, that is, in the space above, inscribe the letter 'Ha'. between the eight petals. Above, 'Ha' place 'U' and 'Krom' and 'Srom'-close to the petals, place 'AUM' and 'Krom' to the left of the Chakra.

1315. Complete the Yanthra with further manthra letters. Place Krom and Srom together to the right of the Chakra thus formed. Surround the Chakra by Hrim. Thus complete the double triangle Yanthra and then worship Sakthi, that is Bhuvanapathi.

1316. Bhuvaneshwari form is the pure red; Her robe is silky. She holds the weapons, goad and noose in Her hands; She gestures in protective pose. She appears, thus adorned with dazzling jewels on Her body. Her body shining as purest gem and Her crown so radiant.

1317. Bare the garment that covers your skin. Seek Her in endearing love and devotion. Offer the milk-rice oblation, chanting the manthra. Form the turn in four directions and pronounce 'Naradayai Suvaha'. Finally serve the food thus offered.

1318. Before serving thus, invoke Her within and place Her firmly in the lotus of your heart, then, pray to Yanthra Raja who is beyond reach. Hold Him fast within you and He will grant all your wishes.

11. Navakkari Chakra

1319. I shall here speak of Navakkari (Nine-lettered) Chakra. The one lettered becomes the nine-lettered, the nine-lettered expands into the eighty-one lettered. Navakkari are the nine letters from KLIM to SAUM.

Navakkari Chakra is of nine letters. This nine-lettered

Navakkari expands into 81 letters.

1320. With KLIM as the manthra: foot, Srim, Hrim, Aim, Gaum, Krim, Haum, Aum, and Saum are the nine manthras. Chant these nine Holy manthras in order, and at the end, chant Sivayanama at every rotation. Then you attain the fruitfulness of Navakkari.

1321. Navakkari is the Chakra on which I practise all that is good arises in Navakkari; when you chant the Navakkari manthra deep within you, the Navakkari Sakthi, confers all blessing, on you.

The Nine Sakthis enumerated are:

1. Navakkari Sakthi (Manthra 1321); 2. Thriu Nayaki (Manthra 1325); 3. Tayyal Nayaki (Manthra 1329); Tatthwa Nayaki (Manthra 1340); 4. Parasakthi (Manthra 1344); 5. Saddhashiva Nayaki (Manthra 1350); 6. Amudeshwari (Manthra 1354); 7. Mingodiyal (Minnal Nayaki-manthra 1359).

1322. The blessings of Navakkari Manthra are related. All knowledge and Gnana, will be yours, the hard karmas shall flee from you; and no more will you perform evil deeds; all boons will be granted to you. Navakkari leads to the vision of divine light.

1323. Earthly gifts of the Chakra are enumerated; Inscribe the Chakra on silver, gold or copper; meditate on it, you will succeed in all your actions and you will triumph in the world. The gifts of the Chakra shall be as rich as your meditation on it is deep.

1324. Chant it with Srim to commence and Klim to end, and as you continuously chant thus, the first syllable becomes the last syllable. Meditate on the chakra with in, offering rice grain and Kusa grass. Perform Archanas thus, and She will accept your worship.

1325. The Srim Sakthi will appear and you will learn of Her hume; She is like a golden flower of smoky hue. She will fulfil all your wishes. Do adore Her and receive Her grace.

1326. All things will fare well with you here below. Kala the God of death, will bypass your reckoned days, your name and fame will spread like shafts of light; draw nearer and nearer to Her and you will reach Her.

1327. Srim Sakthi confers several blessings, Gold, silver and precious stones will be yours. Divine Grace, prosperity and the celestial life of the Devas shall all be yours. Meditate on her constantly that you may attain all these.

1328. They, that meditate on Her, become immortals, the Lord of immortals will bless you, you persevere to reach Him, who wears the Ganga and contains Her.

1329. Worship the letters in the Chakra. Chant the manthra commencing with Hrim and ending with Srim. Meditate on Her, the highly famed one bedecked in garlands and you will see Her as the cloud-laden flower-garden.

1330. Meditate on the incomparable, Sakthi Hrim (Tani Nayaki) and your face will glow in consuming attraction. Seek Her constantly, the eternal one, the one who reposes in the param of Divine Light.

1331. Mediate on Her, who are all blessings, the earthly rulers will be with you and those against you will not flourism. Praise Her who shares the Lord's form.

1332. Chant the name of Hrim Sakthi who is the mistress of eight directions, and attain the life of the celestial Gods, and live so; Abandon the way that leads to this world and reach the Holy Feet of Thani Nayaki Sakthi and flourish there.

Hrim Sakthi pervades all eight directions. Chant Her name and gain the life of celestials. Renounce everything and reach Her feet, you will know the way to reach Her. She is the Thani Nayaki Sakthi.

1333. They who chant Her name in silence, flourish at Her Holy Feet; They who adore Her Feet with flowers know the way to reach Her Holy Feet.

1334. The Chakra expands with 'Aim' to begin with; beginning from 'Aim' it ends in Hrim; to begin you meditate as Aim; meditate on Her, who is dear to the primal Lord.

1335. The Sakthi you adore is Vageswari (Goddess to Logas) whom all Vedas and Agamas praise; She who is within the grasp of the tongues chant shall reveal Herself to you, face to face.

1336. If you hold this Chakra that appears before you, in your tongue its manthra assumes the form of the divine dancer.

If this Vidhya that is in the Golden Hall (Chidambaram will come within the reach of a human, then this man will conquer all and the slender Sakthi will confer Her grace on Him.

1337. She, of the slender form is the Divine Truth, chant Her manthras and meditate on Her constantly; your ways that till now stilled and rolled on in diverse ways, will ascend in steady prosperity and hereafter.

Hail and worship Aim Sakthi, your future will be one of unalloyed joy and steady prosperity.

1338. Chant 'AIM' manthra ceaselessly and all blessings shall follow you. You shall gain the meaning of words, and the understanding that is beyond words; with Her blessings; who is the queen of learning, you will be a master of all learning and you will have no enemies, here below.

1339. There will be no enemies for those who chant the manthra from GAUM to Aim; no more malicious occurences will be directed against them. For those who mediate the vine (GAUM) on the Chakra, all creation, with no exception, shall bow to them. This is no exaggeration.

1340. Adore Sakthi who rules over all Tathwas and all good lives will bend before you, lust-anger and ignorance will all flee in terror and all your actions will be shining.

1341. He who meditates on Her, will alone speak and what he speaks will be the final word and he alone can speak what he thinks is the right; he who meditates on Her shall witness the divine dance of Lord Shiva (Sri Nataraja), and he will become the master of all around.

What you speak will be the final word and the right word.

Meditate on her, witness the dance of Shiva, and become the master of all around.

1342. Gaum Sakthi is the Mother that is all life; She is the mother that created life. Worship at Her feet, all things will be yours, your Karmas will vanish and you will become holy.

1343. You will remain holy and you will walk honoured, far and wide in this world, you shall be benevolent to one and all. So you will tarry close to Her.

1344. I know that they who meditate deeply on the Chakra from KRIM to GAUM will become dear to Parasakthi, the virgin of the sylvan glades, and they shall shine high in the world.

1345. When the luminous Parasakthi makes Her abode within you, your heart dances in joy; Your thoughts are filled with clear visions, copious rains fall and wealth and prosperity smile. This it will be for those who meditate on Her.

1346. Meditate on the Chakra, performing worship, you will overcome all your obstacles; kings will come to you and pay their respects; your thoughts will glow and no sorrows will emanate from you.

1347. For those who meditate on Krim Sakthi in the Navakkari Chakra, they will find their sole refuge and crown of glory in Her. As there is no killing, there will be no hell; there will be none of sorrow's fumes, but a golden light will suffuse, their body.

1348. Those who meditate on Her, do not experience the evils of soaring karma, their egoity perished and their fame glows in all directions; their inner light spreads far and wide and the light of differentiate knowledge is snuffed out for ever.

1349. The Chakra with manthras from Haum to Krim is all light; it is sheer happiness to those who meditate on it, and pure Gnana and clear vision fills their thoughts; meditating on it is like meditating on Panchakshara.

1350. She (HAUM) is the Sadhasiva Sakthi. She is the light behind the Adho-Muka (the downward looking face of the Lord). She, that is immanent in all lives, is the one emanating tastes, sight, feel, sound and smell.

1351. Within, She is in Herself, without, She is in all the world. She is within me; She is within the earth, water, fire, wind and sky filling it all entirely. She is within the eye and within the body too. May you behold Her.

1352. You may well see all that She does, the one that is immanent in our lives. If you hold Her in your thoughts, you may well see Her; if you make way for Her in the depths of your heart, you may well see Her with your physical eyes. Stand firm in seeking Her constantly in Your thoughts.

1353. She stands pervading the seven worlds at once; She

stands immanent in all hearts everywhere; She stands bearing all good things of the world; She stands as the Divine truth that dispels all hard Karmas.

1354. The Chakra runs from AU(M) to HAU (M). It is the Divine Truth. She, AUM is the meaning within that Chakras; She is the self-created Amudheswari Devi, who stands in the centre of the Chakra as good riches.

1355. With your breath coursing upward rouse the kundalini and hold this Amudheswari Devi in your heart, daily you will vision newer and newer things; listen to this; your body will never perish.

1356. Having visioned the rising light in the Chakra, no more harm will come to you; when having lost the sense of time's beginning, there will no more be the spatial consciousness; when having seen the ways of Her grace; there will no more be the differences in power and pelf; when having reached the land of goal, there will be no more the forest of sorrow.

1357. All the space that you sojourn become desolate nothingness; all the space that you have learned there becomes an interminable void; there is no other place, there is not a wee bit of space. Wherever you are, stand firm and unfaltering in HUM Sakthi.

The aspirant engaged in Aum Sakthi worship attains the transcendental state. All space turns into interminable space.

1358. Stand unfaltering and constant in AUM Sakthi, if you incessantly seek and worship Her, She appears as the resplendent light; all your desires and wishes will be fulfilled and your fame will be known in the seven seas and seven worlds.

1359. The Chakra that extends from SAUM to AUM is the light that illumines; this luminous Chakra is the eternal truth. Meditate on Sakthi that is like a shaft of lighting and become luminous.

1360. To speak of the eternal truth that beams high above, is truly this SAUM Sakthi of slender form. Do seek the light that is the truth of Gnana. They who seek the light will themselves be light.

1361. SAUM Sakthi is all spaces, She fills all spaces; She is the space beyond space; She creates all and preserves all. She is the entire universe and all life.

1362. She is immeasurable; She fills vast spaces in the corporeal body in this immense Universe; you may well see many good things in the Mooladhara, yet you may not know that She stands in the very centre of your throat. (Vishuddhi Chakra).

1363. The ignorant do not know Her pervasiveness in the sea-girt world; they do not know Her immanence in the body and life. By seeking other Gods, they fail to know Her anklet; but they are fated to be thus.

1364. To speak of this Chakra, it arose of its own volition. How to form the eighty-one squared Navakkari Chakra is to mark ten horizontal and vertical lines and thus form nine squares on each line. In all they form eighty-one squares.

1365. As you form the Chakra thus, colour the outer circle in the hues of gold, mark the squares in red and the manthra letters in green.

1366. Inscribe the letters of Sakthi on the bark of a tree, fill Sakthi in the eighty-one chambers and offer hot ghee and rice. Worship the Chakra performing Homa (Yagna) and prana oblations.

1367. Hold steadfast to the Sri Sakthi Chakra in calmness; as you meditate on it day by day, you shall be in felicity; and as your name and fame soar like Brahma's, you will be one with Lord Shiva in loved union.

1368. Blend these nine perfumes—sandal, saffronflower, deer musk, fragrant paste, civet scent, ghee, camphor, orpiment and scented water and smear the Chakra with them.

1369. To speak of the worship that you should perform at the Sri Chakra, that holds the virgin Sakthi as its nodal pull, worship the Chakra with incarnations of the Manthra a hundred, hundred times and thus meditate on it constantly.

1370. She beams as Divine Light in your thoughts; She appears with six hands and in them She holds six weapons—the torch, the trident, the goad, the noose, bow and arrow. Chant the manthra KLIM to good begin with and She will appear before you.

1371. This is the form of KLIM Sakthi in the Chakra. She of crimson-hued form and like the choicest pearl is seated on lotus-petals, dressed in fine apparel and bedecked in jewels of gold, with earrings and crown. She is there for those who meditate on the Chakra.

1372. If you meditate on Her with intense feelings; She who pervades all will rise from within the Chakra and bless you, showering Her grace on you, and you shall perceive sound Nadha and light Bindhu enveloping you.

1373. KLIM Sakthi appears in the Chakra surrounded by sixty-four minor Sakthis, including the eight virgins with bows and arrows in each of their two hands. They are seated opposite in the Chakra.

1374. After the Guru has sundered your birth's reckoning. She, the Divine Light leads you to the great way and grants you Tathwa Gnana through the way shown by the Guru.

1375. Sakthi is the luminous One, the dazzling light that stands as light through the entire world. She is of dark-golden hue of the clouds and in soft radiance, emits Her divine brilliance.

1376. Her comely garments are interlaced in pure gems, Her two lovely breasts are decked in pearls and corals, Her two spreading hands hold lotus and flowers and Her two blessing hands gesture in tender grace.

1377. She adorns Herself wearing the jewelled crown on the head and lovely anklets on Her Feet. There is no grace without Her. She appears as Divine Grace in the hearts of those who pray in meekness and to those who seek in devotion, She grants liberation.

1378. The sixty Sakthis are seated around the mighty Sakthi and the eight virgins are seated in concealment around Her too. She bears lotus blossoms in both Her hands, She is the treasure of the SRIM manthra and to the holy ones too, who meditate on Her in devotion.

1379. If you meditate intensely, for a year, on SRIM Sakthi, the treasure of the manthra Chakra, the burden of your worldly cares drops off, your thoughts soar high and your heart attains the brilliance of the sun—this is the true message of the Chakra.

1380. The full flower that rises in the Mooladhara blossoms into effulgent light that pervades all yogic centres, the red flame then reached the sphere of fire.

1381. There, She sits in the sphere of fire (Swadhistana). There She appears in fifty-six forms. There, She is surrounded by fifty-six minor Sakthis and is visioned by fifty-six Sakthis.

1382. She is as one effulgent light, from Her jewelled crown to Her Feet; She wears Her form like lustrous pearls; Her two pendent hands hold a parrot and the Gnana Mudhra and Her two upraised hands bear the noose and the goad.

1383. Severe the roots of your passes and adore Him Her in the recesses of your heart thus, all evils will leave you and in five years of chanting HRIM Sakthi, you will be like Lord Shiva.

1384. If you meditate on the Chakra of the merciful Sakthi, and if you chant in the order done, the heavenly light in this Chakra of the lordly Sakthi where manthra HRIM is invoked, will appear.

1385. Vision and meditate on the light that arises in the Chakra; It is the Sakthi that appears as light within the Chakra, verily She is the support of the Shushmna, the Adharas and the rest within.

1386. The AIM Sakthi abides immanent and all-pervasive in the lotus sphere of the navel centre (Manipoorka) that rises in the Kalas; meditate; there you will be firm in Nadha and you will see the end of your birth-cycle.

1387. AIM Sakthi, Vageshwari decked in a garland of pure gems, is the queen of speech, She is milk-hued and is the queen of songs. She is the queen of Jeevas is seated there in the navel centre.

1388. Then, of youre, She measured Dharma with two hands; now for nonce She holds white pitcher of hermits. They who reach Her by the way to the hall of dance, will verily behold the primal cause of all.

1389. The causal Sakthis are fifty-two, they are the causal virgins; She, the primal causal Sakthi of all, stands as grace, immanent in the Chakra.

1390. If Aim Sakthis is worshipped with intense devotion, then this Sakthi stands in your thoughts; then, within the span of a year you will merge in this flame; if you stand in steadfast devotion, you shall vision the ruby that dances in the hall of vast spaces.

1391. The Sakthi that you vision in the heart's lotus in this (GAUM) Tathwa Nayaki, the queen of all Tathwas. She is seated sweetly in my thought this day and has destroyed my life's enemy-death.

1392. The Sakthi that was thus seated in my mind, appeared with eight hands, holding flower, parrot, noose, battle axe and sword, the shield, bow and the arrow too—she danced in divine rapture.

1393. She stood in rapture, Her form green hued, dressed in richly silks, wearing crown of gold, garland of pearls and corals and Her rising breasts contained in gem-laid corset, and there She stood in all glory.

1394. This green-hued mother has forty eight serving companions and eight vestal virgins that take up Her trains. Her breasts are contained in corset and Her pendant hands in blessing gesture, thus She appears, the sweet one of slender waist.

Here, the letters are given as forty-eight (for 56) in number.

1395. The kundalini fire resides in the Mooladhara, course it to unite in Her in Anahatha, the yogic centre, and in true devotion do penance and Japa GAUM and ascend above the Adhara, then you will rise into the heaven within, that is milky pure white (Solar sphere).

1396. The Koopa (KRIM) Sakthi is seated in the mystic sphere between the navel and the heart centres. She is like the cool waters of a well, there is the fiery sphere of the Sun.

1397. The Sakthi thus seated has ten benignant faces. She appears gently in the Sun's sphere. She assumes twenty protecting hands and she holds the holy trident to Sunder Pasas.

1398. The gleaming sphere that is Gnana, the trident, mace, fiery sword, shining drum, the arrow, kettle-drum, parrot and the bow are all on one side, the bugle flower, noose, battle-axe, knife, couch are on the other side of the pendant hands in protecting gesture. Meditate on these.

1399. She is surrounded by forty-four Sakthis; these forty-four Sakthis meditate on her. She that transcends all thought is seated within the lotus.

1400. She that transcends all thoughts, stands before me, as a girl, adorned, wearing the diadem of gold; Her corset is made of gems, pearls and corals, Her silken dress spreads below Her slender waist and Her feet hold the anklets.

1401. This Sakthi, as She stands constant, here, She sunders the Pasas that bind the ancient Jeeva and Anima, Mahima and the rest of the occult powers arise, and the unitive light of Gnana dawns on those who realize Her.

1402. The Sakthi (Sadhasiva Nayaki) of the Sadhashiva, has five faces and ten hands. Of these, the downward looking face (who muka) is by far divine indeed. HAUM Sakthi is in the Vishudhi (throat region) centre.

1403. HAUM Sakthi receives worship with these—the resounding bell, the trident, the skull and the parrot; the serpent that holds gems; the axe, the knife, the ball, the lotus that is lovely like Her eyes; the kettle drum that She holds in Her hands, and the gem-set garland that adores Her body. This is HAUM Sakthi's form.

1404. The beloved one is seated in the Chakra with forty virgins making the retinue and with forty Sakthis offering worship, and they are there in uninterrupted rapture.

1405. To rouse the Kundalini fire that burns in the Mooladhara and to send it upward over the yogic centres, you must centre your mind on the root manthra (AUM); your mind force then lifts it up, heavenward, like the clouds over the terrestrial sphere.

1406. The Pranava manthra composed of letters A and U arose from the terrestrial sphere, Mooladhara, and ascended upward, it appeared as SIVAYANAMA to the eye; it is not invisible to the naked eyes, but, it rose visible for us to see it.

1407. Thus She, Amudheswari Devi, is seated within the moon sphere of Ambrosia in the cranium; here She is, the ambrosial milk-breasts, of white-hue like the ambrosia; Her throat and hands shine like silver and gold and in Her hands She holds the nectar's pitcher.

1408. Her form is beauteous like Ambrosia, She rises in me as pure crystal; She is like a lily and like the pearl of deep cool waters; She is like rich ambrosia and She is immortal.

1409. The thirty-six noble Sakthis and the thirty-six vestal virgins seek Her who has Her home in the lotus flower; the Yoginis (Female yogis) seek Her, the eternal one from within the lotus of their bosom.

1410. My thoughts stood still in meditation when the Kundalini fire filled the yogic centres; I behold the light above in the Sahashrara, and as I held it in my heart, the Sakthi who is of luminous AUM, appeared in a year.

1411. All the binds in the high Heaven, in all the world, and all the creatures therein bowed before me, indeed, they too will become luminous. I was blessed like Narayana with all noble things. I just cannot recount all that comes from AUM Sakthi.

1412. Above the downward looking face of HAUM Sakthi and above the AUM Sakthi in the lunar sphere is the celestial garden in form of the letter 'U'. Here like the wish fulfilling tree of Kalpaha is SAUM Sakthi of golden vine-like form seated on lotus.

1413. The exulting I-ness leaves you, as you worship this golden vine. You will see Her, the maiden innocence, closely entwined, in the Sahashrara Chakra that represents the vast spaces.

1414. This maiden innocence is the embodiment of woman's perfect beauty. The Lord is Her father and the vast world is Her titak, surrounded by several maidens, She of exotic beauty, takes Her place in the narrow crevice of the Sahashrara.

1415. Surrounded by thirty-two Sakthis and accompanied by thirty-two vestal virgins, She that has several places, sits in the spreading petalled lotus within.

Here, the number of letters becomes sixty-four.

1416. They were there, the Sadhaka (aspirant), basking in the light of the dancer, and visioning Her, the cause of all, they were there, the ancient Vedas seeking Her everywhere, but this day, She has Her home in me and reigns Supreme there. SAUM Sakthi is immanent in Her devotees.

1417. He who has Her in the Home of his heart, lacks nothing, does not go abegging and has no peers among celestials. For him, the Lord alone is his refuge.

1418. The instruments that of enjoyment that tempt Jeevas are sixty-four; the Kalas within the Jeevas are also sixty-four, the chambers of Jeeva's Chakra are also sixty-four as is where Siva-Sakthi are:

Tanthra Four Concluded

5

Tanthra Five (Vaadhulahamam)

1. Suddha Saivam

Man is regarded as the microcosm of the macrocosm. The special column, the central support of the human body structure is, anogagously, symbolished in the Tanthras and in the works of the yoga as the Mount Maru of men in the microcosm. Mount Meru is the king of all mountains.

Esoterically explained, Mount Meru is the Universal hub, the support of all worlds. It is the 'Central Mountain' of Hindu and Buddhists cosmography, around which our cosmos is arranged in seven concentric circles of oceans separated by intervening concentric circles of golden mountains. We may, possibly regard it like the 'Central Sun' of western astronomy, as the gravitational centre of the known Universe.

The Sushumna nadi is the chief of Orthedian nerve situated in the hollow of the spinal column (Sanskrit:— Brahmanandhra) the Mount Meru of the human body.

1419. The Lord created the earth in infinite wisdom, and made it the abode of man. But I am not able to sing His majesty adequately as He is as mightly as Mount Meru, from where He sways the three worlds; and here below He is the four paths of Saivam too.

1420. They stand aloft who tread the path of Suddha Saivam. With their hearts intent on the eternal Para, they transcend the worlds of pure and impure maya, where pure intelligence does not consort with base ignorance and where the lines that divide Real, Unreal and Real-Unreal are sharply discerned.

Suddha Siddhantha is, in other words, Vedanta. The Suddha Siddhanthins receive the constant vision by sealing the heights of the Nada sphere and attain perfection in Nadhantha. They are capable of distinguishing between the real, the unreal and the real-unreal.

1421. Having learned all that must be learned and having practised all yoga that have to be practised, they, then, in sure gradition pursue the path of Gnana and so pass into the world of formless souls beyond, and there, rid of all impurities, they envision the self-created, Supreme, forsooth, these are the true Saiva Siddhanthis.

The path of Sudda Saiviam leads to the Supreme Siddha's pure state, devoid of all base ignorance. Yoga leads Saiva Siddhantha into the path of Gnana, and to pass the sphere of formless sound. Verily, that is the goal of Saiva Siddhantha, to be rid of all impurities.

1422. Suddha Siddhantha is Vedanta, they who have seated the scaled heights of the Nadha sphere have truly had the unwavering vision comprehending tathwas from the world of elemential matter to the finite end of Gnana (Bhodhantha). They become perfection in Nadhantha. They are truly the ardent seekers of Gnana.

Moolar equates his Saiva Siddhantha with Vedanta, which is not to be confused with the Vedanta of the schools of Sankaracharaya, Ramanucharya, etc. Bhodhantha is quite apparently the Meemamsa and spanda schools which emphasize the sound aspect of the ultimate.

2. Asutha Saivam

1423. They who walk the twin paths of Cariya and Kriya ever praise the twin Feet of the Lord. They wear holy Emblems on their limbs, two rings in their ear lobes, twin rudraskha garlands around their neck and sit still and impassive, chanting manthras. They remain in amiable constancy in thought of Shiva and thus their souls ascend to Lord Shiva.

1424. In their ear lobes, they wear the double ring of gold, they wear the double string of rudraskha around their neck, with their body (holy) adorned thus, they sit quiescent, chanting manthras and feel their way inward through the twelve states of consciousness; in the ladder of the soul's ascention to Lord Shiva. It is the states of consciousness in Samadhi state. The twelfth state is the final state of boid from whose bourne there is no returning. Such are the peerless school of Saivas.

1425. Suddha Saivas are those who transcended the nine spiritual centres and truly saw God, whom the nine continents seek. They saw the continent beyond all continents. These, indeed are the Pura Suddha Saivas.

These are known as Avasthas or states of the soul's experience as it travels from the navel to the forehead through the heart and neck Chakra centres. They represent the states of wakefulness, dream, deep sleep and beyond deep-sleep, and so on.

1426. The Gnani holds mastery over all the sacred lore on earth and the sixty-four attainments. He espies the vision of all the worlds and the 'Land of Mauno (Silence)' too. He sees the goal of all Vedas and sees the Lord of Himself united in one.

3. Sanmarga Saivam

1427. The apt insignia of those who stand in the Saiva path are the golden emblems of Shiva and the smear of holy ashes. But the path of the Gnan is the path that no evil can cross. His emblem is the holy path of Sanmarga (Gnana) that is the beloved of Suddhasaiva.

1428. The blemishless Gnani is the king of the realm of wisdom; He is the Sun, whose beams pierce the massive lore of Vedanta Siddhantha. His salvation is the true one. He, the immortal one is truly a devotee to the Suddha Saiva way.

1429. The Agamas of yore are nine and in time they expanded into twenty-eight and then they took three divisions

(Manthra-Tanthra-and Upadesa) to accord into the one truth of Vedanta-Siddhantha that is unique and precious in Suddha Saiva.

By stating that the Agamas provide the base for both Vedanta and Siddhantha (which are equated by him) Thirumoolar makes it clear that the Vedanta he has in mind is not the same as that of the Acharyas. The one things common in Vedanta, Siddhantha and Bodhantha is that they all consider knowledge as the ultimate path to liberation.

1430. She, Paraparai, transcends the world of matter, Pure and Impure, the seven states of Thuriya awareness and the categories of real and unreal. She is ever within and grants the soul deliverance. She, the Lord's Divine grace, is the Arul Sakthi that is all pervasive.

1431. The Siddhas do not cognize either Chit or Achit and so ascend categories real and unreal; they attune themselves to SIVOHAM meditation and attain Mukthi, they are deeply immersed in the bliss of Skathi and there in surpassing prowess abound in all Siddhis.

1432. They that take, to the path of Suddha Saiva contemplate in accord on all these—The self, Para, the Sadhasiva that is Lord, the three categories Pati, Pasu and Pasa, the immaculate ancient one, the Tathwas that bind jiva and the goal of liberation.

1433. Those of the Suddha Saiva way fix their thoughts on perfection and lose consciousness of the Self's existence, thus they have reached the end of the Vedas, they follow the twelve way route to divine rapture, that is their vision.

1434. The Gnani stills the incessant flow of thought that even the severe practice of yoga cannot still, he effaces the self with Gnana and identifies himself with Lord Shiva in Bhava; This, in brief is the story of the worthy Gnani.

1435. The Vedantins adept in Brahmic are envision Brahman and hold all phenomena as entire illusion; those who envision Nadantha are unwavering yogis; but Siddhantha that does not accord with Vedanta, is the common lot of Saivas.

1436. However high the clouds soar, they will never touch the heaven's roof; however be the sights that loom; they will never touch the eye's orbs; even so, neither Pasu nor Pasa will reach him, whom contemplation scarce comprehends.

1437. You and He are not two separate identities but are united as One. You stand thus, freed of all sectarian shackles; so adore the Feet of Paraparai and become One with Lord Shiva—this fulfils the Siddhantha way.

4. Stringent Suddha Saivam

1438. They, of Suddha Saiva way, are not for outward form and attire, pomp and ceremony; they uproot all bond and desire and abide in the immaculate Lord. They bring the beginningless Soul's egoity and its bondage to dire destruction, thus they leap onward, with Shiva's suffused light.

1439. The true way of the Siddhantins is to transcend the five Tathwas that constitute the body, the thirty more that together constitute them and the one Tathwa that is beyond pure maya; they dissolve the thick layers of primal bondage and for certain, realize the Self.

1440. They, forsooth, are Suddha Saivas, who do not tarry in pure maya sphere of Shiva Tathwas, but they attain the status of Gods. And using it as a springboard, their soul reaches farther out to Lord Shiva Himself, and merging in His union, self-effacing, they, themselves become immaculate Shiva.

1441. I sought Him in terms of 'I' and 'You'. But, the Lord who knows that I from you taught me the truth—'I' indeed in 'you' and now the difference I and you effaced, I no more talk of I and You.

1442. When you perceive this truth, which is beyond words, then the five Shiva Tathwas bend below and the light of Supreme Gnana dawns illumining the soul's path to the finite Goal of Sayujya union in the Lord.

5. Chariya

1443. Thirumoolar, the master of many penances, beckons to this beloved disciples Kalangi, Kanja Malayaman and Kanduru. He tells them to understand that the practise of Chariya is basic to salvation and it is truly the breath of Suddha Shiva in this world below.

1444. The luminous path of Gnana is to be one, that is, life within life. To seek the light within life is the mighty of yoga. The external acts investing an image with vibrant spirituality is Kriya (action), and to adore Lord Shiva in intense love is the basic worship of Chariya.

1445. You wander through town and village, seek Him through shrine and temple, sing of Him as "Shiva, Siva, my Lord" and in this way do offer meek worship, and the Lord will make your heart His temple.

1446. The who follow the path of Chariya are Bhaktas; in Kriyas the devoted souls wear holy emblems; they who practise Yama and the rest are yogis and they who reach Sivajnana are true Gnana Siddhas.

1447. The goals of the four paths are: the devotees in the path of Chariya perform many pilgrimages; The devotees of Kriya perform daily worship the yogis alone attain Siddhi and Samadhi and the Gnani's merge the 'I'as in you and find no difference between the two:—

1. Siddhis—miracles; 2. Samadhi:—state of quiescence when breath is controlled and thoughts are centred on God.

1448. Kriya (actions) is the worship of Lord Shiva inform, yoga is the worship of the formless one, Gnana is the advanced path in ripeness of time and Chariya is the adoration of the loving heart; which indeed is exalted.

1449. The four paths of worship give the four states of realization; the six schools of Vedanta—Siddhantha and all those truths are revealed by Nandhi descending from the Golden City, to redeem the doubting humanity.

1450. The ordination rite for self-surrender in Chariya worship in Samaya Dhiksha, the rite of repetition of Lord Shiva manthra in Kriya worship is Visesa in Chariya. Nirvana Dhiksha in Chariya helps purify the Kalas in yoga, and the Abhisheka rite in Chariya is for grace to be reached in Gnana.

6. Kriya

1451. There is One God who pervades the ten directions around. We cannot say that He is not in this direction or that. So, do take refuge under His Holy Feet, then, you will cross the roaring Sea of Karma and safely reach the shores of Beyond.

1452. You may adore Him with exceeding sandal fragrance, that grows atop on peaks in interior forests;You may worship Him with rare flowers that bloom in Heaven's garden's, but you will never reach His Holy Feet that is like flowers that shed 'Honey dew', unless you shed your fleshy attachments and realize Him in the depths of your heart.

1453. The Lord is your guide, so seek His Feet as does the yearning calf, and He will seat you amidst His children of wisdom. The Devas, the heavenly beings, bow low before Him; His love is great, as of the cow to her calf and His grace is bounteous beyond count.

Similar to the cow and the calf to describe the relationship, between God and the individual is as old as the Atharva Veda.

1454. She fashioned this world and all the universe that fills space in all the eight directions. He is one with His consort, sharing Himself with Her; it is the duty of the humans, here below, to adore Him, and it is true Bhakthi that does service a place in the Lord's abode.

1455. To begin with, the Bhaktha practises Chariya, Kriya, then as he is blessed with grace, he takes the pure yoga and in this way he reaches the path of Gnan; and in the end by the grace of the Guru he becomes one with Lord Shiva Himself. These four paths are the steps in the ladder to Shiva union.

1456. The Lord is resplendent as pure gold, His Feet are the lotus bloom, melting in love, I daily adore and pray to them to grant me His grace, and the Lord that is light within my bones, does reveal Himself to me.

Samaya, Videsa, Nirvana and Abhiseka are the four ordinations in Kriya worship also.

7.Yoga

1457. The yogis course the Kundalini through six centres and direct their mind to the singleness of AUM; they sit immobile like a wooden stake, impervious to tickle or to thrust, the Lord grants His grace, to the wise Yogins who thus set their purpose so high.

1458. You never can know Him, albeit through aeons and aeons of time, unless you have realized Him as timeless eternity. The Gods—Hari of the ocean bed and Aya (Brahma), the creator, have in vain sought Him, who is at the pinnacle, through countless vistas of time and He is beyond their understanding, beyond their reach.

1459. Shiva's divine grace blossoms out of Jeevas just so as the hidden fragrance wakes to life from within the flower, the yogi sitting unmoved like a painted picture, realises Him within and He is like the planted pole which the musk-cat embraces, to shed its fragrance.

1460. You say that you have realized God, and yet you have not seen Him who is only within you; but Nandhi, abides as subtley as fragrance within the flower; so, seek Him in singleness of your thought, then your darkness of impurities will vanish and the darkness that is the seed of birth and rebirth will be interminable.

1461. Birth and its accrued bonds can never be sundered either by manthra, song or the sixty-four arts. Then, I took to be path of yoga and here, I met the Sun-moon and fire on the way to the cranium and they showed me the Supreme Way.

1462. If you practise yoga in devotion, and if your yoga is devoted in true penance, then, you will become a true Tapasvin, you shall realize the true word, and of certain, you will be one with the Heavenly beings.

1463. If you practise yoga with care, you will be with the immortals and you will glimpse Him within you, but if you waver, then, you will reach the world of darkness, for truly, the kundalini fire that yoga kindles in you is the Gracious Lord, Himself.

1464. The monarchs that have righteously swayed the sceptre, the devout anchorities unnumbered in thousands, many, many, and many more have fallen due to the pursuit of yoga in fickleness. But, the myriad Siddhas, Devas and the three Supreme Beings, all redeemed, adore Him as their father.

1465. The yogi has three subdivisions in his path, the yoga-kriya that helps him to be the yogi that he is; the yoga-chariya that rids him of all desires and yoga in yoga that centres thought on the Sun within him; and I fixed my heart on the latter.

1466. The Yoga Samaya Diksha is initiation for diverse yoga efforts, Visesha Deeksha is for the achievement of eight-limbed yoga, Nirvana Diksha aids the yogi to glimpse the Divine and when he is granted Abhisheka ordination then, he is ripe for Siddha state.

8. Gnana (Spiritual Awareness or Supreme Wisdom)

1467. Here below, there is no ethical path, other than Gnana; Gnana path is the most exalted, there is no better religious faith too; nothing else, other than Gnana, can confer true liberation. They that are exalted in Gnana are truly exalted among men.

Gnana is the most exalted path and nothing else can confer final liberation.

1468. The mind springs out of the primal principles of sound (nadha) and out of the mind springs intelligence, egoity and will; they who have mastered these three and the mind's cogitational activity as well, have verily mastered Nadha and have truly attained Gnana.

Mastery over consciousness, egoity, will and the mind's cognizational activity is real mastery in Gnana.

1469. They say that by devotion the Jeeva first sojourns in the Lord's world, then, he comes to dwell in the Lord's proximity, further on, he receives the Lord's grace and in the end, he attains Gnana, in Sivohmic I and you union Jeeva will, himself become Lord Shiva.

1470. The unitive attainment of the Gnani is, that, Brahman shall be his impregnable abode, the universe becomes his kith and kin, all the diverse paths the world will present and all will be his of, verily he has realized the pure Gnana, free of doubt.

The Gnani deems Brahman as his impregnable abode, the Universe his kith and kin, and all contending faiths as one. He is truly the realized one.

1471. The Lord is of infinite grace, in His celestial city, there is love, light and eternal peace. The path of Gnana is the true path, to them that seek to know His form, understand His attributes and attain His Holy feet; this is the boat to cross life's turbulent waters.

Lover, Light and peace reign eternally in His celestial city, whose grade is infinite. The ultimate path to cross life's turbulent waters is to have an absolute cognition of the Lord and so to reach His Holy feet.

1472. The life-boat appears and greets him in his path; in whose thoughts Gnana ripens and swells; and thus does He reach the surging waters of the crescent moon's sphere and there rid of impurities, he, himself becomes the effulgent light.

1473. The Gnani embraces all four paths; but it is not so for the yogi until he becomes Mauni (silence); for him; kundalini yoga is performed in ardour; Chariya and Kriya too are his.

Gnana embraces all the four paths; Chariya-Kriya-Yoga and Gnana and the Gnani attains all the four stages they bring in.

1474. The Gnani attains all the four states, in Jnana; Jnana in Jnana is to transcend, the 'I' and 'Mine' yoga-in-jnana is to envision the light of Nadhantha and Kriya-in-Gnana is to seek liberation by good.

1475. He, who realizes Gnana in its four divisions has verily transcended the conflict of virtue and vice, has reached the farthest shores of truth and has glimpsed the mighty object. The Gnani attains unitive wisdom in the absolute, he is the immaculate Siddha, Shiva-Muktha.

1476. There are four initiation, rites in Gnana; Samaya initiates the search for the self, Viseha, the search for the Divine, Nirvana for the descent of the Lord's Grace and Abhiseka for the attainment of the Holy feet of the Divine Guru.

9. Sanmarga (Path of Knowledge)

1477. Only those who evolve thus, that is, glimpsing the light of the holy scriptures, revealing the word of the self-existent Shivam, losing their sense of ego, becoming Siddhas of Sivayoga and triumphing over death, can know the inner meaning of Sanmarga.

1478. The peerless Master-Nandhi of Saivam, who is honoured high, has shown us a holy path for the true redemption of souls; it is the divine path of Lord Shiva, Sanmarga's path for all the world to tread and be free for ever.

1479. They that, in diverse ways, render true devotion to the Guru-thus-seeing Him, adoring Him, Meditating on Him, touching Him, singing of His praises, bearing His Holy feet on their humbled heads, will indeed walk the path of Sanmarga that leads to liberation.

1480. They that have no true vision shall never know Shiva, will never become Shiva, nor will they be even Jeevas, the bondage of their births shall never, never be broken.

Sanmarga gives the true vision, breaking the fetters of birth.

1481. When you scorch the five impurities and listen to the voice of silence, then, you become a pure Mukhta; that I and (Muktha means while living, attain the Supreme Bliss) you merge into one, and by the unsulleyed grace that Gnana grants you will joy in the Divine Bliss. Verily, then you indeed become He by the Sanmarga path.

1482. God is where the Sanmargi is, his visage is the pedestal of Sakthi, I proclaim that to whatever path you follow, to see an assemblage of Sanmargis is to vision the Lord.

1483. Truly, Sanmarga is the purest path, if all paths Sanmarga alone grants God head through knowledge; the rest of the paths are for the unillumined. It is the way of renouncing impurities and transcending the limits of Thuriya consciousness. It is the way of I becoming He (Lord Shiva).

1484. The rest of the three paths open of themselves into that rare seeker in the path of Sanmarga; the path that seeks union with Lord Shiva is alone the true path. So, seek that path as the guiding word that the scriptures proclaim.

1485. Truly, they are the true Sanmargis who see their own selves, and all these, the bondage that keeps the Jeeva an alien to God and the karmas that flow from it, the Avasthas that the Self experiences, the primordial stuff that is matter's nucleus, the consciousness that entwines it and the million,

million mutations that pervade the Universe.

1486. The eternal truth is rending the bonds of the soul as under, conjoining him to the Lord, melting the heart that knows no melting and merging into the primal manifestness (Svaroopa). Sanmarga, truly, gives Jeeva the rest that knows no commotion ever.

1487. Sanmarga path alone is the divine path, for the Sanmargis ordained for the goal. There is no other path than this one, that leads to the one, they that cannot reach in straight, may yet climb, through yoga's path to reach it.

10. Ṣanmarga (Path of Yoga—Consideration of God as Friend)

1488. Sanmarga is itself Sahamarga; so by itself it highly leads to Supreme Mukthi. Other yogas that involve myriad births and deaths do not level to Gnana.

1489. They that do not follow the twelve-tiered path of Sahamarga; will neither know Guru, nor God, nor true faith. The Goddess of grace will frown at them and salvation will never be their portion; they will lose both, their stature and their kin.

1490. Infinite space, abiding light and omnipotent Sakthi are the abiding fruits of yoga-samadhi. They that delight in yoga samadhi are truly great siddhas.

1491. The Yogis may have both yoga and Bhoga (material pleasures); through yoga. Shiva's divine form is attained and through Bhoga they attain all earthly blessings. Thus, they may enjoy both, they, the immortal yogis.

1492. The Yogis, through this path of Sahamarga, pierve the adharas; purify their Nadies, envision the sixteen kalas and glimpse their heavenly radiance; then, their organs of sense; internal and external are all atrophied and they merge in Supreme Cosmic awareness.

1493. The Yogi with the sharp sword of his determinate will harries and subdues the five conflicting senses. The Lord whom the eighteen Gnanas seek emerges in this thought, truly, the yogi deserves our obeisance.

1494. The Lord is hard of shell like the wood-apple fruit. Even for the austere yogi who attains the glossy hue of the rich ripe fruit. He opens all of Himself like a rich mature fruit, to them whose hearts are ripe in love and taste the sweets of divine rapture.

11. Sathputhra Marga (Path of Kriya)—(Father/Son Relationship with God)

1495. The path of filiable piety is the way of true Kriya; the Kriya path, through yoga, leads to Gnana; transcending both, and uniting in Sakthi of the yoga state, is indeed the consummation of Sanmarga path.

1496. Other acts of reverence and these, such as, performing Poojas, reading the holy scriptures, praising the Lord, chanting His Holy name, practising penance, being truthful, bearing no envy, yourself cooking the offering for the Lord with having care, constitute the pure path of filial piety.

1497. They, the humming bees roam unceasingly from flower to flower and the snow-white swans float amidst lotus and blue-bells, they all, seek fragrant flowers, and yet, you who have beheld all this do not, even for a while, adore the Lord with flowers.

1498. His Holy Feet are our rich of refuge; His commandments are our battlements of defence. He is truly the finite shore of the surging tide of Jeevas on earth, thus, He pervades the seven worlds alike.

1499. Adore the Lord in diverse ways; Rise high, bend low, kiss and embrace Him; praise Him; sing Him; and pray at His Holy Feet, this will be your birth's fulfillment. Do adore Him in trembling love and He, indeed shall be your own beloved.

1500. I stand in reverence and adore my Lord; I prostrate in humility and praise Him; forever and ever I shall worship the Divine Light of beauty. You too should seek him with fragrant flowers; the more, you adore Him, the Lord of Heavenly beings, the fuller He reveals Himself unto you.

1501. Listen, you worldly men, the Chariya path that you stand in leads to the Kriya path that exalts you. Then, your primordial Pasas shall lie prostrate and you will live in unending bliss forever.

12. Dasa Marga (Path of Devotion—Master/Servant Relationship)

1502. Lighting the lamps gracefully, gathering fragrant flowers, humbly smearing the holy ground with paste, softing sweeping, singing the Lord's praise and counting the crystal beads, anointing Him in diverse ways—doing all these requirements of temple service, belongs to Dasa Marga (Dasa means servant).

1503. Tossed in doubt, they say this is the Primal Being, that is the Primal Being, saying thus, and not knowing the true path, they move farther and farther away from it, and do not worship. Hold fast to the path of Chariya; pursue this appointed way and seek the king of kings; this, in truth, shall quell all doubts that swell within you.

1504. All these, meditating on the moon Nadi on the left, shifting on to the sun Nadi on the right the Yogins who perform thus, worship at the Feet of the One, and the worship the celestial Beings offer daily to the Lord—all these only begin in the ultimate path of Chariya.

1505. He, the Lord, is sweet melody and appears entwined in divine love to them who adore His Holy Feet in the abiding rapture of their hearts and hold Him as the apple of their eyes. The Celestial Beings seek the Lord chanting His glory in a thousand names.

1506. It is of no avail that you read the holy scriptures, perform Poojas and gather flowers in clusters; you can never realize the Lord so long as your heart is like a pebble dropped into a dark pool over-spread with the mass of ignorance. The Lord who is in your heart's love, is blue-throated (Thiruneelakandam), He is the pure light.

13. Salokyam (In God's World-Oneness with the God)

1507. The four stages of attainment—Salokya, Samipa, Saroopa and Sayujya are reached from Chariya in gradation. The path of Chariya leads to Salokha, that in turn to Sameepa and Sameepa to Saroopa, and ultimately to Para of Infinite Space (Sayujya) beyond which there is no other state.

Saloka, Samipa, Saroopa and Sayujya, respectively, mean'Being in the same world as the Lord', 'Being with Him continually,' 'Adopting His form' and 'united with Him'. These are the different ways of imagining Oneself to be in, during worship.

1508 There are four sacraments in Kriya worship, Samaya sacrament prepares the heart to be a tabernacle of God, Vishesha sacrament installs firm faith, Nirvana helps to realize the truth of faith and Abhisekha confers the state of Supreme Samadhi.

14. Sameebam (In God's Proximity)

1509. Pasa Gnana (worldly knowledge) becomes Pasu Gnana (spiritual wisdom) in Saloka; in Samipa it becomes Arul Gnana (Grace-knowledge) in Saroopa, it is transformed into Pathi Gnana (God-knowledge) and in Sayujya it is dissolved forever.

15. Saarupam (In God's Form)

1510. The state of Saroopa is, no doubt, reached through the eight-fold yoga way. But this Saroopa state cannot be attained unless it be Sanmarga-in yoga. The yoga way only leads to diverse bodily Siddhis. None of these, but only the pure way of Gnan-in-yoga is essential to realize the Saroopa state.

Sanmarga-in-yoga is identical with Gnana-in-yoga. Thirumoolar explains that mere practices of yoga without 'Sanmarga' (worshipful faith and good conduct) will only produce Siddhis (miraculous powers) but will not lead to liberation.

1511. All things, living and non-living, are themselves transformed into gold, as they reach the Golden-Mount of Meru, even so, they who reach the world to the Divine Master attain the divine light form, of the king of Kailash.

16. Saiyujyam (One with God)

1512. The path of Saivam describes four stages in the soul's pilgrimage towards God; it is Saivam, when the self forges a kindred tie with Lord Shiva (in Saloka); it is Saivam, when the soul realizes itself and nears God (in Sanupa); it is Saivam, when it leaves Sanupa (and reaches Saroopa); it is Saivam, when it enjoys the final bliss of Sivanandha, the inextricable union in Saiyujya.

The Saiyujya Marga is, it appears the same as the one termed 'Sahaja' in tantricism which is 'the Marga or way of spiritual exercise which is the earliest or the most natural. It is also the term for ultimate reality among the Sahajiyas'; i.e. those who believe in this path.

1513. Saiyujya is the state of Jagra-Atita-the state beyond consciousness, it is to abide forever in Upasantha, the peace that passes all understanding, and finally to become Shiva Himself, experiencing the infinite power of inward bliss; for ever and ever.

17. Sathinipadham (Descent of Grace)

1514. There, She was the virgin lady of grace in the dark corner of the chamber of primal stiff, intent on consorting with the blind old man—the immortal soul; She rent his veil of night, wooed him with diverse temptations, showered him with many a full favour and took him to Her bosom in Holy wedlock.

In the dark corner of the chamber of primal stuff, the Goddess of grace courted the 'Blind old man'—immortal soul and in marriage took him to Her bosom.

1515. If you meditate on the primal source from whence sprang the evil senses, you will know it is the land of becoming, the ambrosia of the realized. Those who are given the clear vision that is sweet as nectar are truly on the infinite ground of Sakthi's highest seeking.

1516. The primal Sakthi grants abiding grace and releases Jeeva from enveloping gloom. She rows him across the sea of myriad births and lands it on the shores of the bliss of truth, united in the Lord of Heavenly Beings, who are themselves as yet unfree from the obscuration of impurity.

1517. The presence of God and the Goddess of Grace, like a sudden shaft of light pierces and illumines the gloom of bewildering ignorance, like when groping in a chamber enveloped in thick gloom. The Lord Nandhi is worshipped in the blossom of the heart.

Mandhatharam (Slow Pace)

1518. She tempted the soul with guiles, took him to Her bosom, shook him from stupor, dispelled his Karmic hordes and destroyed them to the roots. She filled him with the rapture, lifted the veil of his ignorance, granted him with many a favour and then, bestowed on him Her grace that illumines.

1519. They who have sported in the waters of the virgin grace, will no more wallow in the filthy waters of the virgin's lust; if they but seek to sport in the Holy Virgin's waters of grace, they will not take any more births in future.

1520. He is the Red One (destroyer), the Dark One (preserver) the White One (Creator) the Green One (redeemer). They who know Him thus, will free of doubt certainly seek Him. Remember that His sinewy arms skinned the dark massive elephant and downed it for a vesture; do therefore, seek Him and adore Him.

The Lord plays the multi role of Destroyer, Preserver, Creator and Redeemer. Realization of this truth and adoration of Him will make the Jeeva feel the might of His sinewy arms.

The significance of attributing different colours to Lord Shiva's form is explained here.

1521. The passage of time's flood is infinite, yet they say that He and His consort stand as One. He is verily the unfailing proof of labour rewarded readily for them that adore Him daily in devotion.

Shiva and Sakthi are One and the same, so practise this in pure devotion daily. He is truly the unfailing proof.

1522. To vision the Light that snone from the twin in Unison, was granted to me. It was verily the Divine Light of the Ancient One, in whose matted locks festooned with flowers, the bees dance drunk with nectar; they who waited in patience and prayer indeed saw Him and had their darkness dispelled.

Thiviram (Rapid Race)

1523. This damsel of grace is the garden of the heavenly father. She approaches you, reveals the mystery of the birth beyond count and also destroys their very seed; and then, She makes your vision the Primal One, this, indeed, is the fruit of Her grace.

1524. She, the damsel of shapely breasts and delicate beauty, is of the mountain regions; if you adore Her in devotion, She will cut asunder the bonds of birth, grant the prowess of mighty tapas, scorch the soul's forgetfulness and lead you to liberation's path.

Sakthi is the Goddess of the mountain regions and of exotic blossoms. Vision of the Primal One is the fruit of Her grace. This is granted when the bride of grace, seated in the garden of the heavenly bridegroom, destroys the very seeds of birth.

1525. He is the Lord of all space in eight directions. Bear His Holy feet on your head and He will appear to you with His consort of grace wreathed in clusters of fragrant blooms in Her twisted tresses, and for those who are thus made wise the blue flame of Her floating grace will illumine their path for ever.

Near the Holy Feet of the Lord are all worlds. He will descend with His lady companion—Sakthi of Mighty Grace—who will enlighten the path of the devotees.

1526. Seek very closely, the soft flame of wisdom will grant you, the peerless gift of grace, do as I do, showering flowers at His feet; when you adore Him; then, He will draw near you whom nothing can ever near; He is truly the pervasive life of all worlds.

Wisdom gives the unsurpassable boon of grace and when grace visits, the Lord whom nothing can equal, draws near. When grace descends Jeeva is purififed. He, then mingles in Lord Shiva.

Theevira Tharam (More Rapid Pace)

1527. When the Jeeva attains the state of neutrality to

deeds; good and evil, then divine grace in the form of Guru descends, removing all attributes and implanting Gnana that is like a heavenly cool shade. The Jeeva thus gets rid of egoity and other three impurities and will merge in union with Lord Shiva.

1528. The Goddess of long tresses dances in rapture in the vast space where there is neither night nor day; Make no sound, think of Her and in silence woo Her; She draws you unto Her bosom in all endearment and grants you Her favours. Truly, She is the Paraparai, the Supreme Power.

1529. He is the Sun and the Moon that dispels darkness. He is the peerless flame, that Supreme Lord, the Light on the path. He is the master that illumined the Light within me, He entered in me, lighted up the corporeal body and abided with me forever and ever.

18. Arusamaya Prinakkam (Critique of Formal Religions)

1530. The six faiths congregrate severally and yet, not one of it knows the God within, their adherents drop deep, into the pit of illusion and fastened hard by familiarities of bodndage, they shake and tremble in vain impotence.

The six faiths, being tied fast to the earthly fetters shake and shiver in vain, unable to cognize God, who is within.

It can be safely affirmed that the 'six faiths' that Thirumoolar refers to here are not those described in *Sadharsam Sangaraha*.

1531. He is the Munificient One, who hides in your heart and yet pervades all, The Lord Supreme of austere penance is seated on the lotus of our hearts; in stealth, this cunning Master. Thief enters this hollow abode of human flesh and then leaves it. No one ever knows His deep design.

The Lord, the pinnacle and the magnificent seated in the lotus of our hearts enters this hollow abode of human flesh and then silently parts. This deep design of His is beyond the apprehension of the formal faiths. Intense faith and steadfastness help in the realisation of the omnipresence of the Lord.

1532. Some say, the Lord is within you and without you, then surely, My Lord is within you and without you, to those who say that He is neither within you nor without you, then, surely He is nowhere for them.

1533. They who founded the six faiths, did not find Him; the six faiths do not talk to Him. So you, yourself seek Him in great faith and be resolved of all doubts; then, surely you will enter your father's mansion.

1534. Proclaim that the six faiths are nothing but a dreary waste, that there is nothing except Shiva and there is no penance except it be done for Him. So seek Nandhi of mighty penance and you will indeed by truly redeemed.

Shiva is the only Lord, and the six faiths are but a dreary waste. Being materialistic, the six faith do not lead to the final state. Devotion to Lord Shiva grants certain liberation.

1535. They of six faiths sought the Lord only to gain a heavenly state; they did not seek to be rid of the thorns of bondage, and so they do not know to be rid of this world's materiality.

1536. The path of Lord Shiva alone is the sole path. Other paths only lead to earthly sorrows and for sure birth in bondage returns to you. So you walk in the holy path and when the one appears, the triad impurities that encompass your destruction will of themselves meet their own destruction.

The path of Shiva alone is our defence from earthly sorrows. It is the sole path that leads to ultimate liberation through annihilation of Pasa.

1537. For sooth, here below, the faiths are a hundred in number and the six faiths too are in the swollen stream. All these faiths are not true faiths, they can never take you to the path of Param nor can they take you to the goal they boast of.

Neither the six faiths nor the swollen stream of hundreds of other faiths, tall as their claims are, can lead you to the path of param.

1538. The contenting paths are like the braying asses. They do not seek the pure Shiva, who is all pervasive, by the right path and so, they are not free from impurities, instead, they will grow insane and be entangled in the whirl of birth and death forever.

1539. When those who are assailed by doubts and those

who are freed from doubts comingle together, they persevere in their pursuit and drive the wild beasts of twin Karma to the caves; then, they will reach the Supreme Lord-Goal and be rid of the terrors of the wild; they will then see the path that leads to Param.

1540. God is far away, He is near to hand, He is rid of ailments; He is of immortal name Nandhi; He is transparent to those who have unwavering vision and elusive to those who are tossed in doubt. Such people do not know the mysterious purpose for which this flesh body is fashioned.

1541. Verily, it is the seed of twin Karma and the worst of all curses to be born and to live again and again in this earth below. If you only listen to Him who knows the origin of swil that is birth and death, then, you will no more seek the ways of the perishing man.

The cycle of births and deaths is the lane of the soul, and the seed of the coupled Karma. So, listen to him, who knows the origin of this cycle.

1542. He, that is Nadha and bears the name of Nandhi, is the Supreme Lord. All the Holy ones hail Him as the Great God, you too will make no distinction, but lift your hands in prayer to Him the Supreme Being, and the Primal One shall be such reveal Himself to you.

1543. He is Hara, Divine Father and the Primal Lord Shiva; He entered the heart as implacable truth; but if the hearts of the devotees seek alien path, they do not know Him and He is far, far away from them.

1544. The heavenly Lord who is tender-hearted knows our goal; He is the effulgent Sun who guides the destiny of the heavenly beings of great wisdom. He is of pure crystal hue, so think of Him in unsulled thought for. He has laid for us the path of virtue that is precious.

1545. Do not be tossed in such frail human doubts as this is the right path, that the right path and so on. Seek the being who is beyond the wilderness of doubts for. His is the form that is flawless.

1546. The immortal Devas and the saintly Tapasvins took the true path, and so reached the true goal and merged in

Shiva as One. But they that followed false faiths and did not receive His grace, lost their way and wandered forever.

1547. He is the light within you. The true path of becoming is to know how to reach Him; you will know no contradiction if you know this. The end of your goal is this Supreme Path. They are only folks who are poor in spirit that do not know merging in the Divine Light.

1548. There is a true path for the journey. They who follow the swampy worldly path see only the mirage. They that avoid the sorrowful path of swirling Karma will cross evil safely and will sure worship at the Lord's Feet.

Worldly paths are nothing but a mirage. So give up the sorrowful path of swirling karma and cross evil. Surely you will worship at the Feet of the Lord.

1549. Your holiness consummates in walking in the true path. The hose of your Karmic deeds scatters and flees away. You must leave the torturous path of the Karmic ridden men of the world and journey onward, straight inside. You will for certain stand in the presence of the Lord of the Heavenly Beings.

19. Niracharam (Dissension Refuted)

1550. The heavenly beings who are immortal as the Himalayan mountains, received the six Darshans. They say that they learned them all and thus attained to other world. But, truth is in intimacy within those who have attained divine tranquillity.

1551. They who bow their heads at the feet of the Lord of spreading matted locks bedecked with pure Kondrai bloom, will become like Him. But they do not yearn for Him in constant eagerness, will be immersed in sorrow and will keep sighing eternally here below.

1552. Do not despair, you, who have lost your better nature and thus sit and bewail, but seek the Lord in true penance and the Lord of the Heavens will wipe away your tears and grant you greatness and you will then know no more births.

Neither wail nor despair. This will affect your better nature. Instead, atone for your sins and perform penance. The Lord will wipe your tears and grant you, greatness.

1553. They are His friends, who seek the finite Truth. They who do not seek Him the misery-way of the worldly men; they will in vain be born again and again, enveloped in the darkness of bondage. The Lord is like richly laden clouds that drop gentle rain of Heavenly grace to those, who seek the true path.

1554. The boat of life, guides by divine wisdom, discharges its cargo quickly at the ancient city; these wretched men of ignoble deeds having seen this unerring prospect do not think of His Holy Feet in replete devotion.

1555. When you say that the only being, the eternal being, dwells within you, these ignorant men laugh low; but if these poor folk only seek Him within in prayer, then, they will meet Him—the peerless one.

1556. They who pursue false faiths do not wake to the inner light of AUM within them, they woe not of approaching death and joy not in the ego-effaced ensuring bliss. They do not seek the end of recurring birth. Sadly, they pursued the unending path of contending faiths and stood-forlorn, lost forever, in their false faith.

20. Inner Truths

1557. He, the ancient one, in the days of yore; created the beings of earth and heaven in divine order; the six faiths seek the feet only of the one primal peerless God and He pervades in all of them in appropriate measure.

The ancient Lord, the creator of all worlds, pervades all the six inner faiths.

1558. The Great City is One, the roads that lead to it are six; thus, the six faiths are born. They that contend that this is true, and this is false, are like the dogs that bark in ire to their own echo at the hill-side.

The Lord is the 'Great City' to which the six road (six inner faiths) lead. They who stand in contentions all similar to the dogs that bark at their own echo from the hill-side.

1559. He is the incomparable Lord of the magnificent path of Saivam; He is of Divine lustre who breathes the eternal life of grace, He is the Lord of all Universe, the source of all joy; the beloved of the truly great. Come, stand apart, seek and realize Him and be redeemed.

1560. Shiva laid the ancient divine path that leads to the eternal home. It is He who is sought after by another paths also. Seek Him in this way and you will duly find him within yourself.

1561. The six faiths that profess the means to becoming are by themselves all only blind alleys; no good comes by following them alone. For all life to pursue the true path of becoming is only the path of divine kundalini Sakthi, the blossom-vine that courses through the six centres.

The six faiths that proclaim the means to 'becoming' can do no good by themselves. Kundalini, the blossom vine that courses through the six yogic centres within, is the pervasive force in all of them.

1562. In the past, I sought Him in narrow paths and strayed, but now I have realized the path of Hara ! But, alas ! He has been standing before me like a beacon light in the firmament, guiding my voyage across the sea of my soul's longing.

1563.The path of Lord Shiva is the proven path that leads them to Hara; it is the royal path that renowned souls have walked. Do seek, enter and persevere in the divine path that took the devout to cosmic space.

1564. Still your wandering thoughts, chant the sacred syllable, 'S' and preserve so in the path of Hara and you will envision the effulgent primal light.

1565. The Primal Lord, the tender shoot of Jnana belongs to the lady of lightning form, to the Vedic fire of Brahmins, and to them who think of Him. When you glimpse His loving signs, then you know that you walk in the path of Lord Shiva.

1566. They whose souls are caught in myriad machinations and do not know discrimination, they do not know the mighty Hara's path and do not see the truth. But they who follow Hara's path, certainly reach His Feet of grace with all senses uplifted and He savours the bliss.

1567. The Holy Nandhi who is the acclaimed master of the Saiva faith has shown a way, which is the Master's way of redemption. He did chalk out this, divine path of Saiva, for those here below to walk in the trail of Sanmarga and be free for ever.

1568. When mad men who contend that this is the right faith and that the right faith. My Lord Nandhi thus sees and smiles in pity. Whatever be the place of birth, the form of faith followed is not important. They whose mind is attuned to infinity will surely enter the city of God.

1569. Shiva has five faces and with his downward looking visage for Jeeva, He has six faces in all. The Lord all by Himself sports the garland of heads that truly is the human aspect of the Godly One.

Shiva has six faces (even as there are six faiths). One face (Athomuka—which looks downward for Jeeva's liberation.

1570. The Primal Lord spanned the seven worlds and stands as the sea and the myriad life here below. And in union with Parasakthi, that knows no separation. He pervades all-verily, God is the beginning and the end of all.

1571. Though the immortal beings, Devas and Vidyadharas sought Him, they knew Him not, but pursuing the proven path of Shiva. I reached His Feet of grace to adore Him, and so I realized the bliss of here and hereafter.

1572. The mystery of life's goals is indeed baffling. It is baffling why it is made into six systems. It is a baffling mystery by far how a veritable macrocosm gets imprinted into the shedding sheaths of this body microcosm.

Life's goal is the realization of the macrocosm in the microcosm—the over-soul in the self soul—the mysterious tremendum.

Tanthra Five concluded

6

Tanthra Six (Viyamalaahamam)

1. Holy Darshan of Siva Guru

1573. He taught me meekness of the spirit and infused the light of devotion in me. He granted me the grace of His Feet; after holy interrogation, and testing me entirely. He revealed the real, the unreal and the real-unreal to me. Certainly, the Shiva Guru is the Lord Shiva Himself.

1574. Gathering the strands of my fetters He knotted them together, and then wrenched them off. Freeing me thus from my fond body. He led me straight to Mukthi. Behold, the presence of the divine guru is of such holy potent.

1575. If the Guru confers His grace, you will then attain the miraculous powers of the eight Siddhis, the immaculate purity of the eight Sakthis, the Supreme baptismal act that turns Jeeva into Lord Shiva, and the mystic powers of occult yoga, Manthra Shakthi and Gnans.

1576. He is beyond all worlds and yet, here below He bestows His abundant grace on the good and the devout and works for the salvation of all in love. Thus is the Holy Guru, Shiva, the pure being, whose praise is beyond speech.

1577. The Holy Guru is truly a Deva. By his divine art, He makes me perceive all things in three categories, the

Gurupara in benign compassion Sunders the bonds of Pasu-pasa by His sacred precepts and makes me drink the milk of Mukthi.

1578. The Guru comes, purifies and grants godhead. The witless ones of faulty vision do not see this; but the holy ones take to Him in endearment as like kith and kin, and worship Him as the Lord Himself.

1579. It is only with the blessings of the Guru that the aspirant learns to dissolve the false in the true, to derive the omnipotent might of truth, to possess the bounty of grace of splenderous Lord Shiva and to realize the fantasy of the eight famous Siddhis.

1580. The Shiva Gnani is none but Shiva Himself. And they who seek the feet of Shiva will in sooth gain the wonderous Tathwa Mukthi. The Supreme liberation is their sure reward and they will no more be in the cycle of births.

1581. Nandhi, saying that the Guru is none but Lord Shiva. Many do not realize that guru is Lord Shiva Himself. Shiva will be your Guru and guide too. In truth, the Guru is Lord who surpasses all speech and thought.

1582. Let all your thoughts be thoughts of Lord Shiva, and the Lord by His grace will reveal all to you. If your thoughts are Shiva-Saturated then, He will abide in you closely.

1583. No one knows the intent of Nandhi, My Father, the Blessed, the King of kings, who of Himself came to seek me in the truth's way, to those who rejoice in Him as the Nandhi of heavenly might, truly He is the peerless luminosity of crimson twilight fire.

1584. When the Guru Himself does not impart all these—the Siddhis that are a veritable treasure trove, the Mukthi that is finite salvation the heavenly grace that vanquishes doubts and fears and the Gnana that is the essence of the Vedas, you will never, never learn them at all.

1585. Bhakthi and spiritual resoluteness (Vairagya) are the seeds of the transcendental state; the attitude of oneness with Lord Shiva-Shiva and I are one, in turn, leads to Sivoham and in Sivoham, the Gnana for mukthi shoots, and this shoot shall be easily yours, only if Sakthi bestows Her grace.

1586. The Lord ordained for you, of yore, this life of pleasure here below, that you may attain great pleasure. When in resolve your mind reaches to Him, when He, of Himself, reveals Himself to you.

1587. When you realize the Gnana of Shiva you will achieve the luminous Siddhis and attain the resplendent Mukthi; when your Gnana of Shiva reaches to Supreme Shiva, then, it will yield the bliss of Shivanandha.

1588. I cognized and realized all this infinite space; adoring Him with replete devotion. I received His divine grace; now I have passed all remembrance of exceeding ignorance and have for ever bidden adien to recurring birth.

1589. He is the Lord of all living creation and yet no one knows of His existent state; I cut the tangle that separated Him from me and alas ! I met the Lord, the seed of all causal phenomena.

2. Grace of Guru's Feet

1590. Rise in loving praise of the Holy Lord and having risen; melt for Him in piety; then, the divine Guru who has scorned the fetters of Pasa comes and lays His hand on your head and alas; the rapturous grace of His Holy Feet wells up in you.

1591. Even as my master granted me the grace of His Feet, He made me the head of all and investing me with the Gnana sword of replace might, He placed the crown of abounding grace on my head and proclaimed that I shall forever hold way over this land of deliverance--He did all these, descending here below, on Earth.

1592. Discarding the four divine forms, He assume human form and Himself came as exalted guru, signifying the Mudhra of Gnana; it was He, Nandhi, my good saviour, who of yore blessed me and planted His feet of grace on me.

1593. Like a sea where no wave lashes, there was neither speech, nor feeling, neither self nor over-self and He made me unite in Shivam; He granted me the boundless form that transcends the four states; Nadha and the rest. Alas ! it was all beyond words.

By making me unite in Shivam, He granted me the boundless form that transcends the four states—Nadha, Nadhantha, Kala and Kalanttha.

1594. My divine preceptor Nandhi seized all three forms of life. He assumed the Mudhra of Gnana and drew me to His benign feet; bereft of speech, I melted in bliss-thus did He work my eternal redemption.

All the three forms of life—gross, subtle and causal.

Nandhi, my divine preceptor, transcending all three states—form, formless and form/formless—assumed the Mudhra of Gnana. Drawing myself towards his benign feet, I worked my way to liberation.

1595. He cleansed me of my blemishes, transformed me into Supreme Shivam and immersed me into His infinite bliss that is beyond, beyond words; The fire of His grace scorches not yet the three Seas of my impurities it drank dry and annihilating my primal ego to its traces. He granted me His Feet of grace and abides in me forever.

1596. Nandhi, my Supreme Lord gently planted His loving Feet into my bosom, on my eyes and over my head. He laid the path for me, showed me the truth and settled the course of my destiny. Truly, I cannot describe all that.

1597. He, my Great Nandhi, placed His hallowed Feet on my head, fixed his benign gaze on me and granted me the mighty form, and saw too the end of all births to come.

1598. The Gnana of the Holy Feet frees you from imprisoned impurities, takes you to the world of Shiva and makes you Lord Shiva, Himself, The Gnana of the Holy Feet is Siddhi and Mukthi too.

1599. The Karma of yore that will distort your thoughts when the master does not bless you with the grace of His feet on your crown; Only when the resplendent Lord of milk-white brow places His Feet on you, only then are you truly instructed.

1600. I reached the cool shelter of His triumphant lotus feet, that stands as a crims on pillar of flame, that defied the grasp even of divine Maha Vishnu. And there, the Primal One saw the external denouement of the fleshy cage that held my soul as a hoary captive.

1601. The crowned monarchs at best may sway three worlds; but the power of those who reach His Holy Feet shall know no bounds. Knew that the Heavenly beings attired in kingly diadems only turned his vassels and thus became blemishless free forever.

1602. I treasured His hoary feet in the depths of my heart, and so, shunned the deceitful cause of the scorching senses, swam past the dangerous swirls of good and bad karmas and tasted the nectar of the truth which is the end of all Vedas.

1603. The sages of yore bore the blissful and hoary feet of the lord full of their crowns, trod the path of truth—the goal of the pure ones. May you too reach those Holy Feet.

1604. My Lord's twin feet are truly all manthra and all medicine, all tanthras and all wisdom, all beauty and the pure way.

3. Gnathru-Gnana-Gneaya (Knower, Knowledge-Known)

1605. Do incessantly seek the goal of Sivanandha and the primordial Pasas will not enmesh you here, whenever if envelopes you, you only have to stand firm and throw your egoity out, then, the ambrosial eternal bliss will be yours.

1606. Knowledge and its attributes will be vouchsafed to those who pursue the object knowledge; the subject who seeks the object will merge in the object. They who have cognised the object of knowledge through knowledge will have knowledge of union with the object.

They who have sought and apprehend the object of knowledge through knowledge possess the knowledge of the union with the object.

1607. The two categories:—You and He, see them both in you and He; offer the flowers to 'You' at the feet of He and No more will it be proper for you to say 'Your' and 'He'.

'You' becomes 'He' when the flowers 'You' is offered at the feet of the mighty 'He'.

1608. He, rid of thirty-six Tathwas, elevated me and enveloped me in the infinite expanse of the spirits. Through the subject-object identity, He dispelled my ignorance, imparted the state of performance and transformed me into divine Shiva. Thus, He, Nandhi of blessed memory redeemed me.

Enveloping me in the infinite expanse of the spirit. He, Nandhi of the blessed memory, impated to me the state of permanence, ultimately changing me into Shiva Divine. Thus, Nandhi, worked for my liberation in Gneaya.

1609. I was like the witless here below who knew not knowledge for ignorance. He, Nandhi of hallowed name taught me the distinction between the two and made me know myself (Twam Pada), transformed me into Para (Tathpadha) and made me known to Shiva (Asipadha).

1610. He, the Nandhi of immortal fame showed wonders and blessed me to have the vision that the yes have not seen, the message that the ears have not heard, the rapture that cloys not, the union that has not been had, the Nadha that ceases not and the Bodha that arises at Nadha's end.

1611. They who have mastered the Divine Mauna (utter silence) will reach the very bliss of Mukthi, and all the Siddhis of themselves would evolve in perfection, and seek them into the silent word (Ajapa or Soham). Mastering Mauna thus, they will gain the power to perform, the divine acts—creation, preservation, dissolution, obfuscation and granting of grace.

1612. They who sat in yoga, thus joyous at the luminiscent feet of the Guru, having achieved the three divine Mudhras, having directed, the breath unto the three centres and having coursed its ryhthm in four-finger-measure-have forever sundered all bonds and are never to be born again or die again.

Sambavi, Bhairavi, Kesari or Chimudhra, Gnana Mudhra and yoga mudhra. Some refer to the three categories Jnathuru, Jnana and Jneaya as mudhras—Tripulika Jnana; but it does not seem appropriate here, as the three Mudhras are referred to in connection with yoga. Three centres—Sun-Moon and fire.

1613. As the Supreme Gnani holds the three mudhras of divine potent, He attains three higher forms. The Jeeva that is Jnathru (knower) in rapturous dance enters Jnaeya and Himself becomes the primal form of the spirit.

4. Renunciation

1614. My Lord of resplendent glory, who is beyond birth and death can be reached by the penance of renunciation. Pray incessantly sing His praise and the Lord of the Heavens will show you the land of Dharmas.

1617. By committing a million follies they forget that they are born and die a myriad times and they are closely enveloped in the darkness of Mala. When at last the hidden grace of Shiva bursts forth and chases the night away then it is the right moment for the soul to renounce, and when He does renounce then, He becomes a radiant light.

1618. The renunciate Lord is dharma. He is birthless and kinless. He abides in the wilds and lives by alms. You insensate ones, know that He has renounced all and to all those who renounce, He sunders, their bonds of birth.

1619. He laid the path and planted thorns alongside it, the thorns of temptation will prick those who deviate from the path and those who do not deviate, the thorns do not prick them.

1620. The five senses held me in ambush. Indeed I am not interested in spotting my failings or demanding tribute for my virtues. I stand in penance firmly seeking the hallowed feet of the dancing Lord who rides on the sacred bull.

1621. The Heavens poured when the ploughman ploughed and by the ploughman's ploughing, it flowered in time. Then, the ploughman left it to the ploughwoman, to watch, guard and tender the flowers that are likened to her eyes. Thus, the ploughman forever ceased all efforts at ploughing further.

The ploughman ploughed at the right moment and grace blossomed in abundance. Then he left it to the ploughwoman, to guard and tender, himself ceasing from ploughing further. That is, when grace blossoms, Tapas (penance) ceases.

1622. The Lord of renunciation is the shining light above. He is a friend to all who have surmounted death's days. He is devoid of desires; hence He is the guiding light of all those who have renounced darkness. His Feet will be within reach, only to those who abandon the world.

1623. The four anthakaranas fill the thorny hole of

enjoyment in the one serpent (Jeeva), but with five hoods (senses). It raised its hood and danced away in the twin body—the subtle and the gross. Then it merged (kundalini) into a single hood when the distraction of the senses cease into the very body within.

1624. There is little comfort in the thought that the Primal Lord is the first of all renunciates. It may take many lives to reach the feet of Lord Shiva. It is not that easy that He may come by you. Who knows how and when the Loved One comes.

1625. The nine orifices were sheathed in the armour of Sakthi of lily-wreathed tresses, when the mystic exit opened. The captain that is the breath of life climbed the mast of bitter negation and looked atop from the roof of the cranium and there, He beheld the budded vine bloom as in the sacred and lofty temple within. The yogi climbed the mast of bitter negation, and from the cranium roof watched a distance the mystic flower and the budded vine (grace of Sakthi) bloom as in the sacred temple within.

5. Tapas (Penance)

1626. The heart of the holy, with all passions stilled, does not tremble in fear, but enjoys unruffled calm. There is neither death, nor pain, nor night, nor day, nor fruits of karma to experience; this truly the state of the desire-renounced.

1627. Who knows the mystery of life, the origin of the earth and the might of the pure deeds of penance, except they who receive the grace of the Lord. The rest do not know anything of Supreme Tapas.

1628. The many Tapaswins who perform incessant penance and live by alms have no life hereafter, all blessings of spiritual wealth will be showered on them and they will attain the power to end all births to be.

1629. The Tapaswins perform splendrous penance, being transfixed in mind, tortured in body and stout of heart. They remain impervious to temptations even though the celestials king and others, however mightly, descend to them and tempt them, their determined thought on Lord Shiva remain firm.

1630. The Lord is hidden and yet not hidden. He, of the spreading matted locks, the gold-hued, does not appear to the naked eyes. No one, but only those of hard penance can near Him. So, hasten to adore Him, the Mighty one of the white moon crest.

1631. He—the Primal one, made me reach, here and now, the life of bliss that is to be hereafter. When the mind is transfixed, it reaches God and He of Himself, surely reveals Himself.

1632. The kings, their ministers and their elephantine hordes perished amidst the raging tumult of hatred. But the Tapaswins by fixing their sight on divine Gnana and universal love, became immortals with their eyelids batting not.

1633. Come apart from the clever argumentation of contending theology and for a brief while, look inward; that one look will drive the nail into the coffin of birth and end its recurring cycle forever.

Neither argumentation of contending theologies nor knowledge of scriptures can end the recurring cycle of births. Look inward even for a brief while. That can take you far.

1634. They who do not know to transform the self, do not seek penance. But you need Tapas, when you aspire for Gnana, Tapas is not needed when you are in Sahamarga of yoga and when you attain Gnana Samadhi.

6. Abuse of Penance

1635. You need not pray, if the soul of souls enters in you, you need not adore, if Shiva truly abides in you, you need not die; if you attain samadhi and you need not renounce, if you do not go to the way of the senses.

1636. You need no shouting when you withdraw in understanding; you need no speaking when you are seated in Samadhi, you need no baptismal rites when you stand detached and you need no meditation, when you have reached the actionless state.

Baptismal rites do not matter when you are detached, nor is meditation needed in the stilled actionless—state of Samadhi that transcends all meditation.

1637. They who perform true penance and speak pure truth will know the fruits thereof; they who stand in the righteous way will enjoy the fruit thereof and they who are great on earth will reap heaven's fruit.

1638. I did penance in oneness of mind and witnessed the Lord; triumphant feet; in the eagerness of quest I did penance and witnessed Shiva-State; that you perform in the yearning of your heart is alone penance. Nothing avails the penance of those who do not perform thus.

1639. The true Tapaswins by swimming across the seven seas of the mind, they reached their heaven; let those who are tossed about in the sea of births listen only to the holy commandments of the Tapaswins; then they can for sure see Nandhi face to face.

1640. Unsheath your sword of Gnana from the mind's scabbard, flash it across the bonds of Pasa, hacking both of them and watch yourself, lest your five senses run wild; then the light that is born of penance will become the light of the self.

Unsheath your sword of Gnana from thought's scabbard and snap the fetters of Pasa. Then will the light of penance dawn; which become the light of the Self.

1641. He stands in intimacy within us, so pray that He may grant you Bhakthi, prostrate that He may grant you Mukthi, and truly, it is penance alone that makes Munis divine.

1642. I wove a garland, all for my father, by gathering the tender leaves and variegated flowers, yet, I did not see the gushing waters of His grace; I even scanned the lofty lores of scriptures and still my heart ebbed low, but when I stood in penance, I touched cranium heights and alas ! I met my Lord.

Formal worship and analysing the lofty lores of scriptures will not take you to God. Penance is the Supreme means which confers the vision of the Lord.

1643. The Lord lends His grace and let no harm happen to the devout Tapaswins, who sit in dishevalled locks. If you look at any penance of those who overcame all trials, you will know that it is by the oneness of mind in penance they blocked the births to come.

1644. They, the ignorant of the scriptures, who ran away from austere tapas, for food and roamed in hunger forever are like those, who if fear run away from the crocodile in the river and fall on the bank into the embrace of the bear.

1645. The tiny calf of senses, inside the body sack jumps about for the fruit to ripe and to eat the ripened fruit. They also who can tether the lusty-legged calf to the yard (of knowledge) will have no more pulls within, their thoughts will be centred in oneness on Lord Shiva. This is the real state of penance.

1646. Only by intense penance will your thoughts be all of Shiva. If your thoughts are all of Lord Shiva, then, you need not perform any more penance and if your thoughts find kinship with those thoughts that have tasted Shiva-bliss; then you will be one with Lord Shiva. This is truly Siddhi and Mukthi state.

7. Gnana Flows from God's Grace

1647. If you have the Lord' grace, you have all the riches, true Gnana and greatness too. If you have the Lord's grace, you will become the great God Himself.

1648. Many go about the world exuding Gnana that is beyond the five Tamil mandals. Tamil mandalas are only Shiva Tathwas; it is the blossoming of mind and attainment of Lord's Supreme Gnana.

Tamil is used in the specific meaning of Lord 'Shiva'.

Men go about saying Gnana is beyond the five 'Tamil Mandalas'—spatially. They are very ignorant. The Tamil Mandalas are the five Shiva Tathwas themselves.

1649. Some Gnanis, as they seek God, know that Godly good and evil are two things in this world. As you cognize them as two and uproot them, then you will perceive the Lord's abode that is beyond.

Gnanis realize that God is beyond good and evil, beyond time and space.

1650. He, a benevolent force, stands as the soul of souls. He of Himself will appear at the right time and bless you with His grace still standing by you, He ends our birth to be.

Alas ! He stood before me, and bestowed Mukthi on me.

1651. By Shiva's grace, some become Devas; some are equal Gods and some are freed from their Karmas. When you have Shiva's grace, you will indeed enter His kingdom.

1652. I sought the matchless Feet of the Holy One, the Immaculate one and my father, and alas, Gnana shore forth as a beacon light. You may either remain an earthly being or become a heavenly being, as my Lord's grace dawns.

If you seek the Holy Feet of the immaculate One with Gnana as the beacon light, grace decides your births to be—an earthly being or a heavenly being.

1653. The body-chariot is illusive Chariot, and mind, the charioteer that produces strange fantasises, takes the rein.

They who mount the body-chariot should realize that if they mount the chariot of love instead and receive the grace of the pure one, they will sure be drawn in the triumphant chariot of unity and be one in God, obliterating I and He.

Realization of the truth that the body-chariot is only illusion's chariot that produces fantasise will make men to mount the chariot of love instead, to receive the grace of the pure one, which unites the soul in God.

1654. The Tapaswins if born in the body in the other world, will pursue penance there too and will there reach the Lord's feet and receive His Grace for sure.

1655. The form within the sun-stone is red hot ember, the form within the moon-stone is pearly drop of water, the form within the fire-stone is crackling fire and the form of the Lord that holds fire aloft is of surpassing beauty.

1656. I seek my Nandhi, with love and yearning, seeking Him, I will meet Him as Lord Shiva the Supreme, and then I will catch hold of the valorous feet and hold on to them forever, until He grants me liberation.

8. Apocryphal outfit (Untruthful Posture)

1657. Oh, you fools ! you deceive people with false robes; your pretention only helps you to gorge yourself fast with food; well may you sing and dance and weep and wail and thus seek Lord Shiva, yet, you will never, never glimpse His

Feet.

1658. When those who don the holy robes without having acquired Gnana, and go about the land begging and pursuing evil ways, then the rains fall and famine strikes the land. It is better by far, these evil men straight away de-robe themselves.

1659. A land's weal and woe are in its people, they spring out of their good deeds and evil deeds. And so, if the ruler unceasingly leads the multitude in the ways of virture, then the land will wax in prosperity for ever.

1660. The lowly-born don the rob that they may become high. The high-born don the rob that they may become Gods; The infamy-born are the knaves in robes, they should be disrobed and cast away.

The high born don holy robes to walk in God's path and become gods. The infamy-born knaves put on pseudo-robes to pursue evil ways; They should be disrobed and exposed promptly.

1661. They who perform false penance will not become the holy ones, but they will enter hell. False penance is a vain effort and is deceitful, a ruse for worldly enjoyment. It is only by the truth of Gnana can true Tapas be performed and can one abide in it firmly.

1662. The false don the robes to fill their bellies. The true don the robes and receive exalted oblations above, even if the false done robe to simulate the true, the disserning see through and make themselves free.

Practising false penance is full of deceit and conceit, it is ignoble and unholy too. It is but an artifice to indulge in mundane materialistic pleasures. The discerning eyes are capable of seeing through the false robes, and free themselves from the clutches of the wearers.

9. Robes of Penance

1663. The true Tapaswins are the truly robed, the sinful are only murderous hunters and are not entitled for holy robe. It is none but the true Tapaswins who deserve the true robe.

1664. To smear Holy ash is the first step to penance, the

other embles to reach Lord Shiva are to wear rings of copper in the ears and garland of Rudraksha beads around the neck. Thus do the blemishless Shiva Yogins prepare for penance.

1665. A Sivayogi is accountred thus—a waist strip for an under vest, a long tunic to wrap the body, a matted hair lock done in peacock style, ashes smeared all over, a begging bow of human skull shape and a cowl staff of hard cane.

1666. The Shiva yogi's appurtenances consist of the following ten—Kundalam to adore the ears, Kamandalam (a vessel) to hold holy water, Kandikai to fill the neck, a conch to blow, a bowl to beg and a Kapparai to hold ashes, the yogic sandals, the yogic seat, the yoga sash and the yogic staff.

10. Sacred Ashes

1667. Fools do not know what the thread and the tuft stand for, the thread is but Vedanta and the tuft is Pranajnana. Thus true brahmins who live in accord then, will see Jeeva uniting in Shiva. Chant the sacred manthra 'AUM' and, the two merge in one forever.

1668. The sacred ashes of Lord Shiva, who has bones for His garland, are indeed an impregnable armour. Karmas take flight for those who smear it is joy and Shiva-state comes seeking, and they will reach His handsome feet.

1669. The Holy ash will make you a king and you will have all regalia; those who are purified in its fire will in truth be transformed into Divine Reaching the Holy Feet of the eternal, Immaculate Lord, they will attain Brahman's form and forever be of the divine order.

11. Robes of Supreme Wisdom (Gnana)

1670. With Gnana, the robe only leads to hell; without the robe; yet, Gnana leads to mukthi. When they seek Gnana, they will seek the Lord and pray with their hearts robed in the Gnana way.

1671. They of lowly Gnana assume robes in vain; they of true Gnana filled with grace, do not covet it. The bigots of faiths are of evil Gnana, but those of perfect Gnana do not speak.

1672. It is not necessary for the Lord Shiva Gnanis nor for the Shiva yogins to adopt superfluous ways. In truth, the four Sadhanas (Charya-Kriya-Yoga and Gnana) are indeed needless for them, when they can see the peerless one fully within themselves.

1673. Those of false Gnana-howl about like dogs at the foot of the gallow, peak about like vultures at the carrions and frisk about like monkeys in merriment. But the true Lord Shiva Gnanis are quiescent, dead to the world, though living in the body and the senses.

1674. Those who have attained Shiva Gnana are truly of the holy order. The rest are never, never by any reckoning of the holy order, nor are their robes holy.

1675. Even the gayest attire becomes the Gnani, albeit his own robe is of Shiva Yogin. Whatsoever, robe he adopts, it will aid him to Gnana and nothing is appropriate or non-appropriate for him.

1676. The Shiva Gnani who seeks deliverance through Gnana, is a shrine unto himself of unique status. He observes Mauna (utter silence) and so is a Muktha and Siddha. Other Tapaswins can in no way be like Him.

1677. The stages in the liberation process in the annihilating of the self and the self becoming He in Lord Shiva identity and the Mudhra setting to ultra state. They who receive deliverance at the feet of Nandhi have these and all the rest.

12. Siva Attire

1678. By Hara's (Lord Shiva) grace, they become his liege-me; they seek His golden throne within the body mansion and with darkness dispelled, they do not know of deeds both good and bad. Thus they stand steadfast in the liege-robe of Shiva.

Seek God's golden throne within the body mansion itself. There dies the darkness of Malas (impurities), and you become indifferent to deeds both good and bad. Thus stand steadfast as His liegeman filled with His Grace.

1679. The robe is not for the soul but for the body. When

the body falls, the garb falls with it. Those who do not know that the soul within the body is real, are tossed, about like log caught in a wavy sea.

Polemics against the 'Anatman' concept of Buddhism, Lokayatha (materialistic world), etc.

1680. The holy ones in Lord Shiva's robes remain in solitude, one in Shiva-Sakthi. They are not perturbed by illusions, ignorance, intelligence and allurements of the fish-eyed damsels of the world.

1681. Nothing avails you, Oh ! your vain men, these Holy robes. But rein fast the fleeting mare of the twin breath and seek Holy Nandhi, our beloved Lord, and you will sure attain the eternal Bliss you crave for.

Casting aside all these holy robes, seek Nandhi, the beloved Lord. Then, you will attain the bliss that is final.

13. The Unfit

1682. They do not seek the Guru who, cures blindness. But instead, they seek the guru who does not cure blindness. They are like the blind and the blind shuffled into a blind dance and the blind together fall into a deep pit.

The acts of the unfit are like the blind leading the blind, both finally falling into a deep pit.

1683. The mirror of illusions rises out of the mind. To think of it they cannot even see its shadow, and they do nothing for the fruits of karma to drop, but, they go after the temptations of the backyard drain.

1684. The ignorant multitude that they are do not harken when you beckon them. The mother's milk flows sweetly in the mouth, but even the near and dear ones do not know how the mother's breast become so; verily, it is the formless being that shapes this body-form.

1685. The lips utter one thing, the mind thinks another and the deed does a third, do not behave thus; I know you as the gracious Lord, the rock of all ages, the fire-hued Lord and having known this no one dares to know me as in insensate creature.

1686. These reprobates of the five deadly sins fully deserve the pious ruler's severe punishment. When he fails he does not banish them, the land falls a prey to fell famine.

1687. The who stand in penance-consume away all karmas and stand in Lord Shiva, Himself; even the celestials do not know this. They who do not know Lord Shiva in penance—standing stand in the tangle of births condemned to endless sorrow.

1688. Such things as feeling, thinking, doing, eating, tasting, hurting, falling, rising, and boasting do not come to those who walk in God.

1689. They do not glimpse the dawn, nor the vast spaces nor the visions in spaces; close your inner eyes hard and then see, there you will behold the Light that does not bring another day. The vision of the inner Light ends births.

1690. The false disciple does not think of sundering the fetters of his soul or of annihilating the desires of the world; He does not strive to attain-Mukthi nor anything of the Tathwas and the way ahead, but takes to a wayward course. The gift of grace is not granted to this exceedingly mad disciple.

1691. The other blemishes of the false disciple are, he does not think of ending his five letters nor does he try to deliver himself for the incessant lust that he is immersed in He, a mean liar fears neither birth nor death. Truly, grace will be a stranger to him.

14. The Full-Flegged Disciple

1692. The fit disciples know their job and so find the path with the scriptures to guide them, and find the blemishless Guru. The rest are destined to destruction.

1693. By seeking You, the Supreme Lord Shiva, I lost all my sense of fear; I do not wander any longer and seek the company of another. Oh ! Lord, shatter my karmas, uproot them from my very thoughts and kick them off. Lord own me, grant me, your mighty grace and make me your slave forever.

1694. Even as the body still pulsates with life rally your thoughts to Oneness, stand in love and accord and you will envision high Para, the seed of all seeds. He grants His mighty grace to those who do thus.

1695. When you seek a Guru, seek one who is holy and pure and then give him your all—your body, life and wealth, then, learn clearly in constancy, without distracting a moment, sure you will reach Lord Shiva's state.

1696. Receive the Holy precepts of the Guru, in the asterism of Swathi and Visakha, in the conjunction of *lagnas Vrischika* and Kadacha. The Primal One knows no other than only those who stand in the path of virtue.

Thirumoolar's faith in astrological concepts in demonstrated here.

1697. When your disciple is perfect, your thoughts will be pure crystal and there, the beauteous Lord resides; then all karmas rooted deep like undying weeds will disappear and you will glimpse the grace of the valorous feet of the Holy Lord.

1698. A Sathwic is he, whose thoughts are centred on faith and finite truth, whose vision through the conflicting faiths is clear; who abhores the recurring cycle of births and who easily walks in the straight path of Dharma. He, for sure, is a good and true disciple.

1699. The good and true disciple is the fit one, who scans that which divides the real and the unreal, melts in the soul of his being and with the grace of Lord Shiva to guide, he receives Gnana in true devotion. He humbles himself before the Lord and seeks the bliss of His Sakthi.

1700. This day, I prayed to my Holy Master to grace me with His feet on my head, and as He placed His feet all births vanished. This body that was thus blessed received the grace of Arul Sakthi and I became a ripe Gnani, devoid of all blemish forever.

1701. The holy guru is the master of the four paths that are difficult. He is the incessant seeker of divine Gnana. And as He placed His Feet on my head, my ardour and in Gnana soared higher and higher and my love for Guru Para welled up higher and higher.

1702. The rules of instruction say that the holy Guru imparts divine knowledge only to those who are fully ripe to receive it. Taking the disciple gently to the limits of the vast infinite, He instructs, facing east or south and the disciple facing west or north, the Sakthi of the Lord being centred in his mind.

1703. The disciple humbles himself before the Divine Guru in five ordained postures; he bewails his faults and praises the virtues of his master ; then, the guru who is in Sanmarga; (Jnana Guru) shows the way of deliverance from the mortal prison and imparts Lord Shiva Gnana.

1704. Vedanta is the way of renouncing desires, so, divert the course of your life, take to the Siddhantha-Vedanta way and humble your head at the Feet of the Guru who has renounced all in the spiritual way, then, you become a true disciple.

1705. Truly he is a perfect disciple who follows the true Guru constantly, like a shadow in virtue, truth, compassion, discrimination and love. He, then receives the nectar of crystal clear finite Gnana and witnesses the many miracles it brings in its train.

Tanthra Six Concluded

7

Tanthra Seven
(Kaalottharahamam)

1. The Six Yogic Centres

1706. Coursing the prana breath through, these yogic centres, known as Mooladhara of four petals, Swadhistana of six petals, Manipooraka of ten petals, Anaghatha of twelve petals, Vishudhi of sixteen petals and Agja of two petals (and Sahashrara of thousand petals), in ascending order, the yogi beholds the twin feet of the Timeless One in the twin-petalled Agna Chakra.

There are six Chakras-yogic centres situated at different points along the spinal column of the human body. The yogic centres are symbolized as lotus petals, of varying numbers. The final climax is reached in the "Twin petalled centre finals" (in the cranium between the eyebrows).

1707. The twelve petalled centre is in the Nadha sphere, the sixteen petalled centre is in the Nadantha sphere; the two-petalled Medha centre is beyond the Nadantha where Para sakthi is enshrined. Enter here in indifferentiated Beeda consciousness. Above the Medha centre, is the final supreme truth.

The Anaghatha Chakra is in the Nadha sphere, Vishudhi Chakra, in the Nadantha sphere, Agna Chakra in the Medha sphere, Parasakthi is enshrined here. Above this centre is the final truth.

1708. When the yogis course the Prana breath through the yogic centres he can neither cognize his being as his-self or God, neither can be know his station as being up or down, for the Mighty Parapara who pervades all envelopes him, cool and bounteous as the fruit-laden, Celestial Kalpaka tree (wishing tree in Heaven).

1709. The yogi, with Nadis purified, ascends the yogic centres step by step into the heavenly effulgence of Medha whose twin petals rise into Kalanta sphere, and then you reach the state of Bodha, of unitive awareness, senses petrified. This truly is yoga, the Holy Saha Marga.

1. The spheres of experience in yoga are (a) Nada, (b) Nadhantha, (c) Bodhantha, and (d) Kalantha.
2. The spheres of experiences in yoga are Nadantha (sound sphere), Kalantha (light sphere) and Bodhantha (consciousness sphere).

1710. The yogi does not stop at Medha's (Agna) centre, but he evokes AUM, and now with Prana for support he proceeds beyond the yogic centres and ascends the adhvas. When he practises thus, to the end of perfection his body becomes a doughty receptacle of Eternal joy.

Adhvas are pathways or steps. These are six in number: Kala, Bhuvana, Varna, Manthra, Padha and Tathwa.

1711. Seek the yogic centres in the body where the six centres or atharas are and alive, over the fifty letters rises the one letter (AUM that is the basic to all letters).

1712. As the gross body that decays and the subtle body that escapes are in unseen union., so are the fifty subtle letters to the Tathwas that are gross and so are the six centres to the corporeal body.

1713. There is a jewelled flower of six petals above the discriminating heart's Lotus (Vishudhi adhara). Here, pure awareness turns into bliss of Lord Shiva and it is towards Pure Gnana (Light of knowledge) that is Supreme Reality.

Pure awareness is to be found in the sixteen petalled lotus which is above the heart's lotus. Vishuddha is the nerve plexus above the Anahatha in the neck region. It looks like a sixteen petalled lotus. Its presiding deity (Intantrism) is the Goddess Sakini.

2. Cosmic Lingam

1714. No one knows what the Linga is ! The Linga is the eight directions and the sixteen Kalas. It is as the linga that the Universe merged.

1715. Sadhashiva, who as Linga conceived the world's creation, first manifested His Sakthi, in the world, pervaded it as His Sakthi form and filled it with His Sakthi's powers.

1716. Sadhashiva grantedly, the worldly joys and heavenly pleasures; wisdom and miraculous powers, this body and the state beyond and the thirty-six tathwas—the six yogic centres and the sacred Agamas are all but Sadhasiva.

28 AGAMAS:-KAMIGAM, YOGAJAM, SIVIDHIAM, KARANAM, AJITHAM, DEEPTHAM, SHUTSHUMAM, SAHASHRAM, HAMSHASOOMAM, SUPRAPEEDAM, VIJAYAM, NISVASAM, SWAYAMBHUVAM, AGNEYAM, VEERAM, RAURAVAM, MAGHUDAM, VISHALAM, CHANDRA GNANAM, MUGABHIMBAM, BHIRODAGEETHAM, LALITHAM, SIDDHAM, SANTHANAM, SATHVOKTHAM, PARAMESWARAM, KARANAM AND VAASHULAM.

1717. The countless devas glorify and praise my Lord as the fragrant cool, southern breeze, they adore Him as the Bounteous One, but they do not know that it is He who grants protection, from beyond the vast spaces.

1718 He, the Uncreated Being, is indeed, the Light of life to the resplendent Brahma, Vishnu, Prajapathi, the luminous Sun and Indra and the bright-eye Devas swarming the celestial spheres.

1719. Lord Shiva pervading all nature blesses all, they who do not know this do not adore Him. But to those who adore Him who is immanent, He is the golden stalk of the heart's lotus within.

1720. Those who seek Lord Shiva's form will realize that the pure Vimana (the upper part forming an arc) is the Sthula Linga (manifest Linga) and that the Bali-Peeda (the Altar) is Bhadra Linga (Lord Shiva's throne).

1721. When installing the Linga, pearls, gems, corals, and emeralds sandalwood, hard granite, holy ashes Shiva's agamas and rice in grain and cooked should be poured in and the Linga then fixed. When thus installed, a haunting fragrance will pervade all around.

1722. There are rituals to be observed in the formation of a Linga, and the prescribed materials to shape the Linga's divine form are curd, ghee, milk and pure wax, copper, mercury, fire, conch, hard bricks, shapely Bilva and Kondrai flowers of golden hue.

Vilva—Tamil Villa, a sacred tree. Its leaves are as sacred to Saivas as "Thulasi" to Vaishnavas. Kondrai—genus of flower trees—Cassia.

1723. Lingas for the four Varnas, Brahmins worship Linga made of Crystal; the kings worship Linga made of gold; the Vaisyas worship Linga made of emerald and the Shudras worship Linga made of stone.

1724. They who sought Him in one special way, did not know Him in anyway and it is thus, that the Lord pervades the eight universes and made my heart, a temple too.

Of whatever material the Linga is made, the temple of the omnipresent is actually in the seeker's heart.

1725. The Holy One, who is our refuge, pervades the vast spaces, unknown to anyone, He rapturously resides in the fleshy body, dispels sins and spreads wisdom's Sunlight.

1726. From time's Eternity Beginningless First, the Lord assumed His form thus—The earth is His flower—bedecked feet, the heavens, His Ganga-girt crown, His body fills the vast spaces in unbroken continuity.

1727. The earth is His Sakthi peeta, the heavens the Pure Linga, the billowing Seas are His bathing ghat, the cool waters of the cascading streams on the mountain tops are His heavenly crown, the countless stars are His garland and the eight directions are His limitless raiments.

3. Microcosmic (Pinda) Lingam

1728. The human form itself is truly a Shiva-lingam. It is Chidambaram-Sadhasivam and the Holy Dance Hall as well.

1729. Men are not tired by being reborn over and over again; they still want to live in this fleshy body made of earth, water and other matters, they do not seek to adore the Lord whom the five elements within them, together seek Him.

1730. The day when the Lord entered this fleshy body, a veritable teabernacle of God, the five senses who had taken their places opened the gates and showed you the way of redemption. Like a mother's home, He entered in me and affectionately took charge of the gates (Senses) and became their master.

1731. The expanse of the Vedas lies at the Feet of the Lord who chose this body as His temple, the ten Nadis at the feet of the Lord who made these gates His own; He, my Lord, the Great Nandhi who received our adoration, subduing our five senses entered in me operating the wide gates.

4. Sadhasiva Lingam

1732. Sadhasiva whom we seek and whom the holy praise in songs as a lustrous pearl beyond comparison has His two Feet planted on the earth below. His ten hands are spread in ten directions. His fifteen eyes glow like fiery flames on His five faces.

1733. Sadhasiva comprehends all nine God-forms: Brahma, Vishnu, Rudhra, Sakthi, The Lord takes His seat within the beautiful Sakthi, After the Lord activates Sakthi, the ten directions appear from Him.

1734. The six Vedangas and the four Vedas took their place in the space that opened up. The four paths beginning with Chariya, comprehended in Saiva-truth took their place in the space that opened up.

When Sakthi evolves further, opening up space the four Vedas, the Six Vedangas, the four paths of Chariya, Kriya, Yoga and Gnana comprehended by Saivam—all took their places.

1735. In this Truth arose the ten Avasthas (states of awareness), the twelve (zodiacal houses), the ninety-six Tathwas (body constituents) and this truth arose the Supreme Sadhasiva.

Evolving still further from Sakthi in Shiva Truth, arose the ten Avasthas, the twelve zodiac houses (Rashis) ten ninety-six tathwas (Universals) and the Sadhasiva.

1736. The five faces of Sadhasiva are Central, East, South, North, and West. The central face is of crystal hue. The eastern face is crimson like Kumkum, the southward face is dark like thick pitch, the northward face is red like Aratharam flower and the westward face is white like milky hue. Thus did He reveal to me His lowly Vassal.

Sadhasiva revealed His five faces of five different hues to this lowly vassal (Thirumoolar)—the central face, Isana of crystal colour; the eastward face, Tathpurusha, Crimson, the southward face. Aghora with pitch dark; the northward face, Vama, red and the westward face, Sadhyojatha, milky white.

1737. Entering in my heart with His five faces, fifteen eyes and ten hands holding weapons in them all, Supreme Sadhasiva pervaded within me in fullness.

1738. Aspects of the God-head; Sakthi is this wide world and the infinite universe. Sakthi has form. Shiva is formless conjointly Sakthi and Shiva are the kinetic and the potential aspects. The thirty six-tathwas arose out of them.

1739. The Primal Tathwa is formless. When the primal tathwa has form, it is the world, animate and inanimate; then indeed it is a source of pleasure; Tathwas is all pervasive. Sadhasiva is real tathwa. When in form, that is when the thirty-six fundamental principles of existence devoluted from maya, Sadhasiva is the animate and inanimate world, and the source of all materialistic pleasures (Bhoga).

Tathwa means two things : 1. Basic Truth, 2. The thirty-six fundamental principles of existence evolved from Maya.

1740. Repeat a hundred times that Sadhasiva is One Lord. He will still be beyond anything else you try to say. Sadhasiva, who has entered my heart suffers not those Gods who exalt themselves.

1741. All my dark doubts got dispelled when I contemplated

on the Primal Lord, who is abounding Grace, of dark throat, wearing the radiant crescent moon on His matted russet locks and holding the axe in His hand.

1742. To recount the five faces where His grace abounds it is thus : the northward face is Vama, the westward face is Sadhyojatha; the eastward face is Tathpurusha; the southward face is Aghoram and the upward face is Isana.

These five names, namely Vama, Sadhyojatha, Tathpurusha, Aghora and Isana are regarded as the representations of five different stages of Saivism which originated in immemorial past—A similar idea about the different Yugavatharas of Lord Maha Vishnu is recorded in the Sri Bhagvatha Purana.

1743. Sakthi's crown is in the shining Isana face; Her visage is in the Tathpurusha face; Her heart and waist in the Aghora and Her blessed Feet are in the Vama Face.

1744. The Sakthi's breast, head, long tresses, the eyes, the forehead mark, the armour—these are of glowing green hue. The crowning Sakthi is as dazzling as lightning, and Her ten weapons are fiery bright.

1745. The five Sakthis are seated in Sadhasiva. in the heart is seated the Divine Gnana Sakthi; on the head, the heavenly Para-Sakthi; over His locks, the Adhisakthi; in His armour, is Iccha Sakthi and within His eyes, the Kriya Sakthi.

1746. Sakthi stands in firmness in the quadrilateral Adharas (Mooladhara); She is in sleep in the Hexagonal yogic centre (Swathishtana) and She is agitation in the circular yogic centre (Manipporakaam). Sadhasiva is Sakthi's Mighty form.

1747. Whatsover be the time you seek the great Nandhi, He stands unique with His faces five glowing like the eveing Sun. He stands aloft, upon the lotus top, when you rouse the Kundalini through yogic-breathing and course it upward through the nine centres.

1748. It is His divine nature to ever abide in this fleshy body in inseparable union. His perfection's Feet, I born upon my head and prayed to Him in the depth of my heart.

1749. He is the shining truth. I realized Him in this world below. I brought Him into my heart's temple here below I embraced Him in union and prayed to Him. This is the simple and pure Truth. I sang to Him, the resplendent Sun, in appropriate measure.

1750. He lends His fiery rays to the sun, moon and fire. He supports the fourteen worlds. He stands in the centre of the vast spaces. He is the beginning as well as the end. His own form is as cool as the rays of the Moon.

1751. The Lord is uncreated. He stands with His body as the uncreated Being, Shivalinga, as divine Sadhasiva, as uncreated Shiva, as unalloyed Shivanandha bliss and as Supreme, Eternal Tathpara.

1752. No one knows that Shiva is Akara, the letter 'A' and the pervasive Sakthi is Ukara, the letter 'U'. The two sounds together swell and fill the world as AUM in unrelieved entirely. The Lord is thus the cosmic sound, 'AUM'.

1753. Linga is 'Aum'; its pedestal is *Aumkara*; its centre is 'Akara', 'A'; its inner sound is Ukara 'U'; Makaram 'M' pervading Linga is Bindhu/Nadha.

5. Athma Lingam (Jeeva-Sivam)

1754. All exist, with Akaram (A) as the beginning, all life exists with Ukaram as the beginning. If Akaram and Ukaram are known together, then these two bring the knowledge that Linga is only divine.

All life exists with Akaram 'A' and Ukaram 'U' knowledge of these two brings the knowledge of divine Linga.

1755. Bindhi is the finite support Nadha expanded as the support in Medha. Bindhi that is supported is the pedestal and Nadha conjoint to it is truly Linga's Union.

Bindhi is the support and Nadha the supported; when Nadha is conjoined with Bindhu, the pedestal, the union is Linga.

1756. Linga that is Shiva/Sakthi is static and kinetic. Linga that is Lord Shiva/Sakthi is Sadhashivam and Shiva-Sakthi is Tathpara, the unborn Being.

1757. You may behold the self-illumined Light (AUM) upon the fifty heavenly letters; the light which thus arises with His Sakthi (U) is only He, who is Akara (A)—the finite support, like a golden vine that blooms beautifully.

1758. Bindhu and Nadha together form Linga. Bindhu is the pedestal and Nadha the Linga; with these two as divine support, the five Gods arose, to perform their five functions.

1759. The grand pedestal of Sakthi holds the Athma Tathwas, the central part of Sakthi holds the Vidhya Tathwas, the Linga of Sakthi (Sakthi's Upper part Linga) holds the Shiva Tathwas the divine soul of Sakthi is Sadhasiva.

1760. He entered into the very being of my life. He entered my heart and poured His blessing to my heart's full. You too seek Him along with me, He will enter your home and bless you too.

1761. He, my divine father, who sports the crescent moon, is the Supreme Parapara. He rules the Universe, and the Mighty He also reigns in the heart's temple of His devotees. He, the Hara, whom the immortals bow in worship, resides firm in my heart.

1762. The world will call you a fool if you have this conceit and defiantly deny the Supreme and say that He is not the Lord. He, the Holy One stands in amity with serpent, fire and water in His matted locks and is enshrined in me as tender as the yearning mother cow.

1763. The Immortals in eight directions adore Him, saying He stands there. He lies there, But how shall I praise my Lord who ever resides in my heart's heart.

8. Gnana Linga (Self Realized Shiva)

1764. Parashiva is eminent in all life thus, as form, the formless, and the form-formless. He stands as Guru too. He, the Sadhashiva bestows bounties like the Kalpaka tree.

1765. Parashiva has nine aspects—Sadhasiva is in the centre, that is form/formless Brahma, Mahavishnu, Maheswara are the four formed ones below; and Bindhu, Nadha, Sakthi and Shiva are the four formless above.

1766. He, the Lord of the four Gods (Brahma, Vishnu, Rudhra and Mahesha) is the Lord of the immortals. He is Nandhi that stands in the centre, with faces in all directions. They who adore Him as their Lord will themselves attain His ways. So, seek the Lord's Holy Feet.

1767. I prayed to Him to dispel and destroy my Karmas as He is the One who measures out time's eternity as days, months and years. Even when your folded hands unfold He is the One to you, worthy of your visioning, so seek Him with His virgin Sakthi.

1768. He is the Primal Lord, the God of the Universe. He is the great God of divine justice, whom the illumined devotees praise. He, my Lord the pure One, is as Half and Half in Parasakthi.

1769. The Pure Shiva state, as undimmed light is beyond Sakthi, inside Parasakthi, The Lord's feet are still beyond the beyond. This is the truth of the Supreme Lord.

1770. Seeing the tender Flame is seeing all the Universe. Rise and see His world and you will remain there forever. See the vast expanses and you will see the Lord, who resides in your thoughts, entwined with His Sakthi.

1771. Truly, divine Gnana is to chant the name of the Lord, my father and His Sakthi cluster, my mother in according order. In unceasing rapture, He resides with Her above the navel, in my heart.

1772. They induct the Jeeva into Suddha and Asuddha Maya groups. After disentangling him from the pure Thuriya State, they enter his thoughts and Shiva, then makes His habitation inside him—this is the play of Shiva/Sakthi.

1773. Shiva is Sakthi is Shiva. All the play is manifestation of all Universe, the play of Shiva/Sakthi. There is nomanifest creation with Lord Shiva and Sakthi. It is Sakthi and Shiva that forever assume form.

9. Sivalingam (Shiva, the Sathguru)

1774. He pervades the roaring waters of the Seas, He permeates the spreading winds and the flaming fire. Thus He is immanent in all nature, yet, I do not know Him nor do I adore Him.

1775. There is only one way of knowing Him and adoring Him. They who with water and flowers chant His name will know Him and He, of the matted locks will not separate Himself from them.

1776. I saw the Lord as the One and Only Being, subduing my five senses. I full well adored His Holy Feet and He, the gracious One, the Primal Lord, granted me His blessings.

1777. Brahma, Vishnu, Rudhra, Mahéswara, Sadhasiva of the five faces, Bindhu, Nadha, Sakthi and Shiva—all the nine aspects of Shiva shower their blessings as Nandhi, himself.

1778. If you, accomplish through practise, the rousing of the flaming kundalini and course your prana upward and halt the acts of inhalation and exhalation within the body, then, indeed, you have reached the Supreme Divine State.

10. Sampraḍhayaa (Holy Tradition)

1779. He took from me, through appropriate rituals, my body, wealth, and life, as a sacrificial offering. He directed His spiritual glance at me and dispelled my network of karmas to destruction; and then, He laid His hands on me and in a trice. He imparted spiritual awareness by planting His feet on my head. Thus, through these successive acts of Deekshas, He, the Nandhi ended my cycle of births.

1780. My Gurupara worked for my redemption and for me to attain all these—life and body and Prana and breath that fleets after, Shiva, the mighty and Chit Sakthi that consorts and Param, it is the Supreme Truth.

1781. He seated me to His West (right) and asked me to meditate on Him daily. He said that it was the Truth that lay seated between the crown of the head and the petals of the mouth and that was the true word to be cherished as a divine secret.

Seating the disciple to his right, Gurupara asked him to meditate on the Truth that lay in the Agna centre between the crown of the head and the petals of the mouth. This is the true word. Let the seeker cherish it as a divine secret.

1782. I wandered aimlessly, indulging in indiscriminate talk. He cleansed all my impurities and made me pure. He, a barber, brought me and He to balance which was all to perfection indeed. Then, the disciple and Guru alone remained.

1783. He is the Lord of all life that is existent; but no one knows His true nature. He extricated me from Maya that separates and alas, then I beheld the Lord who is the seed of all.

1784. Intent on the redemption of my body, wealth and life, He sought me and planted His feet on my head and with the grace of divine Sakthi. He exercised my love for the fleshy body. He and I, He made as One intermingling in non-separate Union.

1785. He marked me out to be His vassal. He took my life, possessions and body and made it His own; but as it was He that gave me all my sustenance, I cannot dare say that He took anything from me.

He gave me all and took all, and I granted and gained in the barter, what do I have to complain of ?

1786. Within this body, the Lord is the Prana that is breath and the soul that dwells inside. They do not know the truth of all those that pertains to the perishable body are like the ghosts of the dead.

1787. They who have the awareness, see all worlds and know no sorrows. When they who have realized that awareness will indeed have seen the finite truth.

1788. What shall I say of Nandhi's infinite greatness, who bestows His grace on the souls of those who, having been woken from the primordial Thuriya state (Kevala) have wandered in the bodily state (Sahala) possessing the thirty-six Tathwas.

1789. There is no more approach as I and you for, we are inseparable like body and life. Together, we are like the beauty heavens and the heavenly beings, like the honey and its sweetness that I savour.

The best approach to Him is not in dualistic terms of 'I' and 'you', 'Jeeva' and 'Siva' are as inseparable, as the body and the life, as the heaven and the heavenly being, the honey and its sweetness.

1790. He and she do not know Him; if he knows Him, then he is not the knower; if he knows Him, then, he, the knower and He, the known become one.

So, Long as Shiva and Jeeva are considered as two separate identities, the Jeeva does not know Him. When Jeeva knows

Him, the knower (Jeeva) and the known (Shiva) become one and unitive.

1791. Just as the body and the life feel alike. He stood in me in full identity, I became one, with the heavenly Lord, as He is bounteous like the rains from the heavens. Shiva stands in relation to jeeva like the life and body, and thanks to the bounteous grace of Lord-Shiva, the jeeva can become one in Him in indistinguishable identity.

1792. He, Himself as the Supreme Being, does not stand apart from me and the Lord knows that; we are like the body and the life; This is the truth. He, the Lord of the immortals wrought me to perfection.

11. Conferring Grace (Placing of Grace)

1793. Darkness (ignorance) and light (knowledge) are the two states, life and body are the two forms, dharma and penance are the two graces and truth is only the blessing within.

1794. He, the Nandhi, is beyond our thought so, He is elusive for us to see and distant for us to touch and feel Him. Pray long in the light of your heart, that, the darkness that envelopes you stands dispelled.

1795. All Universe will be revealed to you even in the slightest hint of His Mighty Grace. The Great One stands revealed to you, even when the darkness of ignorance is lifted. When you seek Him, with your swarming thought centred on Him, you will then see the light of Gnana and thus become immortal.

1796. My time rolled on in ignorance, Yet my Lord will in time, know me. He, the bounteous One, will know them by their light of knowledge and intense love.

1797. I do not know when my Karmas will perish. But Nandhi, Himself will know me and when my Karmas will perish. Our Lord of the immortals is sweet like honey, so melt in piety and reach the divine Supreme consciousness.

1798. The celestials tossed in doubt did not know Him. I know the Lord from bygone days. The Lord is the light and He pulsated as Prana in my fleshy body. If I do not know

Him, who else will know Him.

1799. No one knows the measure of grace that is all pervasive, they do not know of the ambrosial sweetness that flows from grace, they do not think of the five actions that grace subtely performs. Indeed, who knows how grace is all-pervasive.

1800. He infuses the sense organs with desire to seek the divine light. He grants the light of knowledge and leads you to enlightenment. He, then seats you in the midst of the devout and holy. They who thus received His grance, truly became Shiva, themselves.

1801. It was of His grace that I was born, grew up, rested in death, remained in obfuscation and then tasted embrosial bliss. Nandhi who entered my heart in His grace, conferred this grace.

1802. By His mighty grace, Nandhi entered my heart, He rested His feet on me, bathed me in the Ocean of nectar, granted me the fervour of devotion and fed me the bliss that is ambrosial.

1803. It was His grace that led me into Pasa and it was the same grace that freed me from this Pasa. It was His grace that in divine love granted me Mukthi. Also, it was His grace that granted me the love for the state beyond Mukthi (liberation).

1804. The Lord who Sundered the bonds of my birth is of infinite grace. He is the dharmic sea. Nandhi is the holiest, of the Holy, the pure one, the Primal Lord who entered my heart in amity.

1805. He entered in my heart with abounding grace. Those devoid of grace do not know Him, even if He is in these. Entering my heart, He filled me with the bliss and I became blissful. He entered my heart as Nandhi, and made me Shivam.

1806. He gave me the intelligence that reasons and the senses that fashions inscrutable Maya. He gave the five elements, the diverse sense organs and the five acts of grace—all these are only the bounties of His grace.

In His bounteous grace, He gave me the instruments to reason out the inscrutable senses, to enjoy the elements and environments for my functioning and performed the five acts for my liberation and attainment of grace.

1807. All manifestations of nature, animate and inanimate, are but His pure-benign grace. The Lord's grace pervades as darkness and as light. All are but the grace of His manifest form.

1808. He assumes all these nine forms—Shiva, Sakthi, the luminous Nadha and Bindhu, the five faced Holy Sadhasivam, Mahesa, Rudhra, Vishnu and the Lotus-seated Brahma.

1809. Those whose eyes are blind do not see even the Sun. But they who have the divine vision see the light everywhere. Those who have not the vision of grace do not see the Lord who is subtle truth. But, they who have the vision of grace see Hara (Lord Shiva) face to face.

1810. The All-Immanent Lord, Himself creates, preserves and destroys and obscures. He, Himself does all these and after that grants Mukthi, that is liberation.

1811. The first four aspects (Shiva, Sakthi, Nadha, Bindhu) are His Formless ones; Sadhashiva is the unmoving form/formless. The abiding last four (Brahma, Vishnu, Rudhra and Mahesa) are the formed ones; all these and the one beyond too are He, Lord Shiva.

1812. He, the indestructable, one being, is immanent in all life. He is in them, but He is not they. All this is His play. He, the desire of my heart, dwells in them as a divine friend.

1813. The immaculate one who dwells in my heart activates the Kundalini (Pure maya) Sakthi and from this act Nadha is born. The imperishable Bindhu is then produced as the seed emanating diverse Kala rays.

1814. The Bindhu that arose thus pervades everywhere. From it rises maya and the Mahamaya and from them, emanate the immortals and their clan, the manthras and the vedas, and the countless, countless worlds swarming in the spread.

12. Luminour Grace (Words of Dispensation)

1815. Those who do not take their firm stand on grace and do not steep themselves in it in conscious determination, will never receive grace nor be freed of the five Pasas. They will not know the greatness that grace gives nor will they be resolute. Those who are born to grace alone know what grace is :

The five Pasas are : the primal impurities—Aanava, Maya and Karma and Tirodayei (Mala of obscuration) and Mayeym are the tangible manifestations of maya.

1816. The great, famed Nandhi barred the way of my future births and gave me the ambrosial bliss that never cloys, He, the Lord of a thousand names told me, in one word, to bathe eternally in the unending Sea of mighty sacred grace.

1817. I sought Him by dancing, singing, weeping and lamenting; and saw the greatness of Shiva. And as I united with Him, He granted me His indefinable form and imparting His grace, He pervaded in me.

1818. I gave up all unworthy knowledge and prostrated at Her Feet and prayed. He, the famed Nandhi saying that I am rid of all these, planted His Feet on me and like a Maya's cloud dispelled, the birth I have taken and all the impurities (Malas) I bore.

1819. Light the lamp and see the space; all pangs will cease to be, before the light of this lamp. Those who have the light to light the lamp are the true shining light, in the Divine Lamp that shines.

1820. Light and darkness are interminable and darkness will cease, only to those who have eyes to see this light. So, too, when the inner light dispells darkness, the Jeeva becomes one with Lord Shiva.

1821. I wandered aimlessly and He entered me in purity and made me pure; He entered me in charity and gave me the bliss of ambrosia. He planted His golden feet on me. Oh, Alas, this act of His is so gracious, I stand bedazed in limitless wonder.

1822. There is no vast space and that is grace, there is a safe refuge and that is the Lord. He entered in me to dispel my darkness. Know Him fully well; then indeed, is Shiva-state attained.

1823. Speak; are all the Gods who are born, live and die, true ones ? You should proclaim that they should leave their bodies as a prey to the vultures and that they save their soul.

13. Shiva Pooja

1824. This heart is the holy sanctum for the bounteous Lord, the fleshy body is a unique temple and the mouth is the power gate. For those who can discern, that is a vision, the jeeva is the Shivalinga and the deceptive senses are but the illuminating lamp.

1825. We offer nothing to Nandhi of the spreading matted locks; who takes the sacrificial oblations. The sacrifice that we can give morning and evening are the songs of praise that melt His Heart. Let us offer this sacrifice, that is sweet as milk.

1826. The Lord who is with His consort of sweet speech is the Supreme Parapara, Enshrine Sadhasiva in Him, consider His upward looking face as Isana and if you perform your worship thus, you will become Shiva, Himself.

1827. Well may you think of Him and speak of His Truth. But rarely indeed you can behold the Holy Feet of the Lord. They who adore Him with flowers and water can but see the Lord of the Holy Feet.

1828. Why is it the Lord has taken His seat in the heart of the Celestial Beings who bear consecrated water and garland of flowers ? With offerings of five sweet dishes, and with sixteen Upachara rituals, they humbly prostrate, in Archana worship.

1829. They are the devout who pray with water and flowers. The Lord, seeing this bestows His grace on them. There are countless sinners who do not know how to approach our Lord thus they slip by in deep ignorance.

1830. They who worship the Lord, reap the reward of bathing in the ine waters of the Lord, Moolar proclaims that Mukthi (liberation) indeed is for those who anoint the Feet of Holy men who are upraised in Gnana.

1831. Oh ! Lord of Immortals, this is my prayer to you. Even if in thoughtlessness, I pursue the world and its ways, do grant me this boon, to unceasingly adore you with flowers and water.

1832. Oh, The Immortals swarm in hordes seeking the Almighty, Him. When you unceasingly chant the thousand names, and the One special sacred name of the primal Lord then, the seas and the unending lands will all be yours.

1833. Bathing Him in the five products of the cow (Panchacowya—Milk, curd, ghee, butter-milk and butter) the celestial beings in clans seek the Lord who knows no end. Oh, He who created the five elements and their attributes, stands revealing His grace within the honeyed flower that is the heart.

1834. The Heavenly beings, bearing the choicest flowers and water traverse over clouds. They stand and pray with subdued pasa and receive the grace of my Lord, unfailingly.

1835. Nandhi with spreading matted locks is in the expanse of waters (Ganges). Renounce the Sea of belief and enter the Sea of Heart's faith. They who do not adore Him with hands laden with flowers will fall in the Sea of sorrow and be immersed forever.

1836. By overcoming all doubts and breaking the marshy banks of the Sea of sorrows, they adore Him with buds and blossoms in true faith. Those who do not know this, fall into great errors. But those who know it will see the Lord seated within the Crown of their Head.

1837. There is one way to reach Him, adore Him with many flowers. This is the way of the Divine, to the Holy Feet of the three-eyed God Lord Shiva. To those who do this, the Lord stands revealed by Himself. Adoring Him thus, He never fails to stand before you.

1838. In endearing love they worship Him at His Feet, as the Lord, the Primal One, the timeless eternity and the Holy one. They adore Him the choicest flowers and deep devotion thus, to receive His grace, Why do not you, too, seek Him in prayer.

1839. The celestial beings seek the earth, laden with flowers and water, and sing the praise of the Pure One. He, the Primal One of the three, blesses Him whoever thinks of His bounteous grace.

1840. You who labour hard, carry pure water, gather flowers and lay them at His shining Feet. Adore the Lord in unfailing piety and stand and pray and like the rain-laden clouds you will be prosperous forever.

1841. Subdue the senses to perform the worship of the Lord in the appropriate manner. Hasten and quickly fall at His Feet, offering water and flowers in daily worship. I said this even in the days of yore. He will surely accept the offerings of your heart.

1842. Adore Him, placing garlands of flowers at His Feet, praise Him as the Primal Lord. Those who have prayed, to Him daily and have yet not known Him, let them adore Him with Athi flowers, so dear to Him and pray that their base nature be cleansed of impurities. This is the way to the Supreme Goal.

Aadhi flower, of the three, *bauhima reacemosa,* is dear to the Almighty Lord Shiva, Himself.

1843. Nandhi of the spreading matted locks abided beyond in bliss above the lotus of the heart. Yet they do not know to chant and muse over the manthra that will lead to Him and there abide in Him.

1844. He is the gem that lies embedded in the cubit of the heart. Yet many do not think of Him and do not see Him. He, the gem-set jewel shines in them who cherish and muse on Him over and over again.

1845. While Nandhi of gracious dualities bestows His gift to the Celestial Beings whom come to Him in prayer, beseeching Him from afar, He, Nandhi is the Chakra (discus) that cuts the darkness (of impurities) and takes the Mighty His abiding seat in my heart.

1846. The Primal impurities (Malas) lose their potency by Samaya Deeksha. They purification of the manthra chanting is insured by Visesha Deeksha, purification of Kalas is affected by Nirvana Deeksha. The Abhiseka Deeksha is for those who have attained the state of Gnana.

1847. Unless anyone has adored Him, who shines beyond time, through aeons and aeons, they will not have become the jeeva that is devoid of karma. Even, Hari's Mighty on the Sea, and Brahma besides seek Him through ages and ages. Yet, He is beyond their reach.

14. Sathguru Pooja

1848. I shall relate the way about 'Upadhesa' that leads to liberation. Also I shall narrate about the performance of Guru Pooja that shows the way to transcend the six yogi centres and to ascend beyond, grasping the lotus feet of Nandhi who blesses me.

1849. Rid of fleshy desires, you may adore Him with the sweet-scented sandal that grows in the recesses of the forest and with rare flowers that blossom heavenward.

1850. Sweet-scented sandals and rare blossoms prove useless; unless you seek Him rid of bodily desires, you cannot reach His Feet that are bedecked with honeyed flowers. Constant worshipping within is indeed great. Reaching the Lord's Holy Feet is to still all actions. But the path of Gnana is all archana when you excel in the path of Gnana that leads to the Supreme Para.

1851. Let the devotee adore the Lord in the morning, at noon and in the evening. While adoring, let him chant the Word 'Holy Nama'—Sacred Name (I worship) and so invoke the famed Nandhi, who is the Supreme Lord, in the three luminaries—the sun, moon and fire.

1852. To perform Pooja in holy places is to be blessed a hundred times. To worship His presence is to be blessed a ten hundred times. To feed those (Gnanies) who have stilled their thoughts is to be blessed a hundred, hundred times. To see that Gnani is fed to contentment is indeed, to be the most blessed of all.

1853. The Poojas you performed when the Sun and Moon Nadis actively beat go to meet the Asuras. The Poojas that you perform when the Sun and Moon Nadis are quelled, in the yoga way, are alone appropriate for Holy Nadhi, The Lord Shiva.

1854. When Prana ascends beyond the spheres of the sun and the moon, Bindhu and Nadha are there. Thus ascending (through six yogic centres) your awareness (consciousness) crosses the frontiers of the waking state. When you continuously worship Nadhi there, that worship is truly divine.

1855. Rouse the kundalini sakthi transcending the

successive gates of awarensss; reduces the perishable body to its elemental (Tathwa) constituents and then discard them. Then does the yogi enter the grace of the Holy One, and there abide in Him. This indeed, is the worship appropriate to Sadhashiva.

1856. The worship that you perform by day and by night, is to the Lord an offering of twin flowers. The worship that you perform where there is neither day nor night, is full of acceptance and is indeed, replete to Him of the flowing matted locks.

In worship, two flowers are offered to the Lord—One at day and the other at night, He, of the matted locks accepts the worship in the sphere where there is neither night nor day.

1857. Seated in the sphere where there is neither day nor night. I imbibed the Supreme honeyed bliss. At the feet of the Holy Lord, where there is neither day nor night, lost in thought to the events outside, I dispelled the twin maya that creates the distinction of night and day.

15. Maheswara Pooja (Worship of the Devotees)

1858. The offering given to the Lord in the high steaped temples do not reach His devotees who are the noble walking temples. But when you offer things to the noble walking temples, this surely reaches the Lord in the high-powered temples (pure devotees).

1859. The great Nandhi has proclaimed that the food received by the tapaswins of blemishless thought is food recieved, by the three worlds, and the offering they cheerfully received are the offerings received by the three worlds.

1860. You will know for certain that the offerings given to the dear devotees of the Lord, are oblations offered to the three Gods, who are seated in Him and to the givers' ancestors for twenty-one generations.

1861. It is certain that though you give a thousand free habitations to hold Brahmins, or you build a thousand temples for the Gods; they are all of no merit when compared to a day's feed given to a holy devotee of the Lord.

1862. You may well feed a hundred thousand Brahmins who wear the holy thread and perform noble sacrifices, but far holier should be the desire to feed in great endearment, albeit a morsel, a true devotee of the Lord who wears the Holy Ashes.

1863. Those who wear the Holy ashes and pray to Him in intense devotion, as their Lord, their God, who rides the Divine Bull, are truly devas on Earth. Those who worship these devas as the Lord Himself, who sports the Ganges on His russet matted locks wilt reach the end of their karmas.

1864. The famed Nandhi's face is of resplendent beauty and His matted locks of glowing sheen, I call His name in intense anguish. I shall neither stop to clamour, nor hail the Mighty Him as my Nandhi, until He appears before me.

1865. Let the yogi worship Shiva's devotees who do not know death for the vestigial ignorace in him will then disappear once and of all. So Unfailingly seek the pure devotees and make obeisance to them. It will be certain that the world will rejoice.

1866. They perform poojas with pride brimming to the full and with no endearment for the holy ones. Though they perform such poojas for ages and ages with their faces turned like hard agitating churns and their hearts filled with extreme egoity, their worship without love for Lord Shiva and His Gnani's temperament leads to nowhere and in the end they only perish.

1867. Moolar in unmistakable, meaningful words has affirmed that the food the holy men partake is the food, for the God, Shiva, MahaVishnu and Brahma and that the sure way to attain Mukthi is to partake unhesitatingly of the leavings of holy men who have realized.the Supreme Truth.

1868. Those who silently persevere in holy penance are not depressed, they are great. So hasten to give away your karmas to them and you will reach that golden land where three karmas, past, present and future do not exist.

The three karmas are:—Sanchitha (stored up), Prarаptha (already bearing fruits), Agaamya (prospective).

16. Grandeur of Holy Men

1869. There are no enemies present, where there is a holy man of divine worth who pursues the Lord, who embraces all spaces. No evil befalls that land; rains fall in abundance and contentment marks the people's way of life.

1870. They are born in this holy land, perform penance in this body and search the reach of the Lord; here in this land, they will receive His mighty Grace.

1871. I sought the goab of Union in Lord Shiva in the peaks of the high mountain (Sahashrara). Then the immortal celestials, the hordes of humans from the eight quarters and the Primal One, too, if they come toward me, and in my hands I hold them, I will be redeemed forever and ever.

1872. The seven universes—the cosmic space beyond them, animate and inanimate lives, the three Gunas, the ancient Vedas, the Gods and who create and preserve and their Primal God who is Shiva—are all in ime only.

1873. The Lord is neither male, nor female, nor hermaphrodite. The grand Light that is concealed within ignorance can never, never cognise Him, who sees without eyes, hears without ears. Only those ripe in knowledge have surely seen Him.

1874. The devotees of the Lord pursue, the sure path in the existent world. They will rule in the heavens above. They become Shiva whose arms stretch embracing the eight directions, whose Feet are in the depths of the neither world whose crown rises in the peaks of the cosmic Universe.

1875. Muse on the Lord who resides in our heart. They who see Him, residing within know no sorrows. The heart that knows His entrance loses its ego and that may be well destroyed too. So strive to reach this state.

1876. He, the Primal Lord, is the finite beginning. He is an endearing companion and in compassion causes dissolution too. I gave up all thoughts of blame, praise and my entire possessions. Then, He did plough my life for an aboundant harvest.

1877. He is my Mother and Father in one. My Seven-fold seven births are willed to Shiva—this document was drawn up even in the days of yore, written by Brahma who created this world and witnessed by Mahavishnu, the cloud-hued.

1878. The Lord abides firm in the hearts of the resolute. He comports in accord, in the handy hearts of those who adore Him. Those who hold and reckon the Primal Lord as their heart's jewel can neither part from Him, ever, nor give Him up.

1879. The celestial beings bore the Nandhi of the flowing matted locks on their heads. Nandhi raised me high on earth, to perform His holy work, He of the spreading locks will lift me higher still, to the very golden Kingdom of purity to rule.

1880. In the days of innocent childhood, I marked out the body ones by their external insignia, became their devotees and rejoined in the act. The holy ones wandered with their matted locks tied in single knot, without a care for this world.

1881. They who seek the holy devotees in endearing love can seek in depth and be near to Lord Shiva. The devotees who seek the Holy One will be merged in Lord Shiva's greatness. The Holy ones wander and do not return to wordly thoughts. They are immersed in the waters of divine contemplation. This is their intense penance.

1882. The eight clans of celestial beings seek the Holy ones and so swarm the earth in surpassing endearment. They earth seems like a crowded heaven for a radium of twelve leagues in eight directions.

"Eight" clans of celestial beings—this is a way of speaking, the number is not to be taken as exact, unless the Lords of eight directions are meant.

1883. No misfortune befalls the land where Shiva yoga Gnanis flourish, new ways of prosperity will dawn and all good will befall this land. It will be a very heaven with no more rebirths for its denizens.

1884. He, who has attained the higher knowledge can even create the world and can transcend several worlds, He who has perceived the divine light is immortal here below. He, indeed, is the true devotee of Lord Shiva, Himself.

17. Rules of Feeding Holy Men

1885. The Lord's devotees receive the food, whatever be it, offered to them as sweet ambrosia. They will ever be engrossed in seeking Shiva and Shiva alone. As unhappy as the husband may feels when the lone plot of land, he owns actually lies uncared for, so should one feel when a devotee is left uncared for.

1886. In order to sustain the body temple where the Lord resides; the holy ones who have savoured the Lord's inner grace will accept alms at noon-tide. They do not think of differences. They are seated in solitude having extinguished all desires.

18. Principles of Receiving Alms

1887. The seed lies in the body-field (Mooladhara—yogic centre) that has a fence. The crop ripens in the crown of the head (Sahashrara). If without feat, they do not harvest and do not feed themselves, they beg only for hunger's sake.

1888. The Lord Shiva begged in Brahma's skull to perpetuate Holy Dharma, so that Lord Brahma may become Brahman.

1889. The Lord created the seven worlds; they called Him a beggar. Why, should the Lord beg ? though. He does it, so that the holy devotees who think of Him constantly might beg and reach His Feet.

1890. The Lord stands waiting for those who come seeking Him. He waits to bestow His bliss on the holy ones. He stands waiting for them to enter. Can any one say that He knows me not.

1891. The devotees of Lord Shiva do not possess such bodily evils as gnawing hunger, greed and anger. They do not remain so either in this world or in the blessed world above.

1892. Tapaswins, though they have received the clear light of pure Gnana, yet they perforce seek the portals of the bounteous for alms. All the world will hold these tapaswins in reverance, for they do not beg for a living.

19. Mudhra Variations

1893. Mudhra is to transcend the cleven Awasthas. Fix the awareness on the silent Pranavam letter 'OM'. All the worldly desires are quelled and you attain Mukthi. This is the way to reach the holy feet of Nandhi.

Fix the Mudhra (that directs the eleven sense organs, five Gnanendhriyas, five Karmaendriyas, and one Manas) on the silent letter Pranava 'OM'. You will reach the Holy Feet of Lord Nandhi's and attain perfection, i.e., Mukthi or eternal liberation.

1894. Insert your tongue inward in the palatal place where the three Thuriya states of awareness subsume, and contain it there. Thus practise the Mudhras, Sambhavai and Kesari. This will result in the flood of light of Divine Gnanam.

1895. Sambhavi Mudhra brings the glance of Nandhi in abounding grace and snaps birth cycle, where true Kesari mudhra 'AUM', the one I practised as Nadha (Guru) divine, is chanted in silence, it brings divine Gnana.

1896. Sadhashiva appears in yogic centres, the Great Shiva appears in Gnana. Shiva's form disappears in the silence of the Mouna Mudhra. Truly, this is the finale Mukthi, the 'Ultimate thule' the last thing.

1897. Mauna is the stillness of both speech and thought, at once. Mouna without speech alone is only a state only when speech and thought are alike in Mauna; But who knows to bring about this Suddha State ?

1898. Sambhavi is the lion among yoga Mudhras that certainly leads to the eight Siddhis. When you seek Gnana Mudhra, it is indeed, Kesari that is landed high by the Holy Vedas.

1899. The yogi, by coursing the Kundalini Sakthi through the six yogic centres within the body, attains the eight Siddhis and experiences the divine Nadha state. He is rid of Karmas and abides in tranquillity and serenity. He pursues the fourth state of Sayujya, that is identity in Lord Shiva. This way, he reaches the Primal One and attains Union in Him.

1900. The yogic way of Dwadasa only leads to Sodasa (Kalas 16) Kala Prasadha which Sunders desires. This in the pure way of Vedanta-siddhantha. Truly, it is pure Suddha Saivism to meditate on the manthra that begins with 'Na' (NAMASIVAYA).

The yogic way of Dwadhasa marga (twelve-states way) sunders desires. It is but the subtle way of performing poojas with sixteen rituals. It subdues the ten organs—motoria and sensoria—that is the end of Vedanta. Yoga is the pure way of Siddhantha-Vedanta.

1901. Mauna is the Mudhra for those who seek mukthi. Gnana (Kesari) the Mudhra for those who are gurus. Siddhantha (Sambhavi) is the Mudhra that draws nectar of grace. All mudhras firm up breath. This Lord Shiva Truth was revealed of yore.

1902. The Holy feet of the Lord will appear in the central Sushumna Nadi. The Lotus centre (Sahashrara) is within a golden sphere. The upward coursing of kundalini lifts the yogi beyond to the moon's sphere that is white and here, he visions the purest one.

20. The Samadhi, Path of the Perfect Cave

This is a very important chapter (all 8 varses 1904 to 1910) describing as it does to what happens when success is achieved in yoga-Samadhi, and also what failure, total or partial involves.

The subject matter of the chapter, is an important one. It explains why the Gnani's body would not be cremated but buried, and what the rituals are that should accompany the disposal of the body in this manner.

1903. When the yogi shuffles his mortal coil, during the phase when the crescent moon waxes. This, He, the soul, will reach this world of the Devas. Abiding there for a while, he subsides into the sphere of Sun; from there he reaches the sphere where the souls of ancestors dwell, and from there he finally abides in the sphere of the moon.

1904. After all these, this life of the yogi ends in Samadhi. But when he fails to reach Samadhi. He will again take refuge (be reborn) in this world and by the Lord's grace resume continual yoga practice and thus complete the unfinised undertaking.

1905. Remaining so in this world, he attains Shivayoga. The Sivayogin merges in Bindhu and attains many miraculous powers. His fleshy body reaching Siddhahood.

1906. If Shiva yogins die while in the pursuit of yoga, they reach the world of Tapas only to return to this world again and to repair yoga. They are indeed blessed, whom the celestial beings esteem highly.

1907. If the Shivayogi gives up life, he enters into Mauna Samadhi to seek the unitive state. He will not be born again in another body, nor remain as Jivan muktha. He is conscious of the here below but remains united with the Lord as one.

1908. They are indeed blessed, who die, if they unite as one in the Lord, Himself, in death. Though dead in the body, they are fully alive in awareness. They who are dead to and dead like the three impurities are true Siddhas who become Lord Shiva.

1909. The Exalted Lord sunders the births of those who intensely seek His Grace. He draws them into the fold of His dear devotees. Likewise, the Gnani, like the Lord, draws His discipline in abounding love and in his own subtle way shapes them towards Godhood.

1910. The heart of the Shivajnani overflows in grace. The Holy man feels Shiva and sees His pervasive presence everywhere. The sky you see may be fragmented, but it engulfs all space. Similarly, the Gnani, though circumscribed by his body, appearing to be rid of consciousness of there and here below, possesses consciousness that is one with the all pervasive Shiva's.

21. Samadhi Rituals

1911. If the body of the Shivajnani is consigned to flames, the entire people will suffer in burning fever. If his body is left a prey to the dogs and jackals, tumultuous war will seize the land and the people will be a prey to dogs and jackals.

1912. If the Gnani's body is consigned to fire, it is like consigning the Lord's temple to fire. Then, no more rains will fall in the land, famine shall fourish the world and countless kings will lose their kingdoms.

1913. It is indeed proper to bury them. If they are consigned to fire, distruction will dog the land. If left the perish, uncared for, the world will lose its prosperity and fall a prey to devastating fires.

1914. As and when the body of the Gnani receives the Lord's grace, let it be seated in a cave, dug appropriately in the earth's bowel. Then stately rules and people in the land receive blessings of infinite grace.

1915. Dig the sepulchure well, heap five cubits around the earth, shape it into a striangle three cubics sides and there seat the body in Padhmasana.

1916. One's own homestead, roadside, tank bund, riverbed, wooded grove, city's common dense forest and high mountain valleys—these are the appropriate sites to shape the sepulchure (Samadhi).

1917. The appropriate dimensions to shape the sepulchure five-feet on all the four sides, nine feet deep and three feet each on the inner triangle's sides at the base.

1918. Spread the five precious metals and the nine rare gems within the cave. Place the seat upon them and scatter Kusa grass and shower with white holy ashes. Above that scatter golden-coloured turmeric powder with rich incenses.

1919. Lay garlands of honey-dew flowers, sandal, musk, civet and diverse unguents upon the cave that is square-shaped inside sprinkling rose water, light the ritual lamp with devotion and affection.

1920. Smear the entire body with white holy ashes to form a protective shroud. Place the body in an appropriate Asana. Sangle with several bright incenses and holy ashes. Having seated the body thus, cover the cave with earth.

1921. Having covered the cave thus, level the four sides. Place his sandals, earrings, and an image with face and eyes decked in suitable dress. Also offer parched rice, food and tender coconut.

1922. Finally pour the white ashes and powdered incense, shower diverse flowers, Kusha grass and Bilwa leaves. Sprinkle holy water and raise a platform three feet by three.

1923. Upon the platform plant the sapling of a peepul

tree, or a holy Lingam. Arrange the Samadhi (face) towards North or East and perform poojas with sixteen rituals in endearing devotion.

22. Arisen of the Mighty Bindhu

The contents of this chapter follow naturally from the preceeding one. Man is called upon to stimulate (imitative magic) the creative process of cosmic Bindhu and Nadha.

This chapter of fourteen verses is also full of meta-physical concepts, dealing especially, with cosmogony viewed from the special angle of evolutes as Bindhu and Nadha of the Primal cause.

1924. When creation commenced, kundalini arose from Para bindhu and from Kundilai the Vainadavam in the vast firmament, nine gods Brahma and the rest with their Sakthis and in corresponding order the Karmas, the Kalas and the sound Vaikarai (Nadha).

1. Kundalini, Kudilai, Tatparai, Vagesi are emanations—the four above. (i.e., Kundalini, etc) and the five Gods: Sadhasiva, Brahma, Vishnu, Rudhra and Maheswara.
2. Sakthis:—five auspicious sakthis of these five Gods—
3. Karanas:—the intellectual organs, Manas, Buddhi, Siddha and Ahamkara.
4. Kalas:—five kala Tathwas and
5. Vaikari:-the unmanifested sound.

1925. Bindhu attains twenty-five modifications. Nadha attains ten modifications. The, rest two—Sakthi and Shiva—attain no modification but activate the other two—Bindhu and Nadha.

1. Twenty-five evolutes of Parabindhu are the nine Vaindavams; the five sakthis of the Five Gods (Manonmani, Saraswathi, Lakshmi, Parameswari and Maheswari); four intellectual organs; five kala Tathwas, Vaikari, the unmanifest sound and niyathi tathwa evolutes of Nadha are kala (time), Vaidhya (knowledge), Ragha (desire), Prusha (the experience of the soul), Maya (illusion), and the five Suddha

Tathwas—Suddha Vidhya, Iswaram, Sadhaakyam, Sakthi and Sivam.

1926. The four ultimate Sakthis—Vagesi, Tathparai, Kudilai and Kundalini evolve from Bindhu. The Parabindhu gives rise to all these manifestations out of Mamaya.

1927. The Kalas Niviriṭhi and the rest in which the sound—'A', 'U', 'M' rest composed, enters there in Nadahantha Bindhu and into the Karanas that include the mind, and the internal intellectual organs evolve manifesting these. The Bindhu's act of creation ceases.

Nivirthikala—this dispels doubts of the jeevas who reach its sphere. Prathista Kala—firms up the Jeeva in truth, Vidhya Kala—confers Gnana, Santhi Kala—confers equipoise and Santyathita Kala—confers manifestations (Swaroopa) beyond equipoise.

1928. The Parapara who is the end and the beginning is immanent. He expands as cause and effect. Well, He is Beeja the causal seed of the five acts too.

1929. The world and the cosmic universe arose by the power of Holy Beeja and that emanated from Bindhu. The five elements—the Sky and the rest arose from out of the causal Asuddha) Maya (Staff of matter) and this Beeja is the Macro and the Micro causal seed.

1930. The Bindhu that shines within the body and without in all nature is white in hue. Nadha is vibrant red. They are embedded within as Sakthi and Shiva. If activated in wisdom they can well grant Mukthi—eternal liberation.

1931. All-pervasive like the Param, the Bindhu stands veiling all like a vast filament and filling everywhere as the space in all pots. Bindhu is Mamaya is the cause and effect, and it pervades all the cosmos.

1932. Nandhi stands in the Bindhu to bestow His manifold blessings and grace. No one that knows Bindhu is within, in their Beejas as the seed that blossoms as a scented flower in the body and a divine swan-SOHAM-in the macrocosm. Beeja is the blessed one, that is the causal seed of all.

1933. There is no embryo without seed. The embryo does not appear except from the seed. The seed and the embryo are only one and never separate. Thus are the Bindhu and the Lord Shiva too. You should know that without the One the Lord, the other cannot fructify or survive successfully.

1934. The food you partake goes in three directions to the body, to the mind and to the excreta. The parts that go to the mind and the body truly become the blood, first.

1935. Out of the sevan constituents food breaks into blood, lymph, bone, skin, flesh, brain and semen. The Bindhu forms in three days like the tiny dew-drops on a blade of grass and matures fully seven times in three days.

1936. When it remains thus in the body, for three days, it becomes a part of the mind. It is retained here and as bright Kala it illumines those who are immersed in holy thoughts. But for those who indulge in sexual intercourses, it departs and their mental powers are deteriorated.

1937. No one knows the destruction that the wasting of Bindhu results in. They do not resolve to prevent their decay by determined will-power. They who thus perish in this perishing body do not give it up and they do not know the way you perish.

23. Subjugation of Bindhu Conformity of Bindhu Flow

1938. Do not look at women who look at you, keep away from women intent on lust. Melt your heart in devotion and uproot the evil desires that sight kindles in you. Light the Kundalini fire and fix it on the source of primal energy. He who does it is truly a Shivayogi who sublimates Bindhu.

1939. He who becomes a slave to lust will be in constant feat; his body deteriorates and his life ebbs away. He will not receive grace nor reach Shivayoga.

1940. Let those who wish to sleep with women, observe the periodicity of the two phases of the moon. The first eight days of the waning moon are not appropriate for union. They can be in union in the last six days, and in the first six days of the waning moon.

1941. Let those who practise yoga avoid the fifth, sixth and the eleventh days after the woman menstruates. For the rest, who seek pleasure, take the six days in the middle of the three weeks that follow.

1942. When they decide on union, it should be for four Muhurthas, following the injunctions of Kama Shasthra. Let them perform the sexual act when the moon's Kalas (left Nadi) shine bright and breath in the Sun's Nadi, runs low. Holding the breath, emit Bindhu and breathe through the right nostril, quelling the left.

'Bindhu' here is semen. Moon's Kala is here, the Pingala Nadi and Sun's Kala is Ida Nadi.

1943. Embrace the damsel conjoining your five senses ograns with hers. But, let your passion for the woman be detached, like the sense that are sublimated Godward. Do not be excited, be clam. Control your breath, senses and mind and concentrate the thought, thus emit your Bindhu.

1944. When in union with damsel of armour, beauty, youth and shapely form, coral lips and breasts that swell, direct your senses inward and emit the Bindhu.

1945. Having emitted, examine the laws of conception and determine in detail the results of the act—the time of union, of pregnancy and delivery, the baby's length of life and death and its character both good and bad.

1946. Having examined these, abstain from worldly concerns, leave the maiden of shapely breasts and do not seek further union. Within two months the baby will take its form and all the rest that you have reckoned will follow.

1947. Except for those who plant the seed, there will be no great wisdom, nor harvest in the future. If they know the seed of seed certainly their body will be preserved like the mango fruit kept in a hanging vessel.

1948. The Lord has great concern for the seed in the womb. He settles, with forethought, its fate and span of life even in the seed. Thus, when the seed itself is the causal thought; it is but a figment of the imagination to attribute cause and effect to outside factors.

1949. Life does not ebb away, if Bindhu stands retained in the body. If Bindhu is truly conserved all these—great strength, energy, alert intelligence, penance, contemplation, silence and enduring siddhis are attained.

1950. Thus conserving the sexual energy, the yogis light the fire of kundalini and coursing it upward through the Sushumna Nadi they reach the state of illumination. They are indeed, true Shiva yogis who in unbroken continuity partake of the ambrosia that flows from within the moon.

1951. Though troubled by passions, the yogi, the Gnani, the Siddha high and the Bhoga yogi who is yet the king of Gnanis. Yet saviour, the ambrosia within, in the yogic way. They who have conserved the Bindhu are all, heroes indeed.

1952. The Lord's body is the fiery Bindhu above (macrocosm) and the Bindhu wasted here below is the vital Prana (microcosm). If these two are mixed, and burnt in the Kundalini fire, then, the yogis consume the very ambrosia. This is true wisdom of yogis.

1953. The folks in ignorance waste it daily, and destroyed by the senses, they weep in pain. But if in wisdom that they consciously perform supreme yoga, the Bindhu that disappears is divinely assimilated.

1954. If you hold women as messengers of death then, love's passion will vanish away. You will be totally rid of your impurities and there will be no death. For innumerable ages, you will be in the Holy Divine Light.

1955. He who has conquered Bindhu has conquered time and he who has wasted it has perished before his time. They do not know that Bindhu that has been preserved becomes one with Kundalini in time, and their breath is controlled in the yogic way.

1956. If you desire woman's love, and in order to excite her intensely, cleanse the woman of her bowel, phlegm and bile, the day before you indulge in sexual union and then, embrace her in union.

1957. Direct the Prana breath upward through the Sushumna nadi to Bindhu and Nadha that arises in the cranium sphere by appropriate devices. Thus you reach to the divine nectar, hold on to it. This Bindhu dissolves in dissolutely in you and your illusions disappear.

This divine nectar is the semenal Bindhu assimilated in the body through yoga.

1958. Those who have realized all these, the ripening of Bindhu, the full result of that ripening, the dire consequences of wasting it and the blessings of retaining it, the Nadha that ensures and the transformation that effects Nadha, have truly conquered Bindhu.

The conquest of Bindhu truly leads to Nadha which effects transformations.

1959. Burn Bindhu (semenal Bindhu) that is Beeja (seed) agreeably in the fire of Kundalini that flames from the Mooladhara, then course it upward into the solar sphere within and touch the lunar sphere beyond where, indeed, the divine nectar is present.

1960. When the Bindhu of the body is destroyed by yoga, it is transformed into divine Bindhu of the ambrosial lunar sphere within. When the Bindhu of the body perishes in the Kundalini fire, the ambrosial waters flow and fill the body. This is indeed Shiva Bhoga that is ambrosial sweet and thus bathed in divine waters of ambrosia the yogi attains rare Siddhis.

1961. When two bodies may unite in union and yet if he does not emit Bindhu, this union is the yoga way. This Bhoga is Shiva Bhoga. The true Bhoga is where the yogi does not emit to quell the passion of the witless woman.

1962. They who seated in yoga way eventhough they unite with women, they do not emit their Bindhu, in passion. The life's passion of these women is unquenched and they will verily pine and droop, still yearning for love, as new lovers do forever.

1963. Vanquish Bindhu by Kundalini Sakthi, kindle the fire in Mooladhara, course it upward straight through the central Nadi, Sushumna. Reach Nadha and swell the ambrosia flowing there. Your Bindhu becomes the divine Bindhu.

1964. When Bindhu and Nadha unite, and the Kundalini fire permeates each minute hair root, you become Lord Shiva Himself, devoid of all thoughts. And the Bindhu then dies in the primal Bindhu of the divine body.

1965. He who pounds the seed and consumes it will not get a good harvest. Different is he who fires it in the Kundalini fire and absorbs it in the body. He has not made a meal of it but had ended the seed of birth.

1966. Bindhu that is the vital Prana courses upward merging in the divine Bindhu. This Bindhu, a swan in the cranium (Sahashrara) unites in Nadhantha, the luminous Bindhu is absorbed into the body.

1967. Bindhu is of two forms for all—the swan (the microcosmic) and Prana (the microcosmic). Those who realize this and absorb one in the other—the Prana (individual) in the Swan (cosmic)—will attain eight siddhis, their body glitters as gold and they become immortal.

1968. Intone the sound 'si' (the first sound of Panchakshara) in your Prana's (life breath) silent thought merging in 'AUM'—the cluster sound of 'A' 'U', 'M', thus you read Parasakthi You hold, this mystic secret (Upadesa) which is indeed, the way to conquer Bindhu.

1969. This is but the mystic sacret, there is none other than this. There is nothing else, but He alone is. Conquest of the Bindhu makes it ascend heavenward. The action of the fourteen organs (five Gnanendhriyas), five Karmendriyas and four Ankhakranas) ceases. Then does Gnana flow and truly this is Shiva state.

The sublimated Bindhu (clan vital) becomes an intellectual and spiritual force. Then the Lord Shiva state is filled with graceful Gnanam.

1970. This vast creation was born in union of Bindhu and Nadha. In this union, the beginning and end of all, and all great manthras too wore born, SIVOHAM is when Bindhu subsides.

1971. The Bindhu is the winning balance of mind, raise it high to the mouth of Sushumna. Try the Bindhu, this way you scorch your interminable Karmas. Then this is the day you pluck away the fruit of fig that holds the seeds of innumberable births.

1972. When Bindhu and Nadha uniting in one enter the sphere of the moon within, the heavenly ambrosia wells and flows. The Manthra (AUM) that rises here is the sacrificial offering to the Supreme Almighty, the Lord.

1973. When mind merges in the Bindhu, then the mind, the ears and all the sensual orgrans will rise together to seek the divine goal. But when thoughts, sounds and words rise in the mind, it seeks lust and is transformed into a thick liquid.

The working of the mind, arising of thought; sound and word, leads to lust, when Bindhu is not sublimated and is transformed into a thick liquid.

1974. No one knows the round (Nadha), the mind that perceives the sound and the place where the undistracted mind discerns Truth. Only the true Gnani's know the place that is truly the Mighty Lord's Seat.

1975. The regions of the five elements are within the body. Earth is where the legs are (Mooladhara), in the navel (Swadhistana) is the region of water, below the breast is the region of the fire, (Manipooraka), above the breast (Anaahatha) and below the shoulder (Vishudhi) is air; and around the neck and beyond (Agna) is the region of the space.

The location and significance of the six yogic centres in the body are: to be noted. Only five elements are involved. The association of space (Akasa-Ether) with Agna Chakra is particularly significant, for it is here, in the two-petalled lotus, that duality is supposed to disappear into non-duality during the Kundalini yoga.

24. The Sun's Position—The Cosmic Sun

1976. The fiery Sun and the rest of the celestials circumambulate the snow-clad mountain Meru, and adore the holy feet of the luminous Lord in severe penance, that they might themselves be illumined.

1977. The Sun is Vishnu, He is Holy Shiva too. He is the Primal energy of all lives, the refuge of all creations. He brings prosperity to the seven worlds in accord.

1978. Chant the thousand names of the 'Sun' in love. He glows in you as a divine spark. The Vedic brahmins pray to Him, the immortal celestials chant His name. He is the Primal Lord who blesses all.

1979. The Primal Lord alone is the uncreated being

(Svayambhu). Who stands as the Tathwas and Sakthi for the World. He is also the Moon of soft Divine Light.

1980. Indeed the 'Sun' within the body rises in the moving centre of the sixteen petalled Vishudhi, above the twin-circle of the Manipooraka centre, the hexagonal centre of Swadhistana, and the triangle of the Mooladhara centre.

1981. The Sun is within. When his beams beat on the Mooladhara triangle it receives the four kalas and when his shafts fall on the Vishudhi the sixteen kalas shine.

The effulgent 'Sun' above can confer the four Kalas on Mooladhara and the sixteen Kalas on Vishudhi.

1982. When you reach the sphere of the 'Sun' your worldly thoughts fade into darkness and the four cognitive organs do not contend any more. The Sakthi in the light within reveals the truth of the Vedas, which you do not seek to understand.

1983. The 'Sun' within the body, takes its route below the earth centre, that is the Mooladhara. Indeed, he is invisible between the fiery centre (Manipoorka) and the watery centre (Swadhistana) within.

1984. Breaking through the Earth (Mooladhra) the Sun penetrates into the yogic centres that are the sky (Vishudhi) and space (Agna) within the body. He is the very source of joy that dazzle the eyes and indeed, he responds to sweet contemplation.

1985. No one knows the route of the 'Sun' that penetrates earth (Mooladhara). They are only versed in worldly lore. Only those who have realized the truth know his real abode and they say that he circumambulates Mount of Meru, (Sahashrara) of the unconquerable Lord.

25. The Microcosmic Sun

1986. The benevolent Nandhi stood incessantly in my thoughts in postures of standing, sitting, walking and lying prostrate. Destroy your impurities (Malas) and ascend the Adharas-yogic centres through the central Sushumna Nadi, and there you will vision the sun, that shines within in nonpareil brightness.

1987. They who say ascending the yogic centres reach

and see where the 'Sun' reposes within the body; they indeed, are the self-realized ones. They who differ from this and say anything they like, are enveloped in darkness, like when the 'Sun' here below, dips the horizon.

1988. They who do not penetrate the yogic centres, nor search the world within, do not know where the Sun is in its midst. Those who know where lies furtively, to them my heart melts in love.

The yogi's heart melts in love for those who contemplate the sun within as worthy of adoration.

26. Mind's Sun

1989. When the Moon spreads its contending rays the luminous Sun becomes dewy cool. My yearning prana commingling in the luminosity that emanates as a beam; is my life's full moon.

1990. To vision the union of the beams of the Sun, and the Moon in the mystic land within is divine. They who have visioned it have indeed, become Lord Shiva himself.

1991. The Kalas become four when the Kala arises from the intermingling of the rays with the three Kalas of the sun, moon and fire. Know that when the sun-moon and fire mingle their rays then it is full moon within.

1992. The light that shines beyond the two orbs, is a light that cannot be perceived in any realm. It is the ethereal light that shines within, piercing the cosmic universe. No one can near it, nor perceive it.

1993. The nine orbs (planets) go round the earth, but none of the nine, knows the Lord. The nine orbs may well propitiate Him, yet they do not receive His Mighty grace. They are surrounded in darkness, devoid of bliss.

27. Cosmic Bindhu (Gnana Sun)

1994. The Bindhu expands into two, Apara and Para. The Apara becomes the Para Nadha, from which in turn arises the Para Kalas: The Gnana Sun dawns within with those Kalas.

1995. The sound that arises when the Sun within dawns

is an emanation from Paranadha. The five sounds—Vaihari and the rest, belong to this Parabindhu that arise in the five Kalas, one in each.

1. Vaikhari:—articulated speech. Its source is below the tongue.
2. Madhyamai:—sound as it reaches the throat. Its source is between the heart and the throat. Its shape is the letter formed articulately inside.
3. Paiysanthi:—through form sound (no letter shape). Its source is the stomach. Its shape is Prana.
4. Sukshmi:—unarticulated sound. It is from the navel point. Its shape in intelligence.
5. Panchamai:—subtle sound-Source. Its source is ultra sutble. Its shape is Pranava. It is located in the Mooladhara.

1996. He is the Head and the Lord of the Devas, He creates the ten directions. Of youre they hailed Him as the Lord, of the Three Mighty Gods (Brahma-Vishnu-Shiva) He is the Lord of the four too (Nadha, Vindhu, Shiva and Sakthi)—the formless four); the immortal celestials say that He stands in them as the central Being. Sadhashiva, of the four Gods.

1997. He is not unreal, He is the Truth. He, my Father is the sun-moon and fire who dispels darkness and the darkness of my all karmas too. He, the Holy Nandhi, appeared to me, to dispel the darkness of my low desires.

1998. He dispelled my darkness with His peerless rays and then the divine fruits honey flowed within. Beaming with benevolent rays—as the Lord of Kailash, He stood aloft, within me too, as resplendent light.

1999. His dazzling light spreads as true wisdom and unhindered it invades all worlds. It is the pervasive light that none can fathom. No one knows it as the Supreme Light.

2000. The Sun (Gnana Sun) that rises in the vast firmament stands within the too shedding divine rays. He constantly traverses in the eight directions. Yet, He stands forever fixed within those that know this Supreme Truth.

2001. The navel, eye, nose tip, in the centre of the eyebrows and within the crown of the head are the five places where the Lord resides as Divine Light. He is the One Lord whom the Devas saw as three—Brahma, Vishnu, Rudhra. The Apara becomes the Para Nadha, from whom the Para Kalas arise and with these Kalas the Gnana sun dawns within.

28. Shiva Sun

This chapter alongwith the proceeding one correlates the energy flow (of the sun) in the cosmos (human body) following yogic and Tanthric principles.

Para 25 (The mind's Sun) Para 26 (Gnana Sun) and Para 27 (Shiva Sun) present a consolidated picture of the roles of the Sun-Moon and Fire in the cosmos, and in the human body (microcosmos) in various aspects such as the mind Jiva Jeeva Gnana (for Supreme wisdom) and finally in the removal of ignorance by the Light of Holy Shiva.

2002. Just as when the luminous sun rises and the murky darkness before him flees, the darkness of contending Pasa and the vast ignorance, flee fast, before the Gnana light of Lord Shiva.

2003. The Sun appears in pot to pot, and you may well close the pots, yet you cannot contain him. So, too, when the Lord who swallowed poison enters this body, you cannot contain Him in this body for He pervades all.

2004. He, Himself stands as three lights (Sun-Moon-Fire); He, Himself stands established as Brahma and Mahavishnu, as indistinguishable life and body and as space, light and darkness too.

2005. The divine fire, Sun, Moon, Earth, Water, Fire, Wind, Space and the countless creations are the ancient abodes of Lord Shiva. Similarly, the five Gods (Brahma, Vishnu, Rudhra, Maheswara, Sadhasiva) and Four Holy Vedas—these nine are also favourite resorts of Shiva Adhithya (Shiva-Sun).

29. Nature of the Jeeva Prana

2006. The One Param whom the Vedas praise and the One whom, I realize in contemplation is the undying light that shines in me and I beheld Him, as the Divine Swan Para Bindhu.

2007. The two swans on the river bank (of life) do not

know of any separation. If one, Jeeva, says that he is by himself, then, this foolish swan, does not receive grace.

This reminds one of Rig Vedic Verse I. 164. There, two birds are seated on a tree, One (Jeeva) enjoys the fruits of the tree (pippalam) and the other (Shiva or Brahman or Supreme Soul) watches, but does not eat.

30. Purudan

2008. Activating the Gnana and Kriya Sakthis, the true Lord, from time immemorial created Vakhari and the rest of the sounds, Maya and the rest of the impurities, and Purusha and the rest of the illusory Tathwas.

The four sounds are:—Vaikari, Madhyamai, Paiysanthi, Sukshma.

Vaikari—articulate sound form.

Madhyamai—sound form proceeding from the throat and indistinctly articulate.

Paiysanthi—sound form proceeding from the lungs struggling towards vocalisation.

Sukshma—subtle source of speech.

This is variously translated as 'the experient self', 'the agent of experience', 'the agent-self', and as 'the world-soul' in (Samkhya Philosophy). We prefer the first one in the context of Shiva Siddhantha.

2009. The Lord is the Beginning of all. He is the Atom—within the-atom. Divine an atom within the atom into one thousand forms. They who can thus divide the atom within the atom may well be near the Lord, who indeed, is the Atom-within-the-atom.

The Lord, the source of all, is the atom within the atom. Only they who are capable of fragmenting an atom can vision this atom within an atom (the Lord).

2010. Jeeva, that is the atom, is like the tiny seed of the spreading banyan tree. If you purify your way by the fire of Gnana, then, the dark Pasa that malign You will be driven away. Seek the divine way that the Dancing Lord shows you.

2011. No one realizes that He is within the Jeeva, atom, and the atom (jeeva) stands comingling in their Him. The peerless Lord, unintermittently pervades in the entirety of all creation.

31. Jeeva (Soul)

2012. To speak of the size of Jeeva is like this; split a cow's soft hair into a hundred tiny parts and then divide each part into a thousand parts. The size of Jeeva equals that one part of the one hundred thousand.

2013. Though my Lord is of infinite size, yet He dwells permeating within the littleness of this body. He is the Lord Supreme whom the celestials cannot know. As such as your penance is so much also is He known.

2014. You may not be inclined for yoga. But if your illuminated Guru teaches you, you may accomplish it and persevere so in several lives. And seeing you practise thus, Shiva's form will arise in your thoughts.

Yoga practise persevered through several lives makes Shiva's form arise in your thoughts.

2015. You are harassed by Maya's manifestations. But when the illumined Guru lights you up by His Grace, your entire troubles will cease. They Jeeva, illumined by Gnana may accomplish it and reach the Thuriya State.

32. Pasu (Jeeva)

2016. The learned cows (Jeevas) may wander about bellowing and the power-giddy cows may strut about displaying their insignia. But the good mature cows (Gnanis) yield a pot of milk (Gnana) that is precious, the rest are indeed, only barren cows.

2017. Take the cows, that graze in the backwoods of desires, beyond them, and lead them, to the feet of the Lord. Discipline them in superior ways and manage the herd thus, until such time, their thoughts do not turn back to the backwards of worldly pleasures.

Lead the cows (Jeevas) that graze in the backwoods of worldly desires to the Holy Feet of the Lord. Instruct them in Supreme disciplined ways. From then, on they will never turn to their previous state.

33. Bhodhan (Lord as Giver of Light of Gnana)

2018. Jeeva and Lord Shiva are not separate; Jeeva does

not know Shiva and when Jeeva comes to know Shiva, Jeeva becomes Lord Shiva.

2019. The Dancing Lord (Sri Nataraja) is the benevolent light. He is the joyous light of all creation. He is the cluster of light that overseas all and adorns the many hooded serpent with gem like shining eyes.

The dancing Shiva is the cluster of benevolent lights that oversees all, and the joyous light that vibrate through the entire creation.

2020. The Lord without the aid of sensory organs, is self-illumined. He is immune from ignorance, is all knowledge and is Himself as knowledge and is Himself as the knower too. He is the Jeeva as well, who stands pervading all.

2021. To me, who did not know the truth of the 36 Tathwas, He, the famed Nandhi taught me the truth of the 36 Tathwas. And when by His grace, I learned the truth of the 36 Tathwas He stood beyond the 36 Tathwas.

2022. Many do not know that Lord Shiva is grace. They do not know of the five Malas (impurities) that are to be rid of. But they perform diverse penance and are lost in distraction. They do not seek the Tathwa (truth) that is ever new.

2023. Men do not think of the divine acts, the Lord performs daily. Neither do they think of the ministering acts that the Lord performs daily. The Lord daily bestows His grace on the good. They who do not know this, do not seek Him daily but are entangled in their interminable work—a—day Karmas.

34. Benefits of the Controlling Five Senses

2024. The elephants (senses) are five that are in rut. Their rut increases for they do not remain tied to the (divine) post. As the Mahout (Jeeva) tires and the elephants (senses) too, become exhausted of their energy, they then turn to the yoga way. So, do not delay to control your senses.

2025. Unless the rider (Jeeva) trains the restless steed, (senses) by coursing the breath in the yogic way and by attentively learning holy lore, it will take its wayward course. They rider may firmly sit on its neck and administer hard punishment, Yet the animal will not move forward.

Unless the rider (Jeeva) trains the restless state, (senses) in the yogic way, it goes astray. The animal seldom moves, though the rider sitting on its back goes on making the punishment more and more severe.

2026. The sensual organs (sensoria) are five and the sense-birds (Jnannendriyas Motoria) are five. The sense-birds seek to feed upon the five sense-fields (potencies), Five are the waters (elements) and-five their function. Yet, they are all of one lineage. The lone hunter (Jeeva) brings the herd together. The exits of the body are nine and the harassing senses bring sorrow to him.

2027. The five lions that roam the forest seek their prey and get filled. The five then return to their caves; if you pull out the claws and teeth of the five, you will surely reach the Lord.

The senses are roaming like lions which feel contented when their stomachs get filled. If their claws and teeth are pulled, they will have no more terrors for you—you will safely reach the Lord.

2028. There are 96 Tathwas within and there are five ministers (senses). The five senses and their brood of sons within seek to rule over you. If the five stand in their fiery passion, the tribute that we pay to the five is indeed endless.

Five senses and the 96 Tathwas reign Supreme over you. The senses are like conspiring ministers that ever plot to usurp the body-kingdom.

2029. I do not praise the Holy Light daily, I do not speak of Sakthi who is within, nor do I conquer the five senses. But I am like an uncontrolled steed running headlong to its downfall.

2030. There are countless holes in this body's dark chamber, my lot will be faulty if I run with the countless holes (desires). But countless indeed, will be the bliss you attain, if you do not run with the countless holes of desires.

Do not run with the numerous holes of desire present in this body. Control will bring countless blessings.

2031. Life here below is of the strength of one's karma. The life in heaven above is of the strength of one's prayer.

Strength of wisdom belongs to man's higher life. And truly, their way of life is on one's strength of grace.

35. Controlling the Senses-Way of Sublimation

2032. The body pond is thus shaped round—its depth is one cubit and its diameter is half cubit. The fisherman (Lord) spreads His net and catches many a fish (of desires). So I do not encounter any more troubles.

2033. The stirring Indhriyas dwell within the body and he who controls them is indeed, immortal. If your thoughts seek the twin pleasures—food and sex, they will last only this far, until your breath lasts.

2034. Those who know nothing just say 'control, control the five senses', None, not even the immortals can control the five senses. Truly, you are an inert mass when you control the five senses. I learned there is an alternate way open. Sublimate them towards the Lord which is wisdom's way.

2035. The elephant in triple (Pasas) rut roared loudly. They became fat, causing destruction in their train and devastating the sweet fields of sugarcane (virtues). Then I applied the goat of knowledge to control them, but they roamped about and escaped in great fury.

2036. It is rare penance, if you sublimate the five senses. This indeed, is the way to receive grace, it is the Lord's Feet too and all the worlds are yours.

2037. The thought is the seed of all things, so why derivel at length and why think of the mirage ? If thought is expanded, the things too expand, All that there is to it is, to contract your thoughts. This is for those who think about it.

2038. The Lord, knowing all well how spent away you are, comes to dwell in the body for the soul to lean on. And He of blemishless fame subdues the five-headed serpent that lies coiled in Pasa and provides the fluted Sushumna that stands central.

2039. Tie the five prancing sensing organs to the post of Gnana that illumines. This is the way of yore that is high and true and thus you attain grace that is bliss.

2040. Daily think of the living Nandhi, gently control your

distracting thoughts and course your thoughts through Mooladhara. Then your thoughts become a temple extending from north to south.

2041. The hours speed away and many a day passes away too. Your possessions are transitory like the writing on the water. So, conquer the senses and quickly give them up. Then even if your troubles, as mountains, roll on you, may bear them, gently indeed.

2042. Praise the Holy form of the purest one, praise Him redeeming the senses by intelligence; welling up in love in your heart, you will become one with Him, the Lord of four directions, and of beings, and in all others.

2043. No one knows that the five senses with engrossing thoughts within the body, slowly eat you away. Do not take them lightly and talk away. They are indeed, like a mountain range that is capped by dark clouds.

2044. There is nothing that your need give up; the five senses are false organs that arise to meet the five cravings; Reach to Him in your thoughts and praise Him in sweet songs.

36. Paths of Unholy Guru

2045. The unholy Guru is indeed, a fool. He has no wisdom, has not realized the truth and is not versed in the way of the Vedas and the Agamas. He speaks ill of God, has no humility and his sole concern is this worldly life.

2046. The holy Gurus seek to know the Manthras, tanthras, Mahayoga, Jnana, bondage and Mukthi. But the unholy gurus do not seek them, do not clear doubts, but are in search of food, and truly they are blind.

2047. The unholy guru, bereft of knowledge, is no exalted teacher. He is a big fool and does not know the way of becoming. He is a vile fellow who is not rid of passions and he teaches vile things to vile men.

2048. If a teacher teaches without driving away the illusory thoughts that breed imagination, he will lose faith in divinity. The great Nandhi of yore has declared that he is an enemy to his own self and an evil for the king and the Kingdom.

2049. The blind (the unholy guru), who leads the blind (foolish disciples) will first fall into the eternal pit; then, the foolish disciples too fail; and in the end, in disorder, they fall together—The blind that lead and the blind that are led—are indistinguishably jumbled together.

37. Way of Holy Guru

2050. He is the Great Holy Guru who takes the Jeeva to the state beyond Tathwas. Placing his Feet on my head the master blesses me, works for my self realization and subdues my Pasas. He who is Truth itself performs all these.

2051. Blessing the disciples with his feet on their head, he extricates them from their Karmas and drives away their evil stars. He keeps the messengers of death at bay from them and ends their miseries of unending birth.

2052. Even as the black iron that is transmuted into gold does not return to black iron, the disciple who once receives the mighty grace of the Holy Guru does not return to births.

2053. The Holy Guru liberates you from Pasas, removes your entire impurities and makes you seek the Lord in Love—such are the Holy Gurus, blemishless. But they who exult in contention are not enlightened gurus.

2054. The Holy Guru is a pure being, so endearing and can give you love that is free from Malas—impurities. He is holy and immortal; He, the High master, assesses the worth of his disciples and bestows his grace on those who are rid of impurities.

2055. All that the alchemist touches turns into gold; just so, the Jeevas blessed by the holy guru, freed from the triple Malas-impurities, become Lord Shiva, Himself.

2056. The holy guru stand as Lord Shiva Himself. In his presence the Jeeva attains his self-realization, If you seek self-realization, think of him, within, as Shiva in fleshy body.

2057. The way of birth, the way of death, the way of Maya, they who have been the way of birth have not seen the way. You can reach the great way that Nandhi speaks of in this way; if you follow your Holy Guru.

2058. He is the Holy Guru, who speaks of the Vedas and

Agamas in entranced bliss, enters into Shiva, yoga, removes the bondage of Pasa (attachment through severe desirements), stills all your thoughts and leads you to the Lord.

2059. The Holy Guru reveals the real (Sath) the unreal (Asath) and the real-unreal (Sath/Asath); he takes Chit (Jeeva) and Achit (Tathwas) into Shiva-para. The blessed words spoken by the Guru are blissful, beyond pure (Suddha) and (Asuddha) impure.

2060. The five impurities arise by the sensations of Pasa. They alone are true aspirants who adore the feet of the Holy Guru in intense love and being purified in the three Thuriya awareness they attain the Supreme State.

2061. Powerful, indeed, are the senses from which arise pleasure sensations. If Jeeva subsides in the silence in the Self, then, he ascends high and will reach the Shiva state. All this is the play of Lord Shiva and Sakthi.

2062. All these—consigning Jeeva to the sorrows of birth, rescuing it by gentle ministrations, assigning it appropriate positions, redeeming it and baptising it in Gnana, establishing it Mukthi and in the end placing it in mystic silence (Utter/absolute Mouna) are but the Lord's work.

2063. The fleshy body is the arena of the Lord's play. He imparts clear knowledge of Chit and Achit to Jeeva; purifies him, wipes off the impurities and consigns him to the Sath (Real) to perform the five acts like Himself—these are the plays of Lord's grace.

2064. There is nothing beyond the state of Isathwa (Shiva state). Realizing this, continue for ever, in intense love for the Lord. My Lord is the Pure One who abides in love. It is the Lord who illumines all directions.

2065. He, the unalloyed Gold stands in the cranium sphere where the garland of scarlet rubies glows. The fine divine nectar wells up here. They who swill it, end their cycle of births, They who do not remain only to gormandize.

2066. He, the Lord attaches the two Mayas—Suddha and Asuddha to Jeeva and activates them to free him from the Asath, Asath and the Sath-Asath and to sunder his Pasa's bonds here. Then he imparts the peerless light of knowledge, too.

2067. The Lord, indeed, is the Supreme Guru, Do seek liberation by ascending the way of the yogic centres and scroching impurities, endlessly chanting His name to dispel the darkness of ignorance and harassing the Pasas (impurities) that the Jeeva is heir to.

38. Unsanctified Conduct

2068. Men perform many evil deeds thinking there is none who over-sees them. In fact, there is no place where the overseer is not present. The Lord pervades all, overseeing all. They who see the Overseer abandon all evil deeds.

2069. Men utter many falsehoods. He who created this sea-girt world knows all. So let them speak the truth. For He, that is of the lustrous dark throat will make celestials revere them.

2070. They sell the love of God and make a daily business of it. Thus they are pride-filled, but they will be in the whirl of births. They who pound and consume the seed (Bindhu), lay their body land to waste. But, truly, for the God-man, there will be no births forever.

2071. There is nothing there in the north for those who repeatedly say 'North'; They walk northward bereft of Gnana. For those who truly possess knowledge, all the world in the north is contained in their heart.

2072. He who made this body-mix is the one who holds this body land. He who shines within the body is Nandhi, They seek and search Him in all lands, not knowing that He stands within the body.

2073. The Lord rises, visible to your eyes, in your very palm. He stands in your thoughts, overseeing all. He guides your way, as light within the Eyes. He embodies love who oversees you ever.

2074. The Lord is seated with the virgin Sakthi on one side, the learned ones on one side, the steadfast Tapaswins on one side and the self-realized beings on one side. But how is it they do not know His true nature.

2075. The eye that does not see is covered by cataract

(ignorance). The Lord is the Unseen Light, even for those whose eye has no sight. He is the Divine Eye, even for those who have not seen Him, They who have seen Him in the inward eye have truly seen the Supreme Truth and are rid of all illusions.

2076. Even as the lunatic becomes lucid by the administerd medicine and realizes his true self, and even as the eye regains its sight, so too, Nandhi by bestowing His grace on me, my thoughts became serene and was heightened to the actionless state.

2077. The Lord pervading eight directions moved all of them. Of this, they do not think of His omnipresence, They are drunk in their inebriate Karmas and so do not wake up from their stupor and also they abandon, forever all thoughts of becoming divine.

2078. The two, I and you, stand in union as one, undifferenciate, as becoming one. For these, there is no more two. I and you. But they who speak of I and you, as two, to them Me is forever two, I and you, He is the Being, the one and one above.

2079. Where do the sensations go, when life ebbs away ? Sentience is lost and the body drops. Life and body flourish as one, they do not know this state.

2080. Prana is apart from pervasive awareness. When you know what Prana is then, you will know what awareness is. Awareness is the Supreme Knowledge, (not prana) that pervades the body. They do not know that the Mighty Lord within this awareness is the Great Lord.

2081. He is the world's axle-pin, the resplendent light and the true Siddha. He pervades the five elements the earth, sky and the rest. He is the Lord of Devas and stands with His Sakthi. To praise Him in high words is to realize your self.

2082. He is the peerless light, the resplendent light, the end of all; He is the goal of this fleshy body, all the worlds and the worldly pleasures that are honey-sweet. Give them up and the Lord of limitless goodness will bestow His grace on you.

2083. He is your beginning the life in your fleshy body,

the God in mount Kailash. No one knows His design; when the Primal One sways you, and your entire ego is effaced, then, you will reach the Lord who is above all Tathwas.

2084. He is not the Indriyas (external sensual organs) nor the Anthakaranas (Internal sensual organs) nor the subtle body that carries life. The inscrutable Maya and the thirty-six tathwas arose out of the might man. The eternal and the everlasting Uncreated being stands above all of them, high at the apex.

39. In Compassion for Mens' Evil Lot

2085. The Ungodly ones germinate the seed and plant the seedlings. They do not think of their own fleeting life, for they are poor in spirit. They know nothing of karmic sorrows and so perish in the blazing fire, truly they are such who do not think of the soul's liberation.

2086. They very well see life fleeting away in a trice; yet they stand in contention. Though what do these men get from it ? They do not stand in the righteous ways, they do not know the Primal one, nor do they adore His Holy Feet in endearing love.

2087. Those who do not care for the soul's well-being borrow grain. Pound it hard, feed their base senses and nourish the body alone. Thus they wander with their lives to live. But in the broad valley, their body of finally lies a prey to the raging flames. They do not realize this.

2088. In the days of yore, the four sages sought the Holy one in Kailash; the Supreme One imparted His teaching there, under the wild Banyan tree, Those who do not think of Him are of evil speech and they stand in wait, ready to march to the burial heap.

2089. The Lord ever bestows imperishable fame and truthful fruit of the true, full penance, only in those who endear Him. Yet the world thinks that this is God and that is God. Getting distracted thus, they fall bruised with hands hitting on the rocks.

2090. The Ungodly do not pursue the way of bliss—of being born in bliss, growing in bliss and being steeped in the thoughts of bliss. They forget this way, and instead hankering after food and ramient are steeped in sorrow. And steeped in sorrow, they slumber insensibly.

2091. Human birth is rare, yet men do not seek the Lord's Feet that are so rare to reach. They who attained the rare human birth have yet missed this rare treasure and they are indeed only crawling creatures.

2092. Considering these—the ardour of mind, ever fresh youth and endearment of heart, as good, they indulge in pleasure and sport in diverse acts of love. They do not think of heavenly pleasures and forget the heavenly bliss the lord bestows and they miss it for ever and for ever.

2093. He is thus, His form like the rising Sun; He is this, the Kundalini fires residing within; He is here, seated in the Lotus of the heart, He is the first truth but we do not seek the Lord.

2094. The unholy ones do not unite in Him in the way the Holy Guru has shown. They do not seek Him, but indulge in aimless talk. They do not sing Him, realizing His benevolent deeds. What do they get from all these, but only dance about and waste away their lives.

2095. He is the great light that fills my heart. Melting in love, I adore Him daily, like if it were the end of my days. If you do not adore Him, the five senses will cause havoc like the elephants that roam lossely.

2096. The birds, beasts and the several humans, all of them, do not at all seek Him in endearment. They who have realized Him in intense penance drink and run in surpassing rapture. These indeed, are the beings who have reaped in fruit of their birth here below.

2097. The unrighteous are they who do not seek His light in unbroken continuity, they are like those who do not cherish Him who is gold; I seek Him the Lord, the Primal One, the fruit of wisdom, the Lord of the celestial beings; forever and ever as my sole refuge.

2098. The bees flit from flowers to flowers and in incessant rapture gather the sweet honey, they do not think of this; that there is a pure honey that is far sweeter, that wells up (In yoga) in their mouth. No one knows this rare honey.

2099. I wasted away my life, by not seeking Him. The Lord of the celestial beings is in my love. He is the One Being for all the worlds, Yet they do not praise Him in their thoughts and so they slip low down.

2100. When the God of death leaps forward, the fated days that are agreeable to him roll away too and you tremble and shake. You may think, what may come of it, but if you seek place then, dip the ladle of your heart into the boiling brth of love.

2101. The field ripened along the banks of the river of life. One should seek the divine bliss before the floods (of age) swell. So practise yoga that takes you to the mountain top where the ambrosial waters flow. Then greying age will seize you no more.

2102. He who knows the origin of all, knows the night (end) that envelopes all worlds. The unholy do not know the self luminous Light, whom the enlightened hold aloft as the one Supreme God, and thus their thoughts still stand on this world.

40. Salutory Doctrine

2103. Forget away this transient life here below; even like the day your life passes away; so think of the Lord, at the very instant. He comes flying to you and your distracting sorrows end. Do, therefore, think of mighty Lord Shiva's holy way.

2104. Think of Him as far as your thoughts go. Speak His truth as far as you can. They may say He is not the Lord. But He is very much, everywhere, So, seek the Holy path of Hara that is ever good.

2105. Intensely uphold this doctrine—One is the family. The family is one, God is one, then there will be no more death. If you can seek with confidence, there is no other refuge than Him. Think of Him holding Him steadfast in your thoughts and you will be redeemed.

This, is extraordinarily modern in tone. Thirumoolar rises here to the highest in grandeur of thoughts.

2106. Praise the benevolent Lord of mount Kailash. Our Lord, stands as central, in the four cardinal directions. Praise the Lord, who, with the Holy Feet spurned the God of death, with the precious body that holds Prana's vital breath and be redeemed.

2107. Seek the way so that you do not enter another body, when this body leaves you. You think of that time when this human body came to you and indeed, you will receive His mighty grace.

2108. The Lord who enters into you and walks with you in the life, surely knows when you will ripen in holiness. Seek the Lord even on the eve of your death and He will be your redemption for the life that is to be.

2109. If your fleeting life is to attain its good goal, then think of the Lord even on your death-bed. Then, Shiva's grace will follow and you will have no more births and the heavenly world will be yours.

2110. Praise our Lord is congregational devotion. Sing His praise within, dance within, and know Him and adore at His feet, then, He yearns after your like the cow after its calf.

2111. When in death, courses yours life breath that ascends upward, through the central Sushumna and seek the feet of the Lord. All your evil Karmas dire perish and He of the blemishless fame will seat you among the immortal beings.

2112. The devotees praise Him as their Lord, God, mounted on the bull. By wearing His holy ashes they, indeed, become celestial beings. For those who adore the feet of the Lord who wears the Holy Ganges in His matted locks, there is no further Karmas.

2113. You, who have laboured hard in worldly pursuits and are entangled in miserable Pasa, know our Lord, be filled with Love, perform penance, attain perfect Gnana that is true and be in eternal bliss.

2114. For all those who seek the higher goal in earnest, there is a high penance that they should seek, there are true Feet that they should adore and there is a true way that they should adopt.

2115. He bestows His blessings on those who seek Him, He gives the sorrows of birth to those who do not seek Him. He reveals the grace of His Holy Feet to those who intensely adore Him. Joining the horde of Devas they seek and realize Him, the Fire-hued Lord.

2116. He is Mukthi (Liberation), Gnana and Nadha that resounds in the three branches of Tamil. As they praise the Lord thus, through unending time. He, the pure one stands within them as the ghee within milk. But they do not seek nor love this Light.

Three branches of Tamil are the three branches of knowledge: which are poetry, mustic and drama. Here the reference is to Nadha of all the three A-U-M.

2117. As the Creator of all, the Pure One has allotted many aeons. No one knows how many there are. So, they leap into the cascade of birth, and beyond this, they know nothing clearly of Shiva.

2118. Life here below is filled with misery. So praise the Pure One, of gen-hued form, When you near the time to sleep in death, Unless you in melting heart hail Him as the Lord, who abides in Divine Light, you will not realize Him.

2119. Some who are knaves in real, seek the holy guru; if there are such people, then famine will strike the land. Even the Lord is appalled at such men and He will consign them to the bottomless hell. Indeed, true Siddhi, is, to meet those who tread the righteous path.

2120. The countless Devas worshipped Lord Shiva. Nothing becomes them by worshipping him. So it is far better that you worship the Holy Guru, who, having himself worshipped the Lord, shows the way of becoming, too. Then, surely indeed, your liberation (Mukthi) is definite.

2121. Inveighed by Pasa, the humans and the celestials perish in Karma. So seeing this, why not hold on to the Guru who is a Gnani, pure and blemishless and is Himself the Supreme Param; then there is nothing more to speak of after this ?

2122. The Guru who admitted the disciple into his loving grace, is the Lord Himself. He works day by day for the disciple's karma to perish. The Guru appears in the form of the Lord of flowing russet locks who wears the dripping Ganges and ends our sorrows.

Tanthra Seven Concluded

8

Tanthra Eight (Supraahamam)

1. Five Divisions of the Body

2123. The body is a bag which holds many ingredients. Yet, there is another bag within the body, it is the Maya bag when the thief, Jeeva leaves the body bag, the Maya bag becomes like dust.

2124. God has shaped the body in two parts. The one is Sukshuma, subtle. This body is of eight constituents—sound, touch, shape, taste, smell, Buddhi (intellect), Manas (mind), and Ahankara (egoity). This is the puriashtha body (subtle).

2125. Of the eight organs thus stated, the first five are Indhriyas (External sensual organs) the rest of the three are Karamas (internal sensual organs). To these, the sentience of Pasa (attachment through desires) is attached. Thus He, the Lord of forehead eye, binds them and unbinds them.

2126. The gooss body is made one shape with these—lymph, blood, flesh, skin, tendons, bones, marrow, fat, brain and semen and it is harassed by sorrows.

2127. No one knows the greatness of His Holy Feet. No one knows that He stands within the body. No one knows this body of sixty-eight Tathwas. No one knows that He is its yeoman guard.

2128. The body spans eight measures with eyes, legs and hands that serve to cover it, in this body of pores and sores. He in divine love, conjoins twenty-four Tathwas. Thus He fashions this body that has four more to speak of:

I. Vital Breath: body (Pramaya Kosha);
II. Mind-body (Manomaya Kosha);
III. Intelligence body (Vijnanamaya Kosha);
IV. Bliss body (Aanandhamaya Kosha).

2129. The Jeeva in all bodies stands as experient spirit, undergoes the five experiences—Jagrat, Swapna, Shushupthi, Thuriya and Thuri Yaatheetha, before it merges in Para. No one knows the way it merges into Param that pervades all like space, inside and out, in every pot.

This is a unique doctrine to Thirumoolar. He says that "Beyond the fourth state (Thuriya) stands the fifth" (Thuriyaatheetha). It is like a "tortoise with the limbs withdrawn, when the *Jeeva* is pervaded by Aum and the divine light beams from within (whereby) the self loses its sentience".

2130. The nine orifices will be tightly controlled, if through the six yogic centres you unite through central Shushumna. The body within the eighteen Kalas will be formed and this will be the body of the Jeeva.

The causal or Kala body is yet another, It is formed of eighteen Tathwas and is truly the body that enters the womb and holds life. The five external senses-three internal organs and ten vayus.

2131. The gross body is prominent with its presence, the subtle body takes invisible shape and the causal boy is all by inference alone. All these bodies merge in the Lord's Feet.

All the three bodies, that is their Tathwas or basic principles of existence—gross, subtle and causal bodies—merge in the mighty Lord's Feet.

2132. Like the prancing steed that leaps forward, the Jeeva, too, traverses far and near; like those who put off one garment and another the Jeeva, too, moves from one body to another body.

2133. Even as the snake sloughs off its skin and assumes another, even as the bird leaves its shell and pursues another life, the Jeeva in its waking state forgets the happenings of the dream state. Thus the Jeeva migrates from one body to another until, with the garee of Sri Hara, it reaches where it is destined to be, and there experiences the two—good and evil Karmas.

2134. Having experienced hell and heaven Jeeva leaves the subtle body and entering into the causal body it continues its course, like the yogi who transmigrates, enters yet another body, thus getting entangled in the cycle of births and deaths.

2135. The 'Jeeva' who realizes that 'I' and 'You' are one, is in the Tathpara state and diverting its inherent course it reaches Param. The rest of Jeevas reaching their destined abodes in heaven and earth, wallow in sorrow.

2136. Shiva is the ground or substrata of the Gnani's body. The ground or substrata of the yogi's body is Nadha and Bindhu. Mukthi (liberation), beyond the three voids, is the substrate of the Mauni's (utter silence).

2137. Aanava (egoity) is the ground of the Vijnani's body. Maya is that of the Pralaya Kalas and Karma is the ground of the Sakalas, Shiva is the ground of the true Gnanis.

2138. They are dumb fools who despise the body as impure and go about seeking other places as holy. But they who consider this body as good and in it seek the Lord, will experience the entire macrocosm, in their tanacious body that is microcosm.

2139. The pure one gently sports in the hearts of those who are of good speech, deed and thought. And those who are of evil ears, speech and mind they live emaciated, with their faces drown in hunger.

2. Relinquishing Body

2140. Course all these—the sweet speech, love intones, the loud sound, airy Prana that articulates and mind that dwells within the fleshy body-upward in the yogic way and your thoughts will no more be of your body.

2141. The body perishes and with it ears, eyes, speech, pulse, fasts and fights and gifts too perish, leaving nothing, for the dying flesh to lean on.

2142. The heart that lusts after slender-waisted damsels will be immersed in distress. They, with pure hearts and will be made of iron, have their body shimmering as lightning and are destined for Lord Shiva's presence.

3. Awastha Differences—Lower State

The lower Awastha pertains to Jeeva in its pre-biological Kevala state and has two aspects, the causal and the caused. The caused state has the five experiences: Jagra (waking), Swapna (dream), Sushupthi (deep sleep), Thuriya (beyond deep sleep) and Thuriyaatheetha (beyond Thuriyaa). Thirumoolar does not refer to Thuriyaatheetha in this context.

2143. In the waking state (Jagdradha) the twenty-four Tathwas take their position in the centre between eyebrows. In the dream state (Swapna) fourteen Tathwas take their hold in the throat centre. In the deep sleep state (Sushupthi) the Purusha (soul) stands alone in the heart centre. In the thuriya state (fourth) He (the purusha) stands in the centre that is the navel plane.

2144. Of the commencing five Jagradha Avasthas that pertain to thirty-six Thathwas, the fourth is the luminous Thuriya. Passing beyond the Thuriyaatheetha the two merge in one as inseparate, with the Jeeva himself becoming Shiva. Do know this order, the Lord Shiva who stands in the beginning truly, becomes the end of all the experiences.

2145. All these instruments of experience—the ten Indriyas and their ten Thanmathras, the ten Vayus (winds) that work secretly, the four Anthakaranas (inner seats of thought) and Purusha of the experient Jeeva—are again and again entangled in the cycle of life's awareness.

2146. Earth is pure gold colour, water is white, fire is red, wind dark and space is smokey. All these five elements stand concealed with in.

The five elements—earth, water, fire, wind and space are concealed with in the body.

2147. The five elements too are an additional function to the sense organs. The five permeate each of the three impurities, three Gunas and six yogic centres. Together with thirty-six

Tathwas, the organs of Avasthas are ninety-six in all.

The ninety-six Tathwas are categorised as follows:—

Athma tathwas 24; Nadis 10; Vikaras 8; Adatharas 6; Datus 7; Vayus 10; Kosas 5; Orifices 9—total 96.

2148. In Jaghra state, the Jeeva of twenty-five tathwas takes its position in the eyebrow centre. The Jeeva with twenty-four Tathwas that is with five elephants (sensory organs), five infantry (motor organs) five cavalry (internal sense potencies), the five elements and the soldiery four Anthakaranas inside, stand at the gate of the waking (Jagra) state. Thus, the Tathwas stand in their respective centres.

2149. No one knows that the bodies (causal, subtle, gross) embrace one another and stand only within the body of Jeeva. They who do not understand the kinship between the body and Jeeva, are truly bewildered like the dog that strays abruptly into a kitchen.

2150. They who are poor in spirit do not know how to be. Those, who, course the Aghna upwards, through breathing in yoga way and sublimate Bindhu, they meet the Lord, who destroyed Kama, the God of love. Their body becomes comely and it remains indestructible here below.

2151. The Pure One appeared and in bounty revealed the fourteen Tathwas that lay concealed in me. He placed, in unknown to anyone, the sixteen Kalas that lend me grace, to centre my thoughts in Him.

2152. In succession you contemplate on the quiteisence of the earth and water expanses on fire that blazes in gold colour, on the wind and space, on the mind, will, intellect and egoity; and then you will stand victorious, vanquishing the elements.

2153. Out of the five elements are born the five senses. One is the child for space—sound; two for wind—sound and touch; three for fire—sound touch and light; four for water—sound, touch, light and taste; and five for earth—sound, touch, light, taste, and smell. This was not yore there, before the beginning of creation before the maiden Sakthi (spirit), loved the maiden Maya (matter).

2154. In the dream state, Jeeva experiences the fourteen Tathwas, the five sense experiences, the five Tanmathras and the four Anthakaranas as well having experienced thus in the dream state, the Jeeva returns to the Jagra state to experience and he stands in full knowledge of the world.

2155. Thus it is, the Jeeva stands in the dream state with fourteen Tathwas. But without the involvement of the ten sense organs, and only with the four anthakaranas and aided by the memory of the earthly life here he, Jeeva visions dreams in the throat centre.

2156. Leaving the throat centre, alone, he (soul) enters the heart centre where egoity Anthekaranas, intellect (Buddhi) and cognition (mind) are lost. In this state, he does not discern—the world and bereft of body consiousness (he) soul reaches the deep sleep state of Shushupthi.

2157. Having reached the deep sleep state of Shushupthi, he remains there with Chitha (will) Prana (vital breath) and sentience of self. Thus he has entered into the heart's centre and there he stands one with the subtle-object in the state of deep Shushupthi.

2158. His movement further continues from the Sushupthi centre, into the Thuriya expanse, leaving thoughts of the world below. He ascends on to the peaks of Nadha (in the Navel centre) and there rid of primordial ignorance, he remains in Mouna (complete silence).

2159. When the silent letters 'M' conjoins with the articulate letters 'A' and 'U'; the five senses are withdrawn, as limbs within the tortoise. Then Jeeva is pervaded by 'Aum' the divine light beams from within the self loses its sentience. This is not known by any one.

2160. The state beyond Thuriya is Thuriyatheetha, experiencing Thuriya in Jagrat, the fourteen foxes (Indriyas etc.,) die of themselves and the swift steed of Prana flees. It is impossible to describe adequately the state of Thuriyatheetha.

2161. The bodies and organs that Maya endows are endless indeed, contaminated by the five primordial Malas (impurities) all Jeevas, experience the five states of awareness. All souls caughts in birth and death are struck alike by karmas.

2162. Maya feed Jeeva with unbroken Avasthas experiences, for the Jeeva to attain Mukthi (eternal liberation) by the Lord's grace. But Maya does not near these Jeevas, who are born in Gnana and they contemplating in Gnana, attain Mukthi directly.

2163. Devoid of awareness, in the primordial slumber state of Gnana, (Kevala state) egoity is activated, giving rise to consciousness, and the Jeeva pursues diverse actions. Thus passing out from the primordial state of Jeeva's deep (Kevala state). He experiences the five states (Avasthas) until he becomes the Supreme Para.

2164. Just as the teacher rouses the pupil, who slumbers in his presence, with his staff, even like it, the benevolent Lord, awakens the soul with Maya, that slumbers in prolonged egoity.

2165. The Jeeva experiences the five states that flee forever. They who say that nothing is left after death are truly surpassingly unenlightened. They might even say that the heavenly Ganges Mandakini, that streams from the clouds, aloft, ends as an empty pot.

2166. When the earthly things' King, that is Jeeva, mounting the swift steed of consciousness arrives at the 'lovely city' of Thuriyatheetha state, all the five senses and the other Tathwas that remain behind, and were once vibrant, only sleep in the body.

2167. In the five states; in purity, vision the five impurities that are not pure. See, that they do not trouble you in the waking state, confront them straight; then you will be directly Para; forever and ever.

4. Mid Jagrath Avastha

This belongs to the Sakala or the living state of the Jeevas on earth. In the four states of consciousness, this Jeeva experiences—Jagrath, Swapna, Shushupthi and Thuriya. Maya manifests herself as Triodhavi (obscuring Sakthi), Mamaya, impure Maya Sakthi that gives differentiated knowledge, Kamya (Sakthi that gives self-delusion) and finally pure Maya (Sakthi that lends grace) in this avastha.

2168. In the waking state—within the waking state Thuriyatheetha (obfuscation of Sakthi) is active. In the dream state—within the waking state is Mamaya (impure), the state of deep sleep—within the waking state is Kamya (of self delusion) and in the fourth Thuriya state within the waking state is Maya (pure).

2169. In this Thuriya state within the waking state of Jeeva, Maya rouses the Kala and Ragas. Then passing back through the states of Shushupthi, dream and waking the Jeeva returns to the Sakala state.

2170. The blind one has eyes, but no vision; and so he gropes for the steps he made of yore. Having found them, he seizes a stick and with its aid finds his way, even like this the Jeevas with three Avasthas to do seek to marck back their way.

2171. The spider standing at the centre of the web, catches its prey, and feeds on it, even so, the Jeeva standing within the body state, where the senses dance in merriment, experiences the five sensations, sounds and the rest of the four.

2172. There is One, who placed the twenty-five Tathwas; I abide with them in my body. I sought Him in endearment as the mad ones; great one, and the birthless one. And I am redeemed by the grace that He granted.

2173. With the twenty Tathwas, the Purusha Tathwa is added to make twenty-five Tathwas in all. Reckoned differently as twenty-five, the Purusha and the void (Viyoma) which is not Para is added. And with Para added to them, there are twenty-eight Tathwas reckoned, in the school of Vedantha.

2174. In appropriate ways course the breath through the Nadis, Idakala and Pingala; seat yourself in comely Asana postures and agreeably direct the breath within, Ascend upward through the Mooladhara, that is triangle shaped. Truly you will see the feet of the Lord, that is timeless eternity.

2175. The ten Padis and the ten Vayus, will subside in ascending breath. Then, your state will be rapturous, your taste agreeable and your mind will be perfect in your good body.

2176. Let them be that are to be; led them die that are to die; Let them leave that are to leave and let them enter that are to enter. The kingly Nandhi of tender love makes us to see all and to see Himself. He witnesses all and does all things that are appropriate.

2177. The twenty sense organs, the thirteen intellectual organs, the Thuriya state, time that is subjectively cognized, the differentiated void and the Thuriyatheetha above are reckoned as twenty-eight Tathwas in another way.

The Tathwas are enumerated as twenty-eight in another way also— ten sense organs, ten subtle potencies—four internal cognitive organs (Anthakaranas) Thuriya state; time, the undifferentiated void and the Thuriyatheetha state.

2178. If the twelve finger length breath ascends upward three hundred and thirty times, as Prana, then the impurities are subdued and so do the Tathwas, accordingly.

2179. If appropriate breath spiranted four crores, forty-eight thousand and five hundred times, then, there will be a cessation for Prana's movement, it subsides in ninety-six Tathwas and the ninety-six in turn merge in the twenty-five Tathwas. By breath control the ninety-six Tathwas subside within the body, which in turn merges in the twenty-five Tathwas.

2180. Overall there are ninety-six Tathwas, out of them, thirty six Tathwas are for the Saivas, twenty-eight of the Vedantins, twenty-four for the Vaishnavas and twenty-five for Mayavadins.

2181. If the Jeeva can make the Tathwas function his way, he will be a wise man. He will be illumined, with illumination divine knowledge in attained. Then there will be no more false devotion. The Supreme Tathwa is the primal letter—sound 'A'.

2182. The thirty-six Tathwas are truly insentient. I am the insentient one and yet I know not myself. The Nandhi declared that I shall know myself. I have known that I am the knower.

Among the thirty-six Tathwas, Jeeva alone is the sentient being.

2183. In the waking state, impurities create five states of experiences. In union with God, Jeeva is disentangled, from these five states and from the thirty-six unreal Tathwas.

2184. There are five impurities for Brahma on the lotus

flower. They are Aanava egoity and the rest (Maya, Karma, Mayeayam and Thirodhayee). There are four impurities for Vishnu. They are Aanava and others (devoid Mayeayam), there are three for Rudhra. They are Aana and others (devoid of Mayeayam and Thirodhaya). There are two impurities for Mahesa.

5. Aathwas (Higher Steps)

2185. The Tathwas are thirty-six, the manthras are seven crores, the Varnas (letter-sounds) are fifty-one, the Bhuvanas, global constellations, are two hundred and twenty-four, the primal Padas are eighty-one and the rare Kalas are five.

Manthram, Padam varnam, Bhuvanam, kalas and Tathwas—these constitute the six yogic centres or the higher paths.

2186. The yogis traverse and in the yogic way, ascend the three spheres within (sun, moon and fire). Having traversed they unite in one with the twenty-five Tathwas. Coursing the breath further upward through the Sushumna they search, and having searched they lose self-consciousness and they remain there.

2187. Waking within the waking state, and experiencing the rest of the states, with the body and breath trained appropriately, they reach the Thuriyatheetha state. Here, they witness the felicitous dance of the Lord. Drinking the fill of bliss they become Lord Shiva, Himself. All these five are the grace-fruits of Shiva.

6. Suddha Jaghrath and Other States

This chapter deals elaborately in 39 verses (2187 to 2226) with the Agamic view of Tathwas, Thuriyas, including the fifth, namely Thuriyaatheetha acquisition of knowledge, and the final merging with Lord Shiva.

2188. The gross body of the waking state, the subtle body of the dream state, together with the twenty-five Tathwas are all truly of Bindhu's power. This power permeating Jeeva penetrates the waking and dream states.

Bindhu power penetrates Jeeva in the waking, dream and

other states, and thus permeates the Tathwas.

2189. They who reach the Thuriyatheetha, within the waking state lie actionless. They who reach the Thuriya state within the waking state crawl towards the goal; they who experience the Sushupthi (deep sleep) within the waking state are Jeevas who are yet developing, they who dream within the waking, state are Jeevas who are hastening towards the good goal.

In dream, Jeeva marches towards the divine goal, in the Sushupthi state, he rises further and still further in the Thuriya state. In Thuriyathitha state, the Jeeva lies impassive.

2190. The acts of Kriya, lead to Shiva Tathwa and the practise of prolonged yoga leads to divine grace and knowledge In Chariya, contemplation of the Lord's form, confers many blessings, and in Jnana, the entire cosmic creation is comprehended at once.

1. Shiva (Nadha); 1. Sakthi (Bindhu); 3. Sadhashiva (Sadhakhya); 4. Iswara (Maheswara); 5. Suddha Vidhya (Rudhra)—these five are the first evolutes of Param. They are known as Lord Shiva Tathwas, and are in the pure Maya sphere.

2191. The beginningless Param brought about this order. Insurpassing wonder and in appropriate graduation, He established these evolutes—Shiva, Sakthi and Sadhashiva, the Pure Isa and the noble Vidhyatatthwas Bodha, Kalas, Niyathi, Time and Mamaya (impure maya).

2192. The luminous Shiva, Sakthi and Sadhasivam, the Maheswara, the Pure Vidhya and Rags, Kalas, Time (Kala)s, knowledge (Bodha), Niyathi (Order) and Mahamaya (impure Maya) the Prusha (soul), these twelve together, must be ascended by the Jeeva.

Below the five Shiva Tathwas in the Para Maya sphere, are the seven Tathwas in the impure Maya (or mamaya) sphere. This sphere is also referred to as Misra (mixed) or pure/ impure Maya. These seven Tathwas are known as Vidhya Tathwas and should not be confused with the Suddha (pure) Vidhya tathwas in the pure maya (or Shiva Tathwas) sphere. These seven are Kala, Naiyathi, Kala, Vidhya or Bodha, raga,

Mamaya and Purusha.

These twelve Tathwas (5 plus 7) are above the 24 Prakritis or Athma Tathwas. Of these, seven belong to the lower strata (Vidhya Tathwas) and five to the upper strata (Shiva Tathwas).

2193. The impurities are Aanava (egoity), Maya (ignorance) and Karma (action). They are like the embryo, the bran and the husk are like the grain of rice. These impurities do not touch the Lord, but stand apart, so be rid of your Pasa (attachment through desires) one by one and adore the Lord.

2194. The colour of cows is many, but the colour of the milk is white only. And the Lord, who is the cowherd, is of peerless hue. When the cowherd who tends the cows shows His guiding staff, the cows will not leave their master.

2195. The soul falls to prey to the body, Indriyas, mind, the intellect, will, egoity and ignorance. If the Pasas further sprout in him, then, he speeds fast, to hell.

2196. The consciousness of the self ceases in the Thuriyatheetha state, In the Thuriya state, the consciousness of the self still burns, through comprehension of the spoken word. In the Shushupthi state, which is bound by Maya, the desire-potency to speak afterwards still exists, and disperate experiences are undergone in the waking and dream states.

2197. The subtle body sees no dream in the waking state of the Thuriyatheetha that is the fifth state. In the Shushupthi state here, the self experiences the self. There, in the Thuriya state is born the Thuriyatheetha *per se.*

Thuriyatheetha state has inner divisions, such as Thuriyatitajaghrath and Thuriyatheetha-Shushupthi. In the Thuriyatheetha-shupthi state, the self experiences the self, and in Thuriyatheetha-Jagrath state, Maya still lingers, but Thuriyatheetha has no dream state.

2198. When six Tathwas out of twenty-five in the waking state within-waking state leave, that is dream state-in-waking. In Shushupthi-in-waking state, five more Tathwas leave and Maya alone function, there.

2199. When the Purusha, experience soul, of Sushupthireaches the Thuriya state next the Maya too leaves, and Bindhu becomes one with Kevela (primordial). Then the body has no more use.

In Thuriya state, Maya too leaves, and Jeeva merges in primodial Bindhu; then the body will be of no use.

2200. In this Thuriyatheetha state, the soul is truly the knower. When he passes beyond from this Thuriyatheetha state, where Jeeva is the knower, he merges into the luminous Thuriya (Shivathuriya) that is the ultimate state.

2201. Add ten Tathwas to the twenty-five Tathwas and they become the thirty-five instruments in Jagrath. With these twenty-five instruments in the throat centre is the dream state. with three instruments the Purusha is in Shushupthi. When the two, Purusha and the Prana, reach the navel-centre, then it is truly the Thuriya state.

Thirty-five Tathwas contribute the Jagrath state. With twenty-five Tathwas Jeeva functions in the throat centre which is the dream state. Purusha is in Shushupthi with three Tathwas. When Purusha and Prana reach the navel centre, then, it is the Thuriya state.

The Jagrath (waking) state, Purusha, the experience soul - functions with thirty-five Tathwas in the eyebrow centre. These thirty-five are: five Jnanendhriyas (sense organs), five Karmendriyas (motor organs), five Anthakaranas (inner intelligence organs), ten Vayus (airs), five Vaks (sounds), One Jeeva (Soul-Purusha), in all 25 Tathwas function in the eyebrow centre. In the dream state, the five senoria, the five motoria are left behind in the eyebrow centre, and the rest of the twenty-five Tathwas stand in the throat centre. In the deep sleep state, (Shushupthi), Chitha, Prana and Jeeva stand in the heart centre.

2202. All the eight Tathwas of the Puriyashtha (subtle body) are in the Jagrath state. In the dream state, the subtle body has three Tathwas. In the Shushupthi state, two Tathwas of the subtle body remain and only one is left behind, in the Thuriya state with Purusha.

The number of Tathwas in each state are sound, touch, shape, taste, smell, intellect, mind and egoity; 2. Intellect, mind and egoity. 3. Intellect and egoity; 4. Egoity only.

2203. Jagrath in Jagrath pertains to the senses, Swapna in

Jagrath is thinking and forgetting, seeking inward is Shushupthi-in-Jagrath; Thuriya in Jagrath is abstaining from seeking and Nandhi is truly in the Turiyatitha state. These are the experiences in the five states of consciousness within Jagrath.

2204. The four inner states of the dream state in Jagrath in dream state, that is to vision in dream as in Jagrath; to vision and forget in dream which is dream-in dream state, then to vision and non-vision which is Shushupthi—in dream state and to infer events which is Thuriya in dream state.

The four inner states of the dream state are jagrat-in-dream state, dream in-dream state, Shushupthi in dream state and Thuriya in-dream state.

2205. Of the four inner divisions of Shushupthi, Jagrath-in Shushupthi is to vision it as non-vision; dream in Shushupthi is to know it as dream; Shushupthi-in-Shushupthi is to know that there is no knowledge of it and the inexplicable void is Thuriya-in Shushupthi.

2206. Jagrath-in Thuriya is external God-consciousness. Swapna in Thuriya is internal God-consciousness; Shushupthi Thuriya is inexplicable void and Thuriya-in-Thuriya is to vision the Supreme Param.

Jagrath-in Thuriya, Swapna-in Thuriya, Shushupthi-in Thuriya and Thuriya-in-Thuriya are God-consciousness external, God-consciousness internal, consciousness of void and vision of Param—these belong to the four sub-states in Thuriya.

2207. Jeeva-knowledge in relation to Para-knowledge in the four states is this; Jeeva-knowledge cognising Para knowledge is Jagrath; Jeeva-knowledge cognising-ceasing is dream; Jeeva-knowledge cognising and yet knowing it not, is Shushupthi, Jeeva-knowledge merging in Para-knowledge is truly Thuriya.

2208. He, Jeeva, then becomes pervasive. Shedding the free impurities, he takes the form of Gnana; experiencing this and abandoning his pervasiveness, He ascends higher to assume the subtle form of Pranava 'Aum'. These are Jeeva's experiences in Thuriya state.

2209. There are thirty-six Tathwas in Jagrath-in-Thuriya; in Swapna-in-Thuriya and in Shushupthi-in-Thuriya. In Thuriya-in-Thuriya the gross body and the subtle body belong to the Suddha Maya. He who attains this Thuriya-in-Thuriya state, indeed, becomes Master.

2210. All these days, I did not know this, when I came to know this, nothing else did I know, when I knew this to be the truth, then I knew that I am it.

2211. He stands all pervasive, as life of life, as form of formless, as Jeeva sentience and knowledge divine. If Sakthi and Shiva are not immanent in the world then all is innert darkness, steeped in entire ignorance.

2212. In wonderous endearment the Lord moved Sakthi into creative activity and conjoined the thirty-six Tathwas to the primordial five Pasas (attachment through desires) and fashioned the body organs too, so that your impurities may be sundered.

2213. No doubt Aanava (egoity) is in the Jagrath state. Even when the soul enters the Thuriya state in the Jagrath-atheetha (Thuriya in Thuriya state) Aanava is still of the Jagrath-Atheetha-state; Jagrath-Atheeta is where the Truth of Para is;

2214. Sakthi was obscured by Mala-contamination; Gnana was obscured by mala-contamination Param and was obscured by Mala-contamination is and he who is freed from Mala-contamination is truly the Enlightened one.

2215. The foes (internal and external) of the thought of God, of the contending mind are the three lions (Lust, anger and ignorance) that are in their bewildering thoughts, the four jackals (mind, intellect, will and egoity) that are in their bouncing thoughts and the five elephants (taste, sight, touch, smell and sound) that are in their sensory thoughts. These are the enemies of thought for God.

2216. Your thoughts wander in distraction with eighteen streaming eyes. Before you tremble in death, take to the true way. You will indeed meet the mighty Lord of your soul.

The five sensoria, the five motoria, the five tanmathras and the three—these eight distract you from God, Give up distractions and take to the true way.

2217. Twenty-five of the Tathwas are left behind in the waking state. The four Tathwas that form the Anthakaranas are in the dream state. Shake these off and enter into yourself, then, the soul stand in Shushupthi devoid of thoughts.

2218. The soul who stands thus has truly become a master. He enters the Thuriya state and remains in the eight-fold yoga. He, then attains the Thuriyatheetha state and further after a while he becomes the pure para.

2219. He who thus became Isa by reaching the Thuriyatheetha state comprehends all the world as pure Gnana. Then, He further attains the five forms, Sadhashiva, Brahma, Vishnu, Rudhra and Maheswara. Having experienced these stages, Jeeva becomes Lord Shiva. Then, further attaining Mauna (Divine silence) state, He merges in the Primal Light.

2220. He is the Lord of Maya Land, where the three spheres sun,moon and fire, are within. He is the one whom I see within and pine for incessantly. He is the lotus that blooms in the cranium, with its stalk stemming deep in my heart.

2221. The birds (Malas-impurities) shrilled unaware of the shimmering dawn, they were bewildered unrecognising their mother (Mighty Sakthi). He, my Lord stood beyond the Vedas. And those who knew the mystic way, of yoga, reached to Him inside their very head.

2222. In deep contemplation, I sought the Lord of all worlds; I saw Him, He, the Lord of all celestials, distinctly in the nine centres within. I sought him intensely, and He stood unfailingly in my thoughts.

2223. Just as one that kindles the lamp's flame, so too you should kindle the lamp's flame in the mooladhara, the yogic starting centre. This lamp in the mooladhara when lighted glows, encompassing the sphere of the moon.

2224. If you ask how the heavenly space within the cranium is, where the inward looking five (senses) abide, then truly it is, like gazing upward, into a mirror, seeing the self reflected in crystal purity at a junction where the five senses in control, meet.

2225. He who knows unknown things, is the knower. He, who is not known to anyone, the Lord makes him know

Him. No one indeed, does know Him? The knower who does not know the self is not a knower. The Jeeva does not know the five Avasthas.

2226. Thus for we spoke of the visioning of the Thuriya state. The void of Thuriya state is a rare state. The states of Jagrath and the rest are unimportant indeed. Great, great by far is the Timeless Para Thuriya state. Transcending it is the Thuriyatheetha state and rarer even by far is this state.

2227. The world of Maya (Prakrithi) belongs to Jeeva. To leave this Maya is to reach the Kevala Maya state. To be born again and again as diverse life forms is the Sakala state. In Para Thuriya is the state of Lord Shiva.

7. Kevala-Sakala-Suddha

2228. He who cognises the self is in the Suddha state. He who does not is in the Kevala state. He who cognises in distracting differences is in the Sahala state. Each, according to his cognising state, conjoin in Sath (real), Asath (unreal) and Sath-Asath (real/unreal) respectively.

2229. He, himself is a foe and a friend to himself. He, himself is the here and the hereafter. He, himself experiences his own Karmas and he himself is a master unto himself.

2230. The soul in Kevala state reposes inertly and the Mamaya (Ashuddha maya) acts on it. By this action, the soul receives powers of cognition. And then mixing with desire (kamiyam) and the objects of desire (Mayeayam) it fully enters in Pasa (attachment through desires). This is the state of Sakala and the evolution of the Sakala state of the soul.

2231. Sakalas are those who are in the Sakala state, they are steeped in the three Pasas. The peerless Brahma, Hari, the numberous celestials, the humans here below and all lives like the tiny worm, all, are truly Sakalas.

The souls are ranked as Vijnakalas, Pralayakalas and Sakalas according to the number of Malas (impurities) they possess.

2232. Pralayakalas abide in the Maya (Ashuddha) world,They are of eternal comeliness. The Srikantha and the eight hundred Rudhras are these Pralayakalas.

2233. Vijnanakalas are numerous other souls. They reside

in the state of Kevala. They are possessed of Aanava (egoity-impurity) alone, These, the eight Vidhyeswaras beginning with Anatha the (Maha) Manthra Svaras that seven crore number, are the Vijnanakalas.

2234. Of them, those who receive the grace of Lord Shiva get liberated from Anava, they, transcending the states of Bindhu (Light) and Nadha (sound), become as 'AUM' (Pranava) and they merge in pure Shiva. This truly is the Suddha (pure) state (Avastha).

2235. When you think of these souls in three gradations, the Vijnanakalas have four divisions. They are shrouded in Kevala (Ashuddha) Maya and are inclined to be gripped by desire. Yet, they leave all of themselves. When the Lord bestows His mighty grace, together they sunder the impurities.

There are four divisions of Vijnanakalas, all shrouded in Kevala state. Some are in pure Kevala (Kevala-in-Kevala). Some more evolved are in Kevala-Sakala by the power of Bindhu. Some even more evolved are in Kevala-suddha, and the furthest evolved, having totally merged in Lord Shiva are the Arul-Kevala state. Although, gripped by Mayaic desire, they are freed by the grace of God and with this they sever the impurities.

2236. Abandoning the thirty-six Tathwas and rid of ignorance, the Jeeva becomes Shiva Himself. And pervading all creation, He enters the true void. This is the Suddha state, which the Jeeva of himself reaches.

2237. Jeeva is now eternal, He is pervasive too. Immersing him in the five eternal impurities, the Lord lifts him from the primordial Kevala state and consigns him to the Sakala state. From thence, freed from the unceasing whirl of birth the Jeeva, reaches the Suddha state.

2238. The Suddha state is the ultimate. The Jeeva that passes through the Kevala when it reaches Thuriya state receives knowledge of Tathpara—who exists beyond Kevala and Suddha states—thus realizing the self within.

2239. The twenty-five Tathwas then involute into the soul. The soul, having realized the Suddha state, will merge in Suddha Vidhya Tathwas. In this category, the first three, Suddha

Vidhya, Iswaram and Sadakyam will involute in Sakthi. Beyond Sakthi Tathwa (Nadha). Thus involving, the soul returns to the Beginning. This is the order in reverse of evolution too.

2240. The twenty-five Tathwas of Purusha involute into the six Vidhya Tathwas. They involute higher above into the three Shiva Tathwas, who in turn merges into Sakthi (Bindhu) who stands with Shiva (Nadha). Thus the ultimate of involution, into eleven Tathwas in reached.

1. Twenty-five prakrithi or Athma Tathwas including the experient soul-Purusha;

2. Suddha-Vidhya. Iswaram..Saadhakyam—they belong to the Shiva Tathwas;

3. Eleven Tathwas—six Vidhya Tathwas plus the five Shiva Tathwas.

The Saiva Siddhantha system of philosophy postulates thirty-six Tathwas, of these, twenty-five, including Jeeva, belong to the body (Athma Tathwas); six to higher knowledge (Vidhya Tathwas); and five to the spirit (Shiva Tathwas). At the time of involution the twenty-five bodily Tathwas involute into the Jeeva (soul), they do not involute into Shiva Tathwas. So, Thirumoolar here skips them and enumerates the Tathwas that involute into the Shiva Tathwas as twenty-five only. Of the remaining five Shiva Tathwas, the important three, namely Suddha Vidhya (spiritual knowledge), Iswaram(Godliness), and Sadhakyam (God-equality) involute into Lord Shiva. As Sakthi stands one with Shiva, it is not considered as a separate categoy. Thus the Tathwas are enumerated in the verse and as twenty-eight in all.

2241. The Kevalas (Vijnanakalas) possessed with Aanava alone are inert. The Pralayakalas have Maya in addition. They see with unseen form. The Sakalas are souls in all three impurities.

2242. The Vijnanakalas possess Aanava Mala (impurity of egoity) alone. The Pralayakalas have Maya too and the Sakalas have all the three Aanava, Maya and Karma. These are their impurities.

2243. The Vijnanakalas who stand in Kevala (inert state) by the power of Bindhu, that is in Kevala, become activated, as Sakalas within Kevala. And so they attain the truth of Mamaya who holds the power of Manthras.

2244. The Pralayakalas who stand with Aanava, reside in Maya (Suddha), yet this Maya does not affect them with Mamaya's (Ashuddha) Kamya desires that the Sakalas possess. They indeed are one hundred and eight Rudhras.

2245. The Sakalas are they who being enveloped, in the three Malas-impurities wallow in the worldly life. Thus like the very worm that enters life's womb are the Devas, the humans and the rest of Brahma's numerous creation—All these are Sakalas who crowd the world.

2246. They who reach the Suddha state, by the luminous grace of Shiva stand dispelled of the triple Malas that are Sath-Asath and having thus rid them entirely of dark Pasas, one by one, they become Suddhas ever.

2247. The Jeeva stands in the Suddha-Kevala-Mukthi state. Afterwards, when the Kalas leave, then is the Suddha-Sakala-Mukthi state. Again, when the soul stands as one in AUM sound, then is the Suddha (Kevala) Jagrath Mukthi state. Still beyond, when the soul, itself stands within itself, then he is in Suddha within-Suddha-Mukthi state.

2248. Jeeva is in dear Kevala-Mukthi state when he is inert without knowledge, unaffected by desires, goalless, everlasting, unattached to Kalas, actionless and incapable of daily experiences, infused by the deceitful Malas—impurities.

2249. The Suddhas here below, although Sakalas, possess Bindhu, Maya and Kriya; the power of interminable Gnana Sakthi substrate (Dhanu) and in Bindhu they attain divine knowledge. Thus are the Pralayakalas of this world.

2250. For those who see into the depth, there are nine subtle divisions for the soul in the three states; To speak of these subtle divisions in the three states; Kevala, Sakala and Suddha; it is like this : Kevala-Kevala; Kevala-Sakala and Kevala-Suddha; Sakala-Kevala; Sakala-Sakala and Sakala-Suddha; Suddha-Kevala; Suddha-Sakala and Suddha-Suddha. These are the nine combinations in all.

2251. Kevala-in-Kevala is Athitha-Athitha state, Kevala-Sakal is the Vaindava manifestations in the Suddha Maya state. This Kevala-Suddha state is the state of holy Vijnanakalas, that leads the soul to embodied grace.

2252. Sakala-Kevala is the Jagrath Atheetha state; Sakala-Sakala is the Jagrath within Jagrath state. Sakala-Suddha is the Tatpara (self-illumined) state. All these occur in the state of Sakala.

2253. The inner divisions of Suddha-Suddha state are: Suddha-Kevala, Suddha-Sakala and Suddha-Thuriya. Suddha-Kevala is the state of Upasantha, Suddha-Sakala is the state of expansive Thuriya-Suddha. Suddha or Suddha-Thuriya is the state of Shiva-becoming. These three states belong to the Suddha-Suddha state of Jeeva.

2254. Transcending all these states—Jagrath-in-Jagrath, dream in Jagrath, Shushupthi-in-Jagrath and the Thuriya-in-Jagrath, is Jagrathateetha that confers divine bliss. Here, the five primordial Malas—impurities vanish away for ever and ever.

2255. In the state of Jagrathatheetha Anava is entirely rooted. Jagrathatheetha, is not Para-Avastha state (Shiva), but surely it confers Upashantha, that is caused by Para. And, thereafter the Jeeva will not ever look at impurities or Gunas.

2256. The Jeeva will subtely experience in the state of bondage (Bodha) of liberation (Mukthi) of Thuriya and Suddha-Atheetha. They will come by the Lord's grace, and when this knowledge dawns by grace, the Jeeva has no more thought or action.

2257. The states of bondage and liberation come of Hara's grace. It is His play to take Jeeva to the Suddha goal, that it might receive God-knowledge.

2258. Those of the five Malas (impurities) are Sakalas; they are bound by Pasa (attachment through desires); they of five Malas rule the celestial world of Swarga and can ultimately attain God-Supreme knowledge.

2259. There is Aanava (egoity) in Jeevas Atheetha state, Maya permeates in the Thuriya state. In the Shushupthi state, desires are planted for Maya experiences. In the dream state, the subtle body functions with eight Tathwas and in the waking state, the gross body is activated.

Although in the dream state, the subtle body has eighteen Tathwas, ten of them (the five sense organs and five Tanmathras (sensual potencies) and the three Anthakaramas (cognitive organs) are active.

2260. In (Kevala) Atheetha state, there is Anava, in Thuriya state, there is Maya too and there he realises that Para. Kamya (seed of Karmas) is there in Shushupthi. In the dream state Mamaya (illusory perception) is also there, and in the waking state Thirodhayaee (obfuscation) joins. Thus the five impurities are attached to Jeeva in the Sakala state.

2261. In the Atheetha state, the Jeeva realizes the primal para. In Thuriya state, the Jeeva stands in Maya (Suddha) that has its origin in Hara. In the Shushupthi state, Karma impurity comes in; in the dream state, Mamaya (Asudha) envelopes him and in the waking state, Thridhayee that obfuscates, comes. Thus stands Jeeva in the Sakala state.

2262. This is the condition of the Sakala state, They get the body form and experience diverse enjoyment. They are pervaded by elements and are conjoined to the mind and the rest of the cognitive organs. Here, they get attached to Karmas and abide in Thanmathras. Thus, these Jeevas are born in the Sakala truth state.

2263. From here. They reach the state when good and bad deeds become equable (Iruvinai Oppu)—when Sakthis' grace descends (Sathini Padam) on them and when they get seated on the pedestal of grace, then with the aid of the Holy Guru they reach the presence of Sakthi's grace. Finally rid of the primordial Aana they reach the state of Shuddha that gives no birth thereafter.

2264. He, the Jeeva, enters the final state of Thuriyatheetha with thirty-six Tathwas and ten states of Avasthas. Then the Jeeva will attain the Divine Gift (Mukthi-Eternal liberation) and merge into the Resplendent Light, which the five gods reach. Here, the Lord Shiva of Holy ashes, is the Jeeva's final refuge.

2265. Knowing not the self, the Jeeva deems body as the self. When he sees the real self, he attains Thuriya state. But even in this Thuriya state, if, he, Jeeva is not united with the

Lord, he will be born again, here below.

2266. If in the waking state the Jeeva realizes the Atheetha state, the Vaindawas (the Tathwas) that impurities caused will shed their malevolence, the birth's whirl will cease, glorious Mukth-Eternal liberation and Siddhi will be attained then, and speech and thought will cease to be.

2267. In the void beyond Atheetha state, Sakthi (water) and Shiva (Fire) will appear. Water and fire do not appear together in space. Then how does water and fire appear in void? This way are Sakthi (water) and Shiva (fire) mingled there.

2268. Of the thirty-six Tathwas, twenty-four are Asuddha (impure) seven are suddha-asudhha (Misera or pure/impure) and five with pure Maya are Suddha (pure). These Tathwas are thus divided in three divisions as Suddha (pure), Suddha-Asuddha (pure/impure) and Asuddha (impure). All these stand with Lord Shiva at the appropriate stages.

Out of the thirty-six Tathwas enumerated in the Saiva Siddhantha School of Philosophy, twenty-four are considered as Athma Tathwas; they belong to this world, and are pervaded by Prakrithi Maya.

Purusha, the experience soul, is considered as another Tathwas. Then, here he is counted with the next category of Vidhya Tathwas, which are six in number. They belong to higher knowledge and are under the influence of Misra (mixed) or pure/impure Maya. In all, the Tathwas in this sphere are numbered here as seven.

The next five Tathwas are known as Shiva Tathwas. They are pervaded by pure paya. They are of the spiritual sphere, par excellence. Paraparam, or the Supreme, is alone the twenty-six Tathwas.

Tathwas are universal principles evoluted from Maya, pure, pure/impure and impure—which they affect the soul in its journey to God.

2269. The Jeeva takes its birth with Para Shiva for father, Maya (pure) for mother and Mamaya (impure) for nurse. And journeying the states of Kevala and Sakala he finally reaches the Suddha state.

8. Para-Avasthas

2270. The Lord is the Para; he is beginningless, is beyond the five states of experience; He is the purest one; seated with in the heart. He is birthless; I came to know the mystery why He parts, and as to why He gave this lovely body and life.

2271. Sakthi in para is Parasakthi; Sakthi in Santhi is Chit Sakthi; Sakthi is in Paranand is Icchasakthi; Sakthi in luminous Bindhu is Gnanasakthi; Sakthi is Maya in Krisya Sakthi; When you Jeeva receives these Sakthis, then he reposed integral in the divine.

2272. They know Him beyond the thirty-six Tathwas truly know Him; They receive His grace when they are beyond the thirty-six Tathwas; He is the divine bliss, only to those who have true knowledge beyond the thirty-six Tathwas. He is Hara who is beyond the thirty-six Tathwas.

2273. The Jeeva slumbers when transcending the five external organs and the four internal organs, within the union of the five Awasthas (states). Then the wonderous Lord appearing with Sakthi of slender form, rid the Jeeva of its poisons (impurities), to rejoice forever.

2274. The Jeeva realizes the self in the Jagrath-Thuriya state. Then beyond this are the state Thuriya-Jagrath, Thuriya-Swapna, Thuriya-Shushupthi and Thuriya-Thuriya. The Jeeva is in this para Thuriya state. Still beyond, in the Thuriya states, Para-Thuriya-Atheetha, the Jeeva becomes Lord Shiva, Himself.

2275. As the Jeeva aspires to the Para-Atheetha,—Thuriya-state, in the desire to be bereft of desires, he perseveres steadfast in it and he becomes beyond—Param (Shiva). The penance doers who do not practise will never become Param. They are forever fettered in several Pasas (attachment through several desires).

2276. The Maya we seek to understand envelops the soul, inside and out, the hypnosis it creates baffles through the world. When you are free form it, your knowledge becomes purified. It is transmuted into Shivanandha and becomes a protective roof over you.

2277. The Jeeva was in the Thuriya state and like swift steed he was led into the Thuriyatheetha Jagrath state. The master thus had the Karmic Jackals chased away, and the Karmas sorely disappointed stood howling.

2278. The Lord of Dance (Sri Nataraja) stands in union with Jeeva in this Thuriyatheetha state. When this union takes place, Maya vanishes away and on this very day, Jeeva attains Shiva form.

2279. In the Jagrath state where the Jeeva is, Maya may well serve as a lamp to light his path. If then, when he reaches the Thuriya state, he realizes his self, albeit in this Thuriya state, Maya will still be, the soul should further ascend to the Thuriyatheetha state.

2280. Not knowing yourself you deem the body as the self. When you enter into the Thuriya state, you will realize the self. Even though you realized the self, you will not leave birth's cycle. Therefore, ascend further upward into the Thuriyatheeta state and unite in the pervasive and pure Lord.

2281. This body is subject to birth. Thuriya state belongs to the body and Jeeva alike. These are subject to birth and death. When the grace of the Holy Guru descends on them, there is no longer two, because Jiva unites in Shiva as one.

2282. If Jeeva in the Thuriya state perseveres further, after having experienced in succession the states of Jagrath, Swapna and Shushupthi within, then he enters Para Thuriya and here Jeeva truly becomes Para.

2283. Succeeding the Para Thuriya Jagrath state is the Para Thuriya Swapana state—that engrosses the entire universe. Then is Para Thuriya Shushpthi state where upasantha (peace beyond understanding) is. Transcending this, Jeeva reaches the Shiva Thuriya state.

2284. Succeeding the Para Thuriya Jagrath state is the Para-Thuriya Swapna state—that engrosses the entire universe, then is Para Thuriya Shushupthi state where Upasantha (peace beyond understanding) is. Transcending this, Jeeva reaches the Shiva Thuriya state (2282 and 2283 verses are the same one stressed by Moolar).

2285. Thus Jeeva, who has become Para, from the Jeeva Thuriya state onward up to Shiva Thuriya state, experiences ten Awasthas (states). Then he enters the eleventh state where he merges into truth of Para Nanthi 'Shiva' and finally goes beyond all eleven states that are thus ensured.

The eleven states, from Jeeva Thuriya-self realization are: Thuriya-Thuriya Jagrath-Thuriyaswapna-Thuriya Shushupthi-Thuriyatita-Para Thuriya-Jeeva become Para. Para Thuriya-Parathuriya-Parathuriya Swapna-Parathuriya Shushupthi-Para Thuriyatheetha-Shivathuriya-Jeeva becomes Para Shiva-Shiva Thuriya.

2286. Beyond Para shiva is Paramam (Brahmam). Beyond Paramam is Paramparam (Para Brahmam). These are the ascending states. From Para Shiva Jagrath, to Para Shiva Swapna, and to para Shiva Shushupthi the Jeeva that has become Para Shiva reaches the final truth that is Para Nandhi.

2287. Pertaining to Para Shiva are the Para Sakthi, Para Nadha and Para Bindhu, and Sashashivam; Brahmam and Hari, and Rudhra the Lord of Devas, and to count to is Maheswara.

2288. Not knowing that they do not rule the spiritual kingdom they indulge in pomp and vanity which is indeed, sorrow. They know not, He pervades all. They do not know the seven-sea girt worlds will be a shamble. They do not know that Lord Shiva stands coming led with Jeeva and body.

2289. Perform the true penances that hold your future. Know your self; and the merciful Lord will confer His grace; when my ego-awareness ended, then I knew myself and now I am bliss.

2290. Think of gold jewelling and there is no thought of the gold metal, think of gold metal and there is no thought of gold jewellery, likewise, think of the sense organs and there is no thought of the self, think of the self and there will be no thought of the sense organs.

2291. Sublimation of thought is when you think of wood the image of the toy-elephant receds; think of the toy-elephant image of wood recedes. Think of the five elements, the thoughts of Param recedes and think of Param, the thought of the five elements recedes.

2292. Transcending the thirty-six Tathwas, abandoning the letters 'Na' and 'Ma' and becoming knowledge, the Jeeva rises thus liberated. As the letters 'Ya' merging in the letter' 'Va' denoting Sakthi and in the letter 'Si' denoting Lord Shiva, the Jeeva 'Ya' becomes SI VA YA that is Mukthi-eternal liberation.

2293. The Thuriya state holds the five letters (Panchakshara). In the Para Thuriya state of Jagrath, there are the fifty-one letters, Nadha is in the Para Thuriya Swapna state and Bodha is in the Para Thuriya Sushupthi state. Beyond appears Paramam (Brahmam) in the Para Thuriya-Thuriya state.

Jeeva Thuriya-Panchakshara-Para Thuriya Avastha 1. Para Thuriya Jagrath-Fifty-one letters; 2. Para Thuriya Swapna-Nadha; 3. Para Thuriya Shushupthi-Bodha; 4. Para Thuriya-Thuriya-Para-Mam (Siva Thuriya beginning of Jagrath).

2294. These five experiences in the Sakala condition of Jeeva are attained by grace. Then the Suddha Avastha state (pure experience) follows. Experiencing this in intensity, the Para Avastha state (Supreme experience) of Nandhi is attained; Then, just as darkness is dispelled before light, the five impurities vanish forever.

2295. The limited sphere of the twenty Tathwas and impure Maya are both unreal, leaving them, the Jeeva should ascend into the sphere of Mamaya (pure experience) that is pure (Suddha). Here the soul is all existence and non-existence at once.

Sakala Awastha—impure Maya sphere (Atma Tathwas) Para Awastha—pure/impure Maya sphere. (Vindhya Tathwas). Suddha Awatha—pure Maya sphere (Shiva Tathwas).

2296. He stands as grace, as Param, as love and stands merged as one form, He, the Lordly Guru, the Natha, of divine Gnana transcended all experiences but He did not abandon me.

9. Triple Gunas and Nirguna

2297. Guna in the waking state is Sathwic; in the dream state it is Rajas; and in the deep sleep state it is Tamas. Nirvana Nirguna is the attribute of the Pure Thuriya state, that destroys the other three Gunas.

10. Cosmic Division

2298. In the vast spaces of cosmos there are numberless universes that evolve and separate. They are countless like the sands that are on the shores of seven seas, sparkling as a jewel of gold that dazzles, they form the seat of the throne for Him, the Lord of the celestials.

2299. On this state of throne, He sits as principle bliss (Tathwas), with His five forms. He pervades the thirty-six Tathwas, nay, He pervades the Tathwas that are eight times by far as numerous as the universes in vast..spaces, and Himself beyond the end of all Tathwas.

11. The Eleventh State is also Avastha

2300. In the fifth state, (Jeeva Thuriyatheetha) there is ambrosia, in the seventh state (Para Thuriya-Jagrath) there is bliss. In the ninth state above (Para Thuriya Shushupthi) there is AUM and in the eleventh state (Shiva Thuriya) the Jeeva stands illumined. Abiding here, He attains the divine body. Listen, Oh damsel, that is red-mouthed as a parrot-these are the attainments of the higher state of the Jeeva.

2301. Even in the Atheetha Thuriya state, the six Tathwas, the Purusha cum Chitta, and the five formless Tathwas, abide formless. The rest of the eight are in the Shushupthi state of Atheetha Thuriya. There is nothing of the Tathwas, only in the eleventh state.

The Supreme Tathwas gradually fade at various stages and in the eleventh state none lingers.

2302. When the eleven states are thus cognised and the Jeeva fixes firm in the Gnana body, there is none but Nandhi contemplates in order this immutable being and surely believes that you can reach the goal.

Nandhi alone is there and Jeeva will have attained the Gnana body. So meditate in order that you surely reach that immutable goal.

12. Uniting and Exiting

2303. The Jeeva in its primal condition is in the Kevala

state, when it mixes with the Tathwas it departs and enters the Sakala state. Released from here, it realizes the self. When it transcends all the three states, it enters the Jagrath Atheetha state, where it is pure (Suddha).

2304. Give up anger, egoity as far as you can, direct your thoughts, Godward, as far as it goes and if you with the Lord's grace slumber, in contemplation, day and night; you will break even mountains and you will vision the interminable space.

13. Pure Awasthas

Forty-one verses constitute this chapter, Pure Avastha (Devoid of impurities). In this chapter, Thirumoolar reiterates much (philosophical, metaphysical and religious material) of what has been mentioned in earlier verses.

2305. Deep in the well of silence, Mauna; is a turtle-Jeeva with the five impurities withdrawn. If you do not deviate from truth and merge in it entirely, you will indeed, live a thousand years beyond the turtle.

2306. They who transcend these five elements: air, fire, water, earth and space and the five Gods : Hari, Rudhra, Maheswara, Brahma and Sadhashiva, and enter into the higher states, will never see death and they will have no other thoughts except those of God.

2307. All the hoary scriptures say Jeeva is the son. They know not that the Jeeva indeed, is the son of Hara. For, without Jeeva, there are no Tathwas that are twenty-five.

2308. The three experiences of waking, dreaming and deep sleep states are like being born, living and dying. When the Jeeva reaches the Thuriya state and abides here, he becomes exceeding pure and enjoys infinite bliss.

2309. If Jeeva experiences the Thuriya state as all within him and he in all without, he will no more return to the thirty six Tathwas. But he will attain divine knowledge (Bodha) and so reach Shiva-State.

2310. You may remove iron from fire but still the iron retains the effect of fire (experience). So too, even if the sense organs are extinguished in the Thuriya state, the impure effect of the Karmic acts will still be there.

2311. The Jeeva's experiences are diverse in the burning state of Jagrath Awastha. Give them up, and with the grace of Nandhi who is embodiment of Vedas, you will reach the Atheetha state bereft of impurities. Then you will be the very Para.

2312. If those who have reached the Suddha Atheetha state relapse to the Sakala state, the Lord's grace will not leave them; still standing close to the Lord, They do not enjoy the pleasures; of the world, and at the end, entering the Samadhi state, they unite in the Lord as one—all these are ultimately attained by grace.

2313. He parted Himself into two halves and created the cluster of Tathwas that pertain to the body. He let me into births and several places. He took me into inert Arul Kevala state and left me there, uniting me in the Lord.

2314. The whirl of leaves made the toy, fire made the wheel of torches, the billowy waves of the blue sea and the curd that stands with the churn—all these are moved by some other force. So too, the Jeeva pushed by impurities, enters heel, heaven and earth and so stands sore troubled—all these vanish away when grace descends.

2315. When this state, where the self becomes Shiva, is attained the impurities, the diverse Pasas (attachment through desires) Gunas and experiences that arise for the estranged Jeeva, will all fade, even as the beams of the moon do in the presence of the rising Sun.

2316. Within those, who have attained the Shiva-State, there fire, water, air, sun and the moon, Hari, Brahma and Rudhra are all seated in their hearts.

2317. He who, subdues the elephants of the five senses, lights up the lamp of Gnana and entering its radiance, drives the darkness within him. For Him, it is easy to ascend the heavenly home, Sivaloka.

2318. All these—the moving breeze that the dancing feet wafts, the vibrant sound that the Damaruka drum emits and the celestial music that the chanting Vedas and Agamas produces—I experienced in the Nadis within.

2319. The effect of goodly penance performed in the past, can be discerned with high knowledge in the present. Self knowledge is true knowledge, the rest is but demented knowledge.

Insight into the past results from true knowledge, Self-knowledge is true knowledge. The rest is but false and demented.

2320. To be actionless is Shiva's bliss. They who are actionless do not seek Shivayoga and will not merge in this world. Oh only to those who are actionless there will be divine message.

2321. When they attain Samadhi, they and He become one, their impurities are sundered and their Jeeva-state will vanish. Their body as divine light will be in Shiva's world. They unite in Shiva devoid of the eight blemishes.

2322. The Sakthi appears at the eternal feet of Hara. And as it appears the interminable darkness of Jiva disappears and light dawns. Then Jeeva incessantly perseveres in the way of time-honoured Jnana and thus reaches the state of Peeda (Jeeva) Mukthi—the eternal liberation.

2323. As the Sakthi aids the Jeeva in Peddha as well as Mukthi, the Jeeva that is doubt tossed in the first state, becomes doubtfree in the second state. And in this condition, Sakthi grants its divine instrument of Gnana to the Jeeva. This truly is the abiding light that transcends Jeeva's flickering light.

Jeeva that is doubt-tossed in Peddha is liberated in Mukthi-eternal liberation.

2324. The thirty-six Tathwas are devoid of knowledge. I do not know the self that knows. And Nandhi blessed me that I shall know. Then I came to know that I am the knower.

2325. He, the Lord of Gnana, the first of the celestials, the resplendent light of the peerless gem, who transformed me into himself, and she, the immaculate, Sakthi—Grace of pure Gnana—I saw them all in this fleshy body.

2326. Light and darkness are Parai and the love within Parai (Sakthi). Transcend the Self and beyond it there is love that is grace; transcend the impurities' darkness and beyond is light that is Gnan; transcend them too, then there is the gift that is the bliss of Lord Shiva.

2327. Let the Jeeva enter in the final Samadhi, that Shiva-Sakthi confers in the bliss of grace. If the Jeeva realizes the inner awareness as the end of fleshy body, it will attain the finite Lordly Shiva state; This is the exalted word (Mahavakyam).

2328. There is no use instructing those who are steeped in ignorance. Also there is no use in instructing those who are filled in Gnana. Instruct only those who know and yet know not, for them they will know and self-realize.

2329. The Jeeva becomes the Chit, Achit and Shiva-Chit, by espousing the Sath, Asath and Sath-Asath. Those who reach this Thuriya state, where there is neither Suddha (pure) or Assuddha (impure) are truly the Suddhas (pure ones). Then transcending these three states, Sath, Asath and Sath-Asath, they surpassingly reach silence (Mauna).

2330. By himself the Jeeva knows nothing, yet he is not without higher knowledge. The knowledge that he, himself has is Sath asath. When the two descend as grace, then, he comes to know himself, and also becomes one with Lord Shiva.

When the two, Shiva and Sakthi descend as grace, Jeeva knows both himself and the Lord.

2331. Only for those who master the knowledge, of the Tathwas (Tathwa-gnana) will be the higher knowledge (god-knowledge). In this higher-knowledge, the self becomes one with Jeeva and from then on, the bliss of God-knowledge has begun for him.

2332. When Jeeva attains self-knowledge, he becomes one with Lord Shiva. Then the malas (impurities) perish and birth's cycle ends. Then grand Mukthi-eternal liberation, the lustrous light of Gnana and the impress of Divine knowledge too (Chin Mudhra) will be his.

2333. Gnana (supreme knowledge) is His form, kriya (action) is His middle part and Ichcha (desire) is His life beat—this is the aspect of this uncreated Being (Tathpara). He is as the seed of the five actions that He performs (of creation, preservation' dissolution, obfuscation and redemption) and so, the Maunis (in utter silence persons), seated in silence receive the Mudhra (impress of God-Supreme Knowledge) that is pure Gnana.

2334. For the Jeeva, Gnana Sakthi gives knowledge, Ichcha Sakthi (desire) gives desire and Kirya Sakthi gives action. All these are subtle, he who grants these to Jeeva is the Lord Himself, and not Jeeva. It is the Lord who acts from within Jeeva.

2335. Action, desire and Gnana of the Jeevas are the work of Mamaya and pure and impure Maya, with Shiva acting within him. But beyond the void of cause-effect, is Shiva, eternal and of exceeding peace (Santha-Atheetha).

2336. He is immanent in the real, the unreal and all. He is Lord who is the real, unreal and the real-unreal. He is the beyond, beyond speech, hasten and realize Him, He will be the life of your life.

2337. Ichcha Sakthi infuses desires and harasses Jeeva. Gnana Sakthi scorches and destroys them. As she who infuses desires into Jeeva is within, do scorch your worldly desires and attain the exalted state.

2338. They who unite with Lord Shiva are rid of the five impurities. They who do not unite are possessed of the five dark impurities. They are destined to be born and on earth, heaven and hell. No one knows that all these things result only from His mighty grace.

2339. They who are caught by the twin forces of Maya (pure and impure) do things accordingly, they who are caught by the forces of Gnana act appropriately and they who are caught by the forces of worldly desires behave that way. All these that they do are the acts of the Lord's grace.

2340. They who are possessed of the wealth of honoured holiness are not destined for dark hell. They who are possessed of the wealth of holiness are not destined for delicious heaven either. They who are possessed of the wealth of holiness depart from the huddle of impurities. They who are possessed of the wealth of holiness depart from all things that are unworthy and so become Lord Shiva, Himself.

2341. Ignorant are those who do not know what is God's

and what is the world's. Only those who know both these are wise, when they come to know both these things, by His grace, they will know of His grace and that they are both these.

2342. Shiva and Sakthi, and are fire and heat. She, with Him as substance, exposes Jeeva's awareness. She is darkness and light. She pervades the three impurities too, and then by the light of grace, She makes Jeeva the very Shiva.

Shiva and Sakthi are like fire and heat. She, is with Him, expousing divine awarness. She is darkness (obfuscation) and light (revealing grace). She pervades the three impurities too, as darkness. Then by the light of grace, she liberates the Jeeva and aids him to become Shiva—the Nandhi that is pure Supreme Truth.

2343. The lotuses wake as the Sun rises; some bloom but others do not. This happens as their conditions are differing. Even though the Sun's beams strike alike on them, the differing effects are a result of the differing states of grace.

The Yogi then beholds in this fleshy body Gnana Shiva—the beginning of celestials and the peerless gem light that shines effulgent—and the immaculate Gnana Sakthi of grace too.

2344. All these—all forms of knowledge Bheda (difference), Abheda (non-difference) and Bheda-Abheda (difference/non-difference), native knowledge, knowledge that comes of learning, God-knowledge, Nadha (sound) and the Nadha-beyond-Nadha, (the Nadantha that is beyond-beyond sound) come by the grace of the holy one.

2345. The play of Hara's grace is like the artificial elephant that played on stilt. With the aid of the elements (Tathwas), it sways Jeevas and makes him dance this way and that, and cognising it to life and worldly ways, infuses the light of Gnana and finally plants Jeeva in the life of grace. All this is the work of His mighty grace.

2346. He, Jeeva, abandonding the thirty-six Tathwas realise the Self. He becomes the finite and pervades, Jeeva in the Tathwas and they in him; yet transcending them, he passes into the beyond and descends on him as grace. He attains doubt-free Gnana and becomes Lord Shiva, Himself.

2347. By His fine grace, he reaches the love of His holy feet, that is beyond reach. Then by journeying the appropriate way, he rouses the mighty steed of Siva gnana and mounting it he passes beyond, and so reaches Shiva Himself.

2348. Those who reached Lord Shiva are the Charanars, Siddhas and Samadhi yogis, the ganais who stood in God-truth, the Anandas who adored Him in love and Nathas—who were all blessed of Divine Grace.

2349. Everyone speaks of two states 'I' and 'He'; but there is a state where 'I' and 'He' are undifferentiated. Those who are in the Higher Kevala (inert) state will not cognise the difference. Effacing the Self, and uniting He and the Self as one, is the state of Suddha (pure).

2350. The great souls who realize Shiva who is the self within. Will seek forth Shiva in the self. They who do not reach Shiva in the self, will never reach Shiva.

2351. Do not lament that you do not know Him. Go the proper way and you will meet Him. He who as twin lights (Sakthi and Shiva) creates all, is united as one light in my heart.

2352. The clay is one, but many are the pots that are made of it. The Lord is one, but He is immanent in all creation; the eyes behold diverse objects, but the objects do not see the eyes. So too is Shiva for Jeeva. God is immanent and omnipresent, yet Jeeva does not see Him.

2353. Standing within, He protects the seven worlds. The good ones who praise Him in love close upon Him. They who do not think of Shiva sob loudly in distress. Those who cannot centre their thoughts in Him, can never, never reach Him.

2354. They who do not see the self within, will not see the goal without. They who do not see the self within, will incarnate several bodies. Effacing the self, unite in the Lord. And in undifferentiated knowledge, you becomes (I and He United) the 'Divine Swan'.

2355. Is it the body or the soul that joys in the bliss, when the lady of the celestials (Sakthi) stands in Maya? The men who think they know all, do not know why they are born and why they die.

14. Dawn of the Supreme Knowledge: Gnanam

2356. With knowledge of the Self there is no harm. But without the knowledge of the Self there he himself is a harm unto himself. When the knowledge that knows the self dawns, you, yourself become Shiva and you are worshipped highly.

2357. There on the leonine throne, Shiva was seated, adored by the mighty celestials. And the lady of exuberant tresses, with bangles of conch shell and resounding anklets sang hailing her Lord.

2358. I did not know that Lord Shiva's form is Gnana; Nandhi by His grace taught one that Lord Shiva's form is Gnana. I sought Gnan's form and I remained in this knowledge.

2359. Gnana has no birth nor death. Gnana has no ground that but Gnana itself. It is Gnana that knows Gnana. Thus all the Vedas conclude in the ultimate.

2360. Above the flower of the heart, Vishuddha yogic centre, this is a flower of sixteen petals, There is pure Gnana, it is utter Sivanandha (Siva-bliss). When the Gnana of self merged in it, Jeeva United in Shiva and remained as one.

2361. To them that firmly fixed their thought in Him, to them He hastened as grace of Sakthi. I praised Him. The Lord too appeared revealing His Golden form and I held fast to Him knowing Jeeva Gnana, then Anima and other Siddhis are attained. Nandhi thus knew Jeeva Gnana as Sivagnana.

2362. Realising this, adore Him and through Jeeva Gnana know Shiva Gnana. Thus Anima and the rest of the eight Siddhis are attained. And thus did Nandhi know Jeeva Gnana as Sivangana.

Siddhis are miraculous occult powers that come in the wake of yoga practice. They are eight: Anima, Mahima, Garima, Laghuma, Prapthi, Prakamyam, Ishthwam and Vasithwam, 1. Anima is to become as tiny as Jeeva, which is atomic in size (Immanence); 2. Mahima : is to become as great as infancy. 3. Garima : is to materialize whole objects (pervasiveness); from diverse fragments; 4. Laghuma : is to become weightless; 5. Prapthi : is to attain all, that is wished for; 6. Prakamyam: is to become all-weight; 7. Isathwam : is to attain vast regal powers; 8. Vashithwas : is to attain powers of total attraction.

2363. Out of ignorance, this world laments about Gnana. They do not know that Gnana of Jeeva is not Gnana at all. When divine Gnana overlays Jeeva Gnana, they both are pure Gnana. After all it is only this much between knowledge and ignorance.

2364. Transcending both knowledge and ignorance, abandoning the five senses and becoming immanent, the Jeeva himself as Gnana, stands as Gnana's pervasiveness.

2365. The heart of the Gnani is the vaste expanse; the heart of the Gnani is rare penance; the heart of the Gnani is the abode of the Lord, for He stands there in the heart of the Gnani.

2366. The Lord is Hari, Brahma and Rudhra. He is the seed of the corporeal world. He is distant and near. He is sweet sugarcane and divine ambrosia. In this way, He stands so close to Jeeva.

2367. All these days, I did not know the self, When I came to know the self, then, I knew nothing else. When I knew the self, He did not leave me and He enquires of my welfare in loving care within me.

2368. The lamp of Maya is flickering, it burns and dies. The pure Lamp is burning steadily, the lamp of the body within is heated but I seek the distant lamp.

2369. I seek the feet of the Lord in goodness, in ten directions I sing that Param is my refuge, and I unite in Him in fullness of mind.

2370. Jeevas were created in the primal play of the Lord. They were all enveloped in mighty impurities. But discarding them, they realized the self and sought the feet of the hoary Lord. Thus, they became Lord Shiva with no more births to be.

Jeevas in Shaiva Siddhantha Philosophy are as eternal as God. What is meant by 'created' is that they are 'activated' from the primordial (Kevala state) inert condition by Shiva acting on Sakthis, and are given the milieu and instruments for development. Such as Thanu (body), Karana (organs), Bhuvana (world) and Bhoga (experiences).

15. The Six Essences

2371. The six ultimate essences are—the essence of Vedanta; the essence of exalted Siddhanta; the essence of Nadhantha; the essence of Bohantha; the essence of the eight branches of Vogantha; and the essence of the Kalas.

2372. The pure ones who are rid of impurities will know the six essences. The impure ones who are bound in impurities will not know the six essences. They who do not know the six essences will not know the Lord, that He is the beginning and the end.

2373. Vedanta says that He is the Supreme One. Siddhantha says that He will become the Supreme One. They realize the self in the Thuriya state and unite in sweet Parapara and in Shiva yoga. Rid of Malas (impurities) and they attain the rare goal-liberation.

2374. Indeed, the truth of Siddhantha is being freed from the Tathwas beginning with the five senses—sound-taste, smell, touch and sight and then contemplating beyond where the Suddha and Asuddha Mayas do not pursue, living daily in the thought of Para and reaching Para who is the Lord.

2375. The ultimate state in Jeeva'a journey is beyond Brahma, Vishnu, Rudhra, Maheswara and Sadhasiva, beyond Para Bindhu, and Para Nadha, beyond the thirty-six Tathwas, when all these are transcended and when the Jeeva is left alone with Lord Shiva.

2376. The Jeeva transcending the tribulations of the thirty six Tathwas reaches the Nadhatha. Ascending still beyond, the Jeeva encounters the darkness of Aanava. When this is dispelled, the peerless divine Gnana dawns. This Nadantha reached beyond is indeed, Gnana (Bodha-Supreme Wisdom).

2377. The Jeeva seeking Yama and Niyama and then going beyond enters into Samadhi. Here Jeeva reaches Para Shiva. And becoming, the Param, abandons all desires, realizes Upasantha that is indeed, the truth of the Yogantha.

2378. When the goal is truth of Kalantha, then this is the way. Ascend the five Nivirithi Kalas and the rest and Medha and the rest sixteen. Here encounter Bindhu. Do merge in it and know vividly the truth of the Kalantha.

The five Kalas Nivirithi—These five are in Shiva Tathwas; Nivrithi, Prastista, Vidhya, Santhi and Santhyatheetha. The 16 Kalas are Medha, Arghisa, Vidha, Bindhu, Artha, Candra, Niropini, Nadhantha, Sakthi, Vyapini, Vyomanprini, Ananthai, Anathai, Anasiruthai, Samanai, Unmanai. These sixteen Kalas within belong to the sixteen Sakthis in the sixteen petalled flower of the Vishuddhi Yogic centre. The realization of these sixteen kalas is known as"Sadsakalaprasada'.

2379. Apart from these paths, there are five others that lead to the light for them who seek. The five paths are dear like Shiva. They are Manthra, serenity (Samadhi yoga) upadesa and pure Gnana.

2380. The Agama Vedas are beginningless. Tanthra is to act in their way, Manthras are the mind and beyond the body and Upadesa is the teaching of Shiva-Gnana.

2381. The way of self-Gnana is to be one with Shiva. In the essence of Kalantha devotional love disappears, without speech, without sentience the Jeeva becomes a great being like Nandhi, Himself who is beyond speech and thought.

2382. In Samadhi, Jeeva and Shiva become one. In Kalantha, in Nadhantha, Yogantha, Bodhantha and Siddhantha the Gnana of knowledge, the knower and the known uniting in one is reached.

2383. The ends of the six Antas, merge in this Gnana, Divine knowledge. This Gnana (knowledge) merges in the knower (Gnani). When knowledge in the knower merges, then Mauna (utter silence) dawns. This is Shiva-Bliss.

2384. Of the sixteen Kalas, Unmanai Kala ends in the sixteenth, Unmanai Kalantha ends beyond in the seventeeth. When Unmanai Kala is reached, then, Nadhantha is born, Unmanai Kala is truly a great goal.

2385. Having been blessed by the grace of Sakthi, that Shiva espoused, the Holy Nandhi, who is Lord of celestials, granted me His Feet. Beckoning me to Him, He revealed the exalted Truth of Vedanta, Siddhantha-Meditate on Him, the Lord.

2386. The doctrinal truth of Vedanta—Siddantha is beyond and penetrating the Prakrithi maya (impure) and Mamaya (pure-impure). The Lord reveals the truth of His agamas to each according to his understanding.

2387. There is no difference in the imprint of Vedanta and Siddhantha, Bodhantha is Gnana, divine knowledge; Yogantha is Jneya; the known, Nadantha is dawning of bliss and the finale imprint is to be immersed in silence (Mauna).

2388. The goal of Vedanta transcends the seven Upadhis (experiences) that are the caused (Kriya). The Nadantha goal rides the Jeeva of Pasas and reaches to the Twam-pada state; Beyond this are the seven causal (Karana) Upathis. The Bodhantha goal leads to the Tathpatha of Real Para. Still beyond is Asipadha.

The causal Upadhis are Ajana (ignorance), Avalana (limit); Vikshepa (separateness); Parokesha Gnana (non-perceptible knowledge); Nityaropagnana (delusion of knowledge); Dakkha-nivrithi (release from sorrow), Ananda (bliss).

The causal (Karma) Upadhis are Sarvajnathwam (total knowledge); Sarvakaranathwam (total causation); Sarva-indriyamitwam (total function); Sarveswarathwam (total worship); Sarachiristi (total creation); Sarvasthithi (total preservation); Sarvasankaram (total destruction) and Asipadha—'I' becoming one (one alone).

2389. Transcending the seven universes and beyond is the great light. The Lord is the light of that light. Of yore, He stood with Parasakthi, here He, and our Lord stands loftily, all by Himself.

2390. Centre on the kundalini in Mooladhara that the Guru taught by his power, perform acts that lead to God, sing His holy praises in full and thus worship Him. Then, you will meet the one being who engrosses, interminable existence.

2391. No one ever thinks of the one beings; they do not think of the Jeeva; the two Karmas (good and bad) and the two Mayas (pure and impure). The one being within fosters and stands as sentience. He is formless and supports all.

2392. Shiva is seated in His devotees. He brings into them the Sakthis that are of Lord Shiva. Then, the Sakthis act in His mighty presence and the devotees remain ever immersed in Shiva bliss.

2393. The Jeeva (Pasu) reaches the Twam Pada state (the two I and He are together), in the Vedanta way, then follows Nadhantha, the holy state when Pasa is rid. Then follows Bodhantha that reaches to the Tathpadha state, where I and He is in one union. Beyond this that follows is the Shiva Sayujya Goal.

2394. Shiva-becoming is the goal of Vedantha and Siddhantha. The rest of the four ends do not lead to Shiva-becoming-Shiva that is Sadhashiva—and so it is that Vedanta and Siddhantha are indeed, wondrous ways.

2395. In Siddhantha, Jeevan Mukthi (Liberation in this body) is attained. Those who stand in Siddhantha have truly reached the Mukthi state. Siddhantha-Vedanta is the exalted path as it leads to the goal of Shiva-becoming.

2396. In the Vedanta-Siddhantha way beyond Shiva aspects in Param and Gnana arises in Jeeva. Only those who stand in penance realize Shiva truth (Tatthwa) in the pure state of experience and that ultimately indeed is Shiva state.

2397. The form and the formless states are Tathwas alike. The Bindhu, Nadha and Sadhashiva too are indeed, Tathwas. So too is Jeeva's (Twam pada and Tath padha). Tathwa is truly where tathpara is in Shive-Sayujya.

2398. The Veda and the Agama alike are revelations of God. This is the truth. The one is general and the other is special. They say their goals are two. Search them both. But for the truly learned there is no difference.

2399. All transcendental states of bliss that the Jeeva experiences are alike, Shiva Bliss (Sivanandham). The three higher states of transcendental bliss are states that come out of the three voids. The bliss that comes of appropriate Mudhras, is the bliss of Shiva's Mighty Dance within. It is the state that fills the soul in rapture.

2400. Kalantha and Nadantha are the two ends (goals). As they are reached, the five Kalas (of Shiva Tathwas) are attained. So the Lord who rises here is known as Panchaktaka. Thus did He speak in the Vedas and Agamas.

2401. Do not wait for the day, to vision the five Kalantas. Take to the way of Vedanta—Siddhantha, that are one. Then you will reach the Yogantha, and there you will envision the Feet of the eternal Dance, who is Shiva.

2402. The Jeeva who is eternal, is freed of five impurities and passes beyond the Tathwas. Here he realizes the eternal self. Then, the primal impurity of Aanava withers away, and with that the Tathwa-Atheeta state ensures, and here becoming one with Lord Shiva is like water that is indistinguishably intermingled with milk. This, indeed, is the truth of Vedanta.

2403. These exalted states, Jeeva, Para and Shiva-know them continuously. You, then reach the states of Twam-Tath-Asi; here you become actionless and you are all Gnana. Thus he merged, says Vedanta-Siddhanta.

2404. The Manthram 'Soham' that the Vedantins in tone is but Shiva yoga that is exalted. Thus says Siddhantha. Truly it is apparent that the Agamas are scriptures filled with Vedic wisdom.

2405. There are two scriptures that Lord Shiva revealed in the beginning the primal Vedas and the perfect Agamas. In appropriate gradation, the Vedanta-Siddhantha evolved, that is indeed, very great.

Moolar has coined the phrase "Vedanta-Siddhantha". He says that it is evolved out of the Vedas and Agamas. It is apparent that Thirumoolar feels keenly the need for somehow reconciling the Agamic and Vedic systems.

16. Path-Pasu-Pasam: Non-Difference

2406. Jeeva is beginning that speaks of knowledge. The Lord is beginningless who is the source of all knowledge; Pasam is the beginningless that binds knowledge and when God-knowledge dawns, there will be no more births.

2407. Countless are the Jeevas (Pasu) from Brahma downward. There are three Pasas (bonds) that bind Jeeva, when these bonds of Pasu are sundered and Jeeva-nature is altered, Jeeva will cling to the Lord and never leave Him.

2408. Even with the three Pasas, there can still be attainments. Daily pray unintermitantly. Praying thus, a light that will be yours will beam as from a high hill top.

2409. In Endearing love they, Gnanis, think of Him, Nandhi, of spreading matted locks, who made the bonds that bind them. Thinking, they shrink from Pasa and seek Godward. This is the reason why He placed the Jeevas in Pasas.

2410. Just as the person that has been extracted, no longer ascends the body, so too, he who saw and shed the truth of Pasu-Pasa will not be in them again. He stands apart and living in the states of Sakala and primal Kevala (inertness) then, he enters the Atheeta Jagrath Para plane which is beyond Pasas.

2411. The Lord you seek is eternal, so too is Jeeva and Pasa. No one knows the nature of the eternal Lord, He is He, Nandhi, who granted knowledge of eternal freedom from eternal bondage to the Saiva Siddhanthins that they truly seek Him with love and pure devotion.

2412. The Pathi (Lord) is the blessed Shivalinga, the Pasu (Jeeva) is the mighty bull that stands in front and Pasa is the altar. Thus does the Lord stand in the temple, for them who are searching.

2413. The Lord daily teaches you that the truth of Pasu-Pasam. The Lord leads the way. The Lord removes entirely the bonds of Pasu-Pasam, to those who realize the truth of Pasu-Pasam; but, Himself stands untouched by Pasu-Pasam.

2414. The great Nandhi of bliss that; wears the crescent moon; placed all these—the truth of Pathi, Pasu and Pasam, the beatitude of Mukthi (eternal liberation) and the way of liberation in Suddha Saiva thought in praise surpassing worthiness.

2415. Everywhere the three classes of Jeevas are possessed of knowledge. The timeless Lord of Divine knowledge too, is everywhere, pervading the three Jeevas; and so, He created them, the three classes, and to each according to his desire granted degrees of knowledge.

2416. This is the way primal creation was, Para, acting on Shiva-Sakthi puts Jeevas to Kevala slumber. Then, the unborn being acting on Sukshma (subtle) Maya rouses them to activity. Finally, the Para acting on pure Maya conjoins impurities of Jeeva.

2417. The act of creation continues. The high five with the Sukshma Maya that arose from Para, Bindhu, Nadha Sakthi and Shiva in the Sukshma also arose the five-faced God who performs the five acts (creation, preservation, dissoluation, obfuscation and redemption)—He, the pure Isanam.

2418. Para Shiva, Sakthi Nadha, Para Bindhu, The five-faced Sadha Shiva, Maheswara, Rudhra, Mal and Brahma were thus in order created, all by Lord Shiva, Himself.

2419. Creation, preservation and dissolution are granted for Jeevas to rest from the birth-and death whirl. Obfuscation and grace redeem Jeevas after below life. All these five acts of His, the beginningless one, that He filled for the Sakala souls.

2420. He placed the thirty-six Tathwas in kundalini and divided the Maya into three categories and with the last of them, Prakrithi Maya, forged the Tatwic instruments, He, the Pathi (Lord) who is apart, then, let them in the Pasas that belong to Jeeva.

2421. The Pasu-Pasam thus released, when it overcomes Jeeva, Pathi works out his redemption, and receives him into His grace. Having made him experience the two Karmas, He consigns him into hell and heaven, and as days Pass Jeeva acquires the love of God (Pathi-Pasam) in which I am steeped.

2422. In the Pasam that binds the Jeeva, anave is 'I'-ness; and possessed of it, the Jeeva longs for Mayaic pleasure experiences. Then heavenly grace descends on him which indeed, is the way to reach His Holy feet.

2423. Not only is grace the means to the Lord's Feet, it is also the source for desires to end; and to attain purification too. Even as the dirt of clothes is removed by earth-dirt (saline earth), Pathi-Pasam-grace works out the purity of Jeevas.

2424. Jeevas who stand in Pathi-Pasam (Arulpasam) reach the Para state. Jeevas that stand in Pasu-Pasam are but; Pasus (in worldly ways). Just as Jeevas who stand in Pathi-Pasam attain Para state, Jeevas who continuously stand in Pathi-Pasam truly become Pasu-Pathi (Lord of Jeevas).

2425. The four Tapaswins—Sanaka, Sanathana, Sanathkurmara and Sanaathanar—of youre sought the way of truth from the Lord. He, the gracious one, gave them the answer of divine gesture (Chinmudhra). And as with their hands, they held fast to His Feet, they reached the way of truth, realizing their self.

The four Tapaswins are the four holy Rishis, said to be the spiritual sons of Lord Brahma, who sought of Lord Shiva the truth of the holy wisdom. Shiva sitting under the wild Banyan tree as Guru, sri Dakshinamoorthy, facing southward, preached them the Divine-Truth by Chinmudhra (gesture of Gnana) in silence. Sri Dakshinamoorthy is held as the Supreme Shive Guru.

17. Head-And-Foot Knowledge

2426. They are miscreants who know neither head nor feet. The Holy say that the Feet are the grace of Sakthi. They say the head is Gnana that unites with the first cause, when the feet of grace shows the head of Gnana to Jeeva, then, there is liberation.

2427. No one knows that the Head and Foot of the Lord is within the body. The Head is in the Sahashrara (cranium) and the foot is in the Mooladhara, Those who visioned thus in the yogic structure, remained in prayer, with their heads bowed at the feet of the Lord.

2428. He stood, encompassing heaven and earth, that the mighty Asuras and Devas may know redemption. He who created this world is the great Nandhi; I bore His Feet on my head.

2429. My father's Holy Feet are within my thoughts. My thoughts are controlled and centred at my father's Holy Feet. If my father does not know me, neither will I know my father.

2430. The place where my loving Lord abides is beyond, beyond the Light that defies all description, He showed me the Light (pure wisdom-Gnana) that is beyond thought. He taugth me that Manthra that is beyond world and I stand, adoring His Holy feet.

2431. Hold the Lord's Holy Feet is your thoughts. Adore

His flower like feet in wisdom, Do wait and pray for the Lord who carries Sakthi on His body with Ganga muffled in His russet matted locks, will in time grant your salvation.

2432. He, the Lord of celestials, stands firm, His feet planted in the thoughts of those who hold Him steadfast. He shuns those wo do not think of Him, He grants His Grace to each according to his devotion.

2433. The lotus of the heart is one, the radiant flowers are three and the father's within are two. Those who can discipline the body in the yogic Kundalini way may well behold Him, even today.

2434. He planted His Feet firmly on my head and broke my fetters into fragments; my heart's impurities were entirely cleansed and it became milky-white. The Lord then sought to take me into His Fold, and now, what more can I say of my Holy State.

2435. The Lord loves Jeevas as His children, eventhough they may wallow in dirt and blemishes. He removes them and mends their ways. Thus is God's love for man and He bestoues His care, in compassion, to each according to his deeds.

18. Three Blemishes

2436. There are three blemishes that harass Jeevas alike, and enveloped in darkness he likes in stupor. They who are liberated from them are the truly liberated, other, entangled in them, will surely perish.

2437. I subdued lust, anger and ignorance and I waxed strong. An ethereal bliss suffused me as though I was within the sound of 'Aum' of a chiming bell, struck swinging.

19. Three States (Padhas) of Realization

2438. He who has attained these three states of liberation—Twam-Padham; Tat-Padam and Asi-Padam—has truly become the Para. Para, Himself, There will be no more birth for him and when he departs he will indeed, be Lord Shiva, Himself.

2439. Aim at Bodha state, discard elements and their

diversities, that are composed of Tathwas, and the ninety-six intruments of experience. Transcend the Nadhantha state of glory and ascend beyond. There indeed, is the Twam-pada State, the truth, that the Vedas speak of.

2440. Beyond the states of Twam-pada and Tat-pada and in the state of Asipada, stands the wonderous, Sakthi. But Shiva remains still beyond, beyond the reach of speech in unimaginable immanence, in all.

2441. When Jeeva and Para reach the Asipada state and merge in the pervasive Jeeva, then, He will in the agreeable silence appear as sweetness compounded of milk, honey and ambrosia.

2442. In the states of twam-pada, tat-pada and asi-pada, the Jeeva, stands as Jeeva, Para and Shiva in the respective order. Beyond them is the Swaroopa Mahavakya (Supreme Word Manifest) (Twam-Tat-Asi) revealing this truth, Nandhi accepted me in His Mighty Grace.

2443. Even some who do not know the fifty letters reach the abovesaid three states, They did so by directing their breath in the yoga way into the Para, thus they become one with Lord Shiva.

2444. Transcending even the thoughts of God is the state of Athitha. Here the sense organs (Indriyas) do not any more cognize the sound and the rest; Jeeva becomes pervasive. All these—the three impurities—the two Karmas, the one Jeeva and the five experiences (Avasthas) all subside. Thus subsiding, the beginningless one wakes into the Thuriyatheetha State.

2445. Beyond the Jagrath (waking) in the Parathuriya state is the dream state within that leads to Upasantha. In the Sushupthi state of Para Thuriya and in Thuriya within Para Thuriya Shiva is reached, then indeed, Asi-pada is attained.

20. Three Paras

2446. The Primal Lord appears in the three encircling spheres within me, I reached Him and was immersed in bliss. I clung to the tender vine of Kundalini Sakthi that She, may shower Her grace.

The three spheres are fire, sun, moon Mandalas.

2447. The vast expanse of Para extended as the divine dance arena. Here Nandhi appeared and stood and filled it. When He came in tender love as a cow that yearns for its calf, Jeeva was beaming, as a lamp placed upon a hill top.

2448. This Para is beyond the thirty-six Tathwas, when the unarticulated Manthra is chanted in silence, then Lord Shiva Para appears, that is still above. He is the God of whom the Vedas speak; Then divine rapture will well up in you. So foster it and enlarge.

2449. By shedding worldly desires, seek Him in intense divine desire. Then, the heavenly kingdom of God (Param) will be yours. When you seek Him in intense divine desire, shorn of worldly desires, then the knowledge of God will be yours. Only those who seek Him in intense worldly desire, bereft of worldly desires, will become Lord Shiva (ParamParam).

2450. Cherish Pathi-Pasam, God Live, that is holy beyond holiness. Then there will be the transcendental Para, and then you will reach beyond Parashiva and there, will be the transcendental Shiva bliss (Para-Shivanandha), Jeeva becoming Shiva is indeed, divine knowledge.

2451. Transcend the five Kalas that appear in the waking state of Thuriya, Reach the lonely state of Higher Kevala (inertness) and be solitary there. Bereft of sentience, ardently enter the Thuriya Atheeta state, then you will be the very Tat-Para.

2452. The purity state that brought Self-Realization, the expansive state within it, the impurities that affected Jeeva before passing all these, seek the Para-Atheeta state, where the Tat para and the time bound Jeeva that became Para comingle into one letter that begins with 'A'—"Aum".

21. Attributes of Para

2453. He, Nandhi is within and beyond Atheetha, He, Jeeva that had become Para Jeeva is within Atheeta, yet without full Gnana. The Para Jeeva attaining Gnana and rid of dark ignorance will be one with God (Pathi)—

2454. The Pathi (Lord) has neither beginning nor end, He

is the resplendent Divine Light; He is seen and yet unseen, Those who attain Gnana of that Para are indeed, holy.

2455. Transcending Thuriya and entering the Thuriyatheetha, is the endless space. Here vision the mighty Lord who dances eternally. They who can peer into the deep well of Pranava (AUM) within, and glimpse Him will have no more birth.

2456. When in contact with red colour, white, too, becomes red. It is like this when Jeeva purified (white) reaches Shiva (that is red). Shiva stands high aloft as a flage planted on the top of mighty Meru mountain, in Gnana's void that absorbs the Universe so unreal.

2457. They, the Kalas and other Tathwas (below) have faded. The two Mayas left behind were sundered, And after taking me into the baptismal fout of Gnana, He made me unite in Him. He, the Holy Nandhi, dispelling my fears, accepted me in His grace.

2458. My Nandhi taught me to realize this self, when I realised the self, He placed me in place where the self is unknown. Here, the light form arose, and He granted me Himself and I became Tat-Para.

2459. Hara stands expanding and contracting, as earth, water, space and wind, as sun and moon, pervasive and immanent, supporting the vast firmament.

2460. Sakthi arose of Herself, Sath (Shiva). In this state, She stands as Tat-Para. In this Iccha (Desire) state, She is Para's material form. Then, She assumes Gnana Sakthi and other forms. Thus acting in surpassing love, She daily, daily moves the world.

2461. Bindhu Sakthi expanded from within Parai. Descending from above, of here below, it imparted sentience to the four cognitive organs. This is the story of Jeevas who have no inherent sentience.

2462. Then Maya arose separately from Parai, and the caused Tathwas and the six experiences are an heir to the body. Feeling, breathing, eating and sleeping are all enjoyments that Maya gives. She is the little light within, that kindles to reach the Great light.

2463. The Primal Lord who is Tat-Para is resplendent light. He is Chit-Para, filled with divine Gnana. He is the Divine sentience that engrosses the universe. Enter into the splendorous light, in the space that is beyond words and there is nothing more to compare.

2464. The hoary scriptures say that expanding space is His Body. He wears the crescent moon. If Jeeva, even after reaching the Thuriyatheetha state, falls a victim to causal experiences of Suddha Maya, He will not, if you ask me, be pure (Suddha).

2465. He pervasively fills space, air, fire, water and earth. He is Tat-Para of infinite love. Sakthi who is manifested in space, air, fire, water and earth is but of His Divine form.

2466. Shiva's mighty grace itself appears to the yogis of intense penance, contemplating on the mystic Meru Mount in their radiant sphere within, in their rare Tapas. so do not move from this way, and there is no other way than this too.

21. Three Thuriyas

2467. Jeeva Thuriya is the Thuriya beyond (In Jagrath) waking, dreaming and deep sleep states. The Thuriya beyond the waking, dreaming and deep sleep states (with Jeeva Thuriya state) is Para Thuriya. Further, beyond the Thuriya (in the Para Thuriya state) is Shiva Thuriya Twam, Tat and Asi states are reached in these respectively.

2468. Twam-Pada is in Jeeva Thuriya of waking state. The end of Jeeva Thuriya is the beginning of Para Thuriya. At the end of Para Thuriya is Para Pada (Tat Pada). Beyond three steps, in the fourth, is Shiva Thuriya (Asi Pada).

2469. The four states of Jeeva Thuriya, the four states of Para Thuriya and the four states of Shiva Thuriya as the end of one Thuriya is the beginning state of the next, which are really ten states in number.

Jeeva or Jagrath Thuriya are 1. Jagrath; 2. Swapna; 3. Shushupthi; 4. Thuriya; the Para Thuriya are 5. Jeeva Thuriya Jagrath; 6. Jeeva Thuriya Swapna; 7. Jeeva Thuriya Sushupthi and 8. Jeeva Thuriya; the Shiva Thuriya are 9. Para Thuriya Jagrath 10. Para Thuriya Swapna; 11. Para Thuriya Shushupthi and 12. Parathuriya Thuriya states.

2470. There are the ten states in the three Thuriyas. You proceed taking them as ends. At the final end of the identity with Para Para, connecting the states in the middle of two each. (Jeeva Thuriya and Para Thuriya Jagrath into one and Para Thuriya Thuriya and Shiva Thuriya Jagrath into one).

State four and five merge with one state. Similarly states eight and nine merge into one state. Thus they become ten Avasthas—the Thuriya of one state being the Jagrath of the next.

2471. Reach the Thuriya land, and be there; if you cannot reach it think of the Lord in the way the scriptures speak of it. Then you will reach the truth that is beyond words.

2472. Do away with the thirty-six Tathwas, that are Asath (unreal) and become knowledge itself; crush the crowding Maya with the Lord's grace. Then, the divine grace will be abiding. This is the way the holy ones knew and followed.

2473. The fourth state of Jagrath in Thuriya (Jeeva Thuriya). Here Jeeva attains Twam-Pada and ends his Karma. Again, commencing from Jeeva Thuriya is the Jagrath state in Para Thuriya. So reach in Para-Thuriya state and here indeed is the Tath-Pada state.

2474. As you reach Twam-Pada and Tat-Pada, you now enter the third Thuriya state (Shiva Thuriya) and at its end you vision the Divine Light (Asi-Pada) the super-subtlety (Shukshma) that words cannot conceive. Beyond this is Lord Shiva who as Nandhi accepted me into His Mighty Grace.

23. Three Mukthis

2475. Jeeva-Mukthi is the Atheetha state, beyond the state of consciousness. Para-Mukthi is Upasantha state (Divine peace). Shiva Mukthi is the Anandha state (Divine bliss). All three are Swaroopa Mukthis that branch from Nadhantha where mighty Pranava 'AUM' is as three letters (A,U,M).

2476. Jeevas do not know the goal of birth. The Jeeva who knows it will be in grace. Here there is nothing to be in the name or outside it. Thus renouncing all, be one with Lord Shiva and this truly is Mukthi (Eternal Liberation).

2477. On becoming Shiva, the triple impurities and the triple Gunas all perish and the Jeeva attains the triple Mukthis, uniting as one with the Tathwas. This is the way of "SO-HAM". Like those who follow this way, the immaculate Shiva reveals Himself.

2478. The work of the Divine gracious Lord, who sunders your bonds, is to grant Siddhi and Mukthi, Suddhi that is pure Shiva, Sakthi of pure bliss, the three fires that extinguish and the exalted Samadhi.

24. Triple Swaroopas

2479. As you ascend, alternate the five impurities and expouse "SO-HAM" that is Gnana filled and be liberated attaining the triple Swaroopa Mukthi. And in the end, vision the truth of eternal Para (Lord Shiva).

2480. The mansions are three and there are three who reside there. Merge the thirty-six Tathwas in the three. The Jeeva may well vision the light that rises from within the three. Then the birth's cycle that was endless will be ended.

2481. The worlds tumbled, aeons passed, the three lights—sun-moon-fire: became one and all merged in the benevolent Lord. No one knows His vastness and greatness.

2482. The primal one, the great indivisible one, divided Himself severally, as form, formless and form-formless, as Guru and as Sakthi—Lord. He became immanent and transcendent too in Jeevas, in numerous forms.

2483. The Jeeva receives divine light in triple Mukthi-Infused with light and brilliance, the crystal shines as a gem. Jeeva is like it when he attains the three Mukthis and the grace of Divine Sakthi. Hold fast to the feet of Nandhi who ordains all these graces.

2484. The Lord, with crystalline hue and radiant brilliance, stands as a gem of the purest serene ray. Seek Him and reach the three Mukthi states. Beyond is void that defies speech.

Here contemplate on AUM in silence for in this Mudhra of Gnana is the final grace.

2485. He is the Light within the crimson lotus of the heart. If with the crimson lotus, you reached Nadha, you will awake the kundalini Sakthi. And closing Muladhara where She is imprisoned, ascend upward (through Shushumana in yogic breathing) and open wide the gate above at the cranium.

25. Mukkranam (Three Phases)

2486. One person functions in three places, yet he may appear as three different persons. Like this are Jeeva, Para and Shiva; they are one but, appear in different forms and places.

2487. The Light within should be brightened to merge in the Light without, to merge in the breath, cosmic solar life, without, the Prana breath within should be roused through the sound potency in 'AUM'. Coursing it appropriately upward, merge the space within into the space without. You will then vision the Shiva state clearly.

2488. My Nandhi ended the pulsations of Kamas by a slight of the hand, as it were. As the lovely Manomani (Sakthi) left, Unmanai (Sakthi Kala) no less lovely entered. So take to Her in inward Samadhi.

26. Three Spaces and Twam-Tat-Asi

2489. All the three states Twam-Pada; Tat-Pada and Asi-Pada arose in Thuriya. One of the three—Jeeva, Para and Shiva stands in respective order in all the three states. Together they are known by the compounded expression, that is, Twam-Tat-Asi (Mahavakyam—Supreme Truth).

2490. The three time-honoured Malas (impurities). Kamiya and the rest, are in the three states Twam-Tat and Asi. The three time honoured Gunas-Tamas and the Rest are in the three states Twam-Tat and Asi. Shiva appears when these impurities and Gunas are seared. They fleet away as He appears like darkness disappears before the Moon's beam.

2491. Attain the state of Twan-tat-Asi through coursing the breath in the yogic way. Consider it as the tenth state of

Thuriya experience. This experience is endless. Alter this experience so that Lord Shiva (Tat) stands first, that is Tat-Twam-Asi or *Tatvamasi.* Thus meditate on it and ascend.

2492. Thus altering the expression into Tatwamasi with Lord Shiva (Tat) first, fix your thought on bliss of Swaroopa and gently hold the Pranava Manthra, that is 'AUM' to your heart. When Jeeva thus practises yoga, he realizes the truth and stands in accepted grace.

2493. Twam-Pada arises in Maya Sakthi. Tat-Pada in comely Parai Sakthi and Asi-Pada leads to Santhi Kala. This Vakya (expression) Twam-Tat-Asi of the celestials is truly attained by yogic breathing.

2494. Deva Datt is one and the same person. But through time and place he appears different. Like this, if Jeeva transcends time and place, He and Lord Shiva become one (SO-HAM). In Twam-Tat-Asi, Jeeva is with primal cause in one body. When attaining true Gnana Jeeva becomes Para Shiva.

Deva Datta is a fictional name used in Vedanta literature. Here the name is used to illustrate how the individual remains the same, though states of time and place may differ. Devadatta was a bachelor in Benares, a householder in Chidambaram, and a Sanyasin in Madurai—all One and the same person in different places.

2495. The three Gunas—Tamas and the rest, the three impurities, Kamiya and the rest, are no more. The three Thuriyas are in those three letters A-U-M (the consonant). All these are of Twam-Tat-Asi.

27. Three Vast Spaces

2496. The Mayas space is left behind, when experiencing the seven caused states. The bodha space is left behind, when experiencing the seven Causal states, the Upasantha space is left behind when experiencing and sundering the cause-caused states (above). Then alone is the end finale.

2497. The Maya space is of Jeeva, the Bodha (Viyome) space is of Para, the Upasantha space (Vyaptha) where Jeeva is one with Shiva-sakthi. All three spaces are of pure manifestations (Swaroopa)—the end of Twam-Tat-Asi that is

Tathwamasi.

2498. The Nandhi that rides the Bull, of Himself, daily blesses you with no impediments. And when I reach His Holy Feet, I cross the space, and I merge in that space that transcends imagination.

2499. This space where Thuriyas merge defies description they call it Paramparam. Those who do not know, say thus. They worship as Paramparam. No one knows, what a wonderous land it is !

2500. The thirty-six Tathwas, devoid of impurities, Anava and Maya are left. Denoted by the letters 'Na' and 'Ma'—Parai granting Her grace to Jeeva ('Ya'), makes it merge into Param ('Ya' Sakthi and 'Si' Shiva). This indeed, is "SI VA YA NA MA" (the five lettered Holy Manthra).

2501. For those who have realized truth, this thought is form and form is thought. For them, there is no descent no ascent and no void. There is neither thought nor form too.

28. Causal-Causal Experiences

2502. When seven caused experiences of Jeeva and seven causal experiences of Para leave, the difference of cause and causal vanish, and then Jeeva becomes Shiva for sure.

2503. Without leaving the thirty-six caused experiences, without leaving Jagrath. Swapna and other states of Thuriya Jagrath, waking and without entering this Shushupthi state that is beyond the thirty-six Tathwas, it avails nothing if the Jeeva speaks of Twam Pada. He on this earth will never, never reach the final goal.

2504. In the three states of Mukthi letter 'A' is Jeeva, 'U' is Para and 'M' is Shiva) 'Si' is Shiva, 'Va' is Para and 'Ya' is Jeeva. Thus the Manthras 'AUM' and Sivaya are interpreted as one.

2505. Isa is vibrant as life of life, interminable and imperishable beyond travails of causal experiences and opposite caused experience. Without His abounding grace, Anava that makes Him-Jeeva tremble never, never leaves him.

2506. Jeeva is immanent in the seven caused experiences. Para Shiva is immanent in the seven causal experiences. In the void that defies cause-caused description, beyond thought and word, is Paraparam.

2507. The seed of Mukthi is Upasantha, knowledge of the Primal One; seed of Bhakti is intense meek adoration; the seed of Siddhi of Siddhi is self, becoming Shiva-Para; seed of Sakthi is the state of Upasantha.

2508. The seven caused experiences lie latent in Maya; the seven causal experiences lie latent in space. When the cause-caused experiences disappear, then it is pervasive Upasantha.

2509. Jeeva's purification of the Self (Athmasuddhi) is in Jagrath Thuriya; vision of Pasam is in Thuriya of the Jagrath; Atheetha (Para Thuriya); this extending into Lord Shiva Thuriya, Upasantha is pervasive.

2510. These acts of purification—removing of Anava (egoity) within entwining with the thirty-six Tathwas and realizing Self knowledge—belong to Jagrath—Thuriya (Jeeva Thuriya).

The grace of Param Guru dawns in the Jagrathatheetha Thuriya (Para Thuriya) state that defies speech. When this is crossed, and Shiva Thuriya is reached, then Upasantha is pervasive.

2511. Entering into the Upasantha experience, Jeeva becomes Shiva, There immersed in Shiva-bliss. Jeeva merges into Shiva. Enjoying this bliss experience it abides here constantly. This experience engrosses all the ten states of Jeeva, from Jagrath upwards to Shiva Thuriya.

2512. Merged in One with Lord Shiva and Sakthi, as cool waters into the wavy Sea, and realizing the truth of the Holy word, that is sweet as ambrosia, Jeeva reaches the shore beyond that indeed, defies speech.

29. Refraining From Vain Speech

2513. A man unsheaths his jewelled sword saying, that he will smite the hare in the moon. Like him there are many who say that they will see the blue-throated Lord and that they know the way. Such will never see, as they do not hold Him in their hearts.

2514. The black-hued serpent in a deep well dies when the black-footed Garuda (vulture) bird passes across the sky. So your heart should stop bragging of your greatness. But be like the river that merges into the wavy ocean.

2515. If you seek to perish your enemies (impurities), why do you fight at the gate of birth. It is silly heroism indeed, If the penance of the holy ones are suitable, then He, who gives all gifts will seat them with the celestials.

2516. Do not be lost in contentions, He, Shiva is our Lord who pervades all worlds. You should hold Him thus. Then truly the eighteen heavenly hosts will worship at your feet. Seek Him and you will be in eternal bliss for ever.

The eighteen heavenly hosts consist of Supernatural beings. They are: Devas (Amaras), Siddhas, Asuras, Daityas, Garudas, Kinnaras, Niruthas, Kimpurushas, Gandharvas, Yakshas, Vinjayas, Bhuthas, Pisachas, Antharas, Munivars, Uragas, Akasa Vasas and Bhoga Shumindars.

2517. The Lord who is dearer than the dearest life in me, the Pure One, who is brighter than the purest gold, the Great One, unvaringly glows in all life; contemplate on Him in appropriate ways.

2518. You may well adore the Pure One standing, sitting and prostrating. Though you, be learned, do conquer your five senses and quickly sunder your contending Pasas. Thus seek Him and know Him and He will be one with you.

2519. My Father, my Lord stands as subtle knowledge, He stands as pervasive knowledge, engrossing the seven worlds, too. He knows all melodies. Sing His praise, the celestials will hold you in endearment.

2520. Think of Him, whom even the celestials do not know, in the waking dawn, continuously think of Him morning, noon and evening. If you thus persevere you will become the very Paraparam.

2521. He pervades all the seven worlds as One. He, of you, conferred His grace on Jeevas. He, the Lord of infinite grace is Supreme in Gnana of the holy ones of constant heart. He, the famed one is festooned in unfading flowers.

2522. I praised Him, hailing Him as my Father, hailing

His golden Feet. And as I praised Him, the radiant lamp of life sparkled within me, and then I heard the bewitching sound, that immersed my body in rapture and there was Divine dance.

2523. I sought my Nandhi within and there I met Him. No one seeks Him within their hearts and so no one knows Him, I entered within me in the yogic way and as created and ascended the yogic centres, my eyes closed in trance and I saw His Divine form and the seven worlds too.

2524. I behold the Mount within; in it was divine glory, abiding Gnana and sweet nectar; for one, who realises Him in unfaltering love. He, the compassionate One, creates the very heaven within me.

2525. The Tapaswins of infinite wisdom stand great in wisdom; they beam pure as the moon's rays, they are in transcendental bliss, themselves becoming divine Gnana; they are encompassed in consciousness of the cosmic universe. And entering Upasantha they freed themselves of impurities and reached the state of quiescence.

2526. They, truly, are Shiva Siddhas, who abandon the three Mukthi states as vain, dispels the enticing darkness of Pasa, rid themselves of Aanava, transcend 'I' and 'Mine' consciousness and remain in constancy.

2527. Siddhas are those who saw Lord Shiva. They are soaked in Suddha-Asuddha and yet not soaked in it. They are Mukthas and in source of Mukthi, too. They are possessed of Mooladhara prowess and are like unto Sadhasiva.

30. Experience in the Eight Petalled Sphere

The eight Gods of the cardinal points of earth are enumerated to indicate that they are seated, within the eight-petalled lotus in the cranium—the microcosm in the macrocosm.

In most books, dealing with Kundalini yoga, the flower in Sahashrara is usually pictured as a thousand petalled lotus. Hence the name Sahashrara (thousand petals). Thirumoolar, however, visions it as an eight petalled lotus. As it is not a centre (Chakra or Adhara). Thirumoolar only refers to the experiences in the eight-petalled lotus of the cranium. The region usually referred to as Shahasrara is directly indicated by Thirumoolar as Mount Meru (In the cranium).

2528. The Gods Indhra, Yama, Agni, Nirudhi, Varuna, Vayu, Kubera and Isana filled the eight cardinal directions in according order.

The eight Gods and their respective eight cardinal directions are:

1. Indhra—God of the eastern quarter;
2. Agni—the God of south-eastern quarter;
3. Yama—the God of the southern quarter;
4. Nirudhi—the God of the south-western quarter;
5. Varuna—the God of the western quarter;
6. Vayu—the God of the north-western quarter;
7. Kubera—the God of the northern quarter;
8. Isana—the God of the north-eastern quarter.

2529. The flower of eight petals, pointing to the eight directions, is in the Maya-land of the body; Contemplate on its radiance, through the lean stalk of Sushumna, and ascend upward, Then you are redeemed.

2530. Here, there are three lotus buds. This spreading Light, sends His rays into the three. The eight-petalled bloom opens within and if the rays of two petals (Agjna) penetrates into them, this body blossoms into a heavenly dream.

2531. The six streams of yogic centres flow into one pond. Thus in a subtle way, it penetrates into the Shiva-state. Here, indeed, is the precious truth, He stands with Sakthi of bouncing breasts and tender vine form.

2532. The Primal One stands as eight directions, eight mountains, eight Gods and eight forms. Reach Him, who blooms within the eight petals and fills from eight to four petalled centres within.

2533. The seven centres are possessed of form (Swaroopa). Transcend them and beyond in the eighth centre is Param. In the ninth centre is Paraparam, that is void. The exalted tenth is the state of Oneness where Aanava is finally shed.

2534. He lasts through countless aeons. He is the Sun. He is the Mighty Lord: Within the major aeons there are many minor aeons. The Universe has passed through several aeons. Bhagavan (God) is unique in the aeon above countless aeons.

2535. He is in this world; yet if He is beyond reach, seek Him in heaven, where the elephants roam and the celestials wander, where fire, rain and wind abide. Seek Him in this space.

2536. A pond which is not fed by any stream is there in the lofty top of the Mount Meru within. And there is a lotus bloom that springs from no mud soil.

2537. When the one and two (Shiva and Sakthi) intermingle, standing and sitting or indulging in worldly talk, the holy Jeevas conquer their senses and seek the Lord, Remaining here or leaving, they are ever blessed.

31. Nine Awasthas and Nine Aspirants

2538. Viswan, Dhaisanthan, and Prajnam are in Twampada state; Virattam, Hiranya Gargbam, Avyakritan are in Tatpada state; Idayam, Prajapathiam and Santhan of the golden world are in Asi-pada state. Yet, they are all but Abhimanis, souls that are still aspirants.

2539. As the nine states, beginning with Jagrath, are experienced, attachment to impurities and Gunas, that emanate birth, vanish. The void (Sathya-Gnana-Bodham) succeeds in the transcendental Thuriya state, filled with truth and Gnana where Jeeva and Shiva are one. Jeeva and Shiva that are now in void in one manifestness (Swaroopa) are two in the rest of the Thuriyas.

2540. As Jeeva merges in the thought of Shiva, the three impurities that give rise to birth flee away. At the end of nine avasthas, Jeeva attains Shiva. Bodha (Awareness of Gnana) and is no more Himself.

2541. Beyond the nine states mentioned earlier there are nine states that defy thought. These will be said in detail below. The Lord who made these twice-nine states is great, indeed.

2542. The nine states evolved from the five states of Jeeva. The Lord spoke of them, and the world rejoiced. I prayed to Him as my Lord, day and night and He severed my strong fetters.

2543. They laid many paths in time's long corridor, many

sects sought to reach Him. Think constantly, day and night, of Him who stands diverse in many lands.

2544. The nine categories that belong to the Primal One are the primal Paraparam, Paraparai, Param and the Light, Jeeva, Tathwas, Kalas and the two Maya and Mukthi (eternal liberation).

2545. He made my inconstant thoughts constant and gave me clear vision. In abounding grace, He created hell and heaven and endless births too. Those who do not perceive these are forever caught in the well of Karmas.

2546. Jeeva stands as an aspirant (Abhimani) in the nine states of experience. The nine categories that are started afterward, belong to the Primal Lord. When you-Jeeva who stands in the nine states reaches the Thuriya states, that are three, then, he will become Shiva. This is the goal of Siddhantha philosophy.

32. Suddha-Ashuddha (Pure/Impure)

2547. No one knows that the breath, twelve finger-breath long, at the tip of the nose (Agna centre) is the Lord's abode. The Holiest Veda that expounds truths in expansiveness, was hesitant to speak of this. Such indeed, is the Lord's greatness.

2548. The Karmas, the right and thoughts and deeds of Karmas are alike the seeds of birth that are to be. Seeing this, keep away from them. Whatever you do after will not reach the Karma pond.

2549. Truth of the Vedas remain hidden, when Maya veils the Jeeva. When Maya leaves, He reveals the truth of Himself. Those who can make Maya vanish merge in God. And thereafter, there is no body and no more mind.

2550. Coursing the Prana stream into the eyebrow centre and opening the vulva cavity where phlegm gathers, and there stilling the breath in the way the yoga-guru taught, and warming it in the Kundalini fire within and restraining it to a low measure is to attain divine strength indeed.

2551. He who is in the body-complex, who rules the body-land; who beams within the body, know that He stands within the body is He, the Nandhi. They seek Him in all the lands.

They do not know that He stands within the body.

2552. The ignorant say that everything is 'unclean'. They do not know the place that is 'unclean'. When they come to know the yogic mysteries of this 'unclean' place, then, they will find that the human birth itself is unclean.

2553. There is no uncleanliness of the Mooladhara for those who observe ritual discipline, who worship Hara, who tend the sacred fire and for those who are versed in Vedic Gnana.

2554. Purity in the Cranium top begins for those who stand in the yogic way. Those who are sunk in the pit of lust will not reach purity's goal. It is only those who have sent the Mooladhara fire up into the central Nadi of Shushumna, will see real purity: Others cannot see it.

2555. The Lord is pure crystal. He is pure fire who emanates rays of purity, No one knows where His source is, they who know the source will themselves become crystal pure, and fire pure.

2556. Primal purity in silence is the way of purity, it is the mighty Lord's name, is the eight Siddhis and is the Holy Feet of the Lord.

2557. My Holy father is the quintessence of truth. Only those who adore Him are accepted in His Mighty Grace. The rest are caught up in the whirl of misery and lie in dark stupor.

2558. Most do not know that Karma brings evil fruits. They do not choose to find Gnana for the liberation from Karmas. They do not know the Vedic teachings to renounce Karma and be liberated. They who wallow in Karma will never reap the rich harvest.

33. Scorn of Eternal Liberation

2559. Those who say that there is no 'Para state' are for sure destined for hell state; all the world knows this. They will go begging from door to door and with the speed of horse, they run in search of food.

2560. Most do not follow the way taught by the Guru. They do not seek the Holy One. They wander indulging in frivolous talk and do not sing His Holy deeds. Those who thus dance about, their desert will be nothing.

2561. He comes and goes into my thoughts. I hold Him as God, in the constancy of my thoughts. I beseech Him, as my Lord and I hold Him close in my heart. He responds to devotion and asks what is here.

2562. Just as the water from the upland flows downward. Truth does not remain in the body. He showed this truth in me just as the ship in the Sea that seeks the shores, the fire-hued Lord, stands as a sure goal to my trouble-tossed soul.

2563. The Param within, is as continuous as thread. Within the lotus stalk. Yet no one seeks Him there, but wander about everywhere. Though the way to reach Him is shown, they do not see it; They are fools who roam about, to reach actions of only evil destiny.

2564. They end their lives with yet, the light within them still unkindled. Such men gather in crowds and do not seek Him. They do not see 'Nandhi', who is immanent in the field, forests and hills.

2565. Men wander about, North and South, seeking Him. Celestials go about looking for Him in the east and west. But fix the divine Manthra (AUM) on to Mooladhara, and rouse the Kundalini fire to stream upward, here you will be as a radiant light.

2566. Even if men of great penance, with gracious looks entreat the men of evil fate who do not practise holy dharma, but indulge in angry speech always, then, they themselves will have to undergo all, all their intractable Karma.

34. Lakshana Thrayam (Ultimate Reality)

2567. The theory of Lakshana is important in all Indian philosophical systems in trying to discuss the nature of the ultimate reality, which is beyond expression. The Vedantins employ this widely in trying to explain expressions like Tatthvamasi, Aham Brahmasmi, etc.

2568. When Jeeva reaches the void, they say, it is Upasantha and Nadantha; this is only to speak on triple grammatical convention.—Lakshana Thraya; when Jeeva reaches void, its state is of total renunciation and of all attributes. When Jeeva reaches Upasantha its state is of renunciation and adherence yet; when Jeeva reaches Nadantha its state is of renunciation and non-renunciation at once. The state of Jeeva, in finite manifestness (Swaroopa) transcends all grammatical conventions.

Lakshana Thraya is a grammatical theory in Sanskrit which states that an expression in a certain context may lend itself to three interpretations of an object in three ways:

(a) The use of the word in its secondary sense—its primary sense having been lost—Tamil, Vitta-Illakkanai.

(b) The use of the word in which the primary sense is retained alongwith its secondary sense—Tamil, Vidatha-Illakkanai.

(c) The use of the word in which the primary sense is partly discarded and partly retained—Tamil, Vithum Vidantha-Illakkanai.

When Jeeva reaches the space, the state that ensues is one of total-effacement of all attributes; Upasantha is the state of non-attachment and attachment yet. Jeeva reaching Nadantha is the state of renunciation and non-renunciation at once. Transcending the grammatical conventions of Lakshnathrayam—that is the same Jeeva being in different places with different experience—is the state of Jeeva in final self-manifestness (Supreme Swaroopa).

2569. Jeeva strung the bow, took aim and with one arrow shot five deadly elephants. He who thus shot, will behold the radiant light beaming like several gems set in splendour.

Jeeva vanquished the five deadly elephants in one shot. He who has shot thus will see the radiant light beaming like gems in diverse colours.

The reference is to the yogic practice of coursing the Kundalini energy through the Shushumna and ascending the yogic centres upto the cranium, where God is visioned.

35. Tatthwamasivakyam

2570. Jeeva attains Twam-pada in Jeeva Thuriya. Beyond in Para Thuriya is tat-pada. Still beyond in Shiva Thuriya is true Asi-Pada. Further, beyond is the Truth that is Tat-Twam-Asi.

2571. Twam-Pada transcends the thirty-six Tathwas, this is Suddha state. Then is Tat-Pada that leads to Upasantha. There is Asi-Pada where Shiva is. The ultimate state is the blessed state of Twam-Tat-Asi that is Tat-Twam-Asi.

2572. The Jeeva (Deva Datta) becomes SO-HAM and by the speech of grammatical conventions it is triple in Twam-Tat-Asi; with attributes thus transferred; here jeeva is jeeva, para and Shiva; all in One.

2573. Twam-Tat-Asi is the same as Tatwamasi. The one comes conjoined as the other. The holy concept of Tat-Twam-Asi (You-Being-I) belongs to Vedanta. The concept of I-Shiva-becoming Tatwamasi is Siddantha-Vedanta.

2574. They who do not know the inexplicable void that is the Thuriya end, call it Param. No, this is not so, There is the wonderous land of Param-Param that rises beyond the three states of Thuriya. No one knows about this properly.

2575. Transcend beyond the states of Twam-Pada, Tat-Pada and Asi-Pada and seek the triple Thuriyas beyond. Then there is the state beyond all states the (one) Truth that is beyond Jeeva, Para and Shiva.

2576. The bliss of manifestness is at the end of Shiva Thuriya state. Here in this state, chant the Manthra that is Pranava (AUM) within your heart. Then, the Supreme awareness Shiva, Himself appears.

2577. Merge the five experiences in Nadha and drop the lowly Malas (impurities) behind. Thus pursuing the onward course, then enter the Suddha state, beyond the Upasantha state (Para Thuriya), is the Shiva state. The Lord Param-Param is further beyond the reach of thought and world. So seek Him, the mighty Lord.

2578. Nature of the confluent state in Tat-Twam-Asi is, it has no completeness, no limits, no speech, no attachment or possession. Of itself, it reveals, uncaused-this, is its nature.

2579. "You Become Truth-That"—thus stood the great expression Mahavakyam (Supreme Sentence). And I became that, Nandhi blessed me thus—to Lord Shiva becoming, and as I became that, I was immersed in infinite bliss.

2580. Jeeva becomes Para and this Para-Jeeva becomes Lord Shiva. And from this Vedic lamp of Shiva-arose the light of Paraparam, and in turn it fills as AUM that no speech can describe.

2581. When the Prana breath from nose tip to cranium passes through the mother Nadi (Sushumna), to the five centres, Uluva, nose tip, eyebrow middle, forehead and cranium, beyond the Primal Nadha and Tathwas; then the Prana breath grows as distant divine light. These truly, are the Jeeva Shiva states.

2582. He dispelled both Jeeva's knowledge and Jeeva's ignorance; and Shiva stood as the all pervasive Supreme Knowledge. So, do not leave Him but adore Him as Lord. Those who do not know the way, will never reach the goal.

2583. They of true knowledge know Lord Shiva who is fire and water at once. They, of true knowledge know Shiva who stands as fire and water, Shiva, Sakthi, comingled. Unless the knower within makes you know, we know that your knowledge avails nothing at all.

2584. He, Nandhi is within Atheetha and beyond it. He, Jeeva, bereft of Gnana, enters Atheetha, attains Gnana and rid of dark ignorance, becomes Para. Then he will be one with God (Pathi).

2585. With head bowed low I worshipped at the Feet of the Lord of celestials, And behold, the Lord stepped forward and said that I shall then see the result of all my prayer and penance, performed of yore, And so, He, the Lord of Fore-head eye, Blessed me.

2586. He, who is holy, birthless, of pure form came in me and said that He received me in His grace. He of golden form, the heavenly Lord whom the celestials praise blessed me with purity and removed my blemishes.

2587. Renouncing all, I entered inward and beheld the Light within. My heart trembled, and I prostrated low, but I never forgot Him. And the Lord of celestials freeing me from the whirl of births and made me immortal, here below.

2588. The five external sense organs, the four internal

cognitive organs, all the worlds and all lives are all swayed by my Lord. He is the pervasive truth form that has neither hand nor mouth.

36. Viswa: Grssam (Absolute Absorption)

2589. Even as the shadow disappears with the body, even as the bubble returns into water and even as the flame of camphor leaves no traces, so it is when Jeeva enters into Param.

2590. When the body and the Jeeva as unbroken in yoga, then, there will be the grace of Shiva-Sakthi, and the Jeeva becomes Param. Jeeva that leaves the body then, becomes pervasive, with no beginning and no end, and it merges in Shiva forever.

2591. The Tathwas that confuse the five sense organs, the expanding internal cognitive organs, finally merge intermittently in Maya, this is the inevitable fate of the whole Universe.

2592. Jeeva becomes Para and this Para stands pervasive and immanent too in all creation. It is mighty power that can dissolve and create vast universe. This boon was granted to me and thus my state is exalted.

2593. If Para can reach Para Shiva by attaining the divine knowledge-form of the Thuriya state and the omniscient experience of the phenomenal universe, then, he belongs to space that is the Supreme Light.

2594. Just as hot iron absorbs water, He absorbed in me in totality. Transcending the Param-Para state, He stands engulfing the three luminous spaces. Here, He is Nandhi who resides in my heart.

2595. Just as the wood apple is consumed by 'elephant' disease, so are Jeeva and Para before Shiva, the supreme Shiva that engrosses all worlds is in the rare state beyond Shiva Thuriya.

2596. Paraparam is the end and beginning, He is Parapara for each and everyone. He absorbed us Jeevas and Para. He, Nandhi was Jnatheru at the end of Jnana-Jneya relationship. This, indeed, is beyond our comprehension.

37. Eternal Truth

2597. Impurities are rid by holy instructions and Jeeva shines like in purified fire. Having been rid of impurities, if Jeeva constantly thinks of Lord Shiva, then, he becomes a radiant flame, that has burnt away all passions.

2598. Nothing avails you if you know all; but not the knowledge that knows everything. When you can say, that you are the knowledge that knows everything, then, you can very well say, that you are God.

2599. I performed penance in the mountain valley within my head and I visioned the Lord with His consort Sakthi. Also I crossed the river of births in this fleshy body and met the 'Thief'hiding in the Kalas.

2600. The Vedas say, that he whose flesh melts in love of God will be Lord of all worlds, will be the Tathwas for all worlds and the heaven will rain because of him.

2601. You ask, how it is that they received the Lord's grace well, it is thus; their bewildered thought wandered in the battle of life, they trained its course, and freed of darkness they sought the Lord and adored His Holy feet.

2602. He, in truth merges in them who are truthful. He never makes his appearance before those who are untruthful. He stands as Lord at the end of time, to work the redemption of all souls. Then, the true ones sport in true joy.

2603. He, the pure one who does not enter false hearts, unites in those who unite in truth, when the prana ascends upward in the Sushumna, and you meet the Lord, then, truly He will abide in your thoughts.

2604. Meditate on Him and night when He abides in your thoughts. Then, He will appear in the cranium above. And if you give up falsehood and fleshy desires, the Lord in truth will reveal Himself to you.

2605. It is the grace of mighty God, whether you reach the yogic climax or not. If you subdue the nine deceptive senses, you may mount the steed of truth. This is the way of redemption that the great Nandhi taught.

2606. Nandhi who entered my Sushumna Nadi, who is ever in my thoughts, who is in my body, is the source of all

Vedas. He, the holy one, does not reveal Himself to men who are untrue. He is the refuge of only those who shed their falsehood.

2607. Nandhi imprinted His Holy Feet on my heart. No one has drawn the bolt of His mighty door and glimpsed Him inside. Give up unreservedly, the thoughts of this deceptive body, which is the receptacle of sorrow. Then unbolt the Sushumna door, and indeed, your reward will be rich.

2608. Adore the Lord with intense feeling, when seeking the way of redemption. For sure, the grace of Hara will be yours. For, He shines in the heart of those who do not utter untruth, and He standing abiding in their midst.

2609. From the fragment flower within, there is a delicious fruit that ripens. The birds within the self hinder you from reaching it. So, shoot your arrow and drive them away. Then you can reach Lord Shiva state that is lustrous as pure as red Gold.

2610. Control the senses that tempt and sunder the Pasas that corrupt. Follow the Lord who ends your confusion, If you do so, my Shiva unhesitatingly says, you are redeemed and He makes your thoughts centre on Him.

2611. They who constantly think of Him will reach into a body, that is glorious and strong. Here, if they adore the Lord in appropriate ways, they, receiving the grace of the Holy One, will reach the world of Supreme Wisdom (Gnana).

38. Ways of Supreme Wisdom

2612. If Karma overtakes them from the past, by patiently experiencing them, they exterminate them. But they should see to it that future Karma is not created. They realise the Self, they are Gnanis who have cognised the Tathwas and have trained the five senses in good ways.

2613. The Tathwa Gnanis realize the self. They cut the gordian knot to past Karmas. They seize and crush future Karmas by the grace of Lord Shiva whom they hold high on their heads.

2614. Karmas accumulate through thoughts, word and deed. Karmas do not abide of thought and word stand consistent. They are the great Gnanis, who conquering thoughts and words, experience Karmas and alter their course.

39. Abnegation of Desires

2615. There is no use in the prattling of breath and Sushumna but sunder your desires and passions. Having sundered them, the Lord's place will be easy to attain.

2616. He is not in stony houses and stately halls. He is not is holy garbs too. Neither is He in deep parlours and massive temples. He is, in the thoughts of those who have relinquished desires. Though they are in this fleshy body, He grants their liberation.

2617. Sunder your desires even like the Lord, The more are the desires, the more are your sorrows. The more you give up desires, the more will be your bliss.

2618. The five senses burn you up and lead you to the way of destruction. So give up desires and scatter them away. Reach to the truth of Supreme Wisdom for this is the way to reach the Almighty Lord.

2619. Like the ocean that rages and foams at full-moon tides, many, many floods rose and passed away through the passage of time. Caught in the floods of pleasure and pain, numberless celestials have perished. Likewise, caught in the floods of desires countless humans have sunk. God alone stands for ever in the ocean of the eternal bliss.

2620. Prolonged activity is suspended when Jeevas are emancipated from Karmas of the past; they reach the Suddha state. Then, by transcending the five acts of God, they receive His direct grace and are forever immersed there. These are the purified ways of the Supreme Wisdom.

2621. Realizing the Supreme Truth in full, these Gnani's attain luminous Siddhi and Mukthi. Being entirely devoid of sexual desire, they achieve the eight mighty Siddhis. As the Lord Shiva Gnani leaves behind this body, divine grace descends on him and then, he remain, forever, in God-Love.

2622. The Jeevas do not in love seek that this Jeeva should become Lord Shiva. They do not know this truth that this Jeeva is Lord Shiva. By not knowing that his Jeeva is Shiva and by not realizing this truth, they take diverse births and wander into several worlds.

2623. The five Gods consign the Jeeva to broiling miseries and then cooling him, again consign him to fresh birth. Thus they ordain them words in the whirl of endless creation. But He severed my desires for limitless learning and He fixed my body, which is restless as the waves, in calmness, in my purified being within.

2624. You say, you are redeemed, But you have not yet seen the appropriate way. Know that Nandhi merges in the fragrant flower within you. So, hold Him in your thoughts in clear vision, then you will have sown the seed of birthlessness.

40. To Be Possessed of Bhakti

2625. He is Gnana and Manthra who confers Mukthi (Eternal liberation). He is the father, the Lord of immortal celestials. He is the pure one, the light that is the Holy way. He is the Pasu-Pathi whom the devotees adore in ardour.

2626. I became a devotee to the devotees of the Lord in continous succession. Giving Myself up thus, I entered into their vassalage and with the grace of the devotees, I reached His Feet. He, then saying that I am His devotee, accepted me in His vassalage of Mighty grace.

2627. He is cooler than water and hotter than fire. No one knows who this ocean of Nandhi is ! He is by far righteous than all bounteous beings in the world. He stands within the heart. He stands as Umapathi, Sakthi's Lord.

2628. No one can say where the Lord is ! Well may the denizens of all the seven worlds, entirely try, yet they cannot know him. No one can dare say, where this peerless pearl is, unless He of Himself appears in devotion of His devotees.

2629. As the calf that searches and calls for its mother, cow, I, in yearning, sought and cried for my Lord. He is the hidden truth of the Vedas who stands eternal beyond heavens. In tender, endearment, He entered into me, in this fleshy body of mine.

2630. The Jeevas have no tasks to perform in the burn condition, their birth comes as of itself. The Jeevas in the eternal liberation state too, by the very condition of this state nothing to perform. The Lord by His mighty grace grants both the states, Then, there is nothing for the devotees to do, except to hold the Lord in their thoughts.

2631. With the Prana breath for seed-energy and the serpent Kundalini, for body, I climb upward, to the resounding music of Nadhia, to the cool mountain within and there I adore Nandhi with the fragrant flower that blooms. I do not let my mind to adore any other God.

2632. Nandhi, the Lord of the Holy celestials, is my protector in need; Seek his protection and be redeemed by ending birth cycle. Think constantly of Lord Shiva's Feet, He, who stands as fire, grants divine protection.

2633. The Dhanavas of the dark world held the Vanavas of the luminous world in fief. But the Lord destroyed the three forts of the evil ones, and the devotees worshipped Him as the Lord of forests and of black mountains. Thus adoring Him in their fleshy body, they united in Him.

2634. This birth is a lasting curse to me. And so, in drooping heart, I seek Him; within and without, in the mountains and the skies, and within the fire too, Thus I stand immersed in Holy thought.

41. To Be in Eternal Liberation

2635. Purified of Tathwas and attaining the Suddha state, the Jeeva receives the grace of Lord in full in Mukthi state. Thus to perform penance is the Jeeva's task, and so rid of Karmas, they stand in true devotion. They are indeed, the Gnanis immersed in transcendental bliss.

2636. The Jeeva-Bird with its feet planted firmly on the Mooladhara seeks the rich fruit, that is Lord Shiva. When it seeks this fruit within the heart, it reaches its great goal, by lighting the Sushumna lamp in the flaming fire of Kundalini within. And thereafter, its four cognitive organs, ever seek, Him alone.

42. Experimentation

2637. This mighty Lord, the great Nandhi granted me His

Feet of indescribable bliss and immersed me in an ocean of grace. Then freeing me from all illusions and secretly guarding me in safety. He born me to the holy banks of silence; this indeed, was a divine experiment.

2638. He is the wise one who fills the rare Vedas. He is the God of countless Gods; He is possessed of divine sense. Transcending the five senses, I seek my union with Him who has these attributes.

2639. This world laments about Supreme Wisdom (Gnana). They do not know that the Gnana of Jeeva is not Gnana at all; but sheer ignorance. But when Siva Gnana overlays Jeeva Gnana, they both become pure Gnana. After all this much is the dividing line between knowledge and ignorance.

2640. I loosend myself into the goal beyond goals, into the assembly where no one assembled and into the knowledge beyond knowledge. In single-minded thought, I merged in Holy Nandhi's mighty grace and there was Shiva in pervasiveness beyond all pervasiveness.

2641. The Lord pervades all as feel within the breeze, as the sweetness within sugarcane, Jeeva within milk as juice within fruit and as fragrance within flower, my Lord is immanent.

2642. He who stood as form of fire abodes as Lord in my thoughts as like the vein of gold in the recesses of a mountain. So, seek Lord Shiva in endearing love

2643. Nandhi seated in the centre of void, descended into my heart's temple and took His place there. And as He descended, I stood up calling Him my father and asking Him to come. Thus as I greated Him, Lord Shiva instantly stood in my thoughts.

2644. He is of mighty attribute. He is the fruit of penance. He is all things good. He resides in the centre of the thoughts. Seek the Great Nandhi, the Holy One, in unfaltering Truth and He will place you as the first of many.

2645. As I searched Him within me, He was with me and stood there continuously. He stands pervasive and transcending beyond too. My father, Paraparam shows me the way.

2646. It is rare for the celestials to reach Him who shows

the way. Here below, He is as father-mother, kith and kin. He is in Shiva Loka the holy way leads too. This is the way the Nandhi is:

2647. Unsheath the world of Gnana and smite and that very instant you will know the Lord. Unite in Him, who is Lord of celestials. You will then be away from the numerous rablle that cling to desires !

2648. Holding the world of Gnana, that the Primal Lord gifted to me, there is no one to separate, me from Him. I searched further, leaving no traces; then Jeeva became one with Primal Shiva.

2649. I scorched Pasa (attachment through desires), the seminal seed of birth, Maya, the invisible one, Karma, that gives birth to desire, the doubts and fears that come in their train and the numerous births, I scorched them all. And thus with my thoughts purified. I searched in calmness. The skillful ones that practise thus shall be one with the mighty Tat-Para.

2650. He taught me the word that is beyond words. He severed my desires for limitless learning. He fixed my body that was restless as the waves, in calmness. He, the Tat-Para entered in my purified being within.

Tanthra Eight Concluded.

9

Tanthra Nine (Maghudaahamam)

1. Darshan of Guru Monastery

2651. Smoke and sound, oblations and sacrificial offerings, all these spread in worship, are for my Lord. The Gurus who thus meditate, who have founded monasteries, have truly reached the Feet of the Lord.

2652. The Lord has no habitation, but the body-house of Jeeva, let them find out if the Lord has any other home. Even after having found out that Jeeva's body is Shiva's home, many say, that He, the Lord is outside.

2653. Having discovered the great way of seeking, I reached the flower-decked feet of Lord Shiva within. He is beyond seeking. Indeed, it is greatness where he resides. He stands as life of the revolving world.

2654. I shall reveal where He is seated and where His mountain is ! I shall reveal where His retreat cave is and where it is located. I shall reveal where His Adharas-yogic centres are, and the forest where He is ! I shall reveal all these eight to the denizens of the world here below.

2655. The guru face is the Lord's pedestal, the monastery is the Lord's Holy land and the holy assembly of blemishless vision is the Lord's abode. The heart that performs the sixteen worships inside is the Lord's sacred throne. The yogic centres within are the Lord's astral cave.

2656. The six yogic centres inward are His pedestal, the pervasive Sakthi is His throne and the universal God within is Lord Shiva, Himself. So it is for those who reflect inward and know it.

2657. The twin Mayas envelope the body of five sheaths when they reach their end. Then the holy light appears of itself. Those who seek the truth, in this manifestness (Swaroopa) are the Gnana's, in exceeding silence.

2. Darshan of Gnana Guru

2658. When the thirty-six Tathwas are subdued, then the holy Guru will appear for you to adore. Shiva-state too will be conferred on you; and then the ineffable bliss will well-up in you.

2659. The Resplendent light is beyond the three Thuriyas. It is the Para Shiva that pervades all. In this land, that knows neither contraction nor expansion are the feet of the Holy Guru that, is beyond speech.

2660. I was gifted this head to bear Nandhi's Feet; I was gifted this mouth to praise the Great Nandhi; I was gifted these eyes to vision the eternal Nandhi; I was gifted this mind, to think of Nandhi afar.

2661. At the thought of the Garuda's form, the serpent's poison leaves its terrors lose. Just like this, the triple Malas (impurities) instantly leave at the thought of Guru's form and the Jeeva then becomes Lord Shiva.

2662. No one knows where the Lord resides. To those who seek where the Lord resides, they will know He resides within them. When they see the Lord, Jeeva becomes Lord Shiva, Himself.

2663. Higher knowledge is to perceive the things that appear and to perceive the things do not appear. To perceive the things in different ways as in waking, dreaming and rest of the states, are the three perceptions that will no longer exist. In the state that the three Thuriyas are transcended, there Nandhi stands firm, in exalted silence.

2664. The sphere of the moon is in the centre between the eyebrows. There the virgin Sakthi is seated, on the flowers of two petals, Her form is radiant as crystal. To vision, Her, seek the Guru who has sundered all bonds.

2665. He entered into the heart, for the seven worlds to rejoice; He entered into earth, to support the heavens; He entered into a rage, for the eight directions to tremble; He entered into the wilderness, to make His abode in the mountains in the north.

2666. The Jeeva's body is of five sheaths—Annamaya-flesh body; Pranamaya—breath body; Manomaya—mind body; Vijnanamaya—knowledge body; and Anandhamaya—bliss-body; This body is a forest where the Jeeva bird has its abode. If the Jeeva seeks the way of sixteen worships then Jeeva's attainments are ten.

The way of sixteen worships is the yogic way of reaching the light with sixteen beams within the Vishuddhi yogic centre, where Sakthi stands, the Ten attainments are the ten states of transcendental consciousness, beyond which is the final goals of Supreme awareness.

2667. Our Holy Nandhi, once He stands and starts loving, does not know of any separation, Think of his form and He melts within you. Enter into His essence and see Him in your heart. For those who can do this, the seminal Karmas die slumbering and the Ego—consciousness perishes forever.

2668. Sunder the strong Pasas (attachment through desires) and cast them away and you may reach our Holy One who is the perfect truth. Seek Him firmly and think constantly of Him within, then, the Holy One who is Dharma will be reached.

2669. Think of Him and He thinks of those who think of Him.Think of Him, that is the radiance of the flower that blooms in the divine fountain within. They may be smaller than the split grain, but if they firmly hold Him, they will surely be great.

2670. When you are seeking to reach the Lord and if you have a miss, take it the work of your evil Karmas in the past, and so persevere in the pursuit of your fervent devotion and you will at last reach the Primal Lord.

2671. On thinking of the Lord, they lose their inconstancy; uniting in the Lord, their existence is lost; when He is in their thoughts their ego is lost, Thus He entered showing them the illumined way.

2672. The Holy Guru's Gnana precept is like a lustrous ray of red gem set on to a green stone. This ray is in the eyebrow centre, it is the light that is within the resplendent light.

2673. The yoga God is as mouth, eye, body and life. The mighty of His form is beyond earth, water, fire, wind, sky and space.

2674. Praise Him, who fashioned this world, as your Pathi, Lord Parasiva's writ runs in all worlds. He lends one half to the great grace and the other half. He gave to His devotees, for them to reach their goal.

2675. He is the Lord of Heavens, surrounded by the vast spatial glades. We know no other Param (Supreme) except Him. Of the celestials, the Vanavas and Danavas, no one has ever seen Him; Only those who have received His grace have seen Him forever.

2676. He made the Jeevas renounce, so that they adore the Lord. He, made them praise Him in meek words so that He the Nandhi confers His grace. Our vision is now clear and we no more adore other Gods. We became the object for other Gnana Jeevas to seek and worship.

3. Pranava Samadhi

2677. The articulate Sthoola Pranavam (AUM) is the mighty key word to the bliss of manifestness (Swaroopa). The inarticulate Sukshumna, Pranava is the Sakthi's divine manifestation (Swaroopa). The Mudhra (Gnana) is the cause of this manifestation. The Prana aloft is the highway of Vedanta.

2678. AUM is the Supreme word/Manthra, it is the form and formless; AUM is the infinite diversity; it is Siddhi and radiant Mukthi (eternal liberation).

2679. The five elements arose in AUM, the entire creation arose in AUM. The three Jeevas merged in the Atheetha (finite) of AUM. It is the form of Jeeva Para and Shiva in union.

2680. This letter-cluster AUM-made up of A-U-M is the bliss of Brahmam. The subtle one expands as the vast invisible creation. All, the yogic centres comprise its form. Thus it is known only to Gnanis of vast knowledge.

2681. My despairing thoughts are thrown into confusion, my steady thoughts lead to clear vision of the Divine Light. My steadfast mind is the place, where environs and devotion appropriate. The Upadesa (teaching) of Sanmarga (Gnana) is great indeed.

2682. To vision the sixteen-petalled centre within is Shodasa, it is the way of the Sanmargis. Beyond this is the end of the nine-centres and still beyond is Pranava; ascending further beyond is the finite and end of Gnana (Supreme Wisdom) and Jneya (known) is in one.

4. Light

2683. Know the light and your form becomes light, know the hidden form and you become that form, know the light's form and you become that light. He stands in love to melt this light within you.

2684. It is easy to enter the universe of eight. This spreading light of immense vastness dispells the primordial darkness entirely. It spreads as daylight in the mystic lotus with-in. My Lord was seated there dispelling contending pasas.

2685. The luminaries such as Jeeva, fire, sun, moon receive their luminosity by the grace of divine light. The light that gives this light is a mighty light of immense effulgence. This light dispells my darkness and stood in me suffused into oneness.

2686. The Lord is the effulgent light, He has no birth. The luminous sun and moon are His eyes, the lustrous fire is His forehead eye. This is His resplendent form of dazzling light.

2687. Below this light above is the wind, earth, fire, sky and water. Rousing the light of Kundalini within, you will be in the Astral sphere. The one light that is there engrosses the light of the five elements.

2688. This light that is within is pure as the light of lightening. It is the light that is great and red and it is the light of Param that beams Supreme wisdom (Gnana). It is the light of the six yogic centres that are ascended; it is the light of constant thought on the pure world 'AUM'. It is the light that is blended of all these lights.

2689. The effulgent light that stands as a sparkling light concealed, within, even points to the shining Lord, it is the light of the heart. It is the light that pervading all pulsates within the body. This is how the Lord stands as Supreme Light.

2690. This light is luminous: It devours the soul's darkness and it is the light of those who adore Him in Supreme Wisdom light. He devours the poison that arises with ambrosia from the milky sea and even holds it in His throat (Thiruneela-kanadam). Like it, is His light too.

2691. Just like the light of the Lord that reposes in Him, is the Light of His Sakthi grace, when the three lights sun-moon and fire shine within by the yogic way, the Lord nears you as one Light in your inner Light:

2692. The light within is only Jeeva. The Lord too who stands within is a gemly effulgent light. Flashing as lightning in the astral sphere, this light merges into one with Sakthi's Light and Jeeva's light.

2693. The Lord who is effulgent light, enterning the dark arena of Pasa (attachment through desires) and dances as light in this darkness. As the forehead eyed God (Lord Shiva) dances thus, He merges as effulgent light is Unmanai Sakthi.

2694. Those who thus went by the secret way of yoga, reached Sakthi, of dark fragrant tresses, who is the Primal Parai. She is the one with the Lord of celestial light—the light beyond the pure space. This light of Hers dispells Pasas' creeping darkness forever.

2695. Some say that there is God; Others say that there is no God; thus do the men of the world hold diverse opinions. Will they who say that there is no Primal, ever reach Shiva state? Even they who say that they have not seen God, if they stand in devotion, then, He, the Light of the astral sphere (mighty Chidambaram) within is in them as the effulgent light.

2696. The effulgent Light that glows afar is the Lord who spreads His beams as like the sun. When He dispells the Maya's darkness, the Jeeva in this very body, becomes a Gnani—Renunciate (Jivan Muktha).

2697. His holy form is of shimmering coral hue. He, the Primal Lord wears the pure white Holy ashes and is brilliant like pure gold and ripe coral. When, I was dispelled of my darkness, I shone as coral red and He, the dancing Lord, Sri Nataraja stood in union in me.

2698. The Lord stood in the heavens and the celestials too, stood there. Yet, they did not know Him and bewildered they stand forever. When Pasa's desires and the odour of past Karmas leave together, then the Jeeva blossoms as a divine flower.

2699. He, Himself alone as the Lord, is in all things; Himself is yourself and thus you should seek Him. He is the very heaven in this vast earth. He is sweet, so may you adore Him.

5. Sthoola (Articulate) Panchakshara

2700. The fifty letters are all Vedas, they are all the Agamas; when the secret of the fifty letters is known; then the fifty letters become the five letters.

The fifty letters are the Sanskrit alphabets and the five letters are NA MA SI VA YA.

2701. With the letter 'A' intoned in commencement, the fifty letters, become fifty-one. With the letter 'U' intoned high with the letter 'A' it ends with the letter 'M'; thus A,U and M as AUM and again rising with letter 'N' it becomes Nandhi's name 'AUM' NAMASIVAYA.

2702.The Parai Sakthi, of the Shodasa flower, within, is in the sixteen letters commencing with 'A'. The Light of the Lord within is in the Unmanai Sakthi beginning with 'U'. The manthra commencing with letter 'SI' (Sivayanama) is Shiva and all Vedas. When commencing with the letter 'NA' and if this order is reversed, it is NAMASIVAYA. This truly is the seminal Manthra that one should seek.

2703. The five letters and the Holy AUM are distributed

in the six yogic centres within. Na—is in the Mooladhara, Ma is in the Swadhistana; Si is in the navel centre,Va is in the heart centre, Ya is in the throat centre and AUM is in the eyebrow centre.

2704. When the seven beams of Prana rise in fury, when the four cognitive senses take their leave and when the hands of death stretch and seize, life ebbs away. Then the five letters above will be the soul's refuge.

2705. Jeevas do not chant the manthra that is to be chanted and mused over. When the Sun and the Moon rise, well they may then chant full-mouthed the wholesome, five lettered Holy manthra, that is so sacred to Sakthi who stands with Lord Shiva, and praise the Lord.

2706. Chant this SIVAYANAMA manthra once with your heart welling up in God love. Then, transparent ambrosia will well up within you. They who do not seek to drink the pure ambrosia, will be like bubbles of a water fall, that know no rest from birth's whirl, forever.

2707. Take to the way the Guru showed and blot out the reckoning of births. The five-letters alone show the way of grace to them who seek to close the way of birth's cycle.

2708. When the miseries of Karmas harass you then, chant the five lettered manthra of the pervasive Nandhi. If you thus seek Him, He will confer the grace of His Holy Feet, and your devotion will lead you to Shiva form.

2709. Think of Him in your heart and prise Him as your Lord. When death approaches you, say, He, the Lord alone in your refuge. Then you will receive the grace of the Lord seated in the five-letters, the Lord who resides in the snow-clad mountain of North (Mount Kailash).

2710. Jeevas not knowing the greatness of our Lord's five letters, question if they will ever dispel their darkness. Such as they are poor in spirit, They will be consigned to the world surrounded by serpents of diverse species.

6. Shookshma (Inarticulate) Panchakshara

2711. They speak of our in slighting terms, But with thoughts centering on the light and hearts melting in love, let them chant His name. And He will, with the alchemic pill of SIVAYANAMA, turn your body into gold.

2712. The letter SI VA YA NA MA denote Siva, Sakthi, Jeeva, Mala and Maya respectively. Chant the five letters SI-VA-YA-NA-MA; for the five Pasas—impurities to disappear. When Jeeva unites with Lord Shiva and Sakthi, that is when you say SI VA YA, the harassing impurities fly away.

2713. The five lettered names of Lord Shiva (SIVAYANAMA) is Shiva-Sakthi (mighty grace)—SI for Shiva; Va for Sakthi; Ya for Jeeva; Na for Thirodayee; and Ma for Maya (impure); thus the five letters denote five relations. As you chant with SI first; that is as SI VA YA NA MA, you are freed of Karmas, there will be no more births and you will become Para-Shiva.

2714. By the mighty grace of Shiva/Sakthi, Sivajnana will be pure when Jeeva is rid of impurities denoted by 'NA' and 'MA' and the primordial Anava too. Respectedly chant SI VA YA and there indeed, is the truth that is Mala-riddance.

2715. NA-MA and the rest (NA MA SI VA YA) pervading Jeeva is his five states of consciousness waking, dreaming and the rest, stand forth as Thirodhayee, the Sakthi of obfuscation and She in turn leads to the Pure Sakthi that is turn leads to grace. The Jeeva reaches the final state of Thuriya in Samadhi. Thus meditating on NA MA and the rest, the Jeeva unites in Lord Shiva.

2716. The Sakthi who confers grace and the Lord together with Her as unseparate Shiva-Sakthi roused Jeeva to life. When you contemplate on SI VA YA, then, the Maya within and the rest of the three impurities are got rid of. This SI VA YA destroys the hard Karmas too.

2717. They who do not chant Shiva, Shiva; are not freed from ignorance. Truly they are dumb beings. Say Shiva-Shiva unintermittently and spontaneously in the depths of your heart. For they who thus chant are in pure Shiva Gnana and the divine grace will be theirs' always.

2718. They who do not chant Shiva-Shiva; indeed, are of evil Karma. Chant Shiva-Shiva; your evil Karmas perish. You become a Deva and the Shiva state too will be yours.

2719. You will no more be entangled in existence when you hold the letters NA MA in the tongue and take the letters SI VA into your thoughts. Further, your goal too will be reached, your ignorance and with it your whirl of births too will end.

7. Athi-Sookshma (Super Subtled State) Panchakshara

2720. Centre your thoughts saying SI VA YA NA MA and all perils will be your vassals.Le the words SI VA YA SIVA, SIVA fill your thoughts unceasingly. Conquering all perils, there will be bliss alone.

2721. He, the yogi, by the yogic centre way, slumbers in yogic Samadhi by penetrating the Sun's fiery sphere and passing beyond into the sphere of cloud-laden Meru. And then articulating the Holy word. He sees the Lord and is forever absorbed in His thoughts.

2722. All that is spoken in Vedas; Vedangas and Agamas are contained in my Lord's one letter that is freed of doubts. If this one letter 'SI' is consummated, then, the boat of life will reach the lovely shore across.

2723. The five letters hang ripe in ancient Vedas. Jeevas do not know the way to slumber-in-waking. They who say that they know the letters are witless. They do not know the letter that unwrites their fate's letter.

8. Darshan of the Holy Lord's Blissful Dance

2724. The only Holy form is everywhere. Shiva/ Sakthi is everywhere; Chidambaram is everywhere. The Divine dance is everywhere. As Shiva is everywhere. Shiva's grace is everywhere. Everything is His divine sport.

2725. He is Chith-Para of divine light, He dances the dance of bliss (Ananda Dance) He is Nadha who is 'AUM'. He dances the dance of beauty known as Sundara Dance. He dances in the Golden Hall (Golden dance) in the Golden Thillai-Chidambaram-(Golden Thillai Dhandavam). No one ever knows Him who dances the wonderous dance (Atdhbhudha dance).

2726. Sakthi of abiding bliss is endless; He dances the Anandha dance, which is honey sweet, with Her. Just you must witness it and having witnessed it, dance transcending all knowledge, you then, become the arena for the Lord to perform the Anandha dance.

Sivanandha Kootthu is the dance of Shiva united, with Sakthi. He dances in boundless space, beyond the frontiers of Supreme wisdom. When this dance occurs, the Agamas and Vedas all, all dance with Him. Out of this dance merges His five-fold acts of creation, preservation, dissolution, obfuscation and revealing.

2727. His dance arena is bliss; the songs melody, the refrain of music and all the musical organs are all bliss. The entire creation is all bliss. It is bliss too for the Lord who dances the Anandha dance.

2728. The Param that is light; the Param that unites in Jeeva, the Param that is Sivaghami who as Sakthi abounds in grace and the bliss of all faiths—are all attained, when the Shivanandha dance is wihnessed, the dance that is the end of pure knowledge.

2729. He, the form-formless performs the dances that are five. The dances the five dance, in order to perform the five acts. He performs the five acts with Sakthi-grace in Him. And so the Lord dances with Sakthi that is of honey-speech.

Lord Shiva's Mighty Dances:—

1. Muni Dhandavam—Thirunelveli;
2. Gowri Dhandavam:—Thiruppatthur;
3. Madhurai—Sandhiya Dhandavam;
4. Thiruvaalangadu—Samhara Dhandavam;
5. Thirukkuttralam—Thiripura Dhandavam;
6. Chidambaram—Anandha Dhandavam;
7. Perur—Oorthuva Dhandavam.

2730. Shiva holds His way. over these universes that He created—all the Universe of five elements, the Universe of other elements and the Universe of Bhoga, yoga, time, Mukthi, passions and appetites. Performing the five acts, He is seated alone as Tatpara in the entire cosmos—Brahmanandha.

2731. When the Lord danced the dance of Divine knowledge-Bliss (Jnananandha) with Nadha Sakthi then the Vedas, the Agamas, the melodies, the seven universes, the elements and the entire worlds dance.

2732. The great Siddha-Lord dances intermingling, in all these, the five elements, the five senses, the five sensual organs in the Vedas and Agamas five together, in Kala and time's eternity and in the five higher Shiva Tathwas—Suddha, Vidhya, Iswaram, Sadhakyam, Sakthi and Shivam.

The Shiva Tathwas are 1. Suddha Vidhya Tathwa, where Gnana predominated and Kriyas is subdued; 2. In Iswara Vidhya Tathwa, Kriya predominates and Gnana is subdued; 3. In Sadhakya Tathwa, Gnana and Kriya are in balance; 4. In Sakthi Tathwa, Kriya is yearned for; 5. In Shiva Tathwa, Gnana exists alone.

2733. When my Lord danced, the Devas, Asuras, Humans, Siddhas and Vidhyadharas, the three primal, the thirty three-godly forms, the seven Rishis, the several faiths and all the creation movable and immovable, all these danced.

2734. Beyond the beyond, the seven universes and high above Sakthi and Sadhasiva, the dark-throated Lord (Thiruneelakandam) embodied, as compassion danced in rapture there for Umadevi to witness.

2735. He danced these eight dances, Kodukkotthi, Pandarangam, Kodu, Samharam and others. He danced the five dances too. You witness all these in the six Nadis (yogic centres) in the yogic ways. He, the Supreme king danced too in the forests of Devadharu, in Chidambaram and in Alavanam.

Sundarakootthu is the dance of compassion: it has eight variations: Kodukotti, Pandarangam, Kapala, Koothu, Zhinathanam, Munthandavam, Anavaratha Thandavam, Anandha Dhandavam and Samhara Dhandavam. All the worlds come into being when this dance begins and come to an end when, the dance ends.

Again, the forests mentioned is where the rishis performed their sacriligious yagnas and challenged the might of Shiva. He destroyed them and danced, Thillai is Chidambaram (in South Arcot District of Tamil Nadu and Alavanam is Thiruvalangadu (In the North Arcot District of Tamil Nadu).

2736. The Holy Feet of Parasakthi are the crest of cosmos of the vast galaxies. The radiant light of Isa is at the crest of cosmos, permeating the cosmos is the expansive nadha. And there through the vast cosmos the Param dances unceasingly.

2737. In yoga, Bodha Gnana is like an elephant goad that subdued the senses. There, in rhythmic cadence arises the drum-beat of Thom-Thom. To this drum-beat, Sankaran dances in accord, within the central Sushumna Nadhi. When, He, thus dances, He enters in you, end abides there, never to leave your everafter.

2738. He danced the delight divas, He danced the nine dances to delight the nine Sakthis. He danced in the forests; He danced in the thoughts of the devotees; He danced in the junction of the Shushumna within. He, my Lord, thus danced away in endless Jeeva.

2739. The Lord dances His ancient dance in all the five Sakthis, five Shiva forms, eight Mukthis, eight primal states, eight Siddhis, eight Shiva states and in the eight Suddhis.

2740. All these—the Seven clouds, the Seven sea girt continents, the Seven bodies, the Seven Shiva-Suns, the Seven appetities and the seven alleviations (Santis)—are contained at the Feet of the mighty dancing Nandhi.

2741. The Tat-Para dances the rare dance in the South-North-East and West and Crest, in the five wondrous faces therein and in the space too, within the pace of peerless bliss.

In Porpathi Koothu, Shiva dances with five faces, and in three stages—form-formless-form/formless. This dance takes place separately on each of the five elements. Those who witness It experience certain physical emotions, such as sobbing, trembling and loss of consciousness.

2742. They are holy devotees, who attained the bliss of Hara's Feet, who have entered in Hara, who cling to Shiva's Holy Feet and who witnessed truly the Lord's dance in the Golden Hall (of the astral sphere).

2743. I was uncontrolled and He controlled me. He blessed me with His Holy Feet and immersed me in immense transcendental bliss. Thus, He dances, our Nandhi, the great dancer of Gnana dance. He made sit still like picture and abided in me.

2744. He dances in excellence in the high heaven. The

valiant Sentinel, in the intimacy of Jeeva, dances in the Red.—Godly Gold Hall; I sought Him, in dive rapture, who dances as Tatpara and adored Him in love.

2745. He dances as a red ruby within; He dances in the flourishing Thillai. He dances in the jewelled Hall, He dances with matted locks in the distant divine Light. He dances in Shivanandha bliss. He dances the pure gold dance. No one can describe Him indeed, who thus dances.

2746. They who dance in the holy temple sob, fear, fall, rise their body exhausted unaware of themselves with their power lost. Thus are the dance emotions of the devotees who in love adore the flower like and golden, Holy Feet of the Lord.

2747. When the devotees withness the Holy dance, they no more hanker after world-seeking, their thoughts are no more bewildered sorrows do not harass their body within, their breath will be trained in the yogic way and their senses are controlled from straying away. They are rid of all desires and their heart elates in bliss-seeking. Thus it is when they witness the holy dance.

2748. Lord dances in the golden Hall with Kali; He dances with demons in the world; He dances in the water, fire, wind and sky; He, the Supreme Lord, dances in the Holy temple day after day.

2749. All these alike—the central spinal column that is Meru; the Nadis Ida (left) and Pingala (right), the Jeeva's delta-shaped Mooladhara the Shushmna cavity, that is like Thillai forest where the cool (southernly) breeze wafts from Mount Malaya—are Shiva's sphere of dance within.

2750. The land of Mount Meru, and the land of the south that lies beyond it are the Ida, and Pingala respectively. The holy hall where the Lord of the crescent Moon dances, is the Shushumna-thus lie the mystic frontiers of this vast universe.

2751. He, that is cosmic Light danced in rapture with the seven universes as His golden abode, the five elements; sky and the rest and His pedestal and the central Kundalini; Sakthi is as the divine hall. This is the inner meaning of the golden Thillai dance.

2752. He danced as bliss in the centre which the Guru indicated, within the head. He danced with her in eternal bliss, in the moving south in renewed ecstasy espousing Sakthi.

2753. The Primal Para danced; the fire in His hand danced, the holy matted locks danced and He danced in intoxication of joy. The crescent moon danced; the heavenly orbs danced; and He is merging with Nadha, danced, the dance of the heavenly Nadantha.

2754. The Lord danced in the holy hall, for the Jeeva to adore. The dance, He dances is the cosmic dance that takes you to the truth of Shiva's boost of realm which truly is the limit of Mauna Gnana bliss.

2755. With the seven universes, the twenty-one worlds, a hundred and eight religions and that show the path of God, then, the four heavenly states of bliss, such as Nadha, Nadantha, Natana and Natananantha and with the Sakthi that is His half, the Para's Holy Feet danced and danced with all of them.

2756. He, that is Paraparam, pervades in all these. Idakala / Pingala— the delta shaped Mooladhara, the central spinal column Meru, where Kundalini Sakthi is and the Shushumna cavity within that is like the Thillai forest—as the primal one.

2757. Kanyakumari, is at the land's end and then the Kaveri and other holy waters that comprise the nine 'Theerthas' and then the seven sacred hills too. In this land, the Veda-Agamas are born, Thus blessed, the south is the Holy Land indeed.

2758. He, the Lord of countless celestials, the blemishless One, dances in Nadha and in the four states—Nadha, Nadantha, Natana and Natanantha. He dances in Veda and on the fire's (Kundalini) top. He dances in Bodha, (pure consciousness) in all the worlds.

2759. He dances in holy ensemble with the celestials, in the Holy temples. He dances with the three Gods and with the assemblage of Munis. He dances in songs in Parasakthi; He, the Lord of dances, dances in Supreme wisdom.

2760. Saying that He is the Lord of the six ways to God and that He is the Supreme Guru, the religions speak of, He chose the holy temple in the south and here danced in resplendence, with no peer to compare.

2761. My Param dances upon the vast spaces, that are His dance arena. The radiance of His two feet ascends to the high heavens and reaches to the five-lettered Nadha's point. He also descends to you and blesses you to confer His Shiva-state on you.

2762. His dances varied, with it the foot-work and the jingle of the anklets, the songs that were sung another forms that He assumed—so, does the Guru Para dance. Seek this dance within and your birth's cycle ends forever.

2763. Just as the Prana that arises in the heart to permeate your hands and feet and all sensual organs—thus He, the red ruby dancer, dances in the arena of nine gems. He danced in rapture as the Holy Guru—in all places.

2764. The form that dances is the Guru's form: it is in truth formless; This formless one shines as Thripurai Sakthi as well, for she is truly Umadevi who is form/formless.

When Lord Shiva dances the Athbhutha (wonder) dance. He is formless and His consort is mingled into Him as Thripurai (or Umadevi). This dance is beyond the comprehension of ordinary human cognition. It can be witnessed only by those who are rid of Maya and Mamaya. In this dance, His partner, Umadevi, first separates Herself from Him during the dance and then later coalesces with Him. He visualisation here is that of Lord Shiva dancing before His consort wearing fire, drum, beads, noose, goad spear, skull, etc, on His body. The five letters SI VA YA NA MA are represented here.

2765. The holy way is form/ formless. The form that dances there in the holy temple of Chittambara, is the form of the Guru within. They who full well know that He is form/ formless receive His Divine grace in the Gnana way.

2766. From within the head, the Prana breath rises high in twelve finger measure, You must seek this highway. This is the place where our Lord of Nadantha dances and this is truly the Holy temple.

2767. All these—the wind, the cloud, lightening, rainbow, sky and thunder arise in space. Like it, He stands concealed in the body as form of light within the rapturous rays blended of six adharas (yogic centres) and without them and separately too.

2768. There is Divine bliss in the five elements, and eight directions and above and below and beyond the intelligent senses. The Lord stands and dances ever for those who transcend Maya and Mamaya, for them to witness.

2769. The Dancer blends in Sakthi of charming bracelets, He blends in blemishless bliss; He blends in blemishless Gnana. The Dancer and His consort blend in dance.

2770. My Lord and His Sakthi that took His half stood dancing and I witnessed this. He stands as redemption, dancing, dancing eternally, for the countless Jeevas that are veiled by Maya.

2771. The form of Sakthi is all bliss. Umadevi's form is of equals bliss, Sakthis form rising in Shiva's form merged as one and so performed one dance, this peerless dance is perfect bliss.

2772. The vast astral space is straight within the forehead between the eyebrows, peer within and there will be the luminous manthra AUM. The place where they sought Him, in yearning, is the place where He is in yearning. This is the holy temple of Chidambaram and I sat there firmly.

2773. The vast universe, the numerous Tathwas, the Sadhashiva the central Shushumna, the Sakthavi Sakthis, the Sambavi Sakthi and the Kundalini Sakthi, that is a plexus in Mooladhara all these seven are Shiva's pedestals. He, the transcendental being, dances on them.

2774. The shedding light of the astral flower that is within, illumines the entire dance arena. The flower indeed, wonderous, for, its four petals in the Mooladhara blossoms into a hundred-petals in the Sahashrara Thala and expanded into two hundred and ten worlds in the vast interminable spaces.

2775. The vast universes are seven crores, the varied life forms are seven crores; the continents of the sea-girt world are seven crores and the Lingas in the eight directions are seven crores—These are the septenary centres or the temples where His cosmic dance is performed.

2776. The space is His body. The Muyalaka (demon) is the darkness in this space. The eight directions are His spreading hands and the three loving eyes are the three lights—sun, moon and fire. Thus, He dances in the space arena, that is His cosmic body.

2777. The arena of the holy dance, is the countless creations, is the Holy Feet of the mighty Lord, is the sphere of water and fire and is the letter five truly.

2778. The drums beat, the pipes played and they hummed 'AUM'. The men danced and they called Him their primal Lord; the crowds of Ganas in serried ranks praised Him and the numerous Bhoothas sang. Thus, He danced the Pandaranga dance, the dance of dissolution, at the ends of the Thiripurai conflagration.

2779. The celestials in the Universe, the celestials beyond, and the holy ones in the Sea-girt world all, all witnessed the golden temple dance of the Lord of the Lotus Feet and adoring them, they reached Lord Shiva state.

2780. Water wells up in the mouth at the right of tamarind. Just like it, is the rapturous experience of all those who witness the Holy dance, they shed tears of joy and melt in love of the Lord, and the ambrosial bliss of divine Light and wells up in their hearts.

2781. Those who witnessed the divine dance become drunk of Shivahandha bliss and stagger about with their senses lost. They who still retain their senses become frenzied. The divine dance is praised by all in the Holy arena and even those who hear of it are like those who witnessed it—all rapture is theirs too.

2782. He dances with fire and drum, with Rudhraksha beads' garland and noose cord, with elephant's goad, trident and skull and with frightening blue throat where there is Gnana. He dances the mighty dance with Sakthi for His inseparate partner.

2783. That dance have eleven accompaniments. The Nadha reverberated with anklet feet with drum in His hand and reached like Para Para in the high heaven. This Holy Nandhi, who danced thus is truly inside your heart and outside too.

2784. The nine centres within, sixteen petalled mystic lotus, the six loving faiths, the seven melodies, SA, RE, GA, MA, PA, DA, NI the twenty-eight rhythmic beats and the love Sakthi too, all danced and He danced the dance of divine bliss.

1. The nine centres within are the six yogic centres and the danced centres of sun-moon and fire.
2. The sixteen-petalled mystic lotus in the Vishudhi centre, where the sixteen Kalas ending with Unmanai, Sakthi are located referred to as Sodasa Kala Prasadham.
3. The six religious states are variously delineated as follows:—Saivam, Vaishnavam, Saktham, Sauram, Ganapathyam and Gowmaram—these are the 'Vaidik' faiths.
4. The seven Primal melodies SA RE GA MA PA DA NI are described as Kurtuttlam, Kaikikai, Uzhai, Ili, Vilari and Tharam.
5. Twenty-eight rhythmic modes commencing from Kandam and Prabandavuru. Kandam has a basic measure and a sing beat. Prabandavuru has no basic measure and has multi beats; In between are permutations and combinations. The twenty-eight rhythmic measures beling to the inner measures of dance Rhythm.

2785. He descended and pervaded as the seven subtle melodies within the articulated seven, as they denote the seven letters, as one harmony in the seven musical notes. In the seventh state beyond the six yogic centres that crosses Gnana Yoga is the AUM Pranjothi (The Divine Light). He danced in the dance of seven melodies.

2786. The three letters A,U and M 'AUM' became the five letters NA, MA, SI,VA,YA and they also became the three hundred and sixty rays; commencing from the Muladhara that hold the waters in through the six centres (yogic) and the three spheres (sun-moon and fire) He danced in the ancient triple Pasas, the dance of Mohantha, (impurity-riddance) so that the triple Karmas may see their end.

Presumably, the reference is to the combined three hundred

and sixty rays of fire (118), Sun (106) and Moon (136); They constitute Kala (time) as the 360 rays or 360 days that comprise a year.

2787. Flowery Feet of the Lord are above the jewelled crowned heads of the celestials. He is a precious jewel who adores the rising heart of His loving devotees. He who transcends all worlds is the Divine tree (Kalpaka Tharau that grants all wishes of heavenly glades).

2788. When the creator dances, all the worlds that He created dance. He dances in our knowledge to the measure our thoughts too dance. When He so endearingly dances in the hearts, the several elements too dance. He dances flaming as the Divine fire, and this we witnessed in surpassing rapture.

2789.The holy ones say He danced that primal dance.But no one has seen Him dance this primal dance of yore. when they witness this primal dance, they dance in grace of this primal Sakthi.

2790. In the nine centres within the nine state, Thuriyatheetha is attained. His twin feet danced in Asi-Pada in the centre that is love. As the anguished Sakthi danced within Him, my loving father danced together with Her in rapture.

2791. The Tathwas, Sadhashiva, the thought, Shiva-Sakthi, the vast creation The Vedas, all these and the Lord too danced the dance of Anandha (Divine Bliss).

2792. He danced in the splenderous temple of Chidambaram, for the two rishis Patanjali (the snaked bodied) and Viyakrapada (the tiger footed) to witness. He danced as form/formless and as cosmic form. He, the Siddha, danced the Ananda within the divine grace of Sakthi. He stood and danced as the form of grace.

2793. Shiva, Sakthi, the worldly desires, even the spaces that do not dance, the Tathwas Nadantha all danced wonderously, when Shiva danced inside of truth, which indeed is Vedanta-Siddhantha.

2794. He, that is Nadha Brahmama, Lord within the sound principle, dances the Shiva Natana in Nadantha—that is the end of Nadha (principle of sound) in Bhodantha that is end of Bodha (Gnanan) in Vedanta that is the end of Vedas, in Shivanananda that is the bliss of Lord Shiva and in Sadhashivananda that is without end. He dances in all of them.

2795. The Holy Para dances everywhere by Himself to make the Jeeva bonds standing afar to depart in prayer and to end the perplexities of the five Gods Rudhra and the rest. This supreme wisdom dance is holy indeed, that Shivanandha fills with bliss.

2796. In times of yore, He stood as the Supreme one, redeeming the countless celestials and earned the name of Lord Vikirtha. He is the One who danced in the three luminous lights and also accepted me in His grace.

2797. Lord is the beginning of the Vedas, He is beyond the Nadha Tathwas, He is the Tathwas placed in order and is their Lord too at once. Not knowing this, the Jeevas seek the pleasures of this world and reveal in them. He stands comingling in that in separateness.

2798. They who say bliss, bliss are witless one. No one knows the dance of bliss; Having witnessed the dance of bliss, the Jeeva ends its separateness and unites in divine bliss.

2799. One hand in the letter 'SI'gestures to the Jeevas to leave this and to be reformed. Another flower-like hand in letter, 'VA' gestures to the Tapasvins to become like him and to be united in him. The golden hand in the letter 'YA' gestures to the celestials to be in Deva, and not to fear. The hand that holds fire gestures the letter 'NA'. The foot on earth that is planted in dance gestures the letter 'MA'. Thus the entire five-lettered Holy manthra 'SI, VA, YA, NA, MA' denotes the divine dance. This is the signification of the five-lettered manthra is Shiva dance.

2800. The hand that holds the drum (SI), the hand that sways (VA); the hand that offers refuge (YA), the hand that holds the blazing fire (NA) and the lotus-foot, planted firmly, on Aanava (egoity) impurity (MA)—this is the added significance of the divine dance form in relation to the five lettered manthra SI VA YA NA MA.

2801. The symbolism of Shiva dance—Hara's drum is creation; Hara's hand gesturing protection is preservation; Haras' fire is dissolution; Hara's foot planted down in obfuscation (thirodhayee) and Hara's foot, raised in dance, is Abiding grace (Redemption).

2802. He is the flaming fire and the sparkling light too within. The Sakthi of youthful eyes saw Him dance, She saw the three Gods merge into the one primal being and she sang all Vedas in such rapture. She witnesses the trinity dance of Lord Shiva.

2803. Nandhi, my father, the Lord of Gnana, entered in the one-lettered manthra AUM and transcending it, He dances, in surpassing comeliness, in the spaces beyond. I am unable to desire this par-sundara dance.

2804. Nandhi is a lion-hearted Guru, He dances in the Holy temples. No one knows His divine form, it is fiery red; smeared to the white. They who see His form reach the haven of refuge.

2805. Sakthi stands as Tat-Para in the Lord. She forges the bond between Para and Jeeva. Standing as Ichcha, Gnana and Kriya She performs many acts. And you reach Hara's loving Feet when She, lends Her grace.

9. Attainment of Space Within

2806. The Lord is in our heart as AUM, He, the one being, is in our heart as fire, order and as space in the body, itself.

2807. The Lord is all pervasiveness as the vast earth vast, universe and is the Lord void beyond. So too, His benevolence is also vast; His feet support the entire world. Yet, He, the primal Lord, His form is invisible.

2808. He is the cosmic light, the light beyond and the light that mingles in the light that is within. My body light merged shattering all landmarks of existence in the spreading light of space that swallows vast immensity. Thus Lord Shiva's light merges in Jeeva's light.

2809. The sparkling light of the primal one is in the delight of the maiden's union. It was immanent in Brahma and Vishnu, yet, they did not know it and but stood contending. Then He revealed Himself to them as Divine light, flaming from earth to heaven.

2810. The transcendental light is knowledge beyond knowledge. When it merges in silence in the three lights, within, that are mighty than Shiva is reached and there if you do not leave His Feet, you may live long.

2811. He, who wears the serpent is the darling of the celestials. He, the Fire hued fills the space, and having filled the space. He stand as outer-space.

2812. As you breathe in the yogic way, you reach the inner light, that is the breath of all worlds. The damsel in the Mooladhara then rises and ascends upward, spreading Her day light brilliance; and my thoughts thus uplifted, merge in space within. In kundalini yoga, Jeeva's thought merges in space.

2813. Move close to the Lord and He does not ever leave you, move close, to the Lord world and He leaves you alone. Move close to the Supreme Lord Nandhi, who is the flashing light within the mystic astral space, and there adore Him; so that you may drink of the divine ambrosia.

2814. The Universe and the world are in the out space. In the inner space, there is the primal Supreme Wisdom; The resplendent light is in the space where Lord Shiva is and Samadhi's destination is in the space that composes the cosmos.

10. Jnanodhayam (Dawn of Supreme Wisdom)

2815. The waking state is in the conjunction of mind, then, there is the dream state, where bliss is experienced. Beyond, it is Shushupthi where bliss experience is certain. Ascend still further and there is the space (Thuriya) where there are only two: bliss and the Lord of Eternal Bliss.

2816. He peeled the elephant hide with His hands and hold the skull in His hands. He adorned the crescent moon on His crest. And I adored the Lord who is rare and great. Beyond this I knew nothing. I have not seen, whether He is black or red.

2817. When the celestials above consumed ambrosia, He consumed poison. Follow the path of penance that the holy men taught and enter within. He will give you Supreme knowledge that is pure and gold. So seek Lord Shiva's holy feet.

2818. Break open the Kundalini light and light the lamp within; kindle the light within this light; They who can thus brighten the light within the light, will reach the feet of Him, who is lustrous lamp of the supreme wisdom.

2819. The Lord of Tathwas is where the Tathwas are present. Where there are no Tathwas, there the Lord is not present. When you know the truth of Tathwa Gnana, then the Lord of Tathwas will appear there.

2820. The ambrosia that wells up from the fleshy body mire is in the astral space that holds true Gnana. He stood with the spreading matted locks of lustrous golden hue and with the hannting perfume of the ruddy (astral) flower.

2821. The light of Lord who is in heaven is blended into the brilliance of all these—pearl, diamond, coral of there three waters and gold of purest fineness and gems. In no other way, can this divine resplendence be described.

2822. I sought Him separately as I and He, As I thus sought, the Lord of Primal Gnana, Himself granted that 'I' and 'He' are not separate and then, there was no more the thought of I and He.

2823. The supreme wisdom way is the Nadantha way, it is the knowledge of the self. The Gnana way of yoga is to centre on Lord Shiva; the Gnana way of silence is the Veda truth of Nadantha.

2824. Sivagnana is the life breath for those who seek liberation. Again Lord Shiva is the life-breath for those who seek liberation. Yet again, Pranava is the centre of divine union for those who seek liberation. Finally, the Lord is knowledge within knowledge of those who seek eternal liberation.

2825. For those who can see Him, He is the light of their eyes; He is the ambrosia of the oceans. The mighty Nandhi never fails those who adore Him; He stands as unfailing support to those who alone yearn for Him.

2826. He is like the sound within the one-letter word AUM. He is the great truth that the celestials long for. He is our Lord, the flaming Light that shines afar. The immortals who adore His Holy Feet are only beings who are devoted to His inner service.

11. Sathya Jnanandham (Sath-Chit-Ananda)

2827. All spaces as space is everything or nothing. Seeking the three spaces above and the three spaces below, and knowing not what this space it like, is the Tat-Para Jnanandha which is this the Supreme Bliss.

2828. In the first Thuriya is Thom Pada state (Twam-Pada) that is, Jeeva, Thuriya, where in the Jeeva realises its spiritual nature, and is in God consciousness, but duality still exists. In the second Thuriya is the state of Tat-Pada, which is Para Thuriya, in which the Jeeva realises Shiva, and is in union with Him, but not united and duality still exists. In the third Thuriya is the Asi-Pada state, which is Shiva Thuriya, where the Jeeva, unites in God totally, himself becoming God the unitive state is reached. In the state of the beyond Thuriya is immense subtlety that transcends space, where the holy truth of Nandhi is present truly. In beyond Thuriya, Jeeva himself becomes undifferentiated in God, and attains the subtle Shiva state of luminous self-manifestness (Sivaroopa state).

2829. The bliss that is in Sathya-Gnana is peerless; it is incomparable to the light of the rays of pure and the like. This bliss-state of the Sathya-Gnana is like these six: lily, blue, purity, beauty, colour, youth fragrance and radiance, blended together.

2830. To speak of Sakthi, Shiva and Parajnana Bliss are that, Shiva Bliss-Anandha is highly infinite, manifestness (Swaroopa) is Sakthi (ath) and Parajnana is which the Holy Guru imparts (Chit) to Jeeva. All the three together are like the flower, blended with the six attributes mentioned earlier (Sath-Chit-Ananda).

2831. When Jeeva blends into Tat-Para, it is like the blue lily blossom that is blended with colour, purity, beauty, fragrance and radiance. Then it is the state of Shiva-manifestness (Swaroopa) that is exalted of the three states, and Sathya-

Gnana-Anandha, arose in Him.

2832. Think of Him as far as your thoughts stretch, adore Him in melting love, praise Him in melodious songs and you may well envelop Him in your heart, My Lord Nandhi, extending His grace on me too, led me to think of Him, to the farthest reaches of my thought.

2833. When Jeeva crosses the triple state of Thuriya and enters in Sathya-Gnana-Ananda, it is like milk-honey-juice of fruit mixed in ambrosial sweetness. It is a sweetness that permeates every root of the body's hair.

2834. The Lord stood all by Himself, transcending the sphere of immortal celestial's the cosmic spaces and the sphere of Nadha. He stood in Sathya Gnana Ananda with Sakthi of coral lips, pearly teeth and dewy cool speech and the unflickering light of Parajnana following.

2835. The Gnanis left behind the thirty-six Tathwas that stand in the eyebrow centre in the waking state. They rid themselves of impurities, were purified in Thuriya, that is pure (Suddha) and freed of the bondage condition (Buddha) they became Shiva. They the true Gnanis, ascended beyond that into Sathya-Gnana-Ananda (truth-knowledge-bliss that is Sat-Chit-Ananda).

2836. With the triple impurities extinguished the Jeeva has become Shiva. Then, ascending into the triple voids with desire and non-desire ceased, he passes into the holy state of Sathya-Gnana-Ananda bliss. There is the Self-illuminating manifestations (Swaroopa) in that farthest Thuriya of Jeeva.

12. Swaroopa Udhayam (Dawn of Manifestness)

2837. The holy master, Parama Guru, interminably pervades all as constant Para. In this immanent state when Jeeva attains the final Thuriya state. He extends His self-illuminating manifestness.

2838. In that primordial flood of waters, at the time of dissolution, He interminably extended in space as waters of the earth, the tempestuous winds, the fire, the sky and the earth. I do not know how to limit Him and thus adore Him.

2839. Parashiva stood as the Gods—Brahma, Vishnu and

others. Whoever stood wherever, praise the almighty Him as the Supreme Lord. My peerless Lord, stood immanent in all of them and He, the Lord of all worlds stood beyond them too.

2840. They do not know the footprints of the faith's way, and are possessed of egoity. They comingle the eight causal sins of: greed, lust, anger, ignorance, hatred, vengeance, miserliness and possessiveness. They who transcend these and attain supreme wisdom truly become the Lord of immortals and in high heavens.

2841. The three Gods: Brahma, Vishu and Rudhra are of the primal one; Yet, He is separate from them. Likewise, the Lord stands in the triple Thuriya as Jeeva, Para and Shiva. One and yet separate; so the scriptures say.

2842. He has no form; yet, He assumes form. He has no birth, yet He is the seed of all births. The elusive Lord, is beyond formlessness too. Unless He reveals Himself; as Holy Guru, no one can ever reach Him.

2843. They who meditate on His Swaroopa, see Him as light within, will attain timeless eternity and will be in company of the celestials. Yet, no one seeks His true Swaroopa, here below in this world.

2844. As I clung to the Lord who is transcendental light, this light entered in me and remained within. And as I sank and sank into this transcendental light, I beheld this transcendental light of proclaiming Himself aloud.

2845. Sathya-Gnana-Ananda (truth-knowledge-bliss) absorbing all these; such as manifestness; form, attributes and the past, arises, blending with the six attributes: flower, purity, beauty, colour, fragrance and radiance. Like this, the bliss of the Holy Guru arises of self-illumined manifestness, when the four Sakthis are absorbed.

2846. He, the self illumined manifestness is the bliss beyond speech; is silence, When He acts on Adhi Sakthi; He becomes the letters—A, U, M and thus defying description as AUM. He shines as the light within.

2847. I stood adoring Him in devout penance in the valleys within the cranium and there I discovered Him, the thief, standing with Sakthi concealed in the Kalas, discovering Him, I ended my birth's cycle.

2848. I knew the way of becoming, I knew the way of seeking of the rare one and also the path of entrance to Him. With no more egoity and with no other the locale, I became the primal one; He and I will be one and the same.

13. Destiny

2849. Even though you cut them, the Holy grace, Gnanas, who have perceived the truth, or chop them and hammer their heads with a chistle, or soften them with cool sandal paste, they remain passive realizing that all these are but my fate, decreed by Nandhi.

2850. There is nothing else that you come by except your past deeds, the heavens cannot desire, otherwise and so I sought the Lord within the head by the Mooladharạ way, and what I did before, took me, to the fair land of bliss.

2851. The sands that the river deposits are carried away by the river; to no one else is this task apportioned and so, I sought Nandhi of holy ashes and erect matted locks, and in intense devotion, stood inseparated with Him.

2852. What if the walking thunders, or the seas rise and foam, or the fires spread and burn, or the tempests roar and blast, I seek the Lord unconcerned and in intense devotion.

2853. What if the elephant pursues or if the arrow pierces or if the wild tiger surrounds me, I will deeply plough the field of supreme wisdom that the Lord has alloted me, in the other hand.

2854. If this body comes to harm, there is One to fashion another, if a land goes to destruction, there is another land to migrate to, if a house falls to pieces, there is another house to dwell in—thus do the thoughts of the Gnanis, who know Nandhi's bounty, run unconcerned.

14. Darshan of Holy Shiva

2855. Shiva reveals Himself in the thoughts of those whose thoughts merge inseparably in Shiva. Shiva is in the thoughts of those who can vision their thoughts that are free of doubts.

2856. This Vedic object is hidden beyond speech and thoughts; Look at it; it is by far a very subtle object. It has no coming no going, no perishing. All blessings are for those who truly seek the Lord.

2857. He, the unknowable as Param, as Paraparam and beyond, as the constant interminable transcendental light, as the definite support of all and as one beyond the knowledge of the self, showers His grace here below as Lord Shiva.

15. Holy Darshan of Shiva-Swaroopa (Manifestness)

2858. This inviolate bliss is beyond difference and non-difference. Its ambrosial sweetness floods in every hair root. He is beyond the initial three manifestations. The vast greatness of this Supreme manifestations, that the Vedas praise so highly is there indeed.

2859. He who stand in the fragrance of the flower within is sentience, is life, is union, is separation and is the continuity beyond the thoughts.

2860. Think of Him who stands thus; seek His presence and He ends the imperfections of those who seek Him. He is the unwritten immutable Veda. He is of great penance; and it is for sure that He stands within the head.

2861. My thoughts within woke up in a lighting flash; and as I woke up the self-illumined Lord, Nandhi of matted locks, the peerless one of golden hued form entered into me and told me that I knew Him; And thus, saying He cast His benign glance upon me.

2862. He who is Sathya-Gnana bliss is Shivanandha light that surpasses thought; It is pure Brahma Thuriya and Thuriya beyond the triple Thuriyas and the transcendental light arises in it.

2863. He is not Param, nor is He, the expanding Paraparam. He, is neither the abiding object. Beyond nor is He, the vibrant light above it. He is not the One who supports all. He is they and yet not they. He is not Hara but He is beyond bliss. He is Swaroopa Shiva beyond the bliss of Sathya-Gnana-Ananandha.

2864. Standing in devotion, standing in Param and standing in the mighty Sakthi, they realise the Tathwas and attain Mukthi.

Siddhi and mature Gnan. Then from this Suddha state, they pass to the Sukanandha Bodha state.

2865. Thuriyattheetha that is void is beyond words, when the state of Ariya Thuriyatheeta still above is reached, the Jeeva blossom shimmering. The form too is altered; it is neither folding nor unfolding. I do not know how to describe it.

"A thing cannot be described and clarified in terms of itself, but only with reference to something else in the Universe.."

The field from which the substance and the form of symbols are taken is nature. There is no other field from which to derive them. Nature takes the two aspects of 'human nature' and the nature of the surroundings of man, Man's animal nature is symbolic of a particular aspect of human nature, derived from the nature of the surroundings of man. Men's animal nature is symbolic of a particular aspect of human nature, derived from the nature of animals in man's surrounding substance and form of symbols belong to external nature. The meaning applies to the internal nature is the mirror of consciousness, and the pictures in the mirror reflect the dynamism of consciousness.

16. Gradations of Liberation (Mukthi-Karma: Nirvana)

2866. Progression of the soul's journey to the five Mukthis is; the reaches to the Jeeva Mukthi first, then possesion to the Param state and thence to the Shiva State. Practised there in the Thuriya state is the primal self-illumined manifestness, and having attained Swaroopa, the state of Nirvana is reached and in the Ariya Thuriyatheetha state.

2867. He is the Param who is reached by those who, leaving their own desire behind, desire only Him; He is the Lord of Forehead eye when the learned who have learned all, still learn about. He is the Transcendental Light whom those who have no bonds surround. He is the one, whom those who have reached, have ceased to prattle about.

17. Dialogue of the Symbolism (Sooniya Sambhakshanai)

2868. Body is the gambling board, five senses organs are

the dice, impurities-Aanav, Maya and Karma are the three channels and fifty-one letters of Nadha pervading the body are the fifty-one squares, thus the Jeeva's play the game. I do not know the mystery of the Lord's play, who thus leads them to it.

2869. The Holy way is covered by thorny bushes and the Jeevas do not know how to remove it. They who know how to remove it are they for whom my heart yearns for.

2870. There are six streets and in their junction, there are four juicy palm trees. Difficult to climb with ladder. I ascended the height of the palm trees and there I saw the seven seas.

Climb the four juicy palm trees (Nadis—sun—moon—Meru and Shuskshmna) in the junction of the six streets (yogic centres). Then you will behold the seven seas, Sahashrara.

2871. In the abnegation of desires leading to liberation through yoga, I sowed the seed of brinjal, meaning renunciation (Vazhu plus Thalai means 'shaven head') and the shoot of the balsam-pear; meaning bitterness-or world negation-arose, I dug up the dust, meaning the Tathwas or the universes that constitute the body and the pumpkin that is Lord Shiva (suggesting a Linga covered with holy ashes) blossomed. The gardner gang, that is, the Indhriyas or sense organs; may also refer to Malas-impurities prayed and ran and the fruit of plantain that is, Mukthi or eternal liberation from birth, ripened fully well.

The plantain is thought of as being seedless (Vazhai comes from 'Yazh' and 'I'—creating a pun on the world to mean life—giving fruit).

2872. There is a field with seed of the Lord where the Jeeva ripens and they do not know of this field. But if there is the grace of the blue-throated (Thiruneelakandam) Lord, in truth it is easy to enter this field.

2873. There is one (Shushupthi state) deep field, there are two (waking and dream states) waste fields and another alien field (Thuriya) lie mingled with them. Those that plough the field of heart for them the field fed with water (ambrosia) lie ripe in rich harvest.

2874. There are three ploughs; namely, the three Nadis:Ida,

Pingala and Shushumna in the triangular field (that is the Mooladhara, the centre that is Thuriya triangle-shaped); yoke the bulls tightly with the rope, that is, control and breath and drive the ploughshare deep, meaning, course the breath through Shushumna Nadi. They who do not hold their tongue, the manner of thrusting the tongue upward into the Uluva—a yogic practise for realisation—known as Kesari Mudhra, do not plough in the centre, the Sahashrara in the cranium, and closing their legs together, (controlling breath) they plough the waste in vain.

2875.There are two Picottahs (Nadis-Ida and Pingala) and seven wells (seven centres—the six yogic centres) leading to the seventh, Sahashrara. The elder (breath) draws out (exhalation) and the younger waters (inhalation). If the water flows into the field, (the central Shushumna Nadi) and flows into waste, (consumed anytime as food in pleasure-seeking) then it is like the fowl that the harlot rears.

2876. There are twenty-four cows (Tathwas pertaining to Jeeva's body) that stray uncontrolled. There are other gentler cows that are higher Tathwas—(seven Vidhya Tathwas and five Shivatathwas) the gentler one may give a whole pot of milk, but the Jeeva only has the uncontrolled straying ones alone.

2877. There are twenty-four cows (Tathwas of the body) that are in calf. A pitcher of milk from the cows (higher Tathwas—vidhya and Shiva Tathwas) the yield is far better. When you know how to milk the cows of breath, in the yoga way to transcend the Tathwas, the other cows (sensual organs) do not come near at all.

2878. In the upper storey (the cranium) of the house of a smith (Jeeva's body house) there is a bud like mass, (the mystic flower bud in Sahashrara) that expands like a copper (Ruddy in colour) sheet. The smith shaped it round, folding it in truth ('Vay' and 'Mai' creates a pun on the word 'VAY' to mean closing the Uluva opening in the mouth) and they made it his own.

2879. Train the flowing water in the eroding, seed bed of sorrow which is a field, and dam it tightly. Then plough it with a good young bull and transplant the cucumber seedling. This will ripe into a good seed.

Ploughing the eroding seed bed (thought that are filled with sorrow) with the good young bull (yoga), and transplant the cucumber seedling (Bindhu). Truly it will ripen into the good seed (macrocosmic Bindhu).

2880. By strewing the seed, applying manure in baskets full, ploughing with the yoked bulls and digging out the weed, rice will thus be produced. Then cooking the rice in big vessels, they should gently consume it. If they do not do this, lying indifferent, how will they harvest the sweet rice crop?

Strew the seed, apply manure, plough it, remove the weeds then rice in produced—How can you reap a good harvest, if you have not striven like this? Liberation will not be bestowed, to those who do not strive in the yogic way.

2881. The seed (Bindhu) for future ripened, the seed ripened over quite a stretch (the mystic astral space within. For those whom the seed ripened in the three states (the triple Thuriya state)—Jeeva Thuriya, Para Thuriya and Shiva Thuriya—the three spheres beyond, one in each of the three Thuriya states too, ripened.

2882. We do not know by why they plough the waste. They who plough the waste do not have any design and so they perish, like the young weeds that shoot in waste. So do not cultivate the waste of wordly pleasures.

2883. Rouse your call, meaning chanting of the manthra 'AUM', within the shed (body) and consign the binding Pāsas to fire (Kundalini). Thus spend the days continuously, then the great mother will appear and you will be well in the home.

2884. It rained on the mountain, the young deer leapt, the rich ripe fruit from the bunch above dropped. It melted like the metal on the smith's furnace and He made if flow over the heart. These are the experiences in the mystic sphere of Sahashrara.

It rained (nectar flowed) on the mountain (cranium) and the deer (Sakthi) leapt. The rich fruit (bliss of grace) dropped from the bunch (Sahashrara) like the metal in the furnace, it melted and sweet ambrosia flowed.

2885. In a Brahmin's home, there are five milk cows, they strayed uncontrolled with none to herd them, if there is a cowherd, and if they are controlled then, the five cows will give milk in abundance.

2886. The five wild bulls (senses) of Jeeva, the thirty fierce lions (the other Tathwas), the two sweet mangoes (Nadis—Ida and Pingala), the nine fraudulent centres (the yogic six centres and the three spheres of sun, moon and fire) and the mind within, if these are all firmly controlled and they become yours, then, the bull (body) will not become old; if not, they put it to fire (death-cremation).

2887. When the immaculate virgin (Kundalini) chanting the truth of the unwritten book (AUM), the nectar of the flower (Shahashrara) unopened until then, gushes forth, and when the bee (yogi) savours this fragrant liquid, immortality ensues.

2888. The deceptive exhaling breath that leaves, the inhaling breath, which is a flase seed, that enters the five senses that eat of the broths which is made, meaning, worldly pleasures actually astringent in taste, the ripe fruit (navel) of the flourishing Jamun tree—all, went the burning life—roof's way, meaning death.

2889. A margosa tree (body) arose from the bamboo shoot (Karma) and very close to that there was a palmyrah (Shushumna). In this palm, there is a snake (Kundalini) and not knowing how to drive the snake and eat it, the margosa withered away (the body perished in yoga is not practised).

2890. This is how the body is: There are ten big tigers, meaning the ten Nadis, fifteen elephants, which are the ten sensual organs (Karmendriyas and Gnanendriyas) and five sensual potencies (Tanmathras); the five learned Anthakaranas (organs of intelligence); the ten jesters, which refer to the ten Vayus; there are three others that are upright (the three spheres sun-moon-fire); there are six physicians (yogic centres) and the other five who are lordly, meaning the Avasthas or experiences such as, waking-dreaming, etc. They all stand in the body.

2891. Control the two bulls (breaths-right, Pingala and left-Ida) firmly. There is one servant for these two bulls. When breath is controlled. They will become one as Prana coursing through the Sushumna.

2892. Level up the mind-garden in equanimity, in devotion's net and plant and the cotton tree. Enter the place of three by the rope of salvation. They who are filled with perfection will practice yoga daily and ascend upward.

Level up the mind-garden, and plant the cotton tree (coursing thread-like Pranam through Sushumna) then enter the place of three (Agjna) by liberation's rope (yoga practice), where Shiva-Sakthi and Jeeva are. Thus, by practising yoga ascend daily. You will become perfect.

2893. All these—the owl, the snake, the parrot, the cat, the mynah and all the quail—dwells within. As the owl nears the mynah, the mouse screeching loud, warns the mynah.

The six base traits like lust, hatred, infatuation avarice, arrogance (egoity), and malice (the owl, snake, parrot, cat, mynah and quail) dwell within. The mouse (Kundalini yoga power) warns the mynah (Jeeva) as the owl (lust) hears it.

Symbolisms for the six transgressions; Kama (lust); Krodha (hatred; Lobha (miserliness); Moha (greed); Matha (Ahankara-ego); Mastsarya (Vengefulness).

The nhrew-mouse is symbolic of the divine, self which works in the 'Unconscious' and interferes with man's Ahankara egoity stores, and in the plane for the future.

2894. He placed the three white rats (Pasas-the rat unlike the mouse which symbolises the divine) in the toddy measure (body) of foul smell that draws a derisive laugh and sends (the senses) to shambles; If they are placed on the fire (Kundalini) they run, or else, they remain. Because they are fleshy born, how else will they ever go away. Kundalini yoga alone drives away the triple Pasas (attachment through desires).

2895. The five steeds (senses) together with the six camels (evils-base traits) enter the dense forest (thought). They were closed up entirely. They will not anymore see the sky above. If they all (senses and evils) leave the dense forest, the three (Shiva, Sakthi and Grace) will come near.

Renounce everything—you will be liberated.

2896. They who see food, raiment and phialled ungents,

necklace, waist band and lovely bangles, as their goal fall into a deep pit of six sins and remain immersed there; for all these earthly riches are like a fragile garment piece laid on a high rock and at the slightest blow of the wind they all fly away. Worldly desires lead to perdition.

2897. They journeyed thrice daily beyond the islet beyond to the mountain on the bank, in order to superintend the field there. And there Shie (Kundalini) is, the one who moves to the mountain obstacle that stands within. We do not know Her place.

Kundalini removes the obstacles to reach the Sahashrara. Her abode is beyond our cognition.

2898. The kite (Parunthu, also meaning bangle of conch worn by women) and parrot (parrot hold by Sakthi symbolizing good and evil in balance) together beat the drum loudly and the shapely virgin (Kundalini) celebrated her wedding (Union in Shiva in the Sahashrara). She attained the form of the holy element and remained rapturous in this state.

2899. The mating bird (Jeeva) pecked at the food (enjoyments) and approaching its partner fed it. Like this, it is easy for those who eat of the ghee (spiritual, energy or ambrosia) in the melting fire (Kundalini) within, to drive away the darkness (ignorance) and reach the goal.

2900. There are no leaves, there are no bees, but there is the flower (Sahashrara) in the cranium. There is no top, there is no sheath, but this is the root (Lord Shiva). There is no bunch, there is this mystic flower to pluck but no head to wear it. The branch (mighty grace) that bends does not wither.

2901. Having visioned the Banyan tree (Lord Shiva) that stands beyond in the Sahashrara, they adore the Holy Lord and unite in Him. They are truly great, who transcend the five exceeding sorrows, they lie low at the Lord's feet and remain there.

2902. There is a forest that stretches two leagues far, in the way of the loud call of Jeeva (seeking). Inside the forest stand robbers'senses) that seize and bind. If the white guard (yoga) chases these black thieves and shout them away loud, then Jeeva will reach the roof of safety.

This simply means to conquer the senses by yoga and reach Lord Shiva, Himself.

2903. In the tank where Kotti and lily bloom are Neem and Nux Vomica too. They who do not eat the salad of sweet plantain mixed with candy and honey, will hanker, after the Nux Vomica fruit.

Sweet ambrosia (eternal liberation) and bitter Nux Vomica (passions) are both there within the body. They who do not taste the salad of sweet plantain mixed with candy and honey (eternal life), will hanker after Nux Vomica (earthly life).

2904. The Lord is seated on the throne as He-Bee (Lord Shiva) and She-Bee (Sakthi), with the Mukthi hued (multi) umbrella canopying aloft. The lowly bee (Jeeva) embodied of Pasa, swills the nectar which the She-bee grants by herglance (mighty grace). This truly is rapture that is surpassing.

2905. What is to be done with those cows (Jeevas) that gaze in the backwoods of desires. Discipline them in superior ways and thus manage the herd. Until, then, they will not turn their thoughts away from the backwoods of worldly pleasures. Then take them beyond and lead them to the Feet of the Lord.

2906. The Lotus (Sahashrara) and the lily (Kundalini) blossomed in the water above (cranium), and the water below (Mooladhara) respectively. To those who can see the light in the cross beam (Agjna) above, they will find the Lord as a cool water melon that flourishes even in dry regions.

2907. Six (the six base qualities; lust, hatred, greed etc.) are the birds in the house of five (body of the five senses), hundred (the Sahashrara of 1000 petals) are the birds at the top of the tree, and having ascended the seven (the six yogic centres and the seventh ultimate centre of liberation) high steps, you will surely reach the Home (eternal liberation).

2908. The roundly earth swells and water springs (ambrosia) within the bathing well (body), where they draw water; bind your breath (coursing breath through Sushumna) and with ropework centre your thoughts. Then the divine light may well dawn.

2909. There are seven circling seas, and eight mountain ranges and in the depths of space, this fire, rain and wind and the expansive land. Visioning it, if you dwell it in, then this itself is a holy temple.

This land (Sahashrara) is expensively vast with seven circling seas (space) and eight mountain ranges (the mystic flower with eight petals) dwell in this land, for it is truly a holy temple.

2910. The body-pole was erected thus by man and embrasing in warmth and developing pregnancy, They made this body and the couple left. It has been sought after by the bewitching birds of the deep well (senses) through successive lives.

2911. There are two things, the wedding drum and the wedding Thali; stronger than the wedding drum and the Thali is the crow bar; the stronger than the drum, Thali and crow-bar is the love that comes of the Lord's grace.

The Lord's love and grace is far superior and greater than the wedding drum, wedding Thali and the crow-bar (sex-union).

2912. They who see the fish (women) remain looking at the fish; they who see the Hare (astral vision of the mystic moon within) are rid of the three Pasas (attachment through desires) and he who controls the tumultuous battle (Indriyas) see the hidden truth (Lord Shiva) and becomes His golden form.

2913. In the body bank filled with creepers (Pasas) that spread and entwine and where reeds (desires) flourish; the Lord is not the stork that walks gently on them. He dives deep into the rocky floor to grant redemption for Jeeva.

2914. The garden below is of three leagues; the forest above is of half a league; frontiers blurring the two routes intermingle and they who can see the frontiers very clearly can cross the backyard very quickly and reach the hamlet safely.

The two routes (right and left breaths) form the garden below (Mooladhara) and the forest above (Sahashrara) intermingled. And they who can discern the blurring frontiers clearly reach the hamlet (liberation) safely and quickly.

2915. No more Karmas will germinate, if when after ploughing, the seed is cast, copious rains fall and it soaks the land. No more Karmas if yoga is attained. If yoga is consummated you will surely reach the Lord of flourishing matted locks.

2916. When Jeeva vanquishes Indriyas by yoga the tiger (Prana breath) that leaps twelve finger measure of length crouches, the billows (mystic waters in the astral sphere) of the hidden Sea spread softly and the rapturous ambrosia that is nectar-sweet swells up. Thus does the Jeeva surround the five Indriyas that harass him.

2917. The good man, Jeeva, boarded a boat and launched out into the sea. He traded well and flourished very fast. This is Jeeva's journey in yoga Sea. While voyaging in the yoga Sea he lost his heart to a she-devil (Mayaic senses) and lost his spirit under her spell. To him the divine water flows that (from the cranium) is like a rich fruit laden with sweet nectar.

2918. There are three plantains trees in the river of three leagues. These trees bore ruddy fruits of triple impurities. They who exceedingly hail the name of the Lord and seek the virgin (Sakthi kundalini) through the central Sushumna will inhale the divine, flower's (Sahashrara) sweet fragrance, This is the triumph of yoga.

2919. There is an Athi tree, (Baumina recemosa), whose flowers are dear to Lord Shiva, (Here it is symblic of the body from Mooladhara, to Sahahsrara) with root and top at the tip of the high and there is the bamboo (the spinal column) through which the Sushumna Nadi runs that is triple crested (the senses and sensual organs) with flag and army who will be destroyed and then the sacred conch will blow in victory (attainment of Nadha state in yoga). This is how yoga vanquishes the Tathwas.

2920. Pig and snake, cow and monkey are together in the herd of the lowly jackal—all these five mean the five senses. The Jeeva does not debase himself by joining them. For when the good and bad deeds are equally weighted in balance, the Jeeva, tinier then the crab's eyes sees its ego diminishing sense should be conquered to reach Iruvinai-Oppu and Nalapari Pakam.

2921. There is an unopened bud. You see that the bud

soon blossoms when it is freed from the plant's fetters. Similarly, unless you give up desires and are freed from the bonds you will not be liberated, so rend the fetters as under and destroy the Tathwas.

2922. Though no water flows, there is a land that is ever green. No one knows of this land. The water that does not flow from rain (grace) does not stand in the land (body) untilled (by yoga). This is the uniqueness of the ambrosial flow in the cranium.

2923. When the owl (Jeeva) gets to the top of the Kurunda tree (cranium) it realizes that desires are the source of the world. Then the snake (Kundalini) standing in the centre of Shushumna teaches supreme wisdom—the Gnana the Jeeva becomes Lord Shiva, Himself.

2924. The plantain tree and the Surai creeper (pepper) together covered space. They say the Surai creeper is stronger by far than the plantain tree, Cutting them down the plantain tree and the Surai creeper together, you will find that the plantain extending will surely flourish. They say that the Surai creeper (Pasa) is stronger than the plantain tree (Jeeva). Cut down the creeper—the plantain tree flourishes well.

2925. The upland 'Kurava' (Inland fisherman) does not dig the earth, instead he sails the seas and catches fatty fish (sensual enjoyments). Let him give up catching fish (worldly pursuits) and rather let him dig the earth; for, there is a way (practice of yoga) to a rich catch that is wealth and food (liberation) for all.

2926. A child (Jeeva) flourishes in the house of goldsmith (Sahashrara). There is a conch of call (Nadha); blow it and call the Lord in joy. The high state is granted to the potter (Brahma, creator) and the titled minister (Vishnu-'Kavi' and 'thi' meaning protector or preserver) alike, so seek and reach Nadha by yoga and attain status of God.

2927. The temple of buffalo (Jeeva) left and shed (yoga) and seeing the army (senses) he turned back half way. The chief (Jeeva) held counsel with the minister (Guru). The nine citizens (Indriyas) closed the gates (orifices) by way of sense control. The Indriyas are the impediments that obstruct the yoga journey.

2928. The eight constituents of the subtle body that ultimately leave, the eighteen Tathwas with purusha immersed in them that sneak in at the time of conception, the nine orifices, the Kundalini that coils like a serpent, the life breath twelve finger measure angula long—if all these are not driven into the womb at conception, by the divine charioteer then truly, the infant born will be far inferior to, less than a human (say a pig).

2929. The sky heron (Jeeva) waking gently, feeds in the lagoon (body) that is covered by moss (Pasa). When the guidance of the marching warrior (guru) is got, Pasas, that are laid to the ground, all flutter away.

2930. On the peaked mountain in a high summit (cranium), a gusty wind (Prana) blows beyond this high summit; there a flower (Sahashrara) that spreads its fragrance blossomed. Within that flower, a bee imbibed its nectar. Here, the Lord draws Jeeva towards Himself.

2931. Jeeva marched ahead within the cranium with the melody of Veena and Flute, intermminglingly that comes of yoga in the Nadha sphere. Even before the bargain talks began, Jeeva and Shiva, the land (liberation) was up, there for Jeeva to possess.

2932. No one knows the trade with the one in Ambrosia; except those who have entered the secret cavern, Moon sphere. They do not know when the moon rises, and that when it rises there will be no more darkness. Some have reached there which is a mystic secret, and have remained there, which is a mystic secret, and have remained there ever. They truly, as the devout holy beings.

2933. The day dawned and it took on a golden hue, the Mast wood shed its golden pollen on the higher banks—this is how the dawn of Gnana is Sahashrara is described. Thus it is where the Holy Lord abides. The damsel (Kundalini) reached this sphere and remained here.

2934. The tibes of Indriyas belong to Jeeva. Each fight with swords and at his gate. If Jeeva is constantly guided, he will take to the true way to the frontier, (Sahashrara) for on one one ever returns from this destination, from this very plane, he reaches the final state beyond the five states of consciousness.

2935. The howling of jackals (senses) outside does not matter anymore; when the mango fruit (Shiva) ripen and drops within this garden (Sahashrara). Like this, when the primal one (Shiva) was reached by the Kundalini fire, this fleshy body that led to Him does not count anymore.

2936. The birds 'Indriyas' shrills that it is dawn (the effulgent light of Gnana in Sahashrara), the flower like damsel (Kundalini fearing separation, bewaits it is dawn. But the Lord joyed in eternal union with her, and for the Jeeva there is no more dawn or any more separation.

2937. There is a boat (body) on the river Ghat (life). The five boatman (senses) plant their feet and row and thus they trade on the river route. But if in the middle the rudder wobbles (pasas leave) then, that becomes this, maning will no more be world trade when Pasas are surrendered, for Jeeva unites in Lord Shiva and Jeeva becomes Lord Shiva.

18. Mauna Samadhi: Utter Silent Transcendental

2938. Their state thus—they stood, they sat, they lay—cannot in any way be described, for their thought is in samadhi's silence. There is a being hidden within; they who reach it (Samadhi); have reached Him indeed. Through Samadhi, the being within is reached.

2939. He is the cause, who is beyond the sings and Mudhras. Unless the Guru Himself leads you to Him; for the Guru alone can show the way, there is no avail describing Him in books, for all these descriptions are like the exerescence of growth on sheep's neck.

2940. They who know the truth, see all the world and have no sorrow at all. When they who thus saw the truth, have indeed, seen the finite truth.

2941. He stands even in my forgetfulness. He who is the Lord of Maya-land is the vast compassion, He who is of great qualities, ended my birth, Himself and His Holy Sakthis sleep in sleepless union in Samadhi.

2942. .He shines beyond the three Thuriyas, in the Thuriyatheeta, that transcends them, beyond waking, dreaming, Shususpthi states; in this state, He is the transcendental light, defying thought and speech.

2943. Attributes of Lord Shiva; He is formless, bodyless, blemishless, richless, harmless. He who is contentionless is the celestial of celestials. He is possessed of Bhootha-army. He, who is attachmentless entered my thoughts.

2944. No one has seen Him and know Him, He, the Nandhi, is within the body; all, in the eight directions praise Him as Lord. The unending bliss of His many devotees, surpasses vast universe. The bliss of His devotees is beyond description; little does anyone know, how much they enjoyed Him.

2945. He is neither Tat-Para nor Sadhashiva. He is formless and He is not formed. He stood in me in union, baffling the imagination and this union of Jeeva and Shiva is wonderous indeed, like enjoying the felicity of Sexual union.

2946. You, fools who see with fleshy eyes know, that it is true bliss to see with the inner eye. A mother cannot tell the daughter of the felicity of the union with her husband. She cannot describe this in any terms. Such is the divine felicity beyond words.

2947. Transcending Param and Paraparam states, I mixed in the Lord, as salt in water, I merged in union beyond word and speech. You ask how it was and I saw it was it.

2948. The fruit of Nux Vomica is lovely to look at, but only those who eat it know its bitter taste. When a virgin matures and becomes a full woman, only then will the husband know of her diverse qualities. These are the deceptive ways of the world.

2949. In the steet-centre of Sahashrara, Samadhi and other ways of union, wnet of themselves into the Light that was Nandhi. I merged, by my Supreme Wisdom, that rises from within the navel centre.

Jeeva Light merges into Shiva light of Gnana, that rises from below the navel centre.

2950. I sit aloof and meditate, and undistracted and free of all doubts, I follow the ancient Vedas, I cross the awesome waste—this is life and I merge beyond into the space, that defines imagination.

2951. The celstials do not seek His Holy Feet that are bedecked in unfading blooms. They do not take to the holy way; neither do they penetrate the radiance of the lovely lotus that is within nor do they seek to drink of the divine ambrosia.

2952. The lovers when they sit and talk for a purposeful union, their passion gushes all of a sudden. The Lord's love gushes, when he of fragrant Kondrai flowers beholds those who determinedly sit to meet Him and He grants His Mighty Grace unhesitatingly.

2953. Myself and my wealth perish, my body and the life perish, Heaven and mind and my ego all perish, with all these perishing, I did not know that this is union of God.

2954. I transcended darkness and space and merged as substance into substance. My entire thoughts firm as immovable rock, went to the Holy Feet of the Lord in abounding grace. Thus I merged into the finite reality.

2955. Meditating in oneness, I visioned Paraparam, realized Shiva state, experienced transcendental awareness and witnessed aeons upon aeons.

19. Greatness of Limitless Beyond

2956. When you have, yourself become limitless, you have no one to see in limit. When you have, yourself become He, You have no one to think of. The eyes that vanquished the God of eternal Love, they have no one, anymore, to look for in longing—tell me, yourself the real truth.

2957. Oh, you dumb ones, you seek to speak of the one who is beyond speech. You can reach the shores of the shoreless vast. He, of the matted locks, appears unreserved for those whose thoughts stand still, like the waveless waters, in the beyond.

2958. Maya is only the mind's work that creates the illusions. When the mind's illusion disappears, there is nothing left to worry about. Neither will there be death nor any more chatter. It is only to seek the self that is the divine truth and Maya creates no illusions there.

20. Greatness of the Realized Souls

2959. There is no impurity, no pride and prejudice, no family, no excellences, no affluence for those who in wisdom plant themselves in Nandhi—form in His love, The realized souls have no possessions.

2960. With the birth ended and the bonds sundered, God and I became one. I have met Shiva the auspicious and so, for me, there is no more the way of rebirth.

2961. We possess sugarcane, fine rice, rich garments and water of green glades too. By the grace of the lovely mother who is peacock shaped, we want nothing, nothing indeed.

2962. The Lord came and entered my thoughts, so no one can intimidate me hereafter, I will now sport and wander in joy and I will not be with anyone else, anymore.

2963. I freed myself of the fetters the creator bound me with and learned the way of reaching Shiva. With the sharp sword of mind I smote Karmas and stood lost of ego. And now I hasten toward the city of God.

2964. He is One; He is the One for all the worlds and the life of all the worlds. The Namashivaya fruit is lovely indeed, it is sweet to those who have tasted it.

2965. The Lord who wears the moon and serpent on His matted hair, is the jewelled Lamp that accepted me in his service. He, the Rare Being, has neither beginning nor end, He entered my thoughts and made me doubt free.

2966. Our Lord created Brahma and Vishnu of yore. He remained there and no one knows why. If the Jeeva renouncing all, appears there and empties all his thoughts, he will have no more births in this carnal body.

2967. Unless the Heavenly Father and Heavenly Mother love, worldly father and wordly mother will not know me, The Father, Mother and I were seated together (Shiva-Sakthi-Jeeva Union). I was adoring my Father and Mother.

2968. The vaste seas, the high mountain peaks, the denizens of the Universe and those who hold their sway there, the primal Sakthi and the people in the eight directions—all, came within my grasp. I am redeemed, high above all. This is the prowess of the redeemed state.

2969. He is the totality, as He, Himself stands as space and celestials; as body, life and matter, as Sea, hill and dale, and Himself as the Supreme Lord of all worlds.

2970. If the God of death comes, I shall smite him with the sword of Gnana; If Fine Shiva comes, I shall surely go with Him. I had sundered Karma long back, which leads to birth. No one can stand against the thought power of the Realized, which is born of intense.

2971. The thoughts of the realized are Shiva-filled. They have destroyed the three impurities and have become Suddha Shiva; so they do not return to the bondage of impurities. Also, they do not indulge in shouts, confusion and fights of this world, but are immersed, in Nadha and Para Bindhu.

2972. The Pure One, who uproots Karmas, stands in the thoughts of those who cognize neither remembering nor forgetting who they are, the eyes that vanquished, the God of Love, to look for in longing? Tell me, the real Truth, Yourself?

2973. I hailed Him as Lord Shiva, My great Lord and the Holy Lord was before me as a Tapaswin; I stood adoring Him; the eternal Lord, the desired Lord, who accepted me in His service.

2974. I adored Him, the Param, the Primal Lord, and I stood determined that I shall seek nothing else. Hence I held Him, the First one, in union in my body, I stood meek in prayer and saw my Shiva's being.

2975. I beseeched the Lord's Feet and He filled my thoughts; as I thus entered His presence. He, the Lord who has no thoughts, ended my birth's whirl; fragmented my fate and sundered my bonds.

2976. He, my Nandhi, resolved my contradictions, ended my disease, age and life's reckoning and thus accepted me in His service. With my contradictions resolved and my life's sorrow laid low, Shiva, of Himself appeared to me.

2977. Shiva entered in me with His celestial retinue and severed my bonds that give rise to births. He, the Primal Lord, is my Father, who accepted me in His service; my heart entered into grace and remained imprisoned there.

2978. In eagerness I sought Shiva bliss and I visioned the

void. Then sugarcane tasted bitter and honey tasted sour, which means that bodily pleasures ceased to interest. Then the fragrance of Lord Shiva bliss sprouted like the sugarcane and honey mixed in this body of pleasures.

2979. Having pursued the way of Chariya and the rest, and having received the grace of the bounteous being; I stand praising Him forever. All that I now do, I see it all as Lord Shiva's doings. With no more Karmas left, I have now crossed the Sea of births.

2980. The Kundalini fire shot up fiereely, into the thousand petalled lotus in the Sahashrara and I made in blaze with the fate of my hearts' love, and She, the Sakthi, the jewel of all worlds appeared. The One, that is my egoity, died and the one, my Shiva, appeared in me.

2981. The six streams of yogic centres, flow into one lake. Thus in this subtle ways, one penetrates into the Lord Shiva-state and here in the cranium sphere is the precious truth-Shiva Himself stands with Sakthi of bouncing breasts and tender vi e form.

2982. With my heart melting, I moan and rave. I adore day and night with my bones melting, I eat, bite and chew Him, my gold, my Guru, my Lord and my God.

2983. The mind blossomed and converged for the Jeeva. Then the mind blossomed and converged in great penance and in yoga breath. When the mind blossomed to describe it beyond words, then, it was finite eternal liberation (Mukthi).

21. Laudation

2984. Mounting the chariot of mind, they seek the divine juggler; they bewail, for they do not know where he has gone. But I, wandering about in the far and near lands and kingdoms, saw Him in this fleeting body land.

2985. Who were they, of youre, who like mountain sat on a kingly elephant and to the accompaniment of sweet music, went in procession, chanting the primal Lord's name in fervour and so attained the exalted status.

2986. They think I am a mad man, for I do not see but rave about my father who is the Pearl of pearls, the Lovely sun rising at dawn, and the Lord whom all celestials adore.

2987. He, the Lord of Gnana's flower, entered in the hearts of his devotees. He, our Holy Lord, entered in me, too, I adore Him who entered in me.

2988. He does not appear in the glasses of the fleshy eye, for He is in the Lotus of the heart. He appears in the glass of Vedic Gnana, as He is in the mind, glass of the righteous ones and that think of Him. I saw Him in the glass of songs and stood enraptured, listening to His divine music.

2989. Chant the Lord's name, a thousand times and a thousand blessings. Shall be yours. For they who chant the lovely 'AUM' a thousand times are rid of thousand, thousand passions.

2990. I praise and laud Gnana who is our refuge, I adore the Holy Feet of the Lord, constantly, in my thoughts; and I expound Shivayoga too. Listen, I chant the one letter (AUM) that is dear to our Lord.

2991. Do seek Nandhi, in diverse ways, by penetrating the Lotus within and going beyond it, you shall reach the celestial world and there, having drunk of the nectar that is exceedingly sweetly. You will return. This is the fruit of practising yoga.

2992. The devotees are more rewarded than the celestials, for, He, the Rare truth, came and stood before. His devotees when they asked Guru, Even if the celestials and their king Indhra ask they will get nothing, but the music of lovely damsels. But that which the devotees get is beyond all their heaven.

2993. These mens' minds are like muddled water, unclear in vision. They cannot see and say that this is the Lord. But if, from the heart's lake that is within, you draw a pitcherful and keep it apart in stillness and you thus purify it, you will become Shiva. It, simply means that you should still your thoughts and be purified, then, you will become Lord Shiva.

2994. I sought Him My Lord, and thus remained yearning for Him, whom the celestials seek in righteous ways. He, the pure one, of the pure penance is transparent as Amala fruit on the palm of those who yearn for Him.

2995. Remaining thus, I attained limitless Gnana. There is no more wavering and as I reach the Holy One, in the land where the Kundalini fire burns, He, the bounteous One, gives me His choicest blessings.

2996. He, the bounteous Lord, monarch of the heavenly kingdom, the Lord of matted locks who carries the flowing Ganga water, the Primal One of the Vedas, hides within the heart that is within, lest those who are devoid of faith should see Him.

2997. They, who adore Him daily a goodness, flourish like me, for my God stretched his flower, feet in grace. He is the divine knight who severs my evil stars and Karmas; my thoughts centered into His sword of Gnana and I do not possess any more cares.

2998. Seek His Feet for they are the reach of the Valnalla warriors, do reach His Feet, for they are the heaven of blessed deeds, do attain His Feet for they are the confluence of holy waters. It is so, for those who constantly adore His Feet.

2999. He, Himself has no home, yet, He pierced the overhanging darkness of ignorance; in this world, He is the Holy preceptor of peerless grandeur; so I ate of the ripe fruit of His Supreme wisdom, and held on to the sweet light within.

3000. It is the goal ultima that you should devoutly seek, for this indeed, is the exalted state, it is where the celestials have their abode; it is sacred and it is where the Ganges too flows and it is the state that rivers roots of karmic desires that come to the past.

3001. The celestials stand above, the great Tapaswins stand below them. Below them are humans who are harassed by sorrow; this is how He is seated. The Bilva garland collected fresh from the forest, festoons the fragrant matted locks. He does what is appropriate for Jeeva.

3002. He, the Lord qualified, quaffed the poison that arose form the Ocean, He pervades the fourteen worlds. He, the Lord is birthless and is seated where the lute, the spring and forest are. He is the king that reigns in the five-lettered Manthra (NAMASIVAYA) that is eternal.

3003. He is life like earth, wind, sun, fire and moon. He is like water. He is like recurring dissolution and creation. He, the Primal One, the Lord of Gods; is in the eight cardinal distinct directions. He is pervasive in all elements.

3004. He pervades fire and sun, wind and moon. He is all pervading. He confers his blessings according to the degree of Gnana that is attained.

3005. Transcending all, yet, He, stands immanent in each. He is the mighty object for the world that is bound in Pasa (attchment through desires) here below. He, Himself is the Supreme Parapara for all the worlds that He gave and thus is the way, His greatness extends.

3006. His crown is high up in the vast pearl-like universes, His form engrosses all the seven worlds and His feet descend deep like the other world; But the ignorant do not know these and do not delight over these.

3007. The Primal Lord is our Lord; He is the resplendent light of the vast spaces, He is the three lights—sun, moon and fire. He is the primal Lord, beyond all universes; he is everywhere— above, middle, below and between them too.

3008. He is great, rising above the vast macrocosm; He is subtle within the fleshy body which is an heir to births; As His devotees see the vision of His Holy Feet and walk toward Him. He goes half way seeking them, on their ways.

3009. He, my Lord pervasively filled all the worlds that are girt by vast oceans and is overseeing all in omniscience. of youre, He created entirely everything and stood diffusing His golden hue, in all worlds everywhere.

3010. He stood as Supreme Paraparam, through several successive aeons. He stood as the Supreme Paraparam protecting all worlds and this world too. No one knows that He stands pervading the Jeevas too, is immanent in them and yet transcending them.

3011. He is the mighty God to adore and there are none beside Him. He is the sense, the feet, the sound, sound's end and the body too, of Jeeva, He, the Lord is immanent in all, as the Prana Breath.

3012. Oh, you men ! why do you speak of someone else, when the cardinal directions are all of Shiva, just as all smoke emanates from fire, all creation arises from our Primal Lord.

3013. The pervasive Shiva, expanding limitlessly, filled in oneness the infinite spaces of the seven worlds, yet, He is not easy to reach. He, our Lord, Shiva, Himself pervades into myriad Jeevas in this world as well.

3014. He is transcendental and immanent, He stands beyond, the three Kalas; seek Him; He is the Lord and master of the Tathwas; He is priceless, peerless and is beyond all celestials. He is Ageless, yet He is within you and you must only seek Him.

The three Kalas in Shiva Tathwa; Nivirthi, Pratishta, Vidhya. Beyond Santhi and Santhiyattitha are the Kalas of Sakthi and Lord Shiva.

3015. He severed the Pasas of this world that Brahma created. He severed the belittling desires that Vishnu gives to Jeevas. He severed the interminable, Karmas in His infinite divinity. Thus, He redeemed me, the lowly and in exceeding endearment, He held me to Himself.

3016. The Lord is light that moves in eight directions; He is the source of all sounds; He is the eternal one. Who pervades the nine universes, as if on one land. He spreads everywhere like the flower's fragrance.

3017. My Lord, He is and He is not. But break your stony heart and He is there. He is pure gem that is ancient, pure and constant. He is light that is beyond speech, and so, He is inscrutable.

3018. The inserutable Lord says that He is, He says that He is within the heart and without it, too. He, Nandhi, of bounteous magnificence, of fragrant matted locks, severs sea of birth of those who adore Him constantly.

3019. The conflicting Devas and Dhanavas adore Him alike and seek Him daily. They yearn for Him with in and without their heart. He, the Lord and lamp of divine light, transforms them into the different celestial beings.

3020. He does not appear in the heavenly spaces, yet, He has form. He is not visible to the naked eyes, yet, He is visible, to the inner eyes. He, the goodly one, is the fruit of music, He is the fruit of all good deeds. He, Lord is endless bliss.

3021. He, the noble one is a sea of joy beloved of all. He is the dark-blue throated (Thiruneelakandam) one, the radiance of pure pearl and Him the holy Siddhas and exalted celestials contemplate over immeasurable time; yet they all do not know Him fully well.

3022. The hues are many and so is the Lord. The goodly deeds are many and so is the pleasure. The vile deeds are many and so are the uniquities. Even, after seeing all these, yet, they do not adore the Lord.

3023. He is the Holy Lord and who is here, there and everywhere. He is in all worlds; He is in the darkness and He is the light, He is in the sun-moon and everywhere. The Lord is benevolent like the rain that falls.

3024. He is sentience, He is gracious. You need subtle wisdom to know our Lord. He is embrace; He is union in divine awareness, He stands as cosmic body.

3025. It is by His might that He supports the seven worlds. It is His might He is subtler than atom. It is by His might that He surpassed the eight mountain ranges in the eight directions and it is by His might that the oceans roar.

3026. My Lord is of infinite greatness; yet, He is within the littleness of this fleshy body. He is beyond the ken of the celestials. Yet, He is prayer and penance and He will Himself appear to you.

3027. The shoot of the tiny banyan seed grew as a mighty tree within thus our body and it bore rich ripe fruit (Supreme Gnana). They who ate it remained to be forever and the foots who did not eat it remained in the body, tossed about from the birth to birth.

22. The All Pervasiveness

3028. There will be Shiva Bhoga, like it a light will be added that suffuses sentient knowledge, The body that has been harassed by Mayaic experience, will be yours, if you have full control over it, Then when you, Jeeva unites in Shiva, its pervasiveness will spread everywhere.

3029. There is no particular place where I can seek that object, I have known. When taking to the astral way, that object will appear as perfection there; when seeking it within the body, it will be a living light there. You, then become omniscent and omnipresent in Shiva-Jeeva union.

3030. Seek the inner light in life that is led here in this sea-girt world that is filled with sorrows and be one in the Lord, for He resides within this body. You may ever meet Him on the waves of the high Seas.

3031. He is the supreme light within the three lights; sun, moon and fire. He, the Lord of celestials is their body too. Yet, leaving the luminosities, He, in great compassion follows Jeevas in the vast expanses and He, the One proliferates as several.

3032. Jeeva gets entangled in the crusted Karma and that comes with their birth. In the end, they realized Him and became golden. He, the Divine Being, is the spark too within the spark of light. If Jeeva reaches His, He will too become a flaming light.

3033. He is the Divine Lightly spark that stands inside desires, He is the Divine spark that waxes into the three lights—sun, moon and fire. He is the Divine spark that is seated in the forehead centre as our thought—the spark of Gnana in Agjna, The great Tapaswins, too, stand like Him.

3034. He is the Lord who is all the ten directions; He is the seven expansive sea-girt worlds too, thus, pervading, He is the voice, the speaker that speaks all, Thus the Jeeva becomes Shiva.

3035. He is like the Garuda Bird, that sees all in an instant, he protects the entire seven worlds. He, the pure one, the birthless one, who removes my Karmas, has no entry, no exit and no stary.

3036. He, the unattached one, who is yet immanent, in all, is of rich matted locks and golden hue. The Holy God is omnipresent, birthless and stands unintermittent in all seven worlds.

3037. He is sentience, He is life, He is union; He is senses and the continuity beyond thought. He is within the fragrance of the flower.

3038. He, the Holy One, is devoid of the odour of the five

senses. My father, the bounteous one, gives all Gnana. He stands diversely, comprehends all, in the precious wisdom of the Vedic sages.

3039. He is the heavenly being who is beyond, the seven worlds. He is the earth too, and is cool like waters of the seven oceans that girdle this globe. He stands united in Jeevas, as the light in their eyes.

3040. He stands as Brahma and Vishnu; as heaven and earth. His limitless expansiveness stands stretching to the fatthest mountains and seven Seas; He stands as the rich ripe fruit too.

3041. He is the Lord of all worlds. The Holy One who is my Father is the Master and Mahout of all Jeeva. He is Jeevas and themselves too. He is the Lord, whom everyone holds in endearment.

3042. He is the spark of Prana breath within. He is the luminous sun in the High firmament. He is the breath of wind and blows on land. He is the thought within all.

3043. The Lord created music and melody in the orderly way of numerals and letters. In His grace and glance, and in His very thought from within He effected the rapturous union of Jeeva and Lord Shiva and united into one family.

3044. The light cardinal directions, the worlds above and the worlds below stand centering in him. Thus, He of the flowing matted locks, bedecked with fragrant kondrai-blooms, immanent in all, pervades all.

3045. The Lord is with and within all creation, and no one knows of his coming and going. He is distant and near. He is Sankara who is constant. He is the primal being. He is our primal Lord, is multiple and yet, the Almighty, He is One.

3046. He is the Jeeva's knowledge, He is the ancient one; and yet no one knows how He is ! He, the Nandhi, our Primal Lord, knows all, in all the eight Universes.

3047. He is water, earth, sky, fire and wind and the spark of the light within the body (soul). He is Paraparam, He is Shiva, our Lovely Lord. He is the walking Jeeva, here below on this earth and yet, He is deathless.

23. The Profit of the Scripture/Classic

3048. The three thousand songs that Thirumoolar composed, the three hundred manthras that he chanted and the thirty instructions that Thirumoolar gave, all these three that Moolar has recited have but one import.

24. Benediction

3049. May our Nandhi's Holy Feet live long; May the Feet of Him who severed impurities live long; May the Feet of Him of Holy Divine Supreme wisdom—the Gnana live long and May the Feet of His Holiness, Lord Shiva who has no impurity Live Long.

Thirumanthiram\Sadhasivaahamam—Notes Concluded
Om Shivarppanam.

Index